THE
POST CARBON
READER

THE

POST CARBON
—— READER ——
MANAGING THE 21ST CENTURY'S SUSTAINABILITY CRISES

RICHARD HEINBERG AND DANIEL LERCH, EDITORS

WATERSHED MEDIA

CONTEMPORARY ISSUES SERIES

Published by Watershed Media in collaboration with Post Carbon Institute.

Watershed Media
Healdsburg, California, USA
www.watershedmedia.org

Post Carbon Institute
Santa Rosa, California, USA
www.postcarbon.org

Library of Congress Control Number: 2010931734

This book is printed on Natures Book Paper. Natures Book
Paper is FSC certified and contains 30% Post Consumer
Waste (PCW). It is acid free and qualifies as a permanent
recycled paper.

Distributed by Publishers Group West.

Cover design by Mike King.
Interior design by BookMatters.

10   9   8   7   6

ISBN 978-0-9709500-6-2
E-book ISBN 978-0-9767510-8-3

We dedicate this book to Rachel Carson, Donella and Dennis Meadows, Jørgen Randers, and William Behrens III, and to all the other pioneers who had the courage and foresight decades ago to warn the people of the world that, if we didn't change course, we would arrive at the crises we face today.

If the present growth trends in world population, industrialization, pollution, food production, and resource depletion continue unchanged, the limits to growth on this planet will be reached sometime within the next hundred years.

—from *The Limits to Growth*, 1972

CONTENTS

FOREWORD

ASHER MILLER

ASHER MILLER *is executive director of Post Carbon Institute. Previously he served as partnership director at Plugged In, international production coordinator at Steven Spielberg's Shoah Foundation, ghostwriter for a Holocaust survivor, and consultant for a number of other nonprofit groups. He currently serves on the board of Transition US, the hub of the Transition movement in the United States.*

❖

Something remarkable happened a few centuries ago. We discovered that fossil fuels—first coal, then oil, and finally natural gas—could be harnessed as an abundant, easily accessible, and cheap source of energy. This discovery led to previously unimaginable advances in transportation, manufacturing, food production, medicine and health care, urban design, and more. In the blink of a geological eye, we radically transformed the way we lived and the world around us. It's like we won the lottery, and like a lot of lottery winners—or other species that suddenly discover an abundant resource—we went crazy for a little while.

We've awakened to find that the bills for this energy bonanza have come due. With an explosion in human population, consumption, economic activity, and environmental destruction, we're beginning to learn the true cost of our industrial binge: climate change, water and food scarcity, biodiversity and habitat loss, social and economic injustice, increasing conflicts over diminishing resources, and an utter dependence on economic growth, which simply cannot be sustained.

Worse still, the very substances that fueled this explosion have "peaked" or are near "peaking," while no alternative energy sources are capable of supplying energy as cheaply and in such abundance as fossil fuels currently yield, in the brief time that we need them to come online. Even while we struggle to address these myriad crises, the cheap and abundant energy we've come to rely on is going into decline.

And rely we have. Look around and you'll see that the very fabric of our lives—where we live, what we eat, how we move, what we buy, what we do, and what we value—was woven with cheap, abundant energy. Those days—the carbon era—are over.

The future is uncertain, but it's clear that profound changes are already under way.

The world almost certainly experienced the peak of oil production in 2008, and peaks in natural gas and coal production are not far off.[1] Meanwhile, climate projections can't keep up with the scale and rapidness of global warming, and leading scientists are now warning us that we need to get below *current levels* of atmospheric carbon to avert threshold events that could tip our climate to the point of no return.

And now the world is reeling from a profound global economic crisis. At the time of this writing, 8.4 million jobs have been lost in the United States alone since the start of the so-called Great Recession, which began in late 2007. To put this into context, for every job available in this country there are six people looking for work. An estimated 16.5 percent of the population is officially classified as "underemployed," the highest level since the 1930s.[2] To return to pre-recession unemployment levels, the U.S. economy would need to generate 10 million new jobs, and that is without factoring in the 1.5 million students and others looking to join the workforce each year.[3]

Economists have hotly debated the shape of the recovery (assuming, of course, that there will be such a thing). But some at least see that this recession is unlike any we've ever known. Mark Zandi, chief economist and co-founder of Moody's Economy.com, and adviser to both Republicans and Democrats, has said:

> This Great Recession is an inflection point for the economy in many respects. I think the unemployment rate will be permanently higher, or at least higher for the foreseeable future. . . . The collective psyche has changed as a result of what we've been through. And we're going to be different as a result.[4]

And former U.S. secretary of labor Robert Reich wrote in July 2009:

My prediction, then? Not a V, not a U. But an X. This economy can't get back on track because the track we were on for years— featuring flat or declining median wages, mounting consumer debt, and widening insecurity, not to mention increasing carbon in the atmosphere—simply cannot be sustained.

The X marks a brand new track—a new economy. What will it look like? Nobody knows. All we know is the current economy can't "recover" because it can't go back to where it was before the crash. So instead of asking when the recovery will start, we should be asking when and how the new economy will begin.[5]

Our starting point for future planning must be the realization that we are living today at a critical moment in the long arc of human history when numerous crises are not only converging simultaneously, they are interdependent and affect virtually every living thing on the planet. The sheer scale and complexity of the challenges at hand are unprecedented. There are no signs to guide us, no road to follow.

It may sound bombastic to say, but it's nevertheless the truth: The success or failure of the human experiment may well be judged by how we manage the next ten to twenty years.

KEY ASSUMPTIONS

Five key assumptions have brought Post Carbon Institute's Fellows together and led to the writing of the book you now hold in your hands:

1. **We have hit the "limits to growth."** This is not a moral question (or not *only* one); nor is it merely a question about the fate of our children and grandchildren. The truth is that we have no choice but to adapt to a world of resource constraints, economic contraction, and climate upheaval. Thus the only question that remains is this: *How will we manage that transition?*

2. **No issue can be addressed in isolation.** Thankfully, recognition of these crises has grown in recent years. However, all too often they are viewed in isolation. We must connect the dots to get to their source—not just their symptoms—and to maximize what little time and resources we have to address the enormous challenges they pose.

3. **We must focus on responses, not just solutions.** As John Michael Greer says, we face a predicament, not a problem. "The difference is that a *problem* calls for a solution; the only question is whether a solution can be found and made to work and, once this is done, the problem is solved. A *predicament*, by contrast, has no solution. Faced with a predicament, people come up with responses."[6]

4. **We must prepare for uncertainty.** While the general trends are clear, it's simply impossible to predict, specifically, how world events will unfold. Therefore, it's critically important that we aim to build resilience on the individual and community scales. Resilient people and resilient communities are characterized by their ability to manage unforeseen shocks while maintaining their essential identity.

5. **We *can* do something.** The bad news is that we simply cannot avoid hardship or suffering in the journey from a world dependent on fossil fuels and growth to communities that live within ecological bounds. The good news is that we can prepare and make positive changes in almost any area of our lives and the lives of our communities. How much and how successful those efforts are all depend upon the thought and effort we invest.

In late 2008 and early 2009, it became abundantly clear to those of us at Post Carbon Institute that the world had begun its inexorable journey to life after growth. To more effectively respond to this challenge and opportunity, we gathered twenty-nine of the world's leading experts to point the way forward through a systems-oriented, interdisciplinary, and collaborative approach.

We believe that in order to manage the transition ahead, we must first understand what brought us here. This book is our effort to integrate this understanding and to point the way forward.

While Post Carbon's role in many ways is to serve as the "think tank for the transition," our Fellows and partners are deeply engaged in the *doing.* We have formed strong partnerships with the Transition movement[7] and other leading innovators and are working with them to transform lives and communities through a powerful combination of integrated thinking and replicable direct action. These symbiotic relationships with on-the-ground leaders and grassroots organizers provide the opportunity to immediately implement and test generated ideas and strategies.

The challenges ahead and the stakes at hand couldn't be more enormous. And yet we feel hope. A real hope renewed with every new community project that's launched, every new Transition initiative formed, and collective action being taken around the world by grassroots groups like 350.org. Together all of these threads can sew a world of resilient communities and relocalized economies that thrive within ecological bounds.

We hope you'll join us.

PREFACE

DANIEL LERCH

DANIEL LERCH *is program director of Post Carbon Institute and the author of* Post Carbon Cities: Planning for Energy and Climate Uncertainty *(2007), the first major guidebook for local governments on peak oil and global warming. He has delivered presentations and workshops on local responses to peak oil to elected officials, planners, and other audiences across the United States, as well as in Canada, the British Isles, and Spain.*

❖

A NEW GAME

The post–World War II global economy has experienced its share of crises, from the oil shocks and "stagflation" of the 1970s to the Asian financial crisis and "dot-com" bust of more recent memory. Each time, the economy has rebounded and gone on to bigger and faster global growth.

But something changed in the summer of 2008. Global economic and energy trends started changing faster and more worryingly than even most pessimists expected. Framed by an oil price spike to nearly $150 a barrel in July and the beginning of the Wall Street collapse in September, that summer has proved to be a major turning point. Few, however, seem to fully understand its significance.

Most analysts of this crisis assumed we were merely in the downward part (albeit a particularly deep one) of a curve of economic activity that would inevitably go back up, if only we could keep the economy from slowing down too much. Despite all the debate about the federal stimulus package in 2009, two underlying assumptions went unquestioned: that the economy would recover within a few years, and that it would function pretty much the same as it had before the crisis (except perhaps for more wind turbines, more solar panels, and a dazzling new selection of fuel-efficient family cars).

And yet, the same people hoping to solve the economic crisis with more spending and/or tax cuts also increasingly acknowledge that we face unprecedented (and growing) energy and climate crises. In fact, the problems at hand require not a few trillion dollars thrown at them but instead fundamental changes in how the modern industrial world works.

We're experiencing a society-wide mental disconnect, a failure to reconcile the pain of the immediate economic crisis with our long-term dependence on cheap fossil fuels and the looming threats of peak oil and climate change. This disconnect means we're not correctly diagnosing the problems we face, and so we're not pursuing the right solutions. We've essentially failed to recognize that the game has changed.

In some ways, the summer of 2008 signaled for the U.S. economy what events like Pearl Harbor and the collapse of the Soviet Union signaled for U.S. foreign policy. They were big turning points that occurred outside the frame of what we had thought was possible. They signaled that the world was no longer working the way we expected and that the old way of doing things no longer applied. This had enormous implications: In December 1941 and in January 1992, much of the previous decades' thinking about how the world worked had to be thrown out. We had to not just learn the new rules of the game but also figure out which new game it was that we were even playing (and hopefully in time to write some of our own rules).

Today we are a few years and a few trillions of dollars into the *new* new game, a game that—this time—is not about geopolitics but about energy, economics, and the planetary ecosystem. Perhaps this new game is called something along the lines of "World without Cheap Oil" or "Beyond the Limits to Growth" (and the recent Deepwater Horizon oil disaster in the Gulf of Mexico suggests we've already started to lose). Yet, most decision-makers in Washington, the state capitals, and the corporate boardrooms seem to feel we're still playing "Global Resource and Capital Bonanza."

We need only look to the last nine years in Afghanistan and seven years in Iraq to see what happens when we flub our first response to a major turning point. Unfortunately, with the new crisis that announced itself in 2008 we will probably get only one try. As my co-editor, Richard

Heinberg, has said, "We've run out of time, natural resources, and capital, so this is our only chance to get things right."

This book is a resource for those who want to try to get things right.

WHAT'S IN THE BOOK

We've organized the contents of *The Post Carbon Reader* in order of their fundamental importance to the human experience.

- Part one is the "Foundation" section, introducing the basics of what we know—and what we think we know—about how our world works.

- Parts two through four are the "Planet" section, covering those natural phenomena most essential to our existence after the sun and the solid earth: the climate, water, and the global biota.

- Parts five through seven are the "Civilization" section. Anatomically modern humans have lived on this planet for more than 100,000 years, but things started really changing around 10,000 years ago when we began the transition to sedentary agriculture. That change was driven in part by the development of our brains and our cultures, two factors that may well hold the key to the long-term success of *Homo sapiens* as our population approaches 9 billion by midcentury.

- Parts eight through fourteen are the "Modern Society" section. How we harness and use energy, how we structure our economies and communities, and how we treat one another have some of the deepest consequences for the health of our life-supporting ecosystems, the wealth of our communities, and the happiness of current and future generations.

- Parts fifteen and sixteen are the "What Now?" section. The book up to this point is a thorough exploration of the complex sustainability challenges we face, with some suggestions for how they can be addressed. But nobody can be a farmer, teacher, doctor, business owner, climate scientist, and elected official all at the same time— so where to start? We believe it starts at the most local level: building resilience and creating solutions for ourselves, our families, and our communities.

This ordering does not imply that the issues covered later in the book are any less important than those toward the front. Far from it. For example, we may someday find the political will to avoid climate catastrophes far beyond the present crises harrowingly described by Bill McKibben in chapter 4, but if we don't change our education system to teach children even the most basic ecological principles, as discussed by Michael Stone and Zenobia Barlow in chapter 30, future generations may well end up creating new sustainability crises for *their* children to solve.

As with any book attempting to cover our multiple sustainability crises, there are many important issues that we simply ran out of room or time for. We would have liked to include chapters on media and communications, for example, to explore how action on even "no-brainer" issues like climate change and peak fossil fuels all too often lives or dies by money and politics, not science and the common good. And I'm personally disappointed that we weren't able to include a chapter on local post-carbon transportation: walking, bicycling, streetcars, carshares, and other options that used to be considered "alternative" but are now recognized as simply "smarter" than dependence on private automobiles. (Visit the companion Web site to this book at www.postcarbonreader.com for supplementary material covering these and other important issues.)

Nevertheless, we're proud that *The Post Carbon Reader* is a uniquely comprehensive, in-depth exploration of the interconnected sustainability crises humanity now faces. The authors in this volume are a diverse group of experts, from big-picture scholars and consultants to on-the-ground farmers and educators. Each brings expertise in a specific field, as well as an integral perspective on our understanding of where the world is currently headed. And all share the view that a transition from a fossil-fueled growth economy to a sustainable, steady-state economy is essential and imminent.

THE UNITED STATES AND
THE POST-CARBON WORLD

This book focuses on the United States, a tough decision we made early on. Although most of the issues we deal with are global in scope, and more and more of the best sustainability solutions are to be found beyond our borders, the fact remains that the behavior of U.S. governments, businesses, households, and citizens has a disproportionate and decisive influence on the rest of the world. Considering the urgency of the crises we face, we determined it would be most effective to focus our efforts where they might have the deepest impact.

And finally, a word about "post-carbon." That term in the title of this book and in the name of our organization refers both to hydrocarbon fuels and to the carbon compounds (most notably carbon dioxide and methane) that their combustion releases into the atmosphere, contributing to global warming. There is no single definition for "post-carbon"; for some it means a purposeful transitioning away from fossil fuels, and for others it's a time when fossil fuels will no longer be readily available. I've occasionally used the definition "no longer dependent on hydrocarbon fuels, and no longer emitting climate-changing levels of carbon into the atmosphere"— but I've also defined "post-carbon cities" as cities that are on a path of resilience for a world of energy and climate uncertainty.

The point is, post-carbon—like sustainability (chapter 2), like resilience (chapter 3), like "Transition" (chapter 33)—is best thought of as a process, not a goal. In many ways, what makes a community or a product "sustainable" ultimately has less to do with the list of "green" characteristics it might boast and more to do with the processes from which it emerges (for this reason I am especially glad we were able to include chapter 3, on resilience, and the box in chapter 2, on the social dimensions of sustainability). If getting to "post-carbon" is a process, the good news is that we can all participate in and contribute to that experience.

People often complain that books (and movies, and lectures) on the various sustainability crises leave them with a bunch of depressing information and nothing meaningful to do except perhaps buy greener products and vote. For most of the chapters in *The Post Carbon Reader*, we asked each of our authors to end with substantive ideas for things people could do in response (indeed, chapter 32, by Chris Martenson, is quite literally a how-to guide on building resilience, starting with yourself). After reading even a few chapters of this book, you admittedly may feel a little more depressed about the state of the world. But you'll also have a clear set of actions you can take to do something about it.

ACKNOWLEDGMENTS

We would like to thank the following individuals: the authors, who patiently endured many months and rounds of edits; the staff of Post Carbon Institute, who provided essential administrative, creative, and moral support; our dear friends P. and L., without whom our work would not be possible; Randall Wallace and the Wallace Global Fund, for supporting the gathering of many of our authors in January 2010; Watershed Media publisher Dan Imhoff; Hannah Love of the University of California Press, our distributor; project manager Sharon Donovan; Suzanne Doyle, for editorial assistance; manuscript editor Debra Makay; Bea Hartman, for the book layout; Chris Hall, for assistance with the illustrations; proof-reader Carrie Pickett; indexer Leonard Rosenbaum; transcribers Simone Osborne, Kristin Sponsler, Laura Bennet, and David Spencer; and Rembrandt Koppelaar and Nate Hagens, who advised on energy and economics data.

Part One

FOUNDATION
CONCEPTS

I

BEYOND THE LIMITS TO GROWTH

RICHARD HEINBERG

RICHARD HEINBERG *is widely regarded as one of the world's most effective communicators of the urgent need to transition away from fossil fuels. He is the author of nine books, including* The Party's Over: Oil, War and the Fate of Industrial Societies *(2003),* Powerdown: Options and Actions for a Post-Carbon World *(2004), and* Blackout: Coal, Climate and the Last Energy Crisis *(2009). He has authored scores of essays and articles, is featured in many documentaries, and has appeared on numerous television and radio programs. Heinberg is Senior Fellow-in-Residence at Post Carbon Institute.*

❖

In 1972, the now-classic book *Limits to Growth* explored the consequences for Earth's ecosystems of exponential growth in population, industrialization, pollution, food production, and resource depletion.[1] That book, which still stands as the best-selling environmental title ever published, reported on the first attempts to use computers to model the likely interactions between trends in resources, consumption, and population. It summarized the first major scientific study to question the assumption that economic growth can and will continue more or less uninterrupted into the foreseeable future.

The idea was heretical at the time, and still is: During the past few decades, growth has become virtually the sole index of national economic well-being. When an economy grows, jobs appear, investments yield high returns, and everyone is happy. When the economy stops growing, financial bloodletting and general misery ensue. Predictably, a book saying that growth *cannot* and *will not* continue beyond a certain point proved profoundly upsetting in some quarters, and soon *Limits to Growth* was pilloried in a public relations campaign organized by pro-growth business interests. In reality, this purported "debunking" merely amounted to taking a few numbers in the book completely out of context, citing them as "predictions" (which they explicitly were not), and then claiming that these predictions had failed. The ruse was quickly exposed, but rebuttals often don't gain nearly as much publicity as accusations, and so today millions of people mistakenly believe that the book was long ago discredited. In fact, the original *Limits to Growth* scenarios have held up quite well, so much so that even the thoroughly pro-business *Wall Street Journal* printed a lengthy front-page reflection on that fact in March 2008.[2]

In any case, the underlying premise of the book is irrefutable: At some point in time, humanity's ever-increasing resource consumption will meet the very real limits of a planet with finite natural resources.

We the co-authors of *The Post Carbon Reader* believe that this time has come.

THE PIVOTAL ROLE OF ENERGY

During the past two centuries, an explosion in population, consumption, and technological innovation has brought previously unimaginable advances in health, wealth, transport, and communications.

These events were largely made possible by the release of enormous amounts of cheap energy from fossil fuels starting in the mid-nineteenth century. Oil, coal, and natural gas, produced by natural processes over scores of millions of years, represent far more concentrated forms of energy than any of the sources previously available to humanity (food crops, human and animal muscles, and simple windmills or water mills) and, with even basic technology, are comparatively easy to access. With this abundant energy available to drive production processes, it became possible to increase rates of extraction of other natural resources—as, for example, chain saws and powered trawlers could harvest timber and fish at rates previously unimaginable. Meanwhile, fuel-fed tractors enabled a relatively small number of farmers to support many specialists in industrial or commercial enterprises, leading to massive urbanization in nearly every country. Modern chemistry (largely based on organic compounds derived from fossil fuels) led also to modern pharmaceuticals—which, together with improved sanitation (likewise dependent on cheap energy), enabled longer life spans and growing populations.

And so, increased consumption of fossil fuels has produced both economic growth and population growth. However, a bigger population and a growing economy lead to more energy demand. We are thus enmeshed in a classic self-reinforcing ("positive") feedback loop.

Crucially, the planet on which all of this growth is occurring happens to be limited in size, with fixed stores of fossil fuels and mineral ores, and with constrained capacities to regenerate forests, fish, topsoil, and freshwater. Indeed, it appears that we are now pushing up against these very physical limits:

- The world is at, nearing, or past the points of peak production of a number of critical nonrenewable resources—including oil, natural gas, and coal, as well as many economically important minerals ranging from antimony to zinc.
- The global climate is being destabilized by greenhouse gases emitted from the burning of fossil fuels, leading to more severe weather (including droughts) as well as melting glaciers and rising sea levels.
- Freshwater scarcity is a real or impending problem in nearly all of the world's nations due to climate change, pollution, and overuse of groundwater for agriculture and industrial processes.
- World food production per capita is declining and the maintenance of existing total harvests is threatened by climate change, soil erosion, water scarcity, and high fuel costs.
- Earth's plant and animal species are being driven to extinction by human activities at a rate unequaled in the last 60 million years.

The exact timing of peak oil (the maximum point of global oil production) can still be debated, as can the details of climate science. Experts can further refine their forecasts for food harvests based on expectations for new crop varieties. Nevertheless, the overall picture is incontrovertible: The growth phase of industrial civilization was driven by the cheap energy from fossil fuels, and the decline phase of industrial civilization (now commencing) will be led by the depletion of those fuels as well as by environmental collapse caused directly or indirectly by the burning of coal, oil, and natural gas.

AT THE END OF ABUNDANCE,
ON THE VERGE OF DECLINE

Our starting point for future planning, then, must be the realization that we are living today at the end of the period of greatest material abundance in human history—an abundance based on temporary sources of cheap energy that made all else possible. Now that the most important of those sources are entering their inevitable sunset phase, we are at the beginning of a period of overall economic contraction.

Limits to Growth foresaw this inflection point nearly forty years ago. But the world failed to heed the warning; as a result, adaptation now will be much more difficult than would have been the case if growth had been proactively curtailed decades ago. Global leaders now face the need to accomplish four enormous tasks simultaneously:

1. *Rapidly reduce dependence on fossil fuels.* We must do this to avert worse climate impacts, but also because the fuels themselves will be more scarce and expensive. Ending our reliance on coal, oil, and natural gas proactively with minimal social disruption will require a rapid redesign of transportation, agriculture, and power-generation systems.

2. *Adapt to the end of economic growth.* This means reworking, even reinventing, our existing economic system, which functions only in a condition of continuous expansion. Banking, finance, and the process of money creation will all need to be put on a new and different footing.

3. *Design and provide a sustainable way of life for 7 billion people.* We must stabilize and gradually reduce human population over time, using humane strategies such as providing higher levels of education for women in poor countries. But even in the best case, this objective will take decades to achieve; in the meantime, we must continue to support existing human populations while doing a better job of providing basic services for those at the bottom of the economic ladder. We must accomplish this in the context of a nongrowing economy and with a shrinking stream of resource inputs, and we must do it without further damaging the environment.

4. *Deal with the environmental consequences of the past 100 years of fossil-fueled growth.* Even if we cease all environmentally destructive practices tomorrow, we still face the momentum of processes already set in motion throughout decades of deforestation, overfishing, topsoil erosion, and fossil-fuel combustion. First and foremost of these processes is, of course, global climate change, which will almost

certainly have serious impacts on world agriculture even if future carbon emissions decline sharply and soon.

Each of these four tasks represents an enormous challenge whose difficulty is multiplied by the simultaneous need to address the other three. The convergence of so many civilization-threatening planetary crises is unique in our history as a species.

LIMITS ARE UNAVOIDABLE

It is unpleasant and unprofitable to talk about limits to the human enterprise. Yet in principle, the argument for eventual limits to growth is comprehensible by nearly anyone.

Simple arithmetic growth is easy to understand. Imagine starting with $100 in a piggy bank and adding to it $10 every year—that's arithmetic growth. By the end of 50 years you will have $600. A debt or a problem that grows arithmetically is much simpler to deal with than one that grows *exponentially*—that's where the quantity expands by a certain percentage per unit of time. Start again with $100 in a piggy bank, but let it somehow magically grow by 10 percent per year, compounded, and the results are quite different: At the end of 50 years, you will have nearly $12,000, or over 20 times as much as yielded by arithmetic growth (figure 1.1). When discussing investments, exponential growth sounds like a very good thing, but when debts or problems grow in this way, calamity has a way of sneaking up on us.

If any quantity grows steadily by a certain fixed percentage per year, this implies that it will double in size every so many years; the higher the percentage growth rate, the quicker the doubling. A rough method of figuring doubling times is known as the "rule of 70": Dividing the percentage growth rate into 70 gives the approximate time required for the initial quantity to double. If a quantity is growing at 1 percent per year, it will double in 70 years; at growth of 2 percent per year, it will double in 35 years; at 5 percent growth, it will double in only 14 years; and so on. If you want to be more precise, you can use the Y^x button on your calculator, but the rule of 70 works fine for most purposes.

Here's a real-world example: Over the past two centuries, human population has grown at rates ranging from less than 1 percent to more

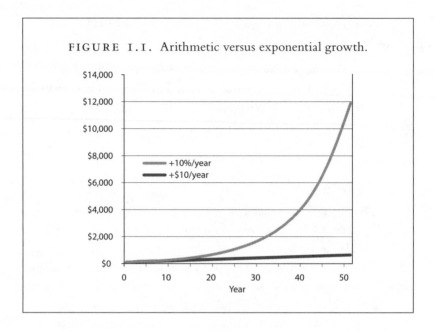

FIGURE I.I. Arithmetic versus exponential growth.

than 2 percent per year. In 1800, world population stood at about 1 billion; by 1930 it had doubled to 2 billion. Only 40 years later (in 1975) it had doubled again to 4 billion; currently we are on track to achieve a third doubling, to 8 billion humans, around 2025. No one seriously expects human population to continue growing for centuries into the future.

In nature, growth always slams up against nonnegotiable constraints sooner or later. If a species finds that its food source has expanded, its numbers will increase to take advantage of those surplus calories—but then its food source will become depleted as more mouths consume it, and its predators will likewise become more numerous (more tasty meals for them!). Population "blooms" (that is, periods of rapid growth) are always followed by crashes and die-offs. Always.

Here is another real-world example. In recent years China's economy has been growing at 8 percent or more per year; that means it is more than doubling in size about every 9 years. Indeed, China consumes more than twice as much coal as it did a decade ago—the same with iron ore and oil. The nation now has four times as many highways as it did, and almost five times as many cars. How long can this go on? How many more doublings can occur before China has used up its key resources—or has simply decided that enough is enough and has stopped growing?

ECONOMISTS TEND TO IGNORE
ENVIRONMENTAL LIMITS

It makes sense that economies should follow rules analogous to those that govern biological systems. Plants and animals tend to grow quickly when they are young, but then they reach a more or less stable mature size. Beyond a certain point, growth becomes more of a problem than an advantage.

But economists generally don't see things this way. That is probably because most current economic theories were formulated during an anomalous historical period of sustained growth. Economists are merely generalizing from their experience: They can point to decades of steady growth in the recent past, and they simply project that experience into the future. Moreover, they have ways to explain why modern market economies are immune to the kinds of limits that constrain natural systems; the two main ones concern *substitution* and *efficiency.*

If a useful resource becomes scarce its price will rise, and this creates an incentive for users of the resource to find a substitute. For example, if oil gets expensive enough, energy companies might start making liquid fuels from coal. Or they might develop other energy sources undreamed of today. Economists theorize that this process of substitution can go on forever. It's part of the magic of the free market.

Increasing efficiency means doing more with less. In the United States, the number of inflation-adjusted dollars generated in the economy for every unit of energy consumed has increased steadily over recent decades.[3] That's one kind of economic efficiency. Another has to do with locating the cheapest sources of materials and the places where workers will be most productive and work for the lowest wages. As we increase efficiency, we use less—of resources, labor, or money—to do more. That enables more growth.

Increasing efficiency and finding substitutes for depleting resources are undeniably effective adaptive strategies of market economies. Nevertheless, the question remains open as to how long these strategies can continue to work in the real world—which is governed less by economic theories than by the laws of physics. In the real world, some things don't have substitutes, or the substitutes are too expensive, or don't work as well, or can't be produced fast enough. And efficiency follows a law of diminishing returns: The first gains in efficiency are usually cheap, but every further incremental gain tends to cost more, until further gains become prohibitively expensive.

Unlike economists, most physical scientists recognize that growth within any functioning, bounded system has to stop sometime.

But this discussion of limits has very real implications, because "the economy" is not just an abstract concept; it is what determines whether we live in luxury or poverty, whether we eat or starve. If economic growth ends, everyone will be impacted, and it will take society years to adapt to this new condition. Therefore it is important to be able to forecast whether that moment is close or distant in time.

Hence the *Limits to Growth* study and book. Its authors fed in data for world population growth, consumption trends, and the abundance of various important resources, ran their computer program, and concluded that the end of growth would probably arrive between 2010 and 2050. Industrial output and food production would then fall, leading to a decline in population.[4]

THE POST-CARBON TRANSITION

Already many farsighted organizations and communities see and understand this long-term trajectory of the human project and are experimenting with ways to satisfy basic human needs in a way that can continue into the indefinite future.

Alternative energy sources and greater efficiencies are important, but the post-carbon transition will not be limited merely to building wind turbines or weatherizing homes, for two key reasons: First, there are no alternative energy sources (renewable or otherwise) capable of supplying energy as cheaply and in such abundance as fossil fuels currently yield, in the brief time that we need them to come online. Second, we have designed and built the infrastructure of our transport, electricity, and food systems—as well as our building stock—to suit the unique characteristics of oil, natural gas, and coal. Changing to different energy sources will require the redesign of many aspects of these systems.

The post-carbon transition must entail the thorough redesign of our societal infrastructure, which today is utterly dependent on cheap fossil fuels. Just as the fossil-fuel economy of today systemically and comprehensively differs from the agrarian economy of 1800, the post-fossil-fuel economy of 2050 will profoundly differ from all that we are familiar with now. This difference will be reflected in urban design, land-use patterns, food systems, manufacturing output, distribution networks, the job market, transportation systems, health care, tourism, and more. It will also require a fundamental rethinking of our financial institutions and cultural values.

LEADING THE TRANSITION

Our new historical moment requires different thinking and different strategies, but it also offers new opportunities to solve some very practical problems. Ideas from environmentalists that for decades have been derided by economists and politicians—reducing consumption, relocalizing economic activity, building self-sufficiency—are suddenly being taken seriously in households that can no longer afford to keep up with the consumerist treadmill.

Quietly, a small but growing movement of engaged citizens, community groups, businesses, and elected officials has begun the transition to a post-carbon world. These early actors have worked to reduce consumption, produce local food and energy, invest in local economies, rebuild skills, and preserve local ecosystems. For some citizens, this effort has merely entailed planting a garden, riding a bike to work, or no longer buying from "big-box" stores. Their motivations are diverse, including halting climate change and promoting environmental preservation, food security, and local economic development. The essence of these efforts, however, is the same: They all recognize that the world is changing and that the old way of doing things, based on the idea that consumption can and should continue to grow indefinitely, no longer works.

Alone, these efforts are not nearly enough. But taken together, they can point the way toward a new economy. This new economy would not be a "free market" but a "real market," much like the one fabled economist Adam Smith originally envisioned; it would be, as author David Korten has said, an economy driven by Main Street and not Wall Street.[5]

Thus far, most of these efforts have been made voluntarily by exceptional individuals who were quick to understand the crisis we face. But with time, more and more people will be searching for ways to meet basic needs in the context of a shrinking economy. Families reliant on supermarkets with globe-spanning supply chains will need to turn more to local farmers and their own gardens. Many globe-spanning corporations—unable to provide a continuous return on investment or to rely on cheap energy and natural resources to turn a profit—will fail, whereas much smaller local businesses and cooperatives of all kinds will flourish. Local governments facing declining tax revenues will be desperate to find cheap, low-energy ways to support basic public services like water treatment, public transportation, and emergency services.

Elements of a transition strategy have been proposed for decades, with few notable results. Usually these have been presented as independent—sometimes even contradictory—solutions to the problems created by fossil-fuel dependency and consumerism. Now that "business as usual" is ceasing to be an option for mainstream society, these strategies need to be rethought and rearticulated coherently, and they need to *become the mainstream.*

What we need now are clarity, leadership, coordination, and collaboration. With shared purpose and a clear understanding of both the challenges and the solutions, we *can* manage the transition to a sustainable, equitable, post-carbon world, though the urgency of the need to fully and immediately engage with the transition process at all levels of society can hardly be overstated.

WHAT IS SUSTAINABILITY?

RICHARD HEINBERG

RICHARD HEINBERG *is widely regarded as one of the world's most effective com-*
municators of the urgent need to transition away from fossil fuels. He is the author of
nine books, including The Party's Over: Oil, War and the Fate of Industrial
Societies *(2003),* Powerdown: Options and Actions for a Post-Carbon
World *(2004), and* Blackout: Coal, Climate and the Last Energy Crisis
(2009). He has authored scores of essays and articles, is featured in many docu-
mentaries, and has appeared on numerous television and radio programs. Heinberg
is Senior Fellow-in-Residence at Post Carbon Institute.

❖

The essence of the term *sustainable* is "that which can be maintained over time." By implication, this means that any society that is unsustainable cannot be maintained for long and will cease to function at some point.

Unfortunately, in recent years the word *sustainable* has become widely used to refer merely to practices that are reputed to be more environmentally sound than others. Often the word is used so carelessly as to lead some environmentalists to advise abandoning its use.[1] Nevertheless, the concept is indispensable and should be the cornerstone for all long-range planning.

It is probably safe to assume that no human living arrangement can be maintained forever. Astronomers assure us that in several billion years the Sun will have heated to the point that Earth's oceans will boil away. Thus *sustainability* is a relative term. It seems reasonable to use as a frame of reference for the durations of prior civilizations, ranging from hundreds to thousands of years. A sustainable society, then, would be able to maintain itself for many centuries at least.

HOW DO WE DEFINE SUSTAINABILITY?

The concept of sustainability has been embodied in the traditions of many indigenous peoples; for example, it was a precept of the Iroquois Con-federacy's *Gayanashagowa*, or Great Law of Peace, that chiefs consider the impact of their decisions on the seventh generation to come.

The first known European use of the word *sustainability* (German: *Nachhaltigkeit*) occurred in 1713 in the book *Sylvicultura Oeconomica* by German forester and scientist Hans Carl von Carlowitz. Later, French and English foresters adopted the practice of planting trees as a path to "sustained-yield forestry."

The term gained widespread usage after 1987, when the Brundtland Report from the United Nations' World Commission on Environment and Development defined *sustainable development* as development that "meets the needs of the present generation without compromising the ability of future generations to meet their own needs."[2] This definition of sustainability has proved extremely influential and is still widely used; nevertheless, it has been criticized for its failure to explicitly note the unsustainability of the use of nonrenewable resources and for its general disregard of the problem of population growth.[3]

Also in the 1980s, Swedish oncologist Dr. Karl-Henrik Robèrt brought together leading scientists to develop a consensus on require-ments for a sustainable society. In 1989 Robèrt formulated this consensus in four system conditions for sustainability, which in turn became the basis for an organization, the Natural Step. Subsequently, many businesses and municipalities around the world pledged to abide by Natural Step condi-tions. The four conditions are as follows:

> In a sustainable society, nature is not subject to systematically increasing:
>
> 1. concentrations of substances extracted from the earth's crust.
> 2. concentrations of substances produced by society.
> 3. degradation by physical means.
>
> And, in that society:
>
> 4. people are not subject to conditions that systematically undermine their capacity to meet their needs.[4]

Seeing the need for an accounting or indicator scheme by which to measure sustainability, Canadian ecologist William Rees and graduate student (at that time) Mathis Wackernagel developed in the early 1990s the concept of the "ecological footprint," defined as the amount of land and water area a human population would hypothetically need to provide the resources required to support itself and to absorb its wastes, given prevailing technology.[5] Implicit in the scheme is the recognition that, for humanity to achieve sustainability, the total world population's footprint must be less than the total land and water area of Earth (that footprint is currently calculated by the Global Footprint Network as being about 40 percent larger than the planet can regenerate, indicating that humankind is to this extent overconsuming resources and operating in an unsustainable manner).

A truly comprehensive historical survey of the usage of the terms *sustainable* and *sustainability* is not feasible. A search of Amazon.com for *sustainability* (April 1, 2010) yielded 8,875 book titles containing the word. A search of journal articles on Google Scholar turned up 108,000 hits, indicating many thousands of scholarly articles with the word *sustainability* in their titles. However, a perusal of the literature suggests that most of this immense body of work repeats, or is based on, the definitions and conditions described above.

FIVE AXIOMS OF SUSTAINABILITY

As a contribution to this ongoing refinement of the concept, I recently formulated five axioms (self-evident truths) of sustainability.[6] My goal was simply to distill ideas that had been proposed previously and put them into a concise, easy-to-understand form.

In formulating these axioms, my criteria were as follows:

- To qualify as an axiom, a statement must be capable of being tested using the methodology of science.
- Collectively, a set of axioms intended to define *sustainability* must be minimal (with no redundancies).
- At the same time, the axioms must be sufficient, leaving no glaring loopholes.
- The axioms should be worded in terms a layperson can understand.

Here are the axioms, each followed by a brief discussion:

The First Axiom

Any society that continues to use critical resources unsustainably will collapse.

Exception: A society can avoid collapse by finding replacement resources.

Limit to the exception: In a finite world, the number of possible replacements is also finite.

Archaeologist Joseph Tainter, in his classic study *The Collapse of Complex Societies* (1988), demonstrated that collapse is a frequent if not universal fate of complex societies and argued that collapse results from declining returns on efforts to support growing levels of societal complexity using energy harvested from the environment.[7] Jared Diamond's popular book *Collapse: How Societies Choose to Fail or Succeed* (2005) similarly makes the argument that collapse is the common destiny of societies that ignore resource constraints.[8]

This axiom defines sustainability by the consequences of its absence—that is, collapse. Tainter defines *collapse* as a reduction in social complexity—that is, a contraction of society in terms of its population size, the sophistication of its technologies, the consumption rates of its people, and the diversity of its specialized social roles. Historically, *collapse* has often meant a precipitous decline in population brought about by social chaos, warfare, disease, or famine. However, collapse can also occur more gradually over a period of many decades or even centuries. There is also the theoretical possibility that a society could choose to reduce its complexity in a controlled, gradual manner.

While it could be argued that a society can choose to change rather than collapse, the only choices that would substantively affect the outcome would be to cease using critical resources unsustainably or to find alternative resources.

A society that uses resources sustainably may collapse for other reasons, some beyond the society's control (as a result of an overwhelming natural disaster or of conquest by another, more aggressive society, to name just two of many possibilities), so it cannot be said that a sustainable society is immune to collapse unless many conditions for sustainability are specified. This first axiom focuses on resource consumption because that is a decisive, quantifiable, and, in principle, controllable determinant of a society's long-term survival.

The question of what constitutes sustainable or unsustainable use of resources is addressed in the third and fourth axioms.

Critical resources are those that are essential to the maintenance of life and basic social functions—including (but not necessarily limited to) water and the resources necessary to produce food and usable energy.

The first axiom's "exception" and "limit to the exception" address the common argument of free-market economists that resources are infinitely substitutable, and that therefore modern market-driven societies need never face a depletion-led collapse, even if their consumption rates continue to escalate.[9] In some instances, substitutes for resources become readily available and are even superior, as was the case in the mid-nineteenth century when kerosene from petroleum was substituted for whale oil as a fuel for lamps. In other cases, substitutes are inferior, as is the case with oil sands as a substitute for conventional petroleum, given that oil sands are less energy dense, require more energy input for processing, and produce more carbon emissions. As time goes on, societies will tend first to exhaust substitutes that are superior and easy to get at, then those that are equivalent, and increasingly will have to rely on ever more inferior substitutes to replace depleting resources—unless rates of consumption are held in check.

The Second Axiom

Population growth and/or growth in the rates of consumption of resources cannot be sustained.[10]

Human population growth has been sustained up to the present. How can we be sure that it cannot be sustained into the indefinite future? Simple arithmetic can be used to show that even small rates of growth, if continued, add up to absurdly large—and plainly unsupportable—population sizes and rates of consumption. For example, a simple 1 percent rate of growth in the present human population (less than the actual current rate) would result in a doubling of population each 70 years. Thus in 2075, Earth would be home to 13 billion humans; in 2145, 26 billion; and so on. By the year 3050, there would be one human per square meter of Earth's land surface (including mountains and deserts). Virtually no one expects this to occur—at some point, population growth will cease. Similar calculations apply to consumption rates.

The Third Axiom

To be sustainable, the use of *renewable* resources must proceed at a rate that is less than or equal to the rate of natural replenishment.

Renewable resources are exhaustible. Forests can be overcut, resulting in barren landscapes and shortages of wood (as occurred in many parts of Europe in past centuries), and fish can be overharvested, resulting in the extinction or near extinction of many species (as is occurring today globally).

This axiom has been stated (in somewhat different ways) by many economists and ecologists and is the basis for "sustained-yield forestry" (see above) and "maximum-sustainable-yield" fishery management.[11]

The term "rate of natural replenishment" requires some discussion. The first clue that harvesting is proceeding at a rate greater than that of natural replenishment is the decline of the resource base. However, a resource may be declining for reasons other than overharvesting; for example, a forest that is not being logged may be decimated by disease. Nevertheless, if the resource is declining, pursuit of the goal of sustainability requires that the rate of harvest be reduced, regardless of the cause of resource decline. Sometimes harvests must drop dramatically, at a rate far greater than the rate of resource decline, so that the resource has time to recover. This has been the case with regard to commercial wild whale and fish species that have been overharvested to the point of near extinction; a moratorium on harvesting these species was necessary for them to recover. If the remaining breeding population is too small, however, even a moratorium is insufficient and the species cannot recover.

The Fourth Axiom

To be sustainable, the use of *nonrenewable* resources must proceed at a rate that is declining, and the *rate of decline* must be greater than or equal to the *rate of depletion*.

The *rate of depletion* is defined as the amount being extracted and used during a specified time interval (usually a year) as a percentage of the amount left to extract.

No continuous rate of use of any nonrenewable resource is sustainable. However, if the rate of use is declining at a rate greater than or equal to the rate of depletion, this can be said to be a sustainable situation because society's dependence on the resource will be reduced to insignificance before the resource is exhausted.[12]

Estimates of the "amount left to extract," mentioned in the axiom, are disputable for all nonrenewable resources. Unrealistically robust estimates would tend to skew the depletion rate in a downward direction, undermining efforts to attain sustainability via a resource-depletion protocol. It may be realistic to assume that people in the future will find ways to extract nonrenewable resources more thoroughly, with amounts that would otherwise be left in the ground becoming economically recoverable as a result of higher commodity prices and improvements in extraction technology. Exploration techniques are likely to improve as well, leading to further discoveries of the resource. Thus, realistic estimates of ultimately recoverable quantities should be greater than what is now known to be extractable using current technology and at current prices. However, it is unrealistic to assume that people in the future will ever be able to economically extract all of a given resource or that limits of declining marginal returns in the extraction process will no longer apply. Moreover, if discovery rates are currently declining, it is probably unrealistic to assume that discovery rates will increase substantially in the future. Thus, for any nonrenewable resource, prudence dictates adhering to conservative estimates of the "amount left to extract."[13]

The Fifth Axiom

Sustainability requires that substances introduced into the environment from human activities be minimized and rendered harmless to biosphere functions.

In cases where pollution from the extraction and consumption of nonrenewable resources has proceeded at expanding rates for some time and threatens the viability of ecosystems, reduction in the rates of extraction and consumption of those resources may need to occur at a rate greater than the rate of depletion.

If the second, third, and fourth axioms are followed, pollution should be minimized as a result. Nevertheless, these conditions are not sufficient in all cases to avert potentially collapse-inducing impacts.

It is possible for a society to generate serious pollution from the unwise use of renewable resources (the use of natural tanning agents on hides damaged streams during preindustrial times), and such impacts are to be avoided. Likewise, especially where large numbers of humans are concentrated, their biological wastes may pose severe environmental problems; such wastes must be properly composted.

The most serious forms of pollution in the modern world arise from the extraction, processing, and consumption of nonrenewable resources. If (as outlined in the fourth axiom) the consumption of nonrenewable resources declines, pollution should also decline. However, in the current instance, where extraction and consumption of nonrenewable resources have been growing for some time and have resulted in levels of pollution that threaten basic biosphere functions, heroic measures are called for. This is, of course, the situation with regard to atmospheric concentrations of greenhouse gases, especially in relation to the burning of coal; it is also the case with regard to hormone-mimicking petrochemical pollution, which inhibits reproduction in many vertebrate species. In the first instance: Merely to reduce coal consumption by the global coal-depletion rate would not suffice to avert a climatic catastrophe. The coal-depletion rate is small, climate impacts from coal combustion emissions are building quickly, and annual reductions in those emissions must occur at high rates if ecosystem-threatening consequences are to be avoided. Similarly, in the case of petrochemical pollution, merely to reduce the dispersion of plastics and other petrochemicals into the environment by the annual rate of depletion of oil and natural gas would not suffice to avert environmental harms on a scale potentially leading to the collapse of ecosystems and human societies.

If a reduction in emissions or other pollutants can be obtained without a reduction in consumption of nonrenewable resources—for example, by using technological means to capture polluting substances and sequester them harmlessly, or by curtailing the production of certain industrial chemicals—then a reduction in consumption of such resources need only occur at the depletion rate in order to achieve sustainability. However, society should be extremely skeptical and careful about claims that untested technologies can safely sequester polluting substances for very long periods of time.

THE FIVE AXIOMS AND A SOCIETY'S SUSTAINABILITY

These axioms are, of course, open to further refinement. I have attempted to anticipate criticisms likely to be leveled at them, which will probably be

BOX 2.1   Defining Social Sustainability

Jesse Dillard, Veronica Dujon, and Mary King

JESSE DILLARD, VERONICA DUJON, and MARY KING are faculty members at Portland State University and co-editors of *Understanding the Social Dimension of Sustainability* (2009), one of the first books in the otherwise ecology- and economics-dominated sustainability literature to explore and define the key elements of social sustainability. Dillard is the Retzlaff Chair in Accounting and director of the Center for Professional Integrity and Accountability; Dujon is chair of the department of sociology; and King is a professor of economics.

Sustainability is often thought of as composed of three overlapping, mutually dependent goals:

a) to live in a way that is environmentally sustainable, or viable over the very long-term,

b) to live in a way that is economically sustainable, maintaining living standards over the long-term, and

c) to live in a way that is socially sustainable, now and in the future.

To date, concerns with environmental and economic sustainability have eclipsed efforts to understand the social aspects of sustainability. As noted by several of the authors of chapters in *Understanding the Social Dimension of Sustainability*, thinking on the social aspect of sustainability has been relatively neglected and is by far the least developed. Yet an increasing number of people are attempting to integrate social concerns into their work on sustainability, both theoretically and in practice. That anthology provides guidance for a developing field of thought from a variety of perspectives.

At present consensus does not exist even on a definition of social sustainability. Polese and Stren, writing up the findings of a UNESCO project on the "social sustainability of cities," identify social sustainability as "policies and institutions that have the overall effect of integrating diverse groups and cultural practices in a just and equitable fashion."[1]

Many analysts have followed Robert Putnam in an exploration of "social capital," asserted by the World Bank, among others, to consist of "the norms and networks that enable collective action."[2] Researchers working in this vein have understood social capital to result from participation in civic institutions. Presumably social sustainability would require that social capital be maintained at "sustainable" levels for future generations, perhaps requiring social support of effective civic institutions to this end.

(continued)

BOX 2.1 *(continued)*

Most business sustainability efforts appear to construe social sustainability as charity, performed as an act of public relations. These are "policies that encourage community involvement, volunteering, [and] development of local communities."[3] According to a recent PricewaterhouseCoopers survey of large U.S. businesses, three-quarters of the firms that responded to the survey were implementing some sustainable business practices, though relatively few are pursuing the social leg of the "triple bottom line"—corporate language for meeting financial, environmental, and social objectives as an organization.[4] Where businesses are attending to the social aspect of sustainability, they are interpreting it as corporate philanthropy and sometimes as policies to help employees achieve "work/family balance" or to avoid burnout.

In urban planning circles, the tripartite understanding of sustainability is sometimes referred to as "the three 'E's, environment, economy, and equity." Social sustainability is conceived of as "equity," without much thought as to what that might require or whether equity alone is sufficient for social sustainability.

A more thought-out and satisfactory definition of social sustainability is provided by Harris and Goodwin: "A socially sustainable system must achieve fairness in distribution and opportunity, adequate provision of social services, including health and education, gender equity, and political accountability and participation."[5] While more solid, this definition still misses the social process required to achieve economic and environmental sustainability that concerns many.

Environmental economists have focused substantial attention on the issue of property rights, with the idea that clear ownership facilitates better environmental management. However, social institutions conducive to better environmental outcomes may have adverse social consequences. Often these social considerations are overlooked, as in the case of ecologists pointing out the ecological advantages of collective management of group resources without noting that the group governance is not democratic, but empowers only a small portion of the community.[6]

Consequently, several contributors to *Understanding the Social Dimension of Sustainability* use a working definition of the social aspect of sustainability developed over time in our workshops and graduate seminars:

The social dimension of sustainability should be understood as both

a) the processes that generate social health and well-being now and in the future, and

b) those social institutions that facilitate environmental and economic sustainability now and for the future.

The processes are both a means to, and an end of, social sustainability. Indeed, for the social aspect of sustainability in particular, processes may often be more important than outcomes. For instance, high rates of literacy achieved by a citizenry engaged in a democratic planning process, as in Kerala, India, may be far more socially sustainable than even higher rates of literacy accomplished in an authoritarian fashion.[7] However, an adequate working definition of the social aspect of sustainability represents only the first step in developing an understanding of the concept.

---

1. Mario Polese and Richard Stren, *The Social Sustainability of Cities: Diversity and the Management of Change* (Toronto: University of Toronto Press, 2000), 229.

2. Robert D. Putnam, *Bowling Alone: The Collapse and Revival of American Community* (New York: Simon & Schuster, 2000); World Bank, *Social Capital Initiative*, http://www.worldbank.org/ (accessed on October 9, 2007).

3. Sully Taylor, "The Human Resource Side of Sustainability," presentation at Portland State University, February 10, 2003.

4. PricewaterhouseCoopers, *2002 Social Sustainability Survey Report*, 2002.

5. Jonathan M. Harris and Neva R. Goodwin, "Volume Introduction," in *A Survey of Sustainable Development: Social and Economic Dimensions,* Jonathan M. Harris et al., eds. (Washington DC: Island Press, 2001).

6. Janis B. Alcorn and Victor M. Toledo, "Resilient Resource Management in Mexico's Forest Ecosystems: The Contribution of Property Rights," in *Linking Social and Ecological Systems: Management Practices and Social Mechanisms for Building Resilience,* Fikret Berkes and Carl Folke, eds. (Cambridge, UK: Cambridge University Press, 1998).

7. T. M. Thomas Isaac and Richard W. Franke, *Local Democracy and Development: The Kerala People's Campaign for Decentralized Planning* (Lanham, MD: Rowman and Littlefield, 2002).

Reprinted with permission from Jesse Dillard, Veronica Dujon, and Mary C. King, eds., *Understanding the Social Dimension of Sustainability* (London: Routledge, 2009), 2–4. Copyright © 2009 Taylor & Francis.

of the sort that says these axioms are not sufficient to define the concept of sustainability. The most obvious of these is worth mentioning and discussing here: *Why is there no axiom relating to social equity* (similar to the fourth condition of the Natural Step framework as noted above)?

The purpose of the axioms set forth here is not to describe conditions that would lead to a good or just society, merely to a society able to be maintained over time. It is not clear that perfect economic equality or a perfectly egalitarian system of decision-making is necessary to avert societal collapse. Certainly, extreme inequality seems to make societies vulnerable to internal social and political upheaval. On the other hand, it could be argued that a society's adherence to the five axioms as stated will tend to lead to relatively greater levels of economic and political equity, thus obviating the need for a separate axiom in this regard (see box 2.1 for further discussion on approaches to the social dimension of sustainability). In anthropological literature, modest rates of resource consumption and low population sizes relative to the available resource base are correlated with the use of egalitarian decision-making processes and with economic equity—though the correlation is skewed by other variables, such as means of sustenance (hunting-and-gathering societies tend to be highly equitable and egalitarian, whereas herding societies tend to be less so). If such correlations continue to hold, the reversion to lower rates of consumption of resources should lead to a more rather than less egalitarian society.

3

THINKING "RESILIENCE"

WILLIAM E. REES, FRSC

WILLIAM REES *is a professor in the School of Community and Regional Planning at the University of British Columbia. He is best known as the co-originator of "ecological footprint analysis," a quantitative tool that estimates humanity's ecological impact in terms of appropriated ecosystem area. He is a founding Fellow of the One Earth Initiative and a founding member and past president of the Canadian Society for Ecological Economics. In 2006 he was elected to the Royal Society of Canada. Rees is a Fellow of Post Carbon Institute.*

❖

THE EMERGENCE OF "RESILIENCE" THINKING

During the past two centuries, life was clearly getting easier and better for many people. The Enlightenment had seemingly abolished superstition as a major influence in the affairs of the Western world while its offspring, modern science, gave humans apparent mastery of matter and the ability to shape the material world to their own purposes. Through much of the twentieth century, progress, or at least what some now call "the progress myth," seemed primed to become a permanent reality. Medicine eliminated many of the scourges that had historically kept humanity's population in check even as industrial agriculture—Malthus notwithstanding—ensured that food production exploded even faster than population. Longevity doubled in many developing countries,[1] while rising incomes, shorter workweeks, unprecedented personal mobility (the private automobile), and the accelerating proliferation of laptops, cell phones, iPods, and other electronic gadgetry ensured that increasingly wealthy millions didn't lack options to fill their longer lives, either at work or at play.

Then the warning signs began to accumulate. Various science-based resource-management strategies that initially seemed successful subsequently crashed and burned:

- Agricultural pesticides once promised to eradicate crop-damaging insects, but dozens of crop-damaging insect species have since evolved immunity and crop losses are as great as ever.
- Fire control, once a mainstay of sound forest management, is now known to turn many protected forests into explosive tinderboxes prone to unstoppable wildfire (as any devotee of a burned-out Yellowstone National Park can readily testify).
- Despite the promise that modern fisheries science and economics could deliver "maximum sustainable yield," we have witnessed the repeated collapse of fisheries around the world, to the despair of both fisheries managers and dependent human communities.

Just as worrisome, various management efforts to reverse these negative trends or repair ecosystem damage have failed. For example:

- The North Atlantic cod stocks that collapsed in 1992 have not recovered despite an eighteen-year-and-counting moratorium on fishing. (The cod are not extinct, but their ecosystems have changed in ways that prevent them from reoccupying their former niche.)
- Massive clear-cuts in the Pacific Northwest have not responded to reforestation efforts as expected.
- The south polar ozone hole shows little sign of recovery, despite the 1987 Montreal Protocol to phase out ozone-destroying gases (regarded as the most successful example of international cooperation to solve a global environmental problem).

As if to underscore the increasing scale of the problem, the oil spills, pesticide scares, and other mainly local pollution incidents that grabbed headlines in the 1960s and 1970s have evolved into the ozone depletion, acid rain, climate change, and other global-scale concerns that have dominated the environmental headlines from the 1980s to the present day.

Ecologists have come to believe that the unexpected systems failures illustrated by these examples are not mere aberrations but are actually the *norm* for ecosystems under steadily increasing exploitation pressure. This implies, for example, that conventional harvesting models based on earlier resource-management concepts are seriously flawed—they do not adequately reflect the functional dynamics of systems under stress. And many critical ecosystems on every continent and in all the world's oceans *are* under stress. The sheer scale of human demands on nature has pushed many socio-ecosystems into unfamiliar and often unfriendly territory.[2] The transition is often unexpected, rapid, and tragic for dependent human populations.

Just what is going on here? One explanation is that overstressed socio-ecosystems gradually lose their "resilience," which is defined as *the capacity of a system to withstand disturbance while still retaining its fundamental structure, function, and internal feedbacks.*[3] Experience shows that, over time, simplified intensively managed systems become more inflexibly "brittle" and thus more prone to erratic behavior (including systems collapse) than they were at earlier stages of "development." To put it another way, excessive human activity—either resource exploitation or waste production—can erode the functional integrity of the same ecosystems that make these human activities possible. Ironically, there are also cases in which human purposes are *frustrated* by natural resilience, such as when insect species evolve immunity to pesticides. The adaptive responses of highly resilient ecosystems or components can thus defeat our best management efforts. Since techno-industrial society remains utterly dependent on ecosystems to continue providing life support, learning how best to cultivate systems resilience must become a key element of sustainability thinking.

Getting at the Root of the Problem

> We have in our hands now . . . the technology to feed, clothe, and supply energy to an ever-growing population for the next 7 billion years.
>
> —JULIAN SIMON[4]

> Can you think of any problem in any area of human endeavor on any scale, from microscopic to global, whose long-term solution is in any demonstrable way aided, assisted, or advanced by further increases in population, locally, nationally, or globally?
>
> —ALBERT A. BARTLETT[5]

How is it that our allegedly science-based culture could produce such a conundrum? Part of the problem is that modern industrial society operates from a "normal-science" perspective that takes a narrowly mechanistic

approach to the biophysical world. For example, most economic thinking and related resource-management policy assume direct, short-term,
reversible cause–effect relationships between human activities and ecosystem responses, and also that the world generally gravitates toward a single
equilibrium. Resource management may acknowledge that ecosystems,
social systems, and socio-ecosystems are complicated, but it also assumes
that, given sufficient data, their "nature" is knowable and predictable. In
any case, our models typically assume that any changes in exploited systems will be incremental, obvious, direct, and manageable.

From this perspective, the role of science is to control the natural
world for human purposes—there are no limits on growth or constraints
on human ingenuity. Standard resource-management models are therefore almost entirely anthropocentric and utilitarian. Traditional management strategies strive to enhance the efficiency of growth by *minimizing*
the annoying variability in natural ecosystems and *maximizing* the production of systems components and variables of value to people (e.g., food
crops, fish catches, GDP per capita).[6] And, of course, once the system has
been engineered into some optimally efficient configuration, the focus is
on trying to keep it there (invariably at the expense of other variables and
system components). The implicit assumption in all this is that "uncertainty in nature [can be] replaced by the certainty of human control."[7]
Little thought is given to the effect of exploitation on non-target systems
components or on events and processes at higher and lower scales in the
total ecosystem complex (see box 3.1).

Traditional production-oriented approaches to resource management
can succeed temporarily—indeed, the North Atlantic cod stocks were
fished for several centuries before they collapsed in the early 1990s. However, the record of modern management failures makes clear that the mechanistic thinking upon which management efforts are based does not capture the full structural complexity and behavioral dynamics of real-world
socioecological systems. Natural ecosystems do not operate continuously in
some optimal state; nature does not set out to maximize specific variables or
particular species. Ecosystems are constantly in flux and are normally able
to function over a wide range of natural variability. Indeed, the adaptability
and tolerance of constituent species have been set by the extremes to which
those species and species complexes have been exposed in the course of
evolutionary history, not by arbitrary "optimal" conditions.

BOX 3.1 Trade and Globalization

Perhaps the most sweeping example of the "growth-through-efficiency" mode of thinking is the modern preoccupation with "free trade" and globalization. Breaking down the barriers among national economies makes it possible for each country to specialize in those few products or services for which it has a domestic "comparative advantage"—that is, products that it can produce with the fewest inputs—and to trade for all the rest. Since each nation will theoretically be operating at maximum efficiency, global output per unit input will be maximized and everyone should be materially better off.

Importantly, this singular emphasis on maximizing growth through trade assumes a stable world and unchanging market conditions—that is, that there are few risks associated with either specialization or trade dependence. Governments thus willingly sacrifice other values such as national diversity and self-reliance on the altar of efficiency.

But what happens if technology or markets change so that demand for Country A's products disappears? What is Country B to do if its customary sources for food imports are jeopardized by climate change and it no longer has a functional domestic agricultural sector to fill the gap? The fact is that the real world is one of rapid ecological and cultural change, and in these circumstances perhaps nations should be asking whether narrow specialization and trade or greater structural diversity for self-reliance would better serve their needs for enhanced socioeconomic resilience.

It therefore should not be surprising that attempting to force the system down some narrow productivity channel in the service of human needs affects how that system functions and behaves. One effect is to make the system more vulnerable to what would otherwise be normal shocks and disturbances. Ecosystems are self-organizing, self-producing systems in which each major component exists in vital relationship with other components. These relationships must be maintained if the components are to continue being able to produce themselves and the system is to retain its functional integrity.[8] When humans maximize the harvest of a particular species, for example, we inadvertently alter that species' relationships to multiple other species (e.g., predators and prey) in the ecosystem, setting off a cascade of feedback responses that can fundamentally erode the system's integrity. Some species may be lost, others may be favored, and, ultimately, the system may cease to function in ways that are necessary to sustain either the target species or their human predators.

In short, the evidence suggests that in addition to overharvesting, efficiency-oriented maximum production strategies simplify both exploited ecosystems and the social systems they support. They eliminate important processes and redundancies, and make the socio-ecosystem more vulnerable to additional stress. The system loses resilience.

The Antidote: Complex Systems Science

> There is no sustainable "optimal" state of an ecosystem, a social system or the world. It is an illusion, a product of the way we look at and model the world. It is unattainable . . . and yet it is a widely pursued goal.
>
> —DAVID WALKER AND BRIAN SALT[9]

Science evolves through experiments, both intentional and unplanned. Resource management based on "normal" linear, reductionist thinking was, in effect, a grand unplanned experiment that has served to test existing theory and assumptions about systems behavior. The ultimate failure of the maximum production model can therefore be interpreted as a signal event that forced a revolution in scientists' thinking about natural systems.

Recent decades have seen the emergence of what is sometimes called "post-normal" science, based on a more refined and humble view of complex systems behavior. The goal is twofold: First, to develop a more comprehensive and integrative theory to explain responses to change in interlinked ecological, social, and economic systems across scales in both time and space; second, to better assist people to adapt resiliently to supportive ecosystems that are themselves constantly adapting (including adapting to human intervention!).

The emerging integrative theory accepts—even embraces—uncertainty and unpredictability.[10] Because living systems exist in changing physical environments, they too are constantly changing and adapting. In these circumstances, reliable prediction is limited to narrow domains of relative stability, and the size and boundaries of those domains may themselves be shifting.[11] Surprise and structural change are inevitable in complex systems, particularly socio-ecosystems in which humans are exploiting nature.

Science has also come to recognize that complex systems behavior is nonlinear—there may be significant temporal lags between cause and effect such that damage is not apparent until long after the causal event.[12] Even more problematic, socio-ecosystems are characterized by moving thresholds or "tipping points" whose existence may be unknown until they have been breached (this is just one form of uncertainty that may be inherently irreducible). The problem is that once some key system component—or even a whole subsystem—has crossed a threshold, it may gravitate into a new quasi-stable regime from which it may not easily be extracted. One of the hardest lessons of our great unplanned experiment is that complex systems generally have multiple possible equilibrium states, some of which may be hostile to human needs and purposes.[13]

In these circumstances, mechanical assumptions must give way to dynamic analysis. The role of science shifts from facilitating the restructuring of nature to helping people adapt to natural variability. On the front lines, resource managers must replace assumptions of certain control with cautious humility as the goal of resource extraction shifts from maximization to sufficiency (and even avoiding catastrophe!). Clearly, planning for sustainability requires that we develop new ways to collect, evaluate, and integrate available information. What do we need to know to enable society to adapt to inevitable change? What kinds of information help to foster novelty and innovation in response to inevitable change? Can we learn to distinguish between useful and dangerous information so that we avoid counterproductive policy decisions?

WHAT IS RESILIENCE THINKING?

"Resilience thinking" is one response to the foregoing questions. "The bottom line for sustainability is that any proposal for sustainable development that does not explicitly acknowledge a system's resilience is simply not going to keep delivering the goods (or services)."[14] Resilience science is based on the simple premise that change is inevitable and that attempts to resist change or control it in any strict sense are doomed to failure. Resilience science is also systems science.

Based on the previous analysis, resilience thinking:

· Accepts that the human enterprise is structurally and functionally
  inseparable from nature. That is, the human enterprise is a fully
  embedded, totally dependent subsystem of the ecosphere—people
  live *within* socio-ecosystems. Human activities can therefore significantly affect the integrity and behavior of supportive ecosystems and
  these changes immediately feed back to affect the state of the human
  subsystem. We can no longer understand the dynamics of either the
  natural system or the human subsystem in isolation without understanding the dynamics of the other component.

· Understands that linked/integrated socio-ecosystems are constantly
  changing in response to both internal and external forces—they
  are dynamic complex adaptive systems. The changes within these
  systems are not linear, smooth, or predictable, particularly outside
  the systems' "normal" regime. Indeed, under sufficient pressure,
  critical systems variables may "flip" (cross a threshold) into a different regime or alternative stable state. In other words, like natural
  ecosystems, socio-ecosystems also have multiple possible equilibria,
  some of which may not be amenable to continued human use or
  existence (remember the collapse of the North Atlantic cod fishery).

· Recognizes that the sustainability of the human enterprise on a
  crowded and resource-stressed planet depends on our ability to
  conserve the resilience of socioecological systems. In this context,
  resilience defines the capacity of the system to assimilate disturbances without crossing a threshold into an alternative and possibly
  less "friendly" stable state. A desirable socioecological system characterized by high resilience is able to resist external disturbance and
  continue to provide biophysical goods and services essential for a
  satisfactory quality of life.[15]

· Further recognizes that, for sustainability, resource-management
  efforts must shift from reshaping nature for the purpose of satisfying human demands to moderating human demands so that they fit
  within biophysical limits. They must do this in a way that is consistent with both the productive and assimilative capacities of ecosystems, and in a way that enhances the long-term resilience of the
  integrated socio-ecosystem.

"Panarchy" and Adaptation

> We are now in an era of transformation in which ecosystem man-
> agement must build and maintain ecological resilience as well as
> the social flexibility needed to cope, innovate and adapt.
> —C. S. HOLLING [16]

Understanding and coping with change is at the heart of resilience thinking, but so far we have discussed change as if it were always random and
unexpected. This is not the most interesting kind of change affecting
complex systems. Researchers around the world have discovered that
the most significant changes in natural systems generally follow a recurring pattern consisting of several phases. These can be described as rapid
growth, consolidation and conservation, release (or "collapse"), and reorganization (see box 3.2). Each iteration of the cycle provides opportunities
for innovation and recombination "experiments," thus enabling species
and whole subsystems to adapt to both external and internal change. In
short, the recurring cycles are inherently adaptive and provide a key to
understanding the evolution of natural systems.

Significantly, adaptive cycles are virtually universal. They take place
at every level within the overlapping/nested hierarchy of subsystems at
scales ranging from a leaf to the ecosphere and over periods ranging from
days to geological epochs. On the human side, they affect individuals,
communities, and entire sociopolitical regions over periods from months
to centuries. Researchers use the term "panarchy" (literally, "ruling over
everything") to describe this nested hierarchy, since it transcends scales
in time and space and extends across numerous academic disciplines. The
emphasis in panarchy theory is to discover the role of recurring dynamics
in systems adaptation: "If we can understand these cycles, it seems possible
to evaluate their contribution to sustainability and to identify the points at
which a system is capable of accepting positive change, the points where
it is vulnerable."[17]

Resilience, Panarchy, and Sustainability

If change is inevitable and resilience is necessary for systems stability, what
can panarchy theory contribute to our quest for sustainability? Does it, in

BOX 3.2 The Adaptive Cycle

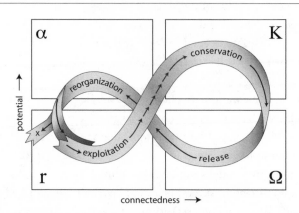

A stylized representation of the four ecosystem functions (r, K, Ω, α) and the flow of events among them. The arrows show the speed of that flow in the cycle, where short, closely spaced arrows indicate a slowly changing situation and long arrows indicate a rapidly changing situation. The cycle reflects changes in two properties: (1) y-axis— the potential that is inherent in the accumulated resources of biomass and nutrients; (2) x-axis— the degree of connectedness among controlling variables. Low connectedness is associated with diffuse elements loosely connected to each other whose behavior is dominated by outward relations and affected by outside variability. High connectedness is associated with aggregated elements whose behavior is dominated by inward relations among elements of the aggregates, relations that control or mediate the influence of external variability. The exit from the cycle indicated at the left of the figure suggests, in a stylized way, the stage where the potential can leak away and where a flip into a less productive and organized system is most likely.

Figure and caption reprinted with permission from L. H. Gunderson and C. S. Holling, eds., *Panarchy: Understanding Transformations in Human and Natural Systems* (Washington DC: Island Press, 2002), 34. Copyright © 2002 Island Press.

Exploitation and growth phase: The early phase in a new adaptive cycle is characterized by the establishment and rapid growth of the stronger opportunistic species (or new businesses) that have flooded in to take advantage of open ecological niches (or unexploited markets) and temporarily plentiful resources. All such "start-ups" are agile and flexible; they may explore numerous available niches or options. In the social domain, new societies or even nations can emerge. Initially, diversity and resilience are high but internal connectivity is low. As it develops, the system gradually creates a stable regime.

Conservation phase: This longest phase of the cycle is characterized by consolidation and accumulation and a change in the character of constituent species. The competitive advantage enjoyed by wasteful generalists/opportunists in the growth phase shifts to efficient specialists. Less aggressive competitors are repressed or eliminated and new entrants to the ecosystem (or market) find it difficult to establish themselves. In ecosystems, internal connectedness and stability increase (though over a narrow range of conditions) and growth slows. Diversity and resilience gradually decline as nutrients and biomass accumulate in a shrinking number of dominant species that compete for ever-scarcer resources. In the economy, establishment firms become complacently unresponsive to changing market conditions or emerging new technologies. Both types of systems become more rigidly homogeneous and monopolistic, which increases their vulnerability to unexpected shocks.

Release phase: "The longer the conservation phase persists, the smaller the shock needed to end it."[1] Subsequent "release" may happen in an instant. With resilience at a minimum, any number of factors—insect outbreaks, prolonged drought, wildfire—can destroy an existing ecosystem, releasing and dissipating stored energy and nutrients. All structure and organization may be lost in the collapse. In the economy, sharp changes in market conditions or new technologies can bring down major corporations or sectors. (For example, in 2007–2009 escalating oil prices and changing consumer preferences brought the North American auto sector to its knees; corruption, lax regulation, and the loss of investor confidence undermined financial markets and bankrupted many firms.)

Reorganization phase: The chaos of release creates numerous opportunities for novelty and experimentation. All options are theoretically open—the future path of the system is up for grabs. In ecosystems, abundant nutrients and access to sunlight create ideal conditions for opportunistic species. Invader species from distant ecosystems or novel combinations of existing organisms may become established and set the system on an unfamiliar course (as seems to have happened to the Atlantic cod ecosystem). In economies, new technologies and aggressive entrepreneurs can move in to fill niches left by failing firms. Often,

(continued)

BOX 3.2 *(continued)*

however, conditions in this phase tend to produce a faithful repetition of the previous cycle. (Think about the U.S. government's trillion-dollar bailout of the financial sector and its rescue of the auto industry in 2008–2009.) In either case, events during the reorganization determine what species/corporations will ultimately dominate the subsequent growth phase.

1. Brian Walker and David Salt, *Resilience Thinking: Sustaining Ecosystems and People in a Changing World* (Washington DC: Island Press, 2006), 77.

fact, suggest points for positive human intervention in the name of resilience, and can it avoid vulnerable configurations in at least some systems?

Recall that contemporary resource-management approaches typically attempt to maximize one or a few desirable systems components at the expense of other species and systems functions—think agricultural or forestry monoculture. Diversity plummets and functions are lost. The managed system becomes inflexibly brittle and vulnerable to unexpected external shocks. While apparently stable, the system's resilience is minimal. In effect, this kind of management approach—aiming for maximum production in the most efficient way possible—creates systems that structurally most resemble the conservation phase of the adaptive cycle in near pre-collapse mode (box 3.2).

Now consider the form of contemporary global economic development. As previously noted (box 3.1), the emphasis here is on maximizing economic growth by exploiting the efficiency gains conferred by local specialization and global trade. This approach tends to maximize resource exploitation and material dissipation (pollution), both of which simplify ecosystems, undermine life-support functions, and erode systems resilience. On the socioeconomic side, the global economy becomes dominated by only a few global enterprises (and their numbers continue to shrink with each merger or acquisition). The sheer economic power of these monster corporations stifles meaningful competition and blocks new players from entering the market: Both local diversity and global diversity plummet. Meanwhile, the economy and society have become deeply dependent on a few declining energy sources (e.g., petroleum) and on energy-intensive systems (e.g., global transportation systems and even the Internet).

So structured, the entire human enterprise appears to be well into the "brittle" conservation phase of an adaptive cycle and highly vulnerable to external shocks.[18] Present globalization strategies represent nonresilience thinking at its best (i.e., "worst"). Perhaps we would do well to recall Joseph Tainter's observation: "What is perhaps most intriguing in the evolution of human societies is the regularity with which the pattern of increasing complexity is interrupted by collapse."[19]

For contrast, let's examine the structure and dynamics of the early growth phase of the adaptive cycle. Here species diversity is high, many organisms are flexible generalists, and the system is characterized by multiple redundancies. Stability and resilience are increasing and operate over a wide range of conditions. The system is least vulnerable to external shocks. Is this not more like what we are trying to achieve?

By understanding the changes in systems dynamics that accompany adaptive cycles in the panarchy we might begin to uncover clear guidelines for structuring sustainability. Remember, the goal is to maintain regional ecosystems and the economy in a structural configuration that promotes diversity and resilience in the face of inevitable shocks such as climate change and global economic turmoil. To achieve this, development strategies must abandon efficiency and maximization as primary goals in favor of social equity and ecological stability. Society should:

· Formally eschew continuous economic growth. The goal of economic activity should be to provide economic security for all within the productive capacity of regional and global ecosystems. This implies creation of a steady-state economy, one characterized by nongrowing throughput of energy and resources.
· Create economic planning regions on a humanly manageable spatial scale. The probability of being able to manage ecosystems and economies successfully decreases as geographic and systems scales increase.
· Manage regional ecosystems to maintain/increase species diversity, systems integrity, and optimal habitat patchiness for the species concerned. Inhibit development of the "conservation phase" of the adaptive cycle.
· Adopt the strong version of the constant-natural-capital-stocks-per-capita criterion for sustainability.[20]

- Strive to maintain economic diversity and multiple employment opportunities within every planning region. This implies balancing the contributions from primary resources and the manufacturing and service sectors. Stabilizing or increasing diversity may require limiting the size of individual enterprises and prohibiting mergers and acquisitions above a certain size.
- Invest in redundant energy systems with an emphasis on sustainable renewable solutions.

It is worth noting that such guidelines speak to the need to decrease regional dependence on imported resources (we are currently importing additional ecological carrying capacity to sustain local communities) and for the "relocalization" of economies. Resilient communities will develop policies that favor greater regional self-reliance, including mechanisms for import displacement when this is ecologically sound. Increased regional self-reliance would produce immediate economic and ecological savings in the form of reduced transportation costs, lower carbon dioxide emissions, and fewer processing and storage facilities. (A useful motto might be: "Trade if necessary, but not necessarily trade.")

Relocalization also brings ecological advantages. Local production for local consumption often has the potential to restore, at least partially, the integrity of local human-dominated ecosystems. For example, depositing urban organic compost on nearby farm- and forestland would close the nutrient cycles broken by the current spatial separation of rural ecosystems and urban populations.[21] It also doesn't hurt that people might once again begin to identify with nearby ecosystems from which they acquire much of their food and fiber. There can be no greater incentive for conservation than knowing one's life depends upon it.[22]

GETTING TO GLOBAL SUSTAINABILITY

Obviously this entire resilience-oriented program flies in the face of conventional wisdom and current trends. But that is precisely the point—the present growth-bound global development paradigm is fatally flawed, inherently unsustainable, and on track for catastrophic implosion, from which there might not be a subsequent "reorganization" phase for billions of people (see box 3.3).

By contrast, if the suggested program were faithfully implemented

BOX 3.3 Fatal Adaptation (or "The Dark Side of Resilience" or "When Resilience Goes Rogue")

The life cycles of everything in the natural world, from cells through organisms to ecosystems, have been described as "never-ending adaptive cycles of growth, accumulation, restructuring and renewal."[1] While this implies recurring opportunities for novelty, particularly during "restructuring and renewal," near-faithful repetition of the previous cycle is more common in nature.

Not so with human-dominated socio-ecosystems. In the face of unwanted exogenous change, human ingenuity generally intervenes and can change the course of history. For example, industrial society's response to "perturbation" typically involves technological innovation or economic restructuring. This may irrevocably alter the character of relevant socio-ecosystems and extend the exploitation/growth and conservation phases of societal development.

Ironically, this characteristically human form of "resilience" is often triggered by problems created by *previous* extended periods of growth— we counter the depletion of soils by applying artificial fertilizers; with peak oil looming, we launch an (increasingly frantic) search for alternative sources of energy. Joseph Tainter argues that the human pattern of adaptation to serial challenges is actually the means by which societies become more complex and subsequently evolve.[2]

But there is a problem. "Adaptation through sequential depletion and substitution" uses up nonrenewable resource stocks and may even extinguish self-producing natural capital vital to long-term societal survival. Indeed, over several millennia we have witnessed the blossoming of numerous large-scale cultures and empires that eventually collapsed, never to reemerge in place.[3] Pre-agricultural societies may have experienced typically repeating adaptive cycles at small spatial and temporal scales, but grander, more technologically advanced societies can so degrade their socioeconomic systems that the "never-ending" cycle of growth to renewal may ignominiously grind to a halt.

This should be of particular concern today. Two hundred years of industrial technology have fueled the explosive growth of both human populations and per capita consumption; globalization—another *initially* adaptive strategy—has extended humanity's "scorched-earth" tactics to the entire planet (see box 3.1). The ecosphere is reeling and,

(continued)

BOX 3.3   *(continued)*

if collapse does occur, it will effectively be global. There can be no "release" of critical assets, no fallback reserves, and no opportunity for subsequent reorganization and rebirth on a comparable scale. It seems that strategies that enhance the resilience of only the "socio-" part of vital socio-ecosystems will ultimately take us down.

Here's what Sir Fred Hoyle had to say on the matter:

> It has often been said that, if the human species fails to make
> a go of it here on Earth, some other species will take over the
> running. . . . [t]his is not correct. We have, or soon will have,
> exhausted the necessary physical prerequisites so far as this planet
> is concerned. With coal gone, oil gone, high-grade metallic ores
> gone, no species however competent can make the long climb
> from primitive conditions to high-level technology. [Civilization]
> is a one-shot affair. If we fail, this planetary system fails so far as
> intelligence is concerned.[4]

---

1. C. S. Holling, "Understanding the Complexity of Economic, Social and Ecological Systems," *Ecosystems* 4 (August 2001), 390–405.

2. Joseph Tainter, *The Collapse of Complex Societies* (Cambridge: Cambridge University Press, 1988).

3. Ibid.; Jared Diamond, *Collapse: How Societies Choose to Fail or Succeed* (New York: Viking Penguin, 2005).

4. Fred Hoyle, *Of Men and Galaxies* (Seattle: University of Washington Press, 1964).

---

region by region across the globe so that each planning region or country achieved a resiliently sustainable steady state, the aggregate effect would be global sustainability. Of course, anyone who reads the paper or watches the news will realize that nothing resembling such a resilience-based strategy is yet being seriously contemplated by any major government or mainstream development organization anywhere. On the positive side, while there may yet be no broad-scale applications, human society is gradually acquiring the knowledge necessary to reorganize itself to our long-term advantage. It is entirely possible to envision a human society functioning in relation to nature such that the resultant socio-ecosystems are resilient and therefore truly sustainable.

Part Two

CLIMATE

4

A NEW WORLD

BILL MCKIBBEN

BILL MCKIBBEN *is an American environmentalist and writer. Scholar-in-residence at Middlebury College and the founder of the international climate campaign 350.org, he is the author of twelve books, including* The End of Nature *(1989), the first book for a general audience about global warming, and* Deep Economy: The Wealth of Communities and the Durable Future *(2007). His latest book,* Eaarth: Making a Life on a Tough New Planet *(2010), explores what it means to live on a planet we've changed fundamentally. McKibben is a Fellow of Post Carbon Institute.*

❖

Imagine we live on a planet. Not our cozy, taken-for-granted earth, but a planet, a real one, with dark poles and belching volcanoes and a heaving, corrosive sea, raked by winds, strafed by storms, scorched by heat. An inhospitable place.

It's hard. For the ten thousand years that constitute human civilization, we've existed in the sweetest of sweet spots. The temperature has barely budged; globally averaged, it's swung in the narrowest of ranges, between fifty-eight and sixty degrees Fahrenheit. That's warm enough that the ice sheets retreated from the centers of our continents so we could grow grain, but cold enough that mountain glaciers provided drinking and irrigation water to those plains and valleys year round; it was the "correct" temperature for the marvelously diverse planet that seems right to us. And every aspect of our civilization reflects that particular world. We built our great cities next to seas that have remained tame and level, or at altitudes high enough that disease-bearing mosquitoes could not overwinter. We refined the farming that has swelled our numbers to take full advantage of that predictable heat and rainfall; our rice and corn and wheat can't imagine another earth either. Occasionally, in one place or another, there's an abrupt departure from the norm—a hurricane, a drought, a freeze. But our very language reflects their rarity: freak storms, disturbances.

In December 1968 we got the first real view of that stable, secure place. Apollo 8 was orbiting the moon, the astronauts busy photographing possible landing zones for the missions that would follow. On the fourth orbit, Commander Frank Borman decided to roll the craft away from the moon and tilt its windows toward the horizon—he needed a navigational fix. What he got, instead, was a sudden view of the earth, rising. "Oh my God," he said. "Here's the earth coming up." Crew member Bill Anders grabbed a camera and took the photograph that became the iconic image perhaps of all time. "Earthrise," as it was eventually known, that picture of a blue-and-white marble floating amid the vast backdrop of space, set against the barren edge of the lifeless moon.[1] Borman said later that it was "the most beautiful, heart-catching sight of my life, one that sent a torrent of nostalgia, of sheer homesickness, surging through me. It was the only thing in space that had any color to it. Everything else was simply black or white. But not the earth."[2] The third member of the crew, Jim Lovell, put it more simply: the earth, he said, suddenly appeared as "a grand oasis."

But we no longer live on that planet. In the four decades since, that earth has changed in profound ways, ways that have already taken us out of the sweet spot where humans so long thrived. We're every day less the oasis and more the desert. The world hasn't ended, but the world as we know it has—even if we don't quite know it yet. We imagine we still live back on that old planet, that the disturbances we see around us are the old random and freakish kind. But they're not. It's a different place. A different planet. It needs a new name. Eaarth. Or Monnde, or Tierrre, Errde, оккучивать. It still looks familiar enough—we're still the third rock out from the sun, still three-quarters water. Gravity still pertains; we're still earth*like*. But it's odd enough to constantly remind us how profoundly we've altered the only place we've ever known. I am aware, of course, that the earth changes constantly, and that occasionally it changes wildly, as when an asteroid strikes or an Ice Age relaxes its grip. This is one of those rare moments, the start of a change far larger and more thoroughgoing than anything we can read in the records of man, on a par with the biggest dangers we can read in the records of rock and ice.

Consider the veins of cloud that streak and mottle the earth in that glorious snapshot from space. So far humans, by burning fossil fuel, have raised the temperature of the planet nearly a degree Celsius (more than a degree and a half Fahrenheit). A NASA study in December 2008 found that warming on that scale was enough to trigger a 45 percent increase in thunderheads above the ocean, breeding the spectacular anvil-headed clouds that can rise five miles above the sea, generating "super-cells" with torrents of rain and hail.[3] In fact, total global rainfall is now increasing 1.5 percent a decade.[4] Larger storms over land now create more lightning; every degree Celsius brings about 6 percent more lightning, according to the climate scientist Amanda Staudt. In just one day in June 2008, lightning sparked 1,700 different fires across California, burning a million acres and setting a new state record. These blazes burned on the new earth, not the old one. "We are in the mega-fire era," said Ken Frederick, a spokesman for the federal government.[5] And that smoke and flame, of course, were visible from space—indeed anyone with an Internet connection could watch the video feed from the space shuttle Endeavour as it circled above the towering plumes in the Santa Barbara hills.

Or consider the white and frozen top of the planet. Arctic ice has been melting slowly for two decades as temperatures have climbed, but in the summer of 2007 that gradual thaw suddenly accelerated. By the time the long Arctic night finally descended in October, there was 22 percent less sea ice than had ever been observed before, and more than 40 percent less than the year that Apollo capsule took its picture. The Arctic ice cap was 1.1 million square miles smaller than ever recorded in history, reduced by an area twelve times the size of Great Britain.[6] The summers of 2008 and 2009 saw a repeat of the epic melt; that summer both the Northwest and Northeast passages opened for the first time in human history. The first commercial ship to make the voyage through the newly opened straits, the MV *Camilla Desgagnes*, had an icebreaker on standby in case it ran into trouble, but the captain reported, "I didn't see one cube of ice."[7]

This is not some mere passing change; this is the earth shifting. In December 2008, scientists from the National Sea Ice Data Center said the increased melting of Arctic ice was accumulating heat in the oceans, and that this so-called Arctic amplification now penetrated 1,500 kilometers inland. In August 2009, scientists reported that lightning strikes in the Arctic had increased twentyfold, igniting some of the first tundra fires ever observed.[8] According to the center's Mark Serreze, the new data "is reinforcing the notion that the Arctic ice is in its death spiral."[9] That is, within a decade or two, a summertime spacecraft pointing its camera at the North Pole would see nothing but open ocean. There'd be ice left on Greenland—but much less ice. Between 2003 and 2008, more than a trillion tons of the island's ice melted, an area ten times the size of Manhattan. "We now know that the climate doesn't have to warm any more for Greenland to continue losing ice," explained Jason Box, a geography professor at Ohio State University. "It has probably passed the point where it could maintain the mass of ice that we remember."[10] And if the spacecraft pointed its camera at the South Pole? On the second-to-last day of 2008 the *Economist* reported that temperatures on the Antarctic Peninsula were rising faster than anywhere else on earth, and that the West Antarctic was losing ice 75 percent faster than just a decade before.[11]

Don't let your eyes glaze over at this parade of statistics (and so many more to follow). These should come as body blows, as mortar barrages, as sickening thuds. The Holocene is staggered, the only world that humans have known is suddenly reeling. I am not describing what will happen if we don't take action, or warning of some future threat. This is the *current* inventory: more thunder, more lightning, less ice. Name a major feature of the earth's surface, and you'll find massive change.

So how did it happen that the threat to our fairly far-off descendants, which required that we heed an alarm and adopt precautionary principles and begin to take measured action lest we have a crisis for future generations, et cetera—how did that suddenly turn into the Arctic melting away, the tropics expanding, the ocean turning acid? How did time dilate, and "100 or 200 years from now" become yesterday?

The answer, more or less, is that global warming is a huge experiment. We've never watched it happen before, so we didn't know how it would proceed. Here's what we knew twenty years ago: the historic level of carbon dioxide in the atmosphere, the level that produced those ten thousand years of stability, was roughly 275 parts per million. And also this: since the dawn of the Industrial Revolution we've been steadily increasing that total, currently raising it more than two parts per million annually. But no one really knew where the red line was—it was impossible to really know in advance at what point you'd cross a tripwire and set off a bomb. Like, say, melting all the ice in the Arctic.

The number that people tossed around for about a decade was 550 parts per million. Not because we had any real data showing it was the danger point, but because it was double the historic concentration, which made it relatively easy to model with the relatively crude computer programs scientists were using. One paper after another predicted what would happen to sea levels or forest composition or penguin reproduction if carbon dioxide levels doubled to 550 parts per million. And so—inevitably and insidiously—that's the number we fixated on. Since it wouldn't be reached until the middle of the twenty-first century, it seemed to offer a little margin; it meshed plausibly with political time, with the kind of gradual solutions leaders like to imagine. That is, a doubling of carbon dioxide would happen well beyond the time that anyone now in power was likely to still be in office, or still running the company. It was when everyone's *grandchildren* would be in charge. As late as 2004, the journalist Paul Roberts, in his superb book *The End of Oil*, was able to write quite correctly that "most climate models indicate that once concentrations exceed 550 ppm we will start to witness 'dangerous' levels of warming and damage, especially in vulnerable areas, such as low-lying countries or those already suffering drought." But by then some doubt was beginning to creep in. Odd phenomena (large chunks of the Antarctic falling into the ocean, say) were unnerving scientists enough that, in Roberts' words, most "would much rather see concentrations stabilized at 450 ppm . . . where we might avoid most long-term effects and instead suffer a kind of 'warming light,' moderate loss of shorefront land, moderate loss of species, moderate desertification," and so on. And since even 450 was still 20 percent above our current levels, "we have a little room to breathe, which is handy."[12]

Or would have been. But as it turns out, we had been like commentators trying to call an election on the basis of the first precinct to report. Right about 2005 the real returns began to flood in, *flood* being the correct verb. And what they showed was that those old benchmarks—550, 450—had been wishful thinking. No breathing room, not when hurricane seasons like 2005 were setting new records for insurance payouts, not when polar ice was melting "fifty years ahead of schedule," not when the tropics "appear to have already expanded during only the last few decades of the 20th century by at least the same margin as models predict for this century."[13] Indeed, "ahead of schedule" became a kind of tic for headline writers: "Arctic Melt-off Ahead of Schedule" (the *Christian Science Monitor*, which quoted one scientist as saying "we're a hundred years ahead of schedule" in thawing Greenland), "Dry Future Well Ahead of Schedule" (the *Australian*), "Acidified Seawater Showing Up Along Coast Ahead of Schedule" (the *Seattle Times*). The implication was that global warming hadn't read the invitation correctly and was showing up at four for the reception instead of six. In fact, of course, the "schedule" was wrong. And of course it was wrong—this was, as I've said, a huge experiment. Twenty-five years ago almost nobody even knew the planet was going to warm at all, never mind how fast.

It was that summer melt of Arctic ice in 2007 that seemed to break the spell, to start raising the stakes. The record minimums for ice were reached in the last week of September; in mid-December James Hansen, still the planet's leading climatologist, gave a short talk with six or seven slides at the American Geophysical Union meeting in San Francisco. What he said went unreported at the time, but it may turn out to be among the most crucial lectures in scientific history. He summarized both the real-world data that had emerged in recent years, including the ice-melt, and also the large body of research on paleoclimate—basically, the attempt to understand what had happened in the distant past when carbon dioxide levels climbed and fell. Taken together, he said, these two lines of inquiry made it clear that the safe number was, at most, 350 parts per million.

The day Jim Hansen announced that number was the day I knew we'd never again inhabit the planet I'd been born on, or anything close to it. Because we're already past 350—way past it. The planet has nearly 390 parts per million carbon dioxide in the atmosphere. We're too high. Forget the grandkids; it turns out this was a problem for our *parents*.

We can, if we're very lucky and very committed, eventually get the number back down below 350. This book will explore some of the reasons this task will be extremely hard, and some of the ways we can try. The planet can, slowly, soak up excess carbon dioxide if we stop pouring more in. That fight is what I spend my life on now, because it's still possible we can avert the very worst catastrophes. But even so, great damage will have been done along the way, on land and in the sea. The Zoological Society of London reported in July 2009 that "360 is now known to be the level at which coral reefs cease to be viable in the long run."[14] We're not going to get back the planet we used to have, the one on which our civilization developed. We're like the guy who ate steak for dinner every night and let his cholesterol top 300 and had the heart attack. Now he dines on Lipitor and walks on the treadmill, but half his heart is dead tissue. We're like the guy who smoked for forty years and then he had a stroke. He doesn't smoke anymore, but the left side of his body doesn't work either.

Consider: On January 26, 2009, less than a week after taking office, Barack Obama announced a series of stunning steps designed to dramatically raise fuel efficiency for cars. He also named a new envoy to aggressively negotiate an international accord on global warming. "This should prompt cheers from California to Maine," the head of one environmental group exulted. "The days of Washington dragging its heels are over," insisted the president.[15] It was the most auspicious day of environmental news in the twenty years of the global warming era. And then that afternoon, the National Oceanic and Atmospheric Administration released a new study showing that a new understanding of ocean physics proved that "changes in surface temperature, rainfall, and sea level are largely irreversible for more than a thousand years after carbon dioxide emissions are completely stopped." Its author, Susan Solomon, was interviewed on National Public Radio that night. "People have imagined that if we stopped emitting carbon dioxide that the climate would be back to normal in one hundred years or two hundred years," she said. "What we're showing here is that that's not right."[16] No one is going to refreeze the Arctic for us, or restore the pH of the oceans, and given the momentum of global warming we're likely to cross many more thresholds even if we all convert to solar power and bicycles this afternoon.

Which, it must be said, we're not doing. The scientists didn't merely underestimate how fast the Arctic would melt; they overestimated how fast our hearts would melt. The Intergovernmental Panel on Climate Change, or IPCC, carefully calculated a variety of different "emissions pathways" for the future, ranging from a world where we did everything possible to make ourselves lean and efficient to a "business-as-usual" model where we did next to nothing. In the last decade, as the United States has done very little to change its energy habits, and as the large Asian economies have come online, carbon emissions have risen "far above even the bleak scenarios" considered in the reports. In the summer of 2008, at an academic conference at Britain's Exeter University, a scientist named Kevin Anderson took the podium for a major address. He showed slide after slide, graph after graph, "representing the fumes that belch from chimneys, exhausts and jet engines, that should have bent in a rapid curve towards the ground, were heading for the ceiling instead." His conclusion: it was "improbable" that we'd be able to stop short of 650 parts per million, even if rich countries adopted "draconian emissions reductions within a decade." That number, should it come to pass, would mean that global average temperatures would increase something like seven degrees Fahrenheit, compared to the degree and a half they've gone up already.

To give you an idea of how aggressively the world's governments are willing to move, in July 2009 the thirteen largest emitters met in Washington to agree on an "aspirational" goal of 50 percent cuts in carbon by 2050, which falls pretty close to the category of "don't bother."[17]

And actually, it's worse than that. What Anderson and others were measuring were the inputs from human beings—the carbon that we pour into the atmosphere when we burn coal and gas and oil. So far we've been the cause for the sudden surge in greenhouse gases and hence global temperatures, but that's starting to change, as the heat we've caused has started to trigger a series of ominous feedback effects. Some are fairly easy to see: melt Arctic sea ice, and you replace a shiny white mirror that reflects most of the incoming rays of sun back out to space with a dull blue ocean that absorbs most of those rays. Others are less obvious, and much larger: booby traps, hidden around the world, waiting for the atmosphere to heat.

For instance, there are immense quantities of methane—natural gas—locked up beneath the frozen tundra, and in icy "clathrates" beneath the sea. Methane, like carbon dioxide, is a heat-trapping gas; if it starts escaping into the atmosphere, it will add to the pace of warming. And that's what seems to be happening, well ahead (need it be said) of schedule. In 2007, atmospheric levels of methane began to shoot up. Scientists weren't sure where they were coming from, but the fear was that those tundra and ocean sources were starting to melt in earnest. In the summer of 2008, a Russian research ship, the *Jacob Smirnitskyi*, was cruising off the country's northern coast in the Laptev Sea when the scientists on board started finding areas of the water's surface foaming with methane gas. Concentrations were a hundred times normal. "Yesterday, for the first time, we documented a field where the release was so intense that the methane did not have to dissolve into the sea water but was rising as methane bubbles to the sea surface," one of the scientists e-mailed a journalist at London's *Independent* newspaper. "These methane chimneys were documented on an echo sounder and with seismic instruments."[18] The head of the research team, Igor Semiletov of the University of Alaska in Fairbanks, noted that temperatures over eastern Siberia had increased by almost ten degrees in the last decade. That's melting permafrost on the land, and hence more relatively warm water is flowing down the region's rivers into the ocean, where it may in turn be melting the icy seal over the underwater methane. The melting permafrost is also releasing methane on land. "On helicopter flights over the delta of the Lena River, higher methane concentrations have been measured at altitudes as high as 1,800 meters," reported Natalia Shakhova, of the Russian Academy of Sciences.[19] In recent winters scientists have reported that far northern ponds and marshes stayed unfrozen even in the depths of winter because so much methane was bubbling out from underneath. "It looks like a soda can is open underneath the water," one researcher explained.[20]

That's scary. Scarier even than the carbon pouring out of our tailpipes, because we're not directly releasing that methane. We burned the coal and gas and oil, and released the first dose of carbon, and that raised the temperature enough to start the process in motion. We're responsible for it, but we can't shut it off. It's taken on a life of its own. One recent estimate: the permafrost traps 1,600 billion tons of carbon. A hundred billion tons could be released this century, mostly in the form of methane, which would have a warming effect equivalent to 270 years of carbon dioxide emissions at current levels. "It's a kind of slow-motion time bomb," said Ted Schuur of the University of Florida in March 2009. At a certain point, he added, "the feedback process would continue even if we cut our greenhouse emissions to zero."[21]

At the same time that we're triggering new pulses of carbon into the atmosphere, we're also steadily weakening the natural systems that pull it out of the air. Normally—over all but the last two hundred years of human civilization—the carbon dioxide level in the atmosphere remained stable because trees and plants and plankton sucked it up about as fast as volcanoes produced it. But now we've turned our cars and factories into junior volcanoes, and so we're not just producing carbon faster than the plant world can absorb it; we're also making it so hot that the plants absorb less carbon than they used to. In a 2008 experiment, scientists carved out small plots of grassland and installed them into labs where they could heat them artificially. "During this anomalously warm year and the year that followed, the two plots sucked up two-thirds less carbon than the plots that had been exposed to normal temperatures," the researchers reported.[22] The same thing may be happening at sea, where in January 2009 scientists "issued a warning" after finding "a sudden and dramatic collapse in the amount of carbon emissions absorbed" in fast-warming areas of the Sea of Japan.[23] Imagine that you desperately need to bail out your boat, but you find that your buckets are filled with holes that keep getting larger. "Fifty years ago, for every ton of CO_2 emitted to the atmosphere, natural sinks removed 600 kilograms. Currently the sinks are removing only 559 kilograms per ton, and the amount is falling."[24] Those are big holes.

THE INTERNATIONAL RESPONSE
TO CLIMATE CHANGE

RICHARD DOUTHWAITE

RICHARD DOUTHWAITE *is co-founder of Feasta, an Irish economic think tank focused on the economics of sustainability. He was instrumental in the development of the "contraction and convergence" approach to dealing with greenhouse gas emissions, which has since been backed by many countries. He is the author of two books,* The Growth Illusion *(1999) and* Short Circuit *(1996). Douthwaite is a Fellow of Post Carbon Institute.*

❖

The nations of the world have agreed that climate change is the most serious threat facing humankind. Before they can develop a joint plan to deal with the problem effectively, however, they must agree on the maximum level of greenhouse gases they should risk allowing in the atmosphere.

THE CHALLENGES WE FACE

The world has warmed by approximately 0.7 degree Celsius in the 200 years since fossil fuels began to be used on any significant scale—but the warming has not been uniform. The biggest temperature rises have been around the North Pole, and some worrying self-reinforcing feedbacks have already developed. For example, the Arctic ice has been melting unexpectedly rapidly, increasing the rate at which the planet is warming because the white ice that reflected solar energy back into space has been replaced by dark, heat-absorbing sea. Similarly, the melting of the permafrost in Russia is now releasing large amounts of methane, a powerful greenhouse gas, into the atmosphere.

Even if its concentration of greenhouse gases was stabilized at its current level, Earth's lower atmosphere would continue to warm by at least another 0.7 degree Celsius. This is because the full heating effect of increased carbon dioxide in the atmosphere—currently around 390 parts per million (ppm)—takes some years to overcome the considerable thermal inertia of Earth's climate system.

The leading American climate scientist, James Hansen of NASA's Goddard Space Institute, points out that the Arctic ice began to melt significantly in the 1970s and suggests that a concentration of 300–325 ppm of carbon dioxide might be necessary for the ice to increase again. Professor John Schellnhuber, the director of the Potsdam Institute for Climate Impact Research in Germany, thinks that almost any concentration above the pre-industrial level of 270 ppm might be too much. He told the *Guardian* in 2008 that even a small increase in temperature could trigger several climatic tipping points:

> Nobody can say for sure that 330 ppm is safe. . . . Perhaps it will not matter whether we have 270 ppm or 320 ppm, but operating well outside the [historic] realm of carbon dioxide concentrations is risky as long as we have not fully understood the relevant feedback mechanisms.[1]

If these experts are right, two things must be done to stop runaway global warming. One is that every ton of carbon dioxide that humans release by burning fossil fuels and clearing forests from now on must be recovered from the air and sequestered safely in the ground. The other is that a lot of past emissions must be recovered too.

Let's put some figures on the size of this formidable task (figure 5.1). Fossil-fuel combustion currently releases about 29 billion tons of carbon dioxide a year: If that was phased out over forty years on a straight-line basis, a total of 580 billion tons would be released before emissions stopped completely by 2050. Deforestation is releasing 7 billion tons a year: If it proves possible to stop that in ten years, it will add 35 billion tons to the atmosphere by 2020. If we ignore other releases from the way we use and abuse the land, including the methane from the cattle we keep and the rice we grow, and the nitrous oxide from the fertilizers we apply, we look set to add 615 billion tons of carbon dioxide to the atmosphere by 2050—even with an incredibly aggressive emissions mitigation program. This 615 billion tons of carbon dioxide will have to be removed together with the excess carbon dioxide that's already in the air. Suppose we take 350 ppm

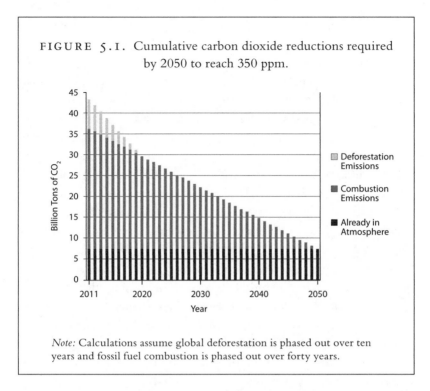

FIGURE 5.1. Cumulative carbon dioxide reductions required by 2050 to reach 350 ppm.

Note: Calculations assume global deforestation is phased out over ten years and fossil fuel combustion is phased out over forty years.

as our initial target, as James Hansen and many others suggest. At present, 2,900 billion tons of carbon dioxide are in the air, so reducing its concentration from 390 ppm to 350 means we've got to take 300 billion tons out.

In total, then, saving life as we know it entails extracting between 900 and 1,000 billion tons of carbon dioxide from the atmosphere and locking it safely away. This amount of carbon dioxide contains about 250 billion tons of carbon—and the only place that carbon can be stored on the scale required is in plants and the soils. Land plants hold 600 billion tons of carbon at present and Earth's soil holds about three times that amount. So at a minimum, we need to find ways to increase the total amount of carbon held by plants and soils from 2,400 billion tons to 2,650, or just over 10 percent. That seems a feasible goal if the political will is there.

A FAILED APPROACH

But the political will is lacking, as the December 2009 United Nations (U.N.) climate conference in Copenhagen showed. The rich countries are not prepared to cut their fossil-fuel emissions by around 7 percent a year, the rate required to put them on track to phase them out completely by 2050. Unless at least 95 percent of every country's fossil-fuel emissions have ceased by then, achieving the 350-ppm target seems impossible. After all, the rough calculations we've just made show that two-thirds of the carbon that needs to be sequestered has yet to be released. Cutting emissions more slowly increases the amount of carbon needing to be recovered and allows the planet longer to warm up, thus increasing the risk that unstoppable feedbacks will develop.

Another problem in Copenhagen was that the rich countries were not prepared to pay countries like Brazil and Indonesia enough to stop cutting down their tropical forests and thus releasing the carbon they contain. This was despite a report in *Nature* earlier in the year showing that the world's remaining tropical forests are not only carbon stores but remove a massive 4.8 billion tons of carbon dioxide emissions from the atmosphere each year[2]—about a fifth of that released by burning fossil fuels. The only proposals on the table at Copenhagen were about slowing the rate of deforestation rather than stopping it entirely.

For their part, the big developing countries—India and China— refused to accept any emissions limits at all, saying that it was up to the richer countries to make deeper cuts to allow them space to raise their people's incomes by increasing their fossil-fuel use. Only about eighty small, poor countries, including the small island states that will disap- pear under the waves because of rising sea levels, pressed for a 350-or-less target.

Copenhagen demonstrated that humanity may not be able to save itself for two reasons—both of which can be overcome. One is that our economies have no reverse gear. While people lived very well at much lower levels of energy use in the past, we cannot return to those levels now without an economic collapse because of the way our money system works.

The other is the way the U.N. process attempted to deal with a world problem on a nation-by-nation basis rather than on a whole-world basis. The process left it up to each nation—or each group of nations such as the European Union—to volunteer to do something to solve the crisis. It did not tell them what to do. As a result, it was scarcely surprising that the sum total of the offers was completely inadequate to reduce the risk that a tipping point will be passed and an unstoppable catastrophic series of changes will take off.

The artificial way the process divided the world into rich countries with responsibilities to act and poorer ones with no responsibilities was particularly unhelpful. Every country in the world has rich people enjoying more than their fair share of the benefits that flow from the use of fossil fuel, and it is these people who should share their benefits wherever they live.

What the U.N. failed to do was to look at the problem in the way we've just done and say: "This is a massive problem that needs a global rather than a piecemeal response. Here's what humanity needs to do to have a chance of survival. Now how can we share out the cost and the work fairly among us all?"

ONE SOLUTION: CAP AND SHARE

"Cap and share" is an attempt to share the cost and the work of fighting climate change among all the nations of the world.[3] It proposes that a Global Atmosphere Trust should be set up to represent everyone's interests, not just those of powerful groups in powerful countries. The trust would cap fossil-fuel emissions at their current level. Then it would take the advice of leading climate scientists on how rapidly it should reduce that cap year by year. Political and economic considerations would have to be ignored as Earth's systems will not take these into account.

The rights to the capped emissions would be shared out around the world each year in three ways. Part (perhaps 15 percent) would be auctioned and the revenue would go to the governments of countries such as Bangladesh, which will be particularly badly hit by rising sea levels and by tropical storms as the planet warms—unless it can pay to strengthen its sea defenses. Another fraction would be sold to fund countries to maintain and increase their soil and biomass carbon stocks, absorbing old and new emissions. Most of the remaining tonnage would be distributed as paper emissions permits on an equal per capita basis to everyone on the planet.

When we get our individual permit—each of us might get the right to release 3 tons of carbon dioxide in the first year—we'd have to decide what to do with it. Do we really want to be responsible for our 3 tons being released? If we decide we do not, we'd just tear our permit up.

However, if we decided that we couldn't afford the financial loss, we'd take it to a post office or bank and sell it for whatever the current market price of our tonnage was, just as if it were a foreign currency note.

The bank would then deposit the permits it had bought in its account with the Global Atmosphere Trust and sell the tonnage to companies producing fossil fuels. For example, the operators of a coal mine would need to buy permits to cover the emissions from every ton of coal they produced, and international inspectors would check to see that they did so. Most of the fossil fuels produced around the world come from two hundred big companies, so policing the system is logistically quite feasible.

The fossil-fuel producers would naturally add the cost of purchasing the permits to their fuel prices, so the price of energy would rise around the world. All other prices would rise, too, because energy is used in the manufacture and delivery of everything we buy. Food prices would be affected, just as they were before oil prices peaked in July 2008, because some crops like corn would be diverted to bioenergy production.

These price increases are one reason that cap and share insists that permits covering the majority of the capped emissions tonnage should be issued directly to everyone. If governments got the money from selling the permits instead and did not pass it on, many people would be squeezed out of the energy and food markets altogether. They could freeze or starve.

Another reason for distributing the permits to people is that, with higher energy prices, every household is going to want to invest in ways to cut its purchased energy use—and the income from the sale of its permits will provide it with the means to do so. Lots of families will be happy to borrow so that they could buy, say, a solar water heater or get insulation work done, knowing that they could use the money earned from selling their carbon permits to pay off the loan.

Cap and share would make anybody financially better off whose lifestyle enabled them to live on less fossil energy than covered by their emissions allocation. In South Africa, for example, 80 percent of the population would come out on top in the year the system started, 10 percent would be unaffected, and the richest 10 percent would lose about 14 percent of their income for a few months until the fact that their tenants, clients, and customers were more prosperous enabled them to make their losses up.

In India, 90 percent of the population would stand to gain, and the more rapidly emissions were reduced, the greater their gains would be. For example, if the pace was rapid and the world price for emissions permits rose to $100 per ton of carbon dioxide, the poorest 10 percent of Indians would see their total income increased twenty times. The incomes of the richest 10 percent would be reduced by only 0.26 percent at that price, and this group would soon make that up through their better business and professional opportunities.

It all sounds too good to be true until you realize that in emissions-intensive countries like the United States and those in Europe, everyone would see their incomes decline because they would, in effect, be buying permits from much poorer people around the world. However, the money they paid would come quickly back as demand for their solar cells and other high-tech goods. Their economies would also become more stable because fossil-fuel-producing countries would not take in more money than they could spend as scarcity drove fuel prices up. The subprime-mortgage fiasco was caused when the U.S. banks with whom the energy producers had deposited their surplus cash resorted to dodgy ways of lending it out.

A problem with cap and share is that it could be *so* effective that energy prices would rise quite a bit and people would start cutting down even more forests to replace fossil fuel. Grazing land might also be plowed to grow biofuels, releasing carbon in the soil. Fortunately, modern aircraft surveillance technology can measure not only the carbon in the trees and other plants growing over entire countries but also—if combined with on-site surveys—the carbon in the soil itself. New Zealand is already using this technique. So, under cap and share, governments of countries that increased the amount of carbon they were storing in their plants and soils would be paid for every extra ton using some of the funds from the permit sales.

Even before the disappointing results of the December 2009 Copenhagen climate summit were known, the United Nations Environmental Program (UNEP) became interested in possible whole-world solutions like cap and share and began to assess them at the request of Norway and the European Union. Besides cap and share, UNEP is investigating "contraction and convergence," which shares out the capped emissions among governments according to the size of their populations, after a transition period in which the emissions-intensive countries get more. Other

BOX 5.1 Cap and Dividend in the United States
Mike Sandler

While cap and share strives to set up a global system to allocate green-house gas emissions equitably among nations, a streamlined national version has found some support in the United States through a concept called "cap and dividend."[1] In this system, the government sets a cap on total emissions and sells (auctions) permits representing those emissions to companies that introduce fossil fuels into the economy—and then the revenues from those permits are returned to citizens through equal per capita dividend payments.

The rationale underlying cap and dividend is straightforward:

· The atmosphere is a resource shared by everyone.

· Companies that emit greenhouse gases into the atmosphere are disposing of a dangerous waste product without having to pay for it, which means they are essentially being subsidized by the public.

· To end this subsidy, companies should pay for a permit to emit greenhouse gases. Because the atmosphere is owned by every-body, everybody should receive a piece of the revenue (the "dividend") generated by the sale of those permits.

Under cap and dividend, companies that emit greenhouse gases would presumably pass the cost of the permits on to their customers, but the periodic dividend everybody receives from the permit sales minimizes that extra cost. This system encourages people to use less fossil fuel, because customers who reduce their use of fossil fuels would be more than compensated by the dividend cash. It especially helps low-income households, which are less able to absorb the increased costs of fuel. Dividends could also help solidify political support for a carbon cap and minimize populist backlash against putting a price on emissions.

Cap and dividend entered the debate on U.S. climate legislation in

MIKE SANDLER is a co-founder of the Climate Protection Campaign, based in Sonoma County, California. He runs a Web site on cap and share and "cap and dividend" at www.carbonshare.org.

late 2009 when Senators Maria Cantwell (D-Washington) and Susan Collins (R-Maine) introduced the Carbon Limits and Energy for America's Renewal (CLEAR) Act.[2] The bill would auction 100 percent of the carbon permits and return 75 percent of that permit revenue to the American people in direct monthly payments. The remaining 25 percent would be invested in conservation, efficiency, transition assistance, and clean energy.

The earlier 1,400-page Waxman-Markey bill had been criticized as a lobbyist-oriented strategy that enriched coal-heavy utilities and polluters and created too many untested "carbon offsets." When the Waxman-Markey bill stalled in the Senate, the CLEAR Act emerged with a different approach: It focused on simplicity (it runs only 39 pages), it placed limitations on Wall Street involvement and speculation in the carbon market, and it returned the proceeds directly back to voters. Some critics have noted that the CLEAR Act's targets need to be strengthened, and the bill as introduced does not specify how portions of the emissions target will be met.

Even if national legislation fails to pass, Californians could receive a dividend. A panel of economists convened by the State of California in 2009 recommended a 75 percent dividend in the state's implementation of the Global Warming Solutions Act (AB 32). More than $7,000 could be returned to a family of four over the eight years of the program. There are still many hurdles before this becomes a reality. Opponents of climate legislation are calling for the suspension of AB 32, utilities want free permits, and legislators may choose to spend the money on other projects instead of providing dividends.

Over the past year, cap and dividend has moved from an abstract idea into a feasible policy option with a bipartisan network of support and reputable endorsements. If this momentum continues, cap and dividend may well become a reality.

---

1. Author and entrepreneur Peter Barnes helped develop the cap-and-dividend concept. More information can be found in Barnes's books *Who Owns the Sky?*, *Capitalism 3.0*, and *Climate Solutions* or at www.capanddividend.org.

2. Information on the CLEAR Act may be found on Senator Cantwell's Web site, http://cantwell.senate.gov/issues/CLEARAct.cfm.

proposals under review include Greenhouse Development Rights and Kyoto 2, both of which propose raising money from energy users across the globe for the massive changes that need to be made.

Whatever carbon-management system the world adopts, farming methods will need to change, and the efforts of hundreds of millions of people will be necessary to get the carbon out of the air. We, the residents of the world's industrialized countries, should not expect our lives to continue in much the same way. While it is going to be extraordinarily difficult to persuade ourselves to reduce our consumption to make the resources available to avert disaster, it's the only way the job can be done.

There is cause for hope: Now that the process which began at the Rio Earth Summit in 1992—and led to the Kyoto Protocol in 1997 and then the Copenhagen climate conference in 2009—is in total disarray, cap and share or some other global-level proposal (see box 5.1) has a chance of becoming the basis for future discussions. The international community certainly needs to move quickly. The time window in which it must act if disaster is to be averted is closing fast.

THE ECOLOGICAL DEFICIT

Creating a New Political Framework

DAVID ORR

DAVID ORR *is the Paul Sears Distinguished Professor of Environmental Studies and senior adviser to the president of Oberlin College. His career as a scholar, teacher, writer, speaker, and entrepreneur spans fields as diverse as environment and politics, environmental education, campus greening, green building, ecological design, and climate change. He is the author of six books, including the widely praised* Ecological Literacy *(1992) and* Earth in Mind *(1994/2004); his most recent book is* Down to the Wire: Confronting Climate Collapse *(2009). Orr is a Fellow of Post Carbon Institute.*

❖

The question of whether technology, politics and economic muscle can sort out the problem is the small question. The big question is about sorting out the human condition. It is the question of how we can deepen our humanity to cope with possible waves of war, famine, disease and refugees.

—ALISTAIR MCINTOSH

As I write, the president-elect and his advisors are pondering what to do about climate change amidst the largest and deepest economic crisis since the Great Depression of the 1930s. Their first round of decisions will have been made by the time you read this book. But whatever policy emerges in the form of cap and trade legislation, taxation, and new regulations on carbon, they are only the first steps, and they will quickly prove to be inadequate to deal with a deteriorating biophysical situation. Emerging climate realities will drive this or the next president, probably sooner rather than later, to more comprehensive measures—as a matter of national and global survival. The problem for President Obama presently

is that we are running two deficits with very different time scales, dynamics, and politics. The first, which gets most of our attention, is short-term
and has to do with money, credit, and how we create and account for
wealth, which is to say a matter of economics. However difficult, it is
probably repairable in a matter of a few years. The second is ecological. It
is permanent, in significant ways irreparable, and potentially fatal to civilization. The economy, as Herman Daly has pointed out for decades, is a
subsystem of the biosphere, not the other way around. Accordingly, there
are short-term solutions to the first deficit that might work for a while,
but they will not restore longer-term ecological solvency and will likely
make it worse. The fact is that climate destabilization is a steadily—perhaps rapidly—worsening condition with which we will have to contend
for a long time to come. University of Chicago geophysicist David Archer
puts it this way:

> A 2°C warming of the global average is often considered to be a
> sort of danger limit benchmark. Two degrees C was chosen as a
> value to at least talk about, because it would be warmer than the
> Earth has been in millions of years. Because of the long lifetime of
> carbon dioxide in the atmosphere, 2°C of warming at the atmo-
> spheric carbon dioxide peak would settle down to a bit less than
> 1°C, and remain so for thousands of years.[1]

But if the record of earlier climate conditions holds true in the future,
it also means, among other things, a 10-meter sea-level rise as well as
warmer temperatures for thousands of years. Climate destabilization, in
short, is not a solvable problem in a time span meaningful for us. But we
do have some control over the eventual size of climatic impacts we've initiated if we reduce emissions of carbon dioxide and other anthropogenic
heat-trapping gases to virtually zero within a matter of decades. Assuming
that we are successful, by the year 2050, say, we will not have forestalled
most of the changes now just beginning, but we will have contained the
scope, scale, and duration of the destabilization and created the foundation
for a future better than that in prospect.

There is no historical precedent, however, for what we must do if we
are to endure. Our biology, and specifically the way we perceive threats,
was honed over the ages to respond to direct physical threats posed by
predators animal or human. It did not equip us very well to perceive and

respond to threats measured in parts per billion that play out over decades, centuries, and millennia. We respond, as noted above, with alacrity to threats that are big, fast, and hairy, and not so quickly or ingeniously to those that are slow, small, subtle, and self-generated. Our understanding of economies was developed in the industrial age and imperfectly accounts for the damage caused to ecosystems and the biosphere, and not at all for the destabilization of climate. Had it been otherwise, we would have known that we were not nearly as rich as we presumed ourselves to be and not nearly as invulnerable as we thought. Our politics are a product of the European Enlightenment and rest on the belief in progress and human improvement, which we now know are not as simple or as unambiguous as we once thought. The political forms of democracy reflect a bedrock commitment to individual rights but exclude the rights of other species and generations unborn. And it is in the political realm that we must find the necessary leverage to begin the considerable task of escaping the trap we've set for ourselves.

The challenge before the president and his successors, accordingly, is first and foremost political, not economic. Our situation calls for the transformation of governance and policies in ways that are somewhat comparable to that in U.S. history between the years of 1776 and 1800. In that time Americans forged the case for independence, fought a revolutionary war, crafted a distinctive political philosophy, established an enduring Constitution, created a nation, organized the first modern democratic government, and invented political parties to make the machinery of governance and democracy work tolerably well. Despite its imperfections regarding slavery and inclusiveness, it stands nonetheless as a stunning historical achievement. The task is now no less daunting, and even more crucial to our prospects. We need a systematic calibration of governance with how the world works as a physical system. Theories of laissez-faire, however useful for short-term wealth creation, have proved to be ecologically ruinous. Henry David Thoreau in our circumstances would have asked what good is a growing economy if you don't have a decent planet to put it on.

Few have even begun to reckon with changes of this magnitude; instead, we place our faith in better technology in incremental changes at the margin of the status quo, hoping to keep everything else as it comfortably is. There is much to be said for better technology and particularly for measured policy changes and doing things piecemeal, mostly because we are often ignorant of the side effects of our actions. Revolutions generally have a dismal history. But in the age of consequences, we have no real choice but to transform our conduct of the public business in at least three ways. First, and most fundamental, as a matter of public policy we must quickly stabilize and then reduce carbon emissions. To do so will require policy changes that put an accurate price on carbon-based fuels and create the incentives necessary to deploy energy efficiency and renewable energy technologies here and around the world on an emergency basis. Success in this effort requires that the president and his successors regard climate policy as the linchpin connecting other issues of economy, security, environment, and equity as parts of a comprehensive system of policies governing energy use and economic development. The details of such a policy were recommended to President Obama's transition team by the Presidential Climate Action Project (www.climateactionproject.com) immediately after the election of 2008, and many of the recommendations subsequently appeared in the president's climate policy. Beyond the policy details the president will need to establish some mechanism by which to reliably coordinate national policies across federal and state agencies whose missions often conflict with the overriding goal of reducing carbon emissions.

Second, the president must launch a public process to consider long-term changes in our systems of governance, politics, and law. The goal is to create practical recommendations that enable us to anticipate and surmount the challenges ahead and ensure, as much as is humanly possible, that we never again stumble to the brink of global disaster. To that end I propose the appointment of a broadly based presidential commission to consider changes in governance and politics, including the necessity of a second constitutional convention. Neither idea is new. Presidential commissions have long been used as a way to engage thoughtful and distinguished persons in the task of rethinking various aspects of public policy and governance. The Ash Council, for one, laid the groundwork for what eventually became the U.S. Environmental Protection Agency. And the idea of a new constitutional convention has been proposed by legal scholars as diverse as Sanford Levinson and Larry Sabato, among many others.[2] In Sabato's words, the founders:

had risked life, limb, fortune, and birthright to revolt against their mother country, determined to stand on principle. . . . But they might also have been surprised and disappointed that future generations of Americans would be unable to duplicate their daring and match their creativity when presented with new challenges.[3]

Facing challenges that dwarf any that the founders could have imagined, we should be at least as bold and farsighted as they were. Whether a presidential commission would propose to reform governance by legislation, amendments to the Constitution, a full-scale constitutional convention, or some combination of measures, their charge would be to reform our system of governance to improve democracy and promote deliberation in ways that soon produce wise and well-crafted public policies that accord with ecological realities. Beyond proposals by experts like Levinson, Sabato, and Robert Dahl that aim to make our politics more democratic and efficient, I propose that the Constitution be amended to protect the rights of posterity to life, liberty, and property. The people of Ecuador went still farther, changing their constitution in September 2008 to acknowledge the rights of nature and permit their people to sue on behalf of ecosystems, trees, rivers, and mountains,[4] an idea that owes a great deal to Aldo Leopold's 1949 essay on "The Land Ethic" and to Christopher Stone's classic article in 1972 in the *Southern California Law Review*, "Should Trees Have Standing?"[5] What first appears as "a bit unthinkable" in Stone's words, however, is yet another step in our understanding of rights and obligations due some other person, or in this case, an entity, the web of life.[6] And not once in our history has the extension of rights caused the republic to tremble. To the contrary, it has always opened new vistas and greater possibilities, with one potentially fatal exception.

That exception is the rights of personhood presumed granted to corporations by the U.S. Supreme Court in the *Santa Clara County v. Southern Pacific Railroad* decision of 1886. Whether the Court actually made such a grant or not, it is long past time to rein in the power of corporations, for reasons that are patently obvious. "The only legitimate reason for a government to issue a corporate charter," in economist David Korten's words, "is to serve a well-defined public purpose under strict rules of public accountability."[7] That some corporations have got the new religion on energy efficiency or greening their operations or carbon-trading schemes pales beside the fact that none is capable of "voluntarily sacrificing profits to a larger public good," in Korten's words. And with very few exceptions they are incapable of helping us to reduce consumption, promoting public health, increasing equality, cleaning up the airwaves, or restoring a genuine democracy. It is time for this archaic institution to go the way of monarchy and for us to create better and more accountable ways to provision ourselves.

The presidential commission will need to carefully consider other bold ideas. Peter Barnes, for example, has proposed the creation of an Earth Atmospheric Trust based on the recognition that the atmosphere is a public commons.[8] Use of the commons as a depository for greenhouse gases would be auctioned, with the proceeds going to a quasi-independent agency and at least partially redistributed to the public, the owners of the commons. As the cap for emissions was lowered, the Trust would generate increasing revenues to help the public pay for the transition. There are other ideas to better harness and coordinate science with federal policy. One such proposal is to create an "Earth Systems Science Agency" by combining the National Oceanic and Atmospheric Agency and the U.S. Geological Survey to better collaborate with NASA. The new agency would be "an independent federal agency . . . with direct access to the Congress and Executive Office of the President, including the Office of Science and Technology Policy and the Office of Management and Budget."[9] The larger goal is to better align earth systems science with the creation and administration of public policy at the highest level as rapidly as possible.

Further, I propose the creation of a council of elders to advise the president, Congress, and the nation on matters of long-term significance relating to the climate.[10] The group would be appointed by the president with the advice of the National Academy of Sciences, the American Association for the Advancement of Science, and the American Bar Association, as well as civic, religious, academic, business, philanthropic, and educational groups. It would consist of persons who are distinguished by their accomplishments, wisdom, integrity, and record of public service, not just by their wealth. Their role would be, as the Quakers have it, to speak truth to power, publicly, powerfully, and persistently. The Council of Elders would be given the resources necessary to educate, communicate, commission research, issue annual reports, convene gatherings, engage the global community, and serve as the voice of the powerless, including posterity. Perhaps one day it could merge with a similar body summoned by Virgin Airlines owner Richard Branson and including Jimmy Carter, Vaclav Havel, Nelson Mandela, Beatrice Robinson, and Desmond Tutu into a Global Council of Elders. But at any scale the point is the same: in difficult times ahead we will need to hear the voices of the wisest among us to guide, cajole, admonish, and inspire us along the journey ahead. And those who govern will need their counsel, steadiness, and vision.

Beyond the details of policy and a reformed governing system, the president must resuscitate the role of the president as educator-in-chief using the office in the way Theodore Roosevelt once described as a "bully pulpit." Americans will need to learn a great deal about climate and environmental science in a short time. By skillful communications and the use of the powers of the federal government, the president can help to raise public understanding about climate science to levels necessary to create a constituency for the long haul. The president and others in leadership positions will need as well to build the case for:

- federally financed elections to remove money from the electoral process;
- reforming the Federal Communications Commission to restore the "fair and balanced" standards for the use of the public airwaves;
- ending the revolving door between government service and private lobbying;
- desubsidizing coal, oil, gas, and nuclear power;
- reducing the Pentagon budget by, say, half to accord with a more modest U.S. presence in the world and a smarter strategy that aims for security by design for everyone not brute force to protect corporations; and
- making more radical changes that might someday lead a more civilized America to confiscate 100 percent of the profits from making weapons.

As educator-in-chief, the president must help to rebuild our civic intelligence, emphasizing why fairness and decency are fundamental to prosperity and our well-being lest under the duress of hard times we forget who we are. The president must also help to extend our notions of citizenship to include our role as members in the wider community of life and knowledge of why being good citizens on both counts is the bedrock for any durable civilization. The president must help us understand the ties that bind us together and extend our sight to a farther horizon.

The challenge of transformative leadership in the age of consequences, however, does not fall only to the president and those in Washington. Far from it! The greater part of the work will be done—as it always has been—by those in leadership positions in nonprofit organizations, education, philanthropy, media, churches, business, labor, health care, research centers, civic organizations, mayors, governors, state legislators . . . virtually all of us. It is mandatory that we all contribute to the effort to minimize and then eliminate carbon emissions, deploy solar technologies, make the transition to a post-carbon economy, reengage the international community, and come to regard ourselves as trustees for future generations. This is a paradigm shift like no other. It is what philosopher Thomas Berry calls our "Great Work." Like that of earlier times, it will be costly and difficult, but far less so than not doing it at all.

From nearly a half century of work in sustainable and natural systems agriculture, urban design, biomimicry, ecological engineering, green building, biophilic design, solar and wind technology, regenerative forestry, holistic resource management, waste cycling, and ecological restoration, we have the intellectual capital and practical experience necessary to remake the human presence on the Earth. From intrepid social examples such as those in Kerala, Curitiba, Saul Alinsky's community organizing in Chicago, and the Mondragón Cooperative in Spain, we know how to build locally based economies that use local resources and local talents to the benefit of local people.[11] Thanks to great educators like John Dewey, Maria Montessori, J. Glenn Gray, Alfred North Whitehead, and Chet Bowers, we have a grasp of the changes in teaching and mindset necessary to make the transition. And from the most prescient among us, like Wendell Berry, Ivan Illich, and Donella Meadows, we know that fast is sometimes slow, more is sometimes less, growth is sometimes ruinous, and altruism is always the highest form of self-interest. This is to say that we are ready to transform our lives, culture, and prospects, and the time is now!

What does this mean on Main Street? I will end on a personal note. I live in a small Midwestern city powered mostly by coal with a struggling downtown threatened by nearby megamalls. The city is roughly a microcosm of the United States in terms of income distribution, ethnicity, and public problems. Run our likely history fast forward, say, 20 years or more and the town would be in disrepair and seriously impoverished. To avoid that scenario, a group of concerned citizens have recently banded together to create another story. They include the president of Oberlin College, the city manager, the superintendent of schools, the director of the municipal utility, the current and former presidents of the City Council, and many others.

The task before us requires solving four problems. The first is to create a practical vision of post-carbon prosperity. Can we make the transition from coal to efficiency and renewable energy in a way that lays the foundation for a sustainable economy? The second challenge is to develop the financial means to pay for the transition, including the capital costs to implement energy efficiency and to build the new energy system. The third challenge is that of actually building an alternative energy infrastructure in Oberlin, which means expanding existing businesses or building new ones. The fourth is to structure private choices so that people have a clear incentive to choose efficiency and renewables over inefficiency and fossil fuels and to buy more locally made or grown products.

In 2007, with outside support, the college launched two studies to help clarify our basic energy options. The first, by a Massachusetts energy firm, examined smart ways by which the city could improve efficiency and switch to renewable energy and thereby avoid joining in a risky, long-term commitment to a 1,000-megawatt coal plant (without the means to sequester carbon) proposed by AMP-Ohio. The second study, specifically on college energy use, examined options for eliminating our coal-fired plant and radically improving energy efficiency to levels now technologically possible and economically profitable. We now have a factual basis on which to build a farsighted energy policy for both the city and the college.[12] The college commissioned a third study to explore the feasibility of developing a new green, zero-discharge, carbon-neutral arts block on the east side of the town square, including a substantial upgrade of a performing arts center and a new green hotel.

What might that future look like ten years from now? Imagine, first, picking up an Oberlin phone book or going online and finding perhaps five new companies offering energy services, efficiency upgrades, and solar installations. Imagine a city economy that includes a hundred or more well-paying green energy jobs filled with highly trained young people from Oberlin High School, the vocational school nearby, and the college. Imagine local businesses using a third of the energy they now use but with better lighting and better indoor comfort at a fraction of the cost, with the savings forming the basis for expanding services and profits. Imagine a city that is sprouting photovoltaic (solar electric) systems on rooftops, installed and maintained by local entrepreneurs. Imagine the local utility (Oberlin Municipal Power and Light) becoming a national leader in improving local efficiency (what is called "demand-side management") while actually lowering energy bills for residents. Imagine the possibility of a new four-star, LEED platinum hotel, conference center, restaurant, and perhaps culinary school as the keystone of a new carbon-neutral, zero-discharge downtown arts district that features great live performances in a new theater and a jazz club featuring student artists from the Oberlin Conservatory of Music. Imagine a revitalized downtown bustling 24 hours a day with residents, shoppers, students, artists, and visitors who came to experience the buzz of the best small town in the United States that is also the first working model of post-fossil-fuel prosperity.

Imagine traveling just outside the city into New Russia township, where dozens of farms form a green belt around the city. In the summer they employ Oberlin teens, providing useful work and training in the practice of sustainable agriculture. Local farms flourish by supplying the college dining service, local restaurants, and the public with organically grown fresh foods. Beyond the green belt there is another forested belt of 10,000 acres that profitably sequesters carbon and provides the basis for a thriving wood products business. Imagine a resilient town economy buffered to a great extent from larger economic problems because it is supplied locally with biofuels, electricity from sunshine and wind, and a large portion of its food. Imagine Oberlin leading in the deployment of new technologies just coming into the market, like plug-in hybrid cars, solar electric systems, and advanced wastewater treatment systems. Imagine hundreds of Oberlin students, equipped with skills, aptitudes, and imaginations fostered in the remaking of the town and the college, spreading the revolution across the United States and the world.

Imagine a town, churches, college, and local businesses united in the effort to create the first model of post-carbon prosperity in the United States, at a scale large enough to be nationally instructive but small enough to be both manageable and flexible. Imagine that model spreading around the United States, cross-fertilizing with hundreds of other examples elsewhere in large cities like Chicago and Seattle, urban neighborhoods, and small towns. If, for a moment, you get very quiet . . . you can feel the transformation going on in the neighborhoods, towns, and cities all over the United States. It has grown into a worldwide movement that rejects the idea that we are fated to end the human experiment with a bang or a whimper on a scorched and barren Earth. It is the sound of humankind growing to a fuller stature—a transformation just in time.

Part Three

WATER

7

WATER

Adapting to a New Normal

SANDRA POSTEL

SANDRA POSTEL *directs the independent Global Water Policy Project. A leading expert on international water issues, she is the author of* Last Oasis: Facing Water Scarcity *(1992), which now appears in eight languages and was the basis for a PBS documentary. She has authored more than one hundred articles for popular, scholarly, and news publications, including* Science, Scientific American, Foreign Policy, *the* New York Times, *and the* Washington Post. *She was recently appointed the National Geographic Society's first Freshwater Fellow. Postel is a Fellow of Post Carbon Institute.*

❖

Water, like energy, is essential to virtually every human endeavor. It is needed to grow food and fiber, to make clothes and computers, and, of course, to drink. The growing number of water shortages around the world and the possibility of these shortages leading to economic disruption, food crises, social tensions, and even war suggest that the challenges posed by water in the coming decades will rival those posed by declining oil supplies.

In fact, our water problem turns out to be much more worrisome than our energy situation, for three main reasons. First, unlike oil and coal, water is much more than a commodity: It is the basis of life. Deprive any plant or animal of water, and it dies. Our decisions about water—how to use, allocate, and manage it—are deeply ethical ones; they determine the survival of most of the planet's species, including our own. Second, also unlike oil and coal, water has no substitutes. The global economy is transitioning away from fossil fuels toward solar, wind, and other noncarbon energy sources, but there is no transitioning away from water. And third, it is through water that we will experience the impacts of climate change most directly.

The rise in global temperatures driven by the last 150 years of humanity's greenhouse gas emissions is fundamentally altering the cycling of water between the sea, the atmosphere, and the land. Climate scientists warn of more extreme floods and droughts and of changing precipitation patterns that will make many dry areas drier and wet areas wetter. They warn of melting glaciers and ice caps that within a few decades could severely diminish the river flows upon which nearly a third of the world's people depend.[1] As if on cue, nature seems to be highlighting these warnings at every turn:

- Floods, droughts, storms, and other climate-related natural disasters forced 20 million people from their homes in 2008.
- Australia remains locked in a decade-long drought deemed the worst in the country's 117 years of record-keeping.
- In late August 2008, India faced the dislocation of some 3 million people when the Kosi River breached a dam and roared out of the Himalayas, causing the worst flooding of that river in fifty years.
- Ten months later, India witnessed its driest June in eighty years with millions of farmers unable to plant their crops.
- In 2009, famine stalked millions in the Horn of Africa, as failed rains led to the worst food crisis in Ethiopia and Kenya in a quarter century.[2]

The United States is by no means immune to these climate-related water risks. While farmers in the Midwest continued recovering from the spring flood of 2008 (in some areas, the second "100-year flood" in fifteen years), farmers in California and Texas fallowed cropland and sent cattle prematurely to slaughter to cope with the drought of 2009. In the Southeast, after twenty months of dryness, Georgia governor Sonny Perdue stood outside the state capitol in November 2007 and led a prayer for rain, beseeching the heavens to turn on a spigot for his parched state. Two years later, Perdue was pleading instead for federal aid after intense rainstorms caused massive flooding near Atlanta that claimed at least seven lives.[3]

Although none of these disasters can be pinned directly on global warming, they are the kinds of events climate scientists warn will occur more often as the planet heats up. Even more worrisome, the effects of climate change are already calling into question the very assumptions that have underpinned water planning and management for decades. In 2008, seven top water scientists argued persuasively in the journal *Science* that "stationarity"—the foundational concept that natural systems vary and fluctuate within an unchanging set of boundaries—is no longer valid for our understanding of the global water system.[4] In other words, when it comes to water, the past is no longer a reliable guide to the future. The data and statistical tools used to plan $500 billion worth of annual global investments in dams, flood-control structures, diversion projects, and other big pieces of water infrastructure are no longer trustworthy.[5]

This is not just a problem for the planners and civil servants who run our local water systems. It raises very serious questions about community health, public safety, food security, and risk management. Will those levees keep the river within its banks? Should that expensive new dam be built when its useful life will be shortened by silt washed down from flooding mountainsides? Will farms get needed irrigation water once the glacier-fed river flows have dwindled? How do we guard against what once seemed unthinkable—the drying up of prime water sources?

In more and more regions of the world, the unthinkable seems to be close at hand. Many Australian water managers now believe that a decade-long dry spell that has sent rice production plummeting, depleted reservoirs, and left the Murray River trickling into the sand is not going away. Increasingly, the question "Down Under" is not when the drought will end, but how this country of more than 21 million people—and its globally significant agricultural sector—can adapt to a permanently drier climate.[6]

In the U.S. Southwest, a similar day of reckoning is on the horizon. Scientists at the Scripps Institution of Oceanography at the University of California, San Diego estimate that there is a 50 percent chance that Lake Mead—the vast reservoir that delivers Colorado River water to tens of millions of people and one million acres of irrigated land—will dry up by 2021.[7] In 2000, Lake Mead stood at 96 percent of capacity; by the summer of 2009, it was down to 43 percent. After analyzing nineteen climate models, a team of thirteen earth scientists concluded in 2007 that the Dust Bowl-like dryness seen in the region in recent years "will become the new climatology of the American Southwest within a time frame of years to decades."[8] As in Australia, it may be folly—and a loss of precious time—to assume that business as usual and life as it's currently lived in the Southwest can continue.

The water challenges confronting us locally, regionally, and globally are unprecedented. They call for fundamental changes in how we use, manage, and even think about water. The good news is that it's within our economic and technological ability to have a future in which all food and water needs are met, healthy ecosystems are sustained, and communities remain secure and resilient in the face of changing circumstances. The path most of the world is on, however, will not lead to this more desirable state.

WHERE WE ARE, AND HOW WE GOT HERE

At first glance, it's hard to believe the world could be in trouble with water. Ever since the Apollo astronauts photographed Earth from space, we've had the image of our home as a strikingly blue planet, a place of great water wealth. But from a practical standpoint, this image is largely illusory. Most of Earth's water is ocean, which provides a multitude of benefits but is far too salty to drink, irrigate crops, or manufacture computer chips. Only a tiny share of all the water on Earth—less than one-hundredth of 1 percent—is fresh and renewed each year by the solar-powered hydrologic cycle.

Although renewable, freshwater is finite: The quantity available today is virtually the same as when civilizations first arose thousands of years ago. As world population grows, the volume of water available per person decreases; thus, between 1950 and 2009, as world population climbed from 2.5 billion to 6.8 billion, the global renewable water supply per person declined by 63 percent. If, as projected, world population climbs to 8 billion by 2025, the water supply per person will drop by an additional 15 percent.[9]

Though telling, these global figures mask the real story. The rain and snow falling on the land is not evenly distributed across the continents or throughout the year (see figure 7.1).[10] Many of the world's people and farms are not located where the usable water is. China, for instance, has 19.5 percent of the world's population, but only 7 percent of the renewable freshwater. The United States, by contrast, has 4.5 percent of the world's population and nearly 8 percent of the renewable freshwater. Even so,

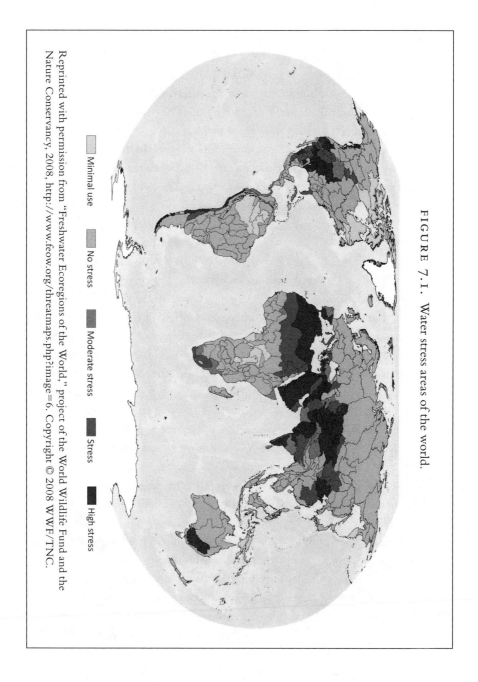

FIGURE 7.1. Water stress areas of the world.

Minimal use

No stress

Moderate stress

Stress

High stress

Reprinted with permission from "Freshwater Ecoregions of the World," project of the World Wildlife Fund and the Nature Conservancy, 2008, http://www.feow.org/threatmaps.php?image=6. Copyright © 2008 WWF/TNC.

most of U.S. farm irrigation and urban growth is in the West, which has much less water than the eastern United States.

For most of modern history, water management has focused on bringing water under human control and transferring it to expanding cities, industries, and farms. Since 1950, the number of large dams has climbed from 5,000 to more than 45,000—an average construction rate of two large dams per day for half a century. Globally, 364 large water-transfer schemes move 400 billion cubic meters (1 cubic meter equals about 264 gallons) of water annually from one river basin to another—equivalent to transferring the annual flow of twenty-two Colorado Rivers. Millions of wells punched into the planet tap underground aquifers, using diesel or electric pumps to lift vast quantities of groundwater to the surface.[11] It's hard to fathom today's world of 6.8 billion people and $60 trillion in annual economic output without such water engineering. It has allowed oasis cities like Phoenix and Las Vegas to thrive in the desert, world food production to expand along with population, and living standards for hundreds of millions to rise.

But the benefits of water development have not been shared equitably. More than 1 billion people lack access to safe drinking water, and some 850 million people are chronically hungry. Moreover, many regions have overshot their sustainable limits of water use. An unsettling number of large rivers—including the Colorado, Rio Grande, Yellow, Indus, Ganges, Amu Darya, Murray, and Nile—are now so overtapped that they discharge little or no water to the sea for months at a time.[12] The overpumping of groundwater is causing water tables to fall across large areas of northern China, India, Pakistan, Iran, the Middle East, Mexico, and the western United States. As much as 10 percent of the world's food is produced by overpumping groundwater. This creates a bubble in the food economy far more serious than the recent housing, credit, or dot-com bubbles, for we are meeting some of today's food needs with tomorrow's water.[13]

This overpumping is particularly serious in India. Using satellite data, scientists have recently estimated that groundwater is being depleted across northern India, which includes the nation's breadbasket, to the tune of 54 billion cubic meters per year. As wells run dry, the nation's food supply—as well as the livelihoods of the region's 114 million people—is increasingly at risk.[14] Likewise, in the United States, the massive Ogallala Aquifer is steadily being depleted. The Ogallala spans parts of eight states, from southern South Dakota to northwest Texas, and provides 30 percent of the groundwater used for irrigation in the country. As of 2005, a volume equivalent to two-thirds of the water in Lake Erie had been depleted from the Ogallala.[15] As in India, most farmers will stop irrigating when the wells run dry or the water drops so far down that it's too expensive to pump.

It is tempting to respond to these predicaments with bigger versions of the familiar solutions of the past—drill deeper wells, build bigger dams, move more river water from one place to another. Indeed, many leaders and localities are responding in just that way. By some estimates, the volume of water moved through river-transfer schemes could more than double by 2020.

China is proceeding with a massive $60 billion project to transfer water from the Yangtze River Basin in the south to the water-scarce north. If completed, it would be the largest construction project on Earth, transferring 41.3 billion cubic meters of water per year—a volume equal to half the Nile River.[16] India's Interlinking Rivers Project would be even more grandiose. Estimated to cost at least $120 billion, it entails building 260 transfers between rivers with much of the water moved from northern Himalayan rivers, including the Ganges and Brahmaputra, to water-scarce western provinces. Though still in the planning stages, the main goal would be to expand the nation's irrigated area by about a third, some 35 million hectares.[17]

In a world of changing rainfall patterns and river flows, substantial hydrologic uncertainty, and rising energy costs, such mega-projects are risky. They often take decades to complete, so payback periods on the large capital investments can be very long (if full payback occurs at all). They often worsen social inequities, such as when poor people are dislocated from their homes to make way for the dams and canals, and "downstream" communities lose the flows that sustained their livelihoods. And serious environmental damage—from soil salinization, water waste, altered river flows, and the loss of fisheries—routinely follows on the heels of such projects.[18] Moreover, large-scale infrastructure built to accommodate river flows today may be poorly matched to climate-altered flows of the future. The Himalayan rivers central to India's Interlinking Rivers Project, for example, will carry greatly diminished flows once the glaciers that feed them disappear.

In addition, giant water projects require giant quantities of energy. Pumping, moving, treating, and distributing water take energy at every stage. Transferring Colorado River water into southern California, for example, requires about 1.6 kilowatt-hours (kWh) of electricity per cubic meter of water; the same quantity of water sent hundreds of kilometers from north to south through California's State Water Project takes about 2.4 kWh. As a result, the energy required to provide drinking water to a typical southern California home can rank third behind that required to run the air conditioner and refrigerator.[19]

Another increasingly popular option for expanding water supplies—desalination—imposes a high energy price as well.[20] Producing 1 cubic meter (about 264 gallons) of drinkable water from saltwater through reverse osmosis requires about 2 kWh of electricity, usually produced from fossil fuels. Although that energy requirement is down from 5–10 kWh twenty years ago, it is still energy intensive. Moreover, today's most energy-efficient desalting plants are approaching the theoretical thermodynamic limit for separating salts from water, so further energy reductions will be modest at best.[21] Currently, the roughly 15,000 desalination plants worldwide have the capacity to produce 15.3 billion cubic meters of water per year, which is less than 0.5 percent of global water demand. Some 47 percent of this capacity is in the Middle East, where many nations can afford desalination—essentially turning their oil into water.[22]

Despite desalination's high costs, carbon dioxide output, risks to coastal marine environments, and production of toxic waste, global capacity roughly doubled between 1995 and 2006. Most U.S. capacity is in Florida, California, and Texas, with many more plants slated to be built.[23] Unfortunately, planners and policy-makers still eyeing desalination as a silver-bullet solution to water shortages apparently miss—or dismiss—the perverse irony: By burning more fossil fuels, desalination will likely worsen the problem they are trying to solve while making local water supplies more and more dependent on increasingly expensive fossil fuels.

A SMARTER PATH TOWARD WATER SECURITY

As with many challenges, finding the best solutions requires first asking the right questions. Typically, when planners and engineers see a water shortage on the horizon, they ask themselves what options exist to expand the supply. The typical answer: Get more water from a distant river, deeper wells, or a desalination plant.

But as the limitations of these "supply-side" options have become more apparent, a vanguard of citizens, communities, farmers, and corporations has started asking a different question: What do we really need the water *for*, and can we meet that need with less? The upshot of this shift in thinking is a new movement in water management that is much more about ideas, ingenuity, and ecological intelligence than it is about pumps, pipelines, dams, and canals.

This smarter path takes many forms, but it embodies two strategic attributes. First, solutions tend to work with nature, rather than against it. In this way, they make effective use of so-called ecosystem services—the benefits provided by healthy watersheds, rivers, wetlands, and other ecological systems. And second, through better technologies and more informed choices, these solutions seek to raise water productivity—the benefit derived from each liter of water extracted from a river, lake, or aquifer.

Working with nature is critically important to building resilience and reducing the energy costs associated with water delivery and use. We can think of a landscape composed of well-functioning ecosystems as "green infrastructure" that provides valuable services to society, just as roads and bridges do. Healthy rivers and watersheds, for instance, filter out pollutants, mitigate floods and droughts, recharge groundwater supplies, and sustain fisheries. They do this work with free energy from the sun—no fossil fuels or manufactured energy is required. By contrast, all the technological alternatives—building and running a treatment plant to remove pollutants, artificially recharging groundwater, constructing dikes and levees, raising fish on farms—require external inputs of increasingly expensive energy.

Of course, one of the most important "services" healthy watersheds perform is the provision of clean drinking water. If a watershed is doing the work of a water treatment plant—filtering out pollutants, and at a lower cost to boot—then it often pays to protect that watershed. New York City, for instance, is investing some $1.5 billion to restore and protect the Catskills-Delaware watershed (which supplies 90 percent of its drinking water) in lieu of constructing a $6 billion filtration plant that would cost an additional $300 million a year to operate.[24] A number of other cities across the United States—from tiny Auburn, Maine, to the city of Seattle—have saved hundreds of millions of dollars in avoided capital and operating costs by opting for watershed protection over filtration plants. In doing so, they have enjoyed many other benefits, such as preserving open space, creating recreational opportunities, protecting habitat for birds and wildlife, and (by preserving trees) mitigating climate change.[25]

Other innovative ideas are coming from Latin America, where some cities are establishing watershed trust funds. For instance, Rio de Janeiro in Brazil collects fees from water users to pay upstream farmers and ranchers $71 per hectare ($28 per acre) to protect and restore riparian forests, safeguarding the water supply and preserving habitat for rare birds and primates. A public watershed protection fund in Quito, Ecuador, started in 2000 in partnership with the Nature Conservancy, receives nearly $1 million a year from municipal water utilities and electric companies. Quito's water fund has become a model for other Latin American cities, including Cuenca, Ecuador, and Lima, Peru.[26]

There are many ways communities can work with nature to meet their water needs while reducing energy costs and building resilience. Communities facing increased flood damage, for instance, might achieve cost-effective flood protection by restoring a local river's natural floodplain. After enduring nineteen flood episodes between 1961 and 1997, Napa, California, opted for this approach over the conventional route of channelizing and building levees. In partnership with the Army Corps of Engineers, the $366 million project is reconnecting the Napa River with its historic floodplain, moving homes and businesses out of harm's way, revitalizing wetlands and marshlands, and constructing levees and bypass channels in strategic locations. In addition to increased flood protection and reduced flood-insurance rates, Napa residents will benefit from parks and trails for recreation, higher tourism revenues, and improved habitat for fish and wildlife.[27]

Similarly, communities facing increased damage from heavy stormwater runoff can turn impervious surfaces such as roofs, streets, and parking lots into water catchments by strategically planting vegetation. Portland, Oregon, is investing in "green roofs" and "green streets" to prevent sewer overflows into the Willamette River.[28] Chicago, Illinois, now boasts more than 200 green roofs—including atop City Hall—that collectively cover 2.5 million square feet, more than any other U.S. city. The vegetated roofs are helping to catch stormwater, cool the urban environment, and provide space for urban gardens.[29]

Many communities are revitalizing their rivers by tearing down dams that are no longer safe or serving a justifiable purpose. Over the last decade some 430 dams have been removed from U.S. rivers, opening up habitat for fisheries, restoring healthier water flows, improving water quality, and returning aquatic life to rivers. In the ten years since the Edwards Dam was removed from the Kennebec River near Augusta, Maine, populations of sturgeon, Atlantic salmon, and striped bass have returned in astounding numbers, reviving a recreational fishery that adds $65 million annually to the local economy.[30]

DOING MORE—AND LIVING BETTER—WITH LESS WATER

Of all the water we withdraw worldwide from rivers, lakes, and aquifers, 70 percent is used in agriculture, 20 percent in industries, and 10 percent in cities and towns. With water supplies tightening, we will need roughly a doubling of water productivity by 2025 to satisfy human needs while sustaining nature's life-support systems. Fortunately, opportunities to get more benefit per drop abound through greater investments in conservation, efficiency, recycling, and reuse, as well as through shifts in what is produced where and when.

But the need to do more with less water is not only a challenge for farmers, utilities, and manufacturers. It is also up to individual consumers to shrink our personal water footprints—the amount of water used to produce all the things we buy. The average U.S. resident uses, directly and indirectly, about 2,480 cubic meters of water per year—about 1,800 gallons *per day*—twice the global average.[31] More conscious choices about what and how much we consume are essential for reducing our global water footprint.

Water for Food

Feeding the world is a very water-intensive enterprise. It takes about 3,000 liters of water to meet a person's daily dietary needs. In the United States, with its high consumption of meat (especially grain-fed beef), the average diet requires some 5,000 liters of water per day. Under some very conservative assumptions, it could take an additional 1,314 billion cubic meters of water per year—equal to the annual flow of 73 Colorado Rivers—to meet the world's dietary needs in 2025.[32]

Once again, the search for solutions needs to begin with a reframing of the question. Instead of asking where we can find 73 Colorado Rivers' worth of water, the question is: *How do we provide healthy diets for 8 billion people without going deeper into water debt?* Framed this way, the solutions focus on getting more nutritional value per drop of water used in agriculture, which is the key to solving the water-food dilemma (table 7.1).

There are many ways we can grow more food for the world with less water, with most falling into four broad categories: (1) irrigate more efficiently; (2) boost yields on existing farms, especially rain-fed lands; (3) choose healthy, less water-intensive diets; and (4) use trade to make the smartest use of local water.

1. *Irrigate more efficiently.* For the last two centuries, societies have focused on expanding irrigation as a key to raising crop production. Today, the 18 percent of cropland that gets irrigation water provides about 40 percent of the world's food—but much of the water withdrawn for farming never benefits a crop. Some of it seeps back into aquifers or nearby streams, while some evaporates back to the atmosphere. There are many ways to reduce the waste: Irrigation can be scheduled to better match crop water needs, for example, or drip irrigation can be used to curb evaporation losses. Reducing irrigation demands by even 10 percent could free up enough water to meet the new urban and industrial demands anticipated for 2025.[33]

2. *Boost yields on rain-fed lands.* Rain-fed croplands have been the neglected stepchild in global agriculture, but this is now changing. Lands watered only by rain produce 60 percent of the world's food. Some, including those in the U.S. Midwest, achieve very high yields. But many rain-fed farms, particularly in poor countries, produce far less than they could. By one estimate, 75 percent of the world's additional food needs could be met by increasing harvests on low-yield farms to 80 percent of what high-yield farms achieve on comparable land. Most of this potential is in rain-fed areas,[34] and it's achievable through small-scale technologies and improved field methods—including, for example, capturing and storing local rain-

TABLE 7.1. Water Used to Produce Selected Products (global average)

Product	Water Used in Production (liters)
1 tomato	13
1 potato	25
1 slice of bread	40
1 orange/1 glass of orange juice	50/170
1 egg	135
1 cup of coffee	140
1 glass of milk	200
1 cup of cooked rice	250
1 hamburger	2,400
1 cotton T-shirt	4,100
1 pair of shoes (bovine leather)	8,000

Adapted from A. K. Chapagain and A. Y. Hoekstra, *Water Footprints of Nations,* vol. 1: *Main Report,* UNESCO Value of Water Research Report Series 16 (Delft: UNESCO-IHE, 2004), 42. Figure for cooked rice adapted from A. Y. Hoekstra, "Virtual Water: An Introduction," in *Virtual Water Trade: Proceedings of the International Expert Meeting on Virtual Water Trade,* Value of Water Research Report Series No. 12, A. Y. Hoekstra, ed. (Delft: IHE Delft, February 2003), 16.

water to apply to crops via low-cost irrigation systems.[35] Because the majority of the world's poor and hungry live on rain-fed farms in South Asia and sub-Saharan Africa, raising the farms' productivity would directly boost food security and incomes.

3. *Choose less water-intensive diets.* Foods vary greatly both in the amount of water they take to produce and in the amount of nutrition they provide—including energy, protein, vitamins, and minerals. It can take five times more water to supply 10 grams of protein from beef than from rice, for example, and nearly twenty times more water to supply 500 calories from beef than from rice. So eating less meat can lighten our dietary water footprint (while also improving our health). If all U.S. residents reduced their consumption of animal products by half, the nation's total dietary water requirement in 2025 would drop by 261 billion cubic meters per year, a savings equal to the annual flow of 14 Colorado Rivers.[36]

4. *Use trade to make the smartest use of local water.* While regional food
   resilience is important, some water-scarce regions may find it makes
   better economic and even environmental sense to import more of
   their food, rather than grow it themselves, and reserve their water
   for drinking and manufacturing. Egypt, Israel, Jordan, and a dozen
   other water-scarce countries already import a good share of their
   grain, saving 1,000–3,000 cubic meters of water for each ton of
   grain they import. Today, 26 percent of the global grain trade is
   driven by countries choosing to import water indirectly in the form
   of grain.[37]

This trade strategy can often be a good alternative to overpumping groundwater or diverting rivers long distances. As water analyst
Jing Ma and colleagues point out, northern China annually exports to
southern China about 52 billion cubic meters of water indirectly through
foodstuffs and other products. This volume exceeds that expected to be
shipped from south to north through the massive water-transfer scheme
now under construction.[38] A rethinking of where, what, and how food is
grown within China might allow the project to be scaled far back, if not
eliminated altogether.

At the national level, however, a food policy that relies on grain
imports can pose significant risks, especially for poor countries. As China,
India, Pakistan, and other populous, water-stressed countries begin to
look to the international grain market to meet their rising demands, food
prices are bound to increase. The food riots that erupted in Haiti, Senegal,
Mauritania, and some half dozen other countries as grain prices climbed
in 2007 and 2008 are likely a harbinger of what is to come and suggest
that a degree of food self-sufficiency may be crucial to food security.[39]
And of course, the rising fuel costs and increased potential for fuel scarcity
associated with peak oil will only make food imports more expensive and
less reliable in the long run.

Water for Homes and Manufacturing

Changes in the production and consumption of manufactured goods can
also shrink our water footprints. For example, Unilever is taking steps to
reduce water use across the life cycle of its products, from raw materials to
manufacturing to packaging to consumer use. Since 1995, water use in its

factories has dropped 63 percent, with some of its factories now treating and reusing all of their process water. Unilever is also working with its raw material suppliers to help conserve water. For example, by installing drip irrigation systems on a Tanzanian tea plantation and on a Brazilian tomato farm, the company is shrinking the water footprint of its Lipton tea and Ragu tomato sauce.[40]

In communities across the United States, conservation remains the least expensive and most environmentally sound way of balancing water budgets—and its potential has barely been tapped. Many cities and towns have shown significant reductions in water use through relatively simple measures like repairing leaks in distribution systems, retrofitting homes and businesses with water-efficient fixtures and appliances, and promoting more sensible and efficient outdoor water use. For example, a highly successful conservation program started in Boston in 1987 cut total water demand 43 percent by 2009, bringing water use to a fifty-year low and eliminating the need for a costly diversion project from the Connecticut River.[41]

The greatest residential water-conservation gains yet to be made lie in smarter landscape choices and watering practices. Turf grass covers some 16.4 million hectares (40.5 million acres) in the United States—an area three times larger than any irrigated farm crop in the country. Particularly in the western United States, where outdoor watering typically accounts for 40 to 70 percent of household water use, converting thirsty green lawns into native drought-tolerant landscaping can save a great deal of water. Las Vegas now pays residents $2 for each square foot of grass they rip out, which has helped shrink the city's turf area by 80 million square feet and lower its annual water use by 18 billion gallons in just four years.[42] Albuquerque, New Mexico, has reduced its total water use by 21 percent since 1995 largely through education and by providing rebates to residents for using water-conserving irrigation systems.[43]

One of the biggest untapped potentials for smarter water management in all types of enterprises lies in more creative use of information technologies: meters, sensors, controllers, computers, and even cell phones. A little book-sized product called iStaq, made by U.K.-based Qonnectis, fits under a manhole cover and measures flow, pressure, and other water variables. If the water pipe springs a leak, the iStaq alerts the utility operator by text message. In farming regions, real-time weather data collection combined with crop evapotranspiration rates and sensors monitoring soil moisture are helping farmers determine when and how much to irrigate their crops. There's even an iPhone application that enables farmers to remotely monitor moisture levels in their fields through sensors placed near the roots of their crops.

In Ugandan villages, farmers lacking computers are getting access to the wealth of information on the Internet by calling their questions in to a free telephone hotline called Question Box. The operators, who speak the local language, search for the answers and call the farmers back. A project of Open Mind, a California-based nonprofit, Question Box enables poor farmers, whose only communication device may be a village phone, to connect to the wired world for information on crop prices, weather forecasts, plant diseases, and more.[44]

The potential uses of information technology to enable smarter water decisions are extensive and have only begun to be tapped. Using GIS (geographic information system) technology, for example, the World Wildlife Fund (WWF) recently identified more than 6,000 traditional water tanks (small reservoirs to capture rainfall or runoff) in a single sub-watershed in western India. WWF determined that if the tanks were restored to capture just 15 to 20 percent of local rainfall, they could hold some 1.74 billion cubic meters of water—enough to expand irrigated area in the region by 50 percent and at a cost per hectare just one-fourth that of an irrigation dam-and-diversion project proposed for the region.[45]

RESETTING THE SIGNALS

Most of the world's water shortages have arisen because the policies and rules that motivate decisions about water have encouraged inefficiency and misallocation rather than conservation and wise use. Without big dams and river diversions subsidized by taxpayers, for example, rivers and streams in the western United States would not be so severely depleted today. And without low, flat rates for electricity, India's groundwater would not be so severely overpumped.

Allowing markets to do what they can do well—send a price signal about water's value—is critical for encouraging investments in water efficiency and more sensible uses of water. Most governments in rich and poor countries alike, however, continue to send the wrong signal by

> BOX 7.1   Ideas to Transition to a
> More Secure Water Future
>
> · Cap groundwater and river depletion.
> · Reduce subsidies; price water to better reflect its value.
> · Protect wetlands and watersheds to safeguard water quality.
> · Re-operate (improve the release of water) or remove dams so as to restore natural river flows.
> · Establish payments for ecosystem services.
> · Offer rebates or tax credits for conservation and efficiency measures.
> · Encourage "green infrastructure" (e.g., roofs, streets) in urban and suburban areas.
> · Reduce individual/corporate/community water footprints.
> · Ensure that decision-making is inclusive, transparent, and accountable to the public.

heavily subsidizing water, especially for irrigation, the biggest consumer. While better pricing is essential, it doesn't automatically account for the many important benefits of rivers, lakes, wetlands, and streams—such as protecting water quality and providing fish and wildlife habitat—that are not recognized in the marketplace. It is the job of governments, as custodians of the public trust in water, to protect these important but often unrecognized values, and it is the job of citizens to demand that their elected officials get busy crafting creative solutions.

Imagine, for example, if U.S. policy-makers propped up farm incomes not with irrigation and crop subsidies that distort markets and misallocate resources, but rather with payments for protecting ecosystem services that benefit society at large. Farmers and ranchers who plant buffer strips along streams, protect soils from erosion, or provide wildlife habitat through wetland protection would receive a payment for providing these services. The Conservation Reserve Program under the U.S. Department of Agriculture (USDA) could be strengthened to secure these water benefits for the long term, perhaps in conjunction with the USDA's new Office for Ecosystem Services and Markets. A tax on water depletion or transfers could help fund the effort.[46]

Current pricing and policy signals are deeply misaligned with the realities of our water predicament—but this means that there are untold opportunities for improvement. Each of the ideas listed in box 7.1 has been implemented by some local, state, or national government somewhere, and has achieved positive results. For example, a cap on groundwater pumping from the Edwards Aquifer in south-central Texas has motivated farmers, businesses, and citizens to conserve. San Antonio has cut its per capita water use by more than 40 percent, to one of the lowest levels of any western U.S. city.[47]

It is critical that policy-makers begin to grapple with the inconvenient truth that supplying water takes energy and supplying energy takes water. Energy and water are tightly entwined, and all too often public policies to "solve" one problem simply make the other one worse. For example, the 2007 mandate of the U.S. Congress[48] to produce 15 billion gallons of corn ethanol a year by 2015 would annually require an estimated 6 trillion liters of additional irrigation water (and even more direct rainfall)—a volume exceeding the annual water withdrawals of the entire state of Iowa.[49] Even solar power creates a demand for water, especially some of the big solar-thermal power plants slated for the sunny Southwest.[50] Clearly any action we take to build local renewable energy sources must be careful not to add additional strain to our already-stressed rivers and aquifers.

The win-win of the water-energy nexus, of course, is that saving water saves energy, and saving energy saves water. The more a community lives on water, energy, and food produced locally, the more options arise for solving multiple problems simultaneously, building resilience through resourcefulness, and preparing for future uncertainties.

Part Four

BIODIVERSITY

PEAK NATURE?

STEPHANIE MILLS, LHD

STEPHANIE MILLS *is a renowned author and lecturer on bioregionalism, ecological restoration, community economics, and voluntary simplicity. She has written or edited six books including* Tough Little Beauties *(2007) and* Epicurean Simplicity *(2002), authored countless articles, and edited a number of publications including* Earth Times *and* CoEvolution Quarterly. *She has lectured at numerous institutions, including the E. F. Schumacher Society, the Chicago Academy of Sciences, and the Harvard Graduate School of Design. Mills is a Fellow of Post Carbon Institute.*

❖

The first rule of intelligent tinkering is to save all the parts.

—ALDO LEOPOLD

Over the vast spans of geologic time much of Earth's surface has been bared and flooded, dried out and iced over. But since life first appeared in the form of bacterial cells 3.9 billion years ago, it has been proliferating, evolving, adapting, and diversifying (or succumbing amidst all these changes).[1]

Nearly 4 billion years' worth of trial and error, calamity, extinction, coevolution, and symbiosis have produced *biodiversity*: the phenomenal multitude of species on Earth. It's estimated that between fifty million and one hundred million different kinds of microbes, fungi, plants, and animals make up this wild richness of life. Just a single hectare of Atlantic Coastal Rainforest may harbor as many as 450 species of trees, to say nothing of its flowers, insects, mammals, reptiles, and amphibians.[2] Moreover, diversity begets diversity—it's a cumulative process.[3] Earth's current biota may in fact be richer than ever before because over hundreds of thousands of years, the evolution of species has, on average, exceeded extinction rates.[4]

Evolution is the process by which species diversify and descend from other ancestral organisms. Over time, populations of different organisms adapt and flourish in their niches. Natural selection preserves the traits that help species flourish. A critter whose chance markings provide better camouflage in its native environment, for instance, is likelier to survive to produce offspring that may bear those traits forward. Eyes, noses, claws, fins, tentacles, pigments, scales, leaves, buds, needles, pheromones, gestation, metamorphosis, and sensation are among evolution's countless feats. Geographic isolation combined with successful reproduction can eventually give rise to new species, organisms different enough from their precursors that they cannot interbreed.

ECOSYSTEMS

Ecosystems are interdependent ensembles of organisms engaged in give-and-take where all beings are in dynamic relation in space and time. They exist at various orders of magnitude, from the microscopic to the planetary. At the grandest scale is Earth's ecosystem. According to atmospheric chemist James Lovelock's Gaia hypothesis, Earth acts like an organism, trending toward conditions favorable to life. Gaia, says Lovelock's colleague Lynn Margulis, is "a convenient name for an Earthwide phenomenon: the regulation of temperature, acidity/alkalinity, and gas composition. . . . the series of interacting ecosystems that compose a single huge ecosystem at the Earth's surface."[5]

Closer in are the distinct microbial ecosystems flourishing in various regions of the human body, from the crooks of our elbows to our lower intestines. The crucial point is that ecosystems—of any size—are made up of interrelated organisms evolving and adapting to their particular environments as communities.

The vast majority of species comprising Earth's biodiversity are wild. Without them we humans would not and could not exist. These wild species provide "ecosystem services" such as food from soil and sea, production and maintenance of oxygen and other gases in the atmosphere, filtration and detoxification of poisons, climate moderation, regulation of freshwater, decomposition of wastes, recycling of nutrients, soil creation, control of pests and disease vectors, and storage of solar energy in food and fuels. They also serve as an immense trove of the genetic information that will allow for future evolution.[6]

THE BENEFITS OF BIODIVERSITY

The word *biodiversity* usually conjures up images of fantastically colored rainforest frogs, immense denizens of the deep ocean like giant squid and great whales, and the "charismatic megafauna" of countless nature shows—great beasts like lions and wolves and the hoofed animals like zebra, antelope, elk, and big-horned sheep on which they prey. But, critically, biodiversity also includes myriad inconspicuous beings like bacteria, insects, bats, and rodents, whose roles in the web of life are fundamental. A fourth of the fearsome grizzly bear's annual calorie intake comes from hordes of Miller moths.[7]

Our own calorie intake also depends on insects. About 70 percent of Earth's flowering plants depend on insect pollination. These plants include most of the crop species that provide about a third of the foods and beverages we consume.[8] Many wonderfully elaborate and exclusive relationships—called mutualisms—have coevolved between wildflowers and pollinators. Deeply hidden nectars lure in the long bills of hummingbirds or proboscises of moths. Some tropical orchids draw bees to gather their special scents, and then festoon the insect with pollen to carry away to another blossom. Such wild pollinators—including not only insects but bats and birds as well—are essential to the survival of the plants they've evolved with.[9] But many pollinators are threatened, including the all-important domesticated honeybee. A syndrome called colony collapse disorder began threatening beehives around the world in 2006. Some commercial beekeepers have lost 30 to 90 percent of their hives. In Maoxian, China, one place where honeybees have vanished entirely, hand-pollinating a hundred apple trees now takes as many as two dozen human workers to do the work of two beehives.[10]

In nature there is no waste, but rather death and transformation. Without the ecosystem services of what are called detritivores—critters that dine on organic debris—and other reducers of carrion and leaf fall, we'd be neck deep in corpses and dead vegetation. Vultures, fungi, bacteria, larvae, and beetles are among biodiversity's undertakers, consuming the dead and transforming them into the makings of soil and future creatures. One such wild mortician is the endangered American burying beetle, big as a thumb, which can scent a small carcass from as far as two miles away. The male and female beetles, ace recyclers, cooperate to bury the corpses they find and feed them to their larvae.[11]

All the intricately related functions and life-support services of wild nature are "on so vast a scale that there is no way we could recreate them or are so complex that we barely understand how they work."[12] To replace or synthesize affordable substitutes would be impossible. Beneficial relationships abound. In ponderosa pine forests, for example, chickadees and nuthatches foraging for insect larvae that dwell in cracks and crevices in the trees' bark in effect groom the trees by devouring pests. Pines visited by these tireless avian predators enjoy relatively greater health and growth.[13]

THE WILD ROOTS OF AGRICULTURE

Every plant, animal, or insect (like the honeybee) that we depend on for food and fiber descended from a wild ancestor. We are heavily dependent on just a handful of domesticated plants and animals. Nine-tenths of global livestock production is made up of only fifteen mammal and bird species, and three-quarters of our food supply comes from only twelve plant species.[14] Raised in monocultures and selectively bred for hundreds of years, these domesticated plants and animals are much less resilient to parasites and diseases than their wild ancestors. The Irish potato blight of 1845–1852 wiped out the single crop that multitudes of people had come to depend on, helping kill or exile millions. Given such vulnerability, we need to preserve not only the diversity of plants and livestock developed by the farmers and gardeners around the world who bred varieties adapted to their specific bioregions, but also the diversity of the wild lands where these stocks originated as reservoirs of genetic diversity. The wild matrix bordering fields and human settlements harbored animals that maintained ecological balances important to human health. By converting wild land to cropland, and by battling organisms that consume or compete with crops and livestock, agriculture reduces biodiversity. Habitat conversion can eliminate predatory animals, which, relative to their prey, are few in number and not prolific. And in the absence of predators, populations of prey species—some of which, like rodents, can harbor human infectious disease—may irrupt.[15]

THE GROUND OF BEING

Whether we live in the town or in the country, our lives depend utterly upon the living soil. Soils, as diverse as the geologies underlying them and the latitudes where they are found, are created as vegetation slowly colonizes bare ground. Plants live, die, and decay to become the humus that will grow other ensembles of plants, also mortal, whose remains will supply yet more nutrients and texture to the earth. Healthy soil is rife with biodiversity, teeming with billions of organisms per cubic meter—galactic numbers of nematodes, earthworms, mites, protozoa, algae, fungi, and bacteria. Together these creatures maintain the soil's structure, regulate the movement of water within the soil, sequester carbon, control plant growth, and provide food and medicine.[16]

Soil that's unprotected by vegetation is vulnerable to erosion. The mudslides that can follow forest clear-cuts and the countless tons of heartland topsoil sent downriver since the plow broke the plains so testify. Thus soil conservation is another crucial ecosystem service provided by biodiversity. Even in seemingly stark, arid lands, living, photosynthesizing communities of organisms called cryptogamic crusts protect desert floors. Composed of algae, cyanobacteria, and fungi, these subtle alliances of communities protect the crumbs of soil where they, the cacti, grasses, mesquite, and other desert plants grow.[17]

Vegetation and precipitation are interdependent: Plants draw soil moisture up through their roots, stems, trunks, and branches and emit water vapor from their foliage. The process, called evapotranspiration, influences cloud formation over landmasses. Thus deforestation generally leads to a decrease in rainfall.[18] "Forests precede civilization, deserts follow," remarked Chateaubriand. Plants sequester carbon dioxide, which, in excessive amounts (along with other greenhouse gases), destabilizes the climate. Hence the biodiversity embodied by forests and other plant communities has provided the tolerable climate and the water cycles that life depends on.

WATER AND LIFE

Sooner or later, most animals, including us, are drawn to streams, shores, ponds, and rivers. Water is life. Yet as human settlements grow, streams and the never-too-popular swamps and sloughs come to be used as sewers and seen as nuisances. We capture watercourses in culverts, drain wetlands, and fill shorelines.

But the biodiversity found where land and water meet can make a life-and-death difference for oceanic ecosystems and coastal settlements. Marshes, swamps, and everglades filter and clean runoff from the land and help mitigate the intensity of floods, which now affect more people than all other natural or technological disasters combined.[19] Fresh- and saltwater wetlands structurally mediate the encounter between sea and shore in different ways, gentling the forces of floods, waves, and storms.

Tidal marshes and mangrove forests, in particular, provide niches for plants and animals that can take advantage of fluctuating water levels, and varying concentrations of salt. Mangrove trees with all their roots buffer shorelines and are nurseries for commercially important fish. They also provide habitat and nesting sites for birds and host communities of mollusks, like snails, and crustaceans, like crabs. Yet assaults from shrimp aquaculture and logging have eliminated half or more of the mangrove swamps in some countries.[20]

Beyond the coasts and over the ocean horizon, marine biodiversity is in trouble. Coral reefs, "rainforests of the ocean," are created by colonies of calcium-depositing spineless (invertebrate) wonders. In the deep seas, corals provide habitat for other invertebrates like sponges, anemones, and countless fish, as well as for wondrous critters like feather dusters and basket stars.[21] Unfortunately, increased atmospheric carbon dioxide is being absorbed by the world's oceans, acidifying their waters and making calcium deposition more difficult. Some algae—the plant life at the base of marine food chains—also are severely affected by this change in the oceans' chemistry.[22]

Overfishing has catastrophically depleted species like cod, halibut, tuna, and billfish. But by keeping food webs intact, marine reserves—high-seas regions where overfishing and pollution are controlled—help fish populations rebound and support the resilience of the corals those fish depend on. In such reserves, corals are more resistant to the killing effects of climate change.[23]

CLIMATE CHANGE

Phenology studies the recurring periodic phenomena of the wild—the landfall of the first monarch butterfly, the first flowering of the milkweed, the hatching of the first clutch of killdeer. Long-term phenological observations now supply definite evidence of climate change. Distribution of species, the size of their populations, and the timing of migration and mating have all been variously affected. Throughout the Northern Hemisphere, spring is beginning earlier. Pest and disease outbreaks have increased in frequency, especially in forested areas.[24]

Because we human beings—given our high-functioning brains and the technologies we have developed with them—are among the most adaptable animals of all, we may not comprehend that climate change can happen too rapidly for evolutionary adaptation to occur among other, less generalist organisms.[25] Timing can be everything. The direct and indirect effects of climate change, say Stuart Pimm and his colleagues, will result in the extinction of 15 to 37 percent of Earth's species by 2050.[26] One example is the adorable pika, a rabbit relative whose hibernation in its montane scree crevices is being cut short by earlier spring thaws and warmer temperatures. Exposed to intolerable early heating, pikas are running out of higher, cooler elevations to retreat to, and extinction threatens.[27]

CONSUMPTION

Virtually every human threat to other species and their habitats is driven by economic growth and by our consumption, be it of food, energy, products, or even scenery. Sustaining what remains of the planet's biodiversity ultimately will require a paradigm shift in economics and far better public understanding of the connections between the things we consume, their places of origin, and the consequences of their extraction and production.

Some threats to biodiversity, like climate change, are planetwide and civilizational. Others are more localized and have particular causes, like the logging of nearly 2 million acres of the northern temperate and Arctic (boreal) forest annually. Some three hundred species of birds breed—and about five billion birds summer—in this vast forest, which stretches from Newfoundland to the Yukon. Two-thirds of the logs extracted from these rich terrains are pulped for mail order catalogs, facial tissue, and toilet paper.[28]

In an age of extinctions, some forms of consumption—fashions in wild furs, virility medicines made from endangered animals or plants, and gourmet dining on rare fish and game—are blatantly unconscionable. Less elite consumers can help conserve biodiversity by dietary change: eating little or no meat, avoiding palm oil (its cultivation for food and biofuel is converting vast tracts of Asian rainforest to plantations), and selecting shade-grown coffee and organic bananas (whose cultivation is friendlier to tropical environments).[29] Because gold mining causes massive damage to lands and cultures, resulting in millions of tons of waste for every ton of gold produced, refraining from purchasing new gold can be a gesture toward protecting lands, waters, and human rights.

Even if we do diminish our consumption and find more sustainable ways of producing our necessities, a decline in human population is ultimately essential for biodiversity to rebound. A reduction in the number of births per woman to replacement level or less should be the aim. Fortunately, the means to that end coincide with female emancipation: Free and universal access to health services, including contraception, abortion, and maternal and infant care, as well as education and economic opportunities for women all are conducive to smaller families and greater equity and well-being.

POLLUTION

In the dwindling of fossil fuels there's good news and bad news for biodiversity. Rapid, drastic disruption of habitats with heavy equipment may become prohibitively expensive. Slowing industrial production, and the deepening scarcity of oil as a feedstock for the petrochemical and plastics industries, may mean a decline in the production of persistent organic chemical pollutants. A reduction in the variety and quantity of immortal waste being dumped on the planet would reduce the suffering of countless beings. For instance, gazillions of tiny pellets of plastic called "nurdles" now pervade the world's oceans. Raw plastic is shipped to manufacturers in the form of nurdles, which are about the size of fish eggs. Hapless sea life ingest nurdles (loosed in the wild from spills and careless handling in the plastics industry) as well as other fragments of broken-down plastic (blown out of open landfills, dropped down sewer grates, fallen off ships). This garbage often fatally blocks their digestive systems.[30]

The present ensemble of life forms evolved in the absence of the high levels of noise, artificial light, electromagnetic radiation, radioactive fallout, synthetic chemicals, nanoparticles, and transgenic organisms that have been unleashed in recent decades. These novel phenomena can spell disaster for wild beings. Across North America, city and suburban lights lure a hundred million migratory birds to their deaths annually in collisions with buildings.[31] Nanoparticles cross the blood-brain barrier in vertebrates, genetically engineered crop plants hybridize to create herbicide-resistant weeds, and hormone-mimicking chemicals affect reproductive physiology across a wide range of animals, from alligators to *Homo sapiens*.

In light of such unintended consequences, the precautionary principle should govern the allocation of intellectual and material resources to shaping the technologies of sustainability. This holds that "where there are threats of serious or irreversible damage, lack of full scientific certainty shall not be used as a reason for postponing cost-effective measures to prevent environmental degradation."[32] ("An ounce of prevention is worth a pound of cure," in the vernacular.)

THE EXTINCTION CRISIS

As it has grown in numbers and technological might, the human race has become a force of geophysical proportion, on par with the asteroid that struck the Yucatán during the Cretaceous era, dethroning *Tyrannosaurus rex*.[33] Extinction is final. Yet no species is immortal. Extinction has been part of evolution since life emerged on Earth. Over the billions of years of life's history, innumerable life forms have flickered out, sometimes individually, occasionally en masse. Heretofore there have been five extinction events so massive that 50 to 95 percent of all species died out.[34] These mass extinctions all seem to have involved long-term pressures on ecosystems, like ice ages, global warming, or continental drift, combined with sudden catastrophes like volcanic eruptions, gamma-ray bursts, and impact events like the asteroid collision that put paid to the dinosaurs.[35]

The normal rate of extinction is about one in a million species per year.[36] The extinction rate today is between 100 to 10,000 times that. (The numbers vary so because an accurate census of life on Earth is likely impossible. Of the 50 million to 100 million species living on Earth, only about 1.75 million have been described.[37])

Our species has deforested, plowed, bulldozed, dredged, drained, dammed, polluted, or paved one-half to one-third of the land surface of Earth.[38] "The structure and function of the world's ecosystems," states the United Nations' Millennium Ecosystem Assessment, "changed more rapidly in the second half of the twentieth century than at any time in human history," resulting in a "substantial and largely irreversible loss in the diversity of life on Earth."[39] Because the richness of biodiversity is directly related to the extent of wild or undamaged habitat, human activity is causing Earth's sixth mass extinction.

These changes and losses are driven by population growth, increased economic activity, and cultural and technological changes. These variously result in conversion of forests to cropland, intensified fishing, building of more dams and reservoirs, accelerated movement of invasive species around the world, and increased nutrient loading in water bodies (which causes algal blooms and a proliferation of "dead zones" offshore).[40]

ALIEN INVASIONS

Conservation biologists rank alien species invasions as second only to habitat loss in threatening the survival of biodiversity. Alien or weedy species are simply "plants [or animals] out of place," by one definition. Transported deliberately or inadvertently to new lands beyond their normal range, these organisms may find themselves free from the predators, parasites, or diseases that formerly kept their numbers in balance. Invasive plants may multiply so plenteously that they outcompete the diverse native flora and end up changing ecosystem processes, indeed changing "the rules of the game."[41] Thirsty alien trees like tamarisk, melaleuca, and eucalyptus, for example, can drastically change the hydrology of their new homes. Invasive animals like the green iguanas, boa constrictors, cane toads, and dozens of other exotic reptiles and amphibians now reproducing in Florida upset the ancient balance of nature.[42]

Once introduced, alien plants and animals are virtually impossible to extirpate. With effort, their numbers can be controlled and new infestations nipped in the bud. Around the shores of the Great Lakes projects to control spreading infestations of the common reed, *Phragmites australis,* are under way. This brawny plant forms dense single-species stands whose rhizomes (rootlike structures) may grow six feet a year, and, when broken up by natural or human action, readily grow into new plants. *Phragmites* colonies degrade wildlife habitat and dry up marsh soils as they spread. Herbicide application, not an activity for amateurs, is considered to be necessary to control *Phragmites.* In areas where the infestations are minor, hands-on community involvement in the monitoring and control of the plant can become part of a cultural commitment to maintaining a region's ecological resilience. (And who knows? Post peak oil, if asphalt shingles are priced out of the market, thatched roofs might make a comeback, creating a demand for *Phragmites.*)

WILDLANDS PRESERVES

Biodiversity preservation must undergird serious strategies for transitioning to the post-fossil-fuel world with its rapidly changing climates. This means securing wild places where ecosystems can persist or recuperate. In the near term, saving biodiversity will require strategic intervention, cooperation, and commitment at the international level. There's broad consensus that a global system of ecological preserves and heritage sites must include healthy, representative examples of the planet's many types of ecosystems, or biogeographical provinces, as well as species-rich biodiversity hotspots (see box 8.1).

Conservation biologist Michael Soule nominates habitat fragmentation and degradation, climate change, and the extirpation of large predators as the three major causes of "ecological wounds."[43] This implies that ecosystem preserves not only must be representative, they must be unfragmented, sufficiently large, strategically oriented with respect to climate change, and interconnected.

"One of the few straightforward laws of ecology," writes paleontologist Anthony Barnosky, is "bigger pieces of real estate support more species. This is called the species area relationship. . . . [U]se it to predict

BOX 8.1   The United Nations' Year of Biodiversity

Recognizing that the threats posed by the loss of the planet's biodiversity are quite as grave as the consequences of climate change, the United Nations declared 2010 to be the Year of Biodiversity. The aim was to produce a binding agreement on targets to curb biodiversity loss at an October 2010 meeting of the 193 countries that have signed the U.N.'s Convention on Biological Diversity.[1]

1. Stephen Leahy, "Biodiversity: A Tipping Point on Species Loss?" *Inter Press Service News Agency*, January 17, 2010, http://www.ipsnews.net/print.asp?idnews=49964.

how many species you might lose if you reduce the size of the real estate that contains suitable habitat."[44] To establish adequately large preserves, landscape-scale restoration, of which we'll learn more later, will likely be necessary. Within biomes or ecoregions, preserves must be connected, particularly along north-south axes to allow for both normal and climate-driven migration. "A parcel of geography," writes Barnosky, "won't preserve a particular assemblage of species if their needed climate at that locus disappears."[45] Thinking big enough for North America, Michael Soule proposes "saving the Spine of the Continent, a 5,000 mile long cordillera extending from the North Slope of Alaska to the Sierra Madre Occidental of Sonora . . . from the Arctic to the subtropics."[46]

To function naturally, ecosystem preserves must be big enough to support a full complement of plants and animals, including "keystone species." Keystone species are plants or animals that play a pivotal role in their ecosystems and often require extensive territories. When they are removed, as with the removal of the keystone of an arch, the whole structure is weakened. Keystone species may be trees whose nuts provide food at a critical time, like the dead of winter, tiding other important members of the community through. They may be habitat-reforming species like elephants, whose foraging and trampling keeps grasslands and savannas open to sustain all the grazing animals that depend on them, or like beavers, whose dams create wetlands, replenish aquifers, and provide habitat for fish, frogs, and waterfowl. When keystone species perish, the ecosystems that pivot on them lose diversity, resilience, and function.

PREDATORS AND PREY

Eat *and* be eaten is the first rule of life's game. Biodiversity depends on the dynamic balance between predator and prey species. "The world is green," writes Julia Whitty, "because carnivores eat herbivores." Wipe out predators, which may be seen as competitors vying with humans for economically valuable plants or animals, and ecosystems deteriorate. On the land, these "trophic cascades" (*trophic* means relating to feeding and nutrition) can unfetter populations of hoofed vegetarians like the white-tailed deer and midsized or "meso"-predators like feral and house cats, skunks, raccoons, and foxes.[47] Among their other misdeeds, meso-predators can decimate bird and reptile populations. The larger herbivores aren't much better, as unconstrained browsing of plants changes everything, including watercourses where streamside vegetation is stripped away. When wolves were reintroduced to Yellowstone National Park, elk backed away from the rivers, and shrubs and trees grew back to shade the water. Cooler water helped trout recover, which gladdened the fly fishermen.[48]

HOTSPOTS

Much of Earth's wealth of species is concentrated in what are called biodiversity "hotspots." Many but not all of these are forested or tropical. Conservation biologist E. O. Wilson's strategy for protecting Earth's remaining biodiversity calls for salvaging the hotspots, protection for lakes and river systems everywhere, identifying centers of marine biodiversity, keeping intact the five remaining "frontier forests"—the rainforests of the Amazon Basin and the Guianas region, the forests of the Congo and New Guinea, and the temperate conifer forests of Canada, Alaska, Russia, Finland, and Scandinavia—and ending all logging of old-growth forests.[49]

A more recent (and perhaps too modest) proposal suggests that preserving just twenty-five biodiversity hotspots (under 2 percent of Earth's land) would help protect nearly half of all vascular plant species (these being plants complex enough to have circulatory systems) and more than a third of all vertebrates. The annual cost of protecting and preserving these ecosystems, and doing so in ways that don't alienate or impoverish their human neighbors and inhabitants, would be only a trifling half billion dollars—which is cheap compared to bailing out the global financial system.[50]

In earlier times and cultures, the practice of venerating particular animals or plants as totems or regarding certain places as sacred deeply informed the human sense of landscape and set ritual limits on the exploitation of those beings. The ancient custom in China of setting aside temple groves, for instance, secured the survival into the present of the venerable gingko tree, a plant that evolved 270 million years ago but has few wild stands remaining.[51]

In our day, human calamities have created de facto wilderness preserves. The 151-mile-long, 2.5-mile-wide demilitarized zone between North and South Korea—a no-man's-land since 1953—has become a wildlife refuge where Amur leopards, Chinese water deer, Asiatic black bears, Eurasian lynx, musk deer, and yellow-throated martens survive. Red-crowned cranes winter there, and probably wouldn't survive without its protection.[52] "Eden with a million land mines," one writer calls it.[53]

SENSE OF PLACE

Among species, *Homo sapiens* is something of a latecomer, having descended from hominid ancestors about 100,000 years ago. (Some other organisms, like the *Triops* tadpole shrimp, have been around in their present form for 400 million years.[54]) Fishing, hunting, and gathering wild foods nourished and stimulated human beings to develop strength, skill, intelligence, and material culture. Reaping biodiversity in the form of game, edible plants, medicinal plants, or useful fiber still is an essential part of daily life for many people around the world, supplementing and enhancing diets and health, and providing food, shelter, and clothing independent of the money economy.

While the industrial era of cheap energy has accelerated urbanization and sprawl, removing humans from natural environments (and vice versa), research mounts that argues the obvious: Optimum human development requires time in the out-of-doors amid green and growing things. Children and adults who spend time in nature—in woods, vacant lots, or even gardens—are happier, healthier, calmer, less prone to obesity, and have a greater ability to focus and reflect.[55] As the late cultural historian Thomas Berry put it, "If human consciousness had evolved on the moon, it would be barren as the moon."

Although you don't have to know the birds or the plants to tell when you're on the front range of the Rockies, in the Mojave Desert, or at the shore of Lake Michigan, learning the flora and fauna of a place can make for a much richer sense of place. This kind of knowledge is vital. As we have seen, Earth is paying a heavy price for modern ecological illiteracy. The transition to a post-carbon, post-growth future means relocalizing and *reinhabiting* certain places, learning where we're at (see figure 8.1).

For many reasons, wonder and pleasure not least among them, we may be turning our attention toward the natural history of our surroundings to form working and supportive alliances with all the other living creatures that make our places what they are. Outdoor education is critical and, when offered, immensely popular. Schoolchildren avidly monitor the minute life in streams to help assess water quality. Volunteers across the country join in annual bird, frog, and butterfly counts, helping to monitor the condition of whole families of organisms.

Given the gravity of the wounds to the planet's ecosystems, future ecosystems are unlikely to resemble those that enlivened Earth during the Cenozoic era, when mammals and flowering plants came to dominance. Still, humanity will need to learn how to reinhabit post-Cenozoic ecosystems and to participate in them rather than living at their expense. Natural history is the original festival calendar. The sustainable cultures to come are likely to take their diets, occupations, themes, calendars, and boundaries from their natural surroundings, just as cultures did before imperialism, industrialization, and globalization. The more biodiversity that remains in our terrains, the more possibilities there will be for discovery, inspiration, and resilience in this geologic era of our doing.

In the Sky Islands wildlands of the southwestern United States and northern Mexico, several hopeful ventures in evolutionary diplomacy are under way. Some ranchers are restoring creeks in these rugged grasslands, reintroducing extirpated species from Sonoran mud turtles to prairie dogs, modifying their range-stocking and grazing practices, and, in some cases, also reintroducing predators like Mexican wolves, mountain lions, and exceedingly rare jaguars. The ranchers know what's at stake: "The loss of one species is usually an indicator of an ecosystem out of balance and a larger domino effect to come, to which cattle will also ultimately fall victim."[56] More than just a good business or environmental decision, the Sky Islands ranchers' actions represent a cultural shift toward appreciating that the land's natural biodiversity has intrinsic value and can ultimately add

FIGURE 8.1. "Where You At?" quiz.

WHERE YOU AT?

What follows is a self-scoring test on basic environmental perception of place. Scoring is done on the honor system, so if you fudge, cheat, or elude, you also get an idea of where you're at. The quiz is culture bound, favoring those people who live in the country over city dwellers, and scores can be adjusted accordingly. Most of the questions, however, are of such a basic nature that undue allowances are not necessary.

1. Trace the water you drink from precipitation to tap.

2. How many days till the moon is full? (Slack of two days allowed.)

3. What soil series are you standing on?

4. What was the total rainfall in your area last year (July-June)? (Slack: 1" for every 20".)

5. When was the last time a fire burned your area?

6. What were the primary subsistence techniques of the culture that lived in your area before you?

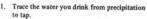

7. Name five native edible plants in your region and their season(s) of availability.

8. From what direction do winter storms generally come in your region?

9. Where does your garbage go?

10. How long is the growing season where you live?

11. On what day of the year are the shadows the shortest where you live?

12. When do the deer rut in your region, and when are the young born?

13. Name five grasses in your area. Are any of them native?

14. Name five resident and five migratory birds in your area.

15. What is the land use history of where you live?

16. What primary geological event/process influenced the land form where you live? (Bonus special: what's the evidence?)

17. What species have become extinct in your area?

18. What are the major plant associations in your region?

19. From where you're reading this, point north.

20. What spring wildflower is consistently among the first to bloom where you live?

SCORING

0-3	You have your head up your ass.
4-7	It's hard to be in two places at once when you're not anywhere at all.
8-12	A fairly firm grasp of the obvious.
13-16	You're paying attention.
17-19	You know where you're at.
20	You not only know where you're at, you know where it's at.

Quiz compiled by: Leonard Charles, Jim Dodge, Lynn Milliman, Victoria Stockley.

Reprinted by permission of the authors; originally from *CoEvolution Quarterly* (winter 1981), 3.

economic value to diversified ranch or farm operations. These foresighted ranchers understand that by shedding the stockman's historic hostility to predators and managing their lands regeneratively they are strengthening the greater ecosystem on which their livelihood depends.

RESTORATION

Regaining local knowledge is the practice of ecological restoration: learning about the primal condition of our bioregions' past, assessing their present conditions, envisioning the persistence of their native ecosystems, and then doing the work to ensure it. Full ecological restoration, say biologists, is "nothing less than the reestablishment of a completely functional ecosystem, containing sufficient biodiversity so that it could continue to mature and evolve over time."[57]

Ecological and wildlands restoration is both labor and intelligence intensive. It involves weeding out exotic species, propagating and planting natives, rehabilitating watercourses, protecting recovering areas, and sometimes seeing them gloriously rebound. Restorationists hope to preserve endangered plant and animal species. Communities that have done their natural-historical homework can engage in various forms of restoration work from gathering seeds and propagating native wildflowers to planting and tending native tree species and "de-roading" wildlands. Sensitively planned and locally directed, ecological restoration could be the basis of a planetary jobs program.

The hope of "rewilding" large landscapes follows on such restorative activities as removing roads from lands such as forests and other habitats healthy enough to knit themselves back together once motorized vehicle access is eliminated. If large enough expanses of certain kinds of ecosystems, like prairies, can be reassembled, and natural disturbances like fires restored, then their earlier, richer, more resilient character—not to mention a measure of excitement—can be achieved by reintroducing large animals, like the bison on the plains, to resume their ecological roles.

The basic precepts of protecting, enlarging, restoring, and reconnecting natural ecosystems can be applied at the municipal and even backyard levels as well. Suppose there's a remnant handful of native tree species or shrubs in the backyard or city park. Identifying those plants, learning and celebrating their natural and cultural history, and then working

---

BOX 8.2 Nature's Right to Life

The Endangered Species Act (ESA) is perhaps the most biocentric law on the books. (Ecuador's new constitution, however, goes further in principle by situating nature's right to continuance at the foundation of governance.) The ESA sailed through Congress in 1973. Intended to prevent extinctions, it mandates certain federal agencies to identify and list endangered and threatened plant and animal species according to strictly biological criteria, without regard to economic considerations, and to conduct programs, which may involve designating and protecting habitat critical for the recovery of these species.[1] It bars federal activities that might threaten listed species or their critical habitat. Its protections extend to private lands, to the oceans, and across national frontiers. Although the government's enforcement of the law has been limited and, depending on who's in power, willfully lax, the ESA has a strong citizen-enforcement provision. This has empowered biodiversity activists to litigate successfully on behalf of endangered species ranging from the polar bear, whose sea ice habitat is threatened by climate change, to the Peterson's milk vetch, a fragile desert flower—and to get millions of areas of critical habitat designated.[2]

---

1. Tyler Miller Jr. and Richard Brewer, *Living in the Environment*, 15th ed. (Belmont, CA: Wadsworth Publishing, 1988), 303.
2. Douglas Bevington, *The Rebirth of Environmentalism: Grassroots Activism from the Spotted Owl to the Polar Bear* (Washington DC: Island Press, 2009), 161–164.

---

to preserve, protect, and increase their territory would strengthen local biodiversity.

Perhaps there are native bird species in your vicinity whose numbers might increase if properly proportioned nest boxes were provided and feral and outdoor cats removed. Pollinator gardens and nectar corridors can be created to support native invertebrates—like wasps, bees, beetles, moths, and butterflies—providing the flowers they need for nectar, or the foliage their larvae need for food. Landscaping with native plants is multipurpose action for biodiversity. Not only does it increase the population of non-weedy species and increase habitat for smaller wildlife, but, once established, native plant landscapes (which consist of species evolved to be resilient locally) generally require less water and maintenance.

While many of the changes needed to make human communities stable, self-reliant, and carbon neutral will reduce the pressure on natural systems, ecological restoration could enrich and positively transform land uses like farming, gardening, and forestry. By reinstating some richness to damaged lands, restoration might promise future livelihoods for wild-crafters gathering herbs, basketry materials, mushrooms, and other edibles. With careful, concerted action on and help from nature's phenomenal capacity for regeneration, the transition beyond fossil-fuel-dependent industrial civilization to a stable world of flourishing, land-based communities may find our descendants inhabiting a planet that still hosts a wild variety of life and culture.

Naked new volcanic islands born out of the spreading seafloor by and by receive bird, plant, spider, and insect colonists that multiply and are eaten or simply die—all becoming soil to host more variations of form and greater diversity. We can take some comfort from such patterns. Life wants to live. Recovering from mass extinctions is nothing new for planet Earth, although it may take 10 million years or so for such a richly diverse community of organisms to evolve again. For our part, and for the sake of the world to come, we must become a constituency for wild nature and do everything within our power to mitigate the extinction crisis we are causing (see box 8.2).

Part Five

FOOD

GETTING FOSSIL FUELS OFF THE PLATE

MICHAEL BOMFORD

MICHAEL BOMFORD *is a research scientist and extension specialist at Kentucky State University and an adjunct faculty member in the University of Kentucky Department of Horticulture. His work focuses on organic and sustainable agriculture systems suitable for adoption by small farms operating with limited resources. His projects examine practical ways to reduce food-system energy use and meet farm energy needs using renewable resources produced on the farm. Bomford is a Fellow of Post Carbon Institute.*

❖

I learned about photosynthesis early in grade school, but its implications didn't sink in for some time. When they finally did, I got excited.

Suddenly I lived in a magical world filled with plants using energy from the sun to assemble themselves out of thin air. I was among the innumerable living beings interacting with one another on a solar-powered planet shaped by life itself. I could breathe because billions of years of photosynthesis had enriched my planet's atmosphere with oxygen stripped from carbon dioxide molecules. The carbon from those molecules had been reassembled into energy-rich chains that made up the bulk of living things and could be rendered to fuel my body. With every breath I took, my body released a little energy that had once been stored by a plant, reuniting carbon with oxygen to make carbon dioxide. Eating and breathing were photosynthesis in reverse. Without plants, I could do neither.

My grade school years were mostly spent in northern British Columbia, where the growing season is short, but good land is cheap, soils are fertile, and summer days are long. Each spring farmers rushed to plant vast fields of grains and oilseeds as soon as the snow melted. The summer fields turned brilliant yellow with canola flowers and lush green with fast-growing wheat, oats, flax, and barley. By fall the plants were spent, stalks were dry and golden brown, and farmers rushed to collect the energy-rich seeds before the snow returned. The short summer's sunshine could be stored as grain for the long winter ahead. It would feed our animals, so we could have fresh meat, eggs, and milk in the depth of winter. It would feed us, as my dad reminded me with his bumper sticker: "Don't complain about farmers with your mouth full."

My parents gardened. Half of our giant backyard was filled with vegetables every summer. The garden filled our plates with fresh produce, and there was plenty left over to fill our freezer and root cellar for the winter ahead. Before we said grace, Mom often proclaimed with delight, "Everything in this meal is from the garden." It all came from photosynthesis.

Agriculture is an important part of the economy in northern British Columbia, but oil is even more so. My grubby little town was full of young men in big trucks and muscle cars who had come north to make their fortunes in the oil fields. During oil booms they kept the bars hopping and the hookers busy, dropping hundred-dollar bills like candy. They didn't have gardens—they seemed to live in a realm separate from sunlight—but somehow they managed to eat and breathe. When the wells ran dry the young men disappeared, shops shuttered their windows, and the town shrank. New oil discoveries brought them back, with all of the gold-rush excitement and disarray that accompanied them. In the seven years I lived there, I saw two cycles of boom and bust.

I left home for university, brimming with idealism and determined to serve humanity. I took a degree in plant science: What could be more fundamental to human existence than plants? There I studied farm management, greenhouse management, weed management, and pest management; fruit production, vegetable production, agronomy, and agro-forestry. I learned about the wonders of the Green Revolution and the promise of genetic engineering. I learned about innovations that allowed fewer farmers to grow more food on less land, to meet the ever-expanding appetite of a growing human population. It all came from photosynthesis.

Or so I thought. I remember the sunny day—well into my PhD work—when I first read that each calorie of energy I got from food required seven to ten calories from fossil fuels to get to my plate. I was stunned. Surely this couldn't be true. I, like other living organisms, got my energy from plants, which got it from the sun. Of course I knew it took some petroleum to farm, process, package, haul, and market food, but I still considered food a renewable resource.

I checked other sources, and found that anybody who took a serious look at the energy balance of an industrialized food system reached a similar conclusion: My food was much more nonrenewable than renewable. The young men in the oil patch were doing more to feed me than the farmers.

I knew how fickle those young men were. The sun would keep shining, but the oil would run out, and they would be gone. I didn't want my food supply to depend on them, and I knew it didn't have to.

For most of human history we, like other animals, got by on renewable energy. We used muscle power for farm tools and food hauling. We ate fresh food when it was available, keeping what we could in root cellars or storing it longer by pickling, salting, fermenting, and drying. We cooked and heated with wood fires. We packaged our food in ceramic jars, wooden boxes, leaves, and paper. Our diets were shaped by where we lived, and changed with the seasons. We lost a lot of food to spoilage.

Only in the past century and a half did we start to invest a lot of fossil energy in our food system. The 1840s brought a diverse array of new factory-made farm machines that made farming easier but demanded that farmers raise enough cash crops to pay for them. The wheel-blade can opener was patented in 1870. A glass-bottle blowing machine made mass production of jars possible in 1903. By 1910 we were beginning to make synthetic nitrogen fertilizer and use gasoline-powered tractors. Frozen foods, fridges, freezers, and refrigerated trucks showed up in the early 1930s and 1940s.

Each ingenious new invention made it easier to get food to the plate—at an energy cost. In 1840 the U.S. food system depended almost entirely on renewable energy sources, including labor from 70 percent (12 million) of the 17 million Americans of the day, more than 2 million of whom were enslaved.[1] By 1900 the population had grown to 76 million, less than 40 percent (30 million) farmed, slavery had finally been abolished, and the food system consumed about 3 quadrillion Btu of fossil fuel.[2]

Today less than 1 percent of the population farms, and those 2 million farmers feed more than 300 million of their fellow citizens. The entire U.S. food system consumes about 10 quadrillion Btu from fossil fuel every year: 1 quadrillion to make farm inputs like fuel, fertilizer, and machinery; 1 quadrillion to farm; 1 quadrillion to haul; 4 quadrillion to process, package, and sell food; and 3 quadrillion to run the fridges, freezers, stoves, and the other appliances that fill our home kitchens.[3] The vast majority of energy used to get food to our plates is used after the food leaves the farm. Our kitchens consume far more energy than our farms.

The past century in America was characterized by rising crop yields that more than kept pace with a growing population, despite a dramatic decline in the number of farms and farmers. It isn't easy to determine how essential fossil-fuel energy inputs were in achieving this remarkable feat. Although the energy used by the American food system increased over the course of the century, the energy used to feed each American declined. Energy consumption by U.S. farms peaked in 1978 and has fallen almost 30 percent since, while yields continue to rise.

There are some obvious ways to further reduce farm energy use. Making nitrogen fertilizer is an energy-intensive process, accounting for most of the indirect energy consumption of U.S. farms. Some give synthetic nitrogen fertilizer the lion's share of the credit for increasing crop yields over the past century, but even without it organic farms today achieve yields comparable to those of conventional farms. Studies that show organic farming to be more energy efficient than conventional often find that most of the difference comes from eschewing synthetic nitrogen.

In places like Kentucky, where I live now, it is possible to grow cold-tolerant winter cover crops that build soil health, protect soil from erosion, and convert atmospheric nitrogen to plant-available forms using energy from photosynthesis. These soil-building crops can be killed in the spring to release plenty of nitrogen for a summer cash crop, eliminating the need for synthetic nitrogen applications. Very few farmers use this energy- and soil-saving strategy in Kentucky today because applying synthetic nitrogen is cheaper and easier than managing a nitrogen-fixing winter cover crop. That changed when the price of nitrogen fertilizer spiked along with energy prices in 2008, giving the economic advantage to those who had planted a nitrogen-fixing winter cover crop. I fully expect that less nitrogen fertilizer will be applied to U.S. farms as energy prices climb, with conventional farmers adopting techniques used mainly by organic growers today.

In northern British Columbia, the growing season is too short, and the winter too cold, to allow nitrogen-fixing winter cover crops. There, the organic farms have to plant nitrogen-fixing cover crops that grow through the summer, like alfalfa. This precludes production of a grain or oilseed crop on the same land that year, but still generates income for the farmer, who can cut alfalfa hay for sale while the plant's roots add nitrogen to the soil.

Some types of agriculture are much more energy efficient than others. The typical meat-centered diet is an energy-intensive luxury. By the time it reaches the plate, a serving of beef consumes about twenty times more energy than an equivalent serving of bread.[4] Grain farming accounts for most of the energy used for beef but only 10 percent of the energy that goes into bread (the rest is mostly for milling and baking). In fact, very little of the grain grown in the United States is destined for bread, or other human food: It's far more likely to be fed to animals.[5]

This is wasteful. The digestive system of cattle evolved to process grass, not grain. Cattle allowed to graze on grass use less energy than cattle fed on grain. Grass-based cattle operations use more land than grain-based systems, but they are often on marginal land planted to sustainable perennial mixtures. In contrast, confinement-based animal agriculture systems relying on grain are not just energy intensive and cruel, they compete directly and unnecessarily for grain harvests that could feed people. Meat and dairy products from pasture-raised animals tend to be healthier, too: They are leaner and richer in the omega-3 fatty acids often lacking in our diets.[6]

A grain- and vegetable-based diet almost always consumes less energy than a meat-based diet, yet vegetables can be energy hogs too. North America's big vegetable greenhouses—marvels of Dutch technology—are a case in point. Tomato, pepper, cucumber, and lettuce plants flourish in the nearly ideal environments the greenhouses maintain: never too hot or too cold; roots bathed in scientifically perfected nutrient solutions; no wind or rain; air enriched with carbon dioxide; human-reared beneficial insects released constantly to devour pests. It's plant heaven, but it comes at a hellish energy cost. The energy used to get one serving of greenhouse-grown tomatoes to the plate is about the same as for a serving of chicken, or twelve servings of field-grown tomatoes.[7] A local vegetable grown out of season in a heated greenhouse usually uses considerably more energy than its imported field-grown equivalent, trucked or shipped from afar.

It doesn't have to be this way. Innovative farmers around the world are developing low-energy alternatives to the Dutch greenhouse system. Perhaps the simplest is the high tunnel—a low-tech, unheated, plastic-covered structure that extends the growing season for soil-based fruit and vegetable systems. Plants grown in high tunnels lead a more stressful existence than those grown in Dutch-style greenhouses, and they don't yield as well, but the energy savings compensates for the yield reduction many times over. High-tunnel-grown vegetables offer health benefits, too: Beneficial phytochemicals are often more concentrated in plants that have experienced stress than in plants that are pampered.[8]

High tunnels extend the growing season but do not allow winter production of warm-season crops, like tomato, in most of North America. Vegetable farmers in China may have a low-energy solution. Rejecting the Dutch model, Chinese farmers are increasingly constructing low-input solar-heated greenhouses with thick walls of concrete or brick on the north face to absorb solar radiation by day and warm the growing area at night. Before the sun goes down the farmer lowers an insulating blanket of rice straw over the clear plastic cladding to trap daytime heat, then returns at sunrise to roll the blanket up. Using this passive solar system, Chinese farmers keep tomatoes and other warm-season crops growing through winters similar to those in much of North America, without burning fuel for heat.[9]

The Chinese-style greenhouse is probably superior to the Dutch-style greenhouse from an energy efficiency perspective, but paying somebody to roll an insulating blanket up and down every day may be more expensive than paying for heating fuel. Organic farmers may use energy more efficiently than conventional farmers, but they also use more labor—a trade-off that is often justified by premium prices available for organic products. Labor has been one of the most expensive inputs in North American agriculture over the past fifty years, and farmers have responded by developing labor-optimizing systems, capable of producing more and more food with fewer and fewer people. Such systems will stop making sense as energy prices continue their inevitable long-term climb in response to declining fossil-fuel supplies.

I am concerned about the increasing fossil-fuel dependence of

American farms that characterized most of the twentieth century, but impressed by the marked reduction in farm energy use that followed the energy price shocks of the 1970s—and confident that many more opportunities exist to reduce farm energy use. Elimination of fossil-fuel consumption by U.S. farms, and replacement with renewable energy sources, appears to be a realistic and achievable goal in the near term.

But farms are just a small part of our industrialized food system. Animal feedlots and heated greenhouses are exceptional examples of farming systems that account for most of the energy used to get food to our plates. Weaning our food system of fossil fuels demands a hard look at the journey food takes after it leaves the farm. Too often, this analysis is limited to an attempt to measure the distance that food travels between farm and fork. The "food mile" has caught the popular imagination as a simple indicator of food-system sustainability. But it is not a very useful one.

How food travels is much more important, from an energy perspective, than how far it travels. Oceangoing freighters are more efficient than trains, which are more efficient than semi-trucks, which are more efficient than small trucks. Air freight would be the worst way to move food, if it weren't for individuals driving big cars to carry small quantities of food. Far less energy is needed to import bananas by boat than to fly fresh fish from the same tropical starting point. A quick jaunt in the SUV to fetch a few of those bananas at the grocery store two miles down the road uses more fuel per banana than the journey of thousands of miles over water that brought them from their tropical home.[10] Taking fewer trips to the grocery store, or getting there by foot, bike, transit, or carpool, has far more impact on food-system energy use than obsessing over paper versus plastic bags. (We should be reusing cloth bags, anyway.)

Food often takes a convoluted route to get from farm to fork, traveling twice as far as the direct distance between the two points.[11] Even so, transporting food accounts for just 10 percent of our food-system energy use. We need to find ways to reduce this energy cost—and we can—but doing so will not wean our food system of fossil-fuel dependency.

Recognizing the relatively small and tremendously variable impact of food miles on food-system energy use is important to avoid fetishizing the "local" instead of conducting rigorous analyses of food-system energy use. It is easy to find gee-whiz renderings of urban skyscrapers filled with plants, increasingly billed as the answer to our food energy woes.[12] These fantastical vertical farms would be obscenely expensive structures, dependent on synthetic fertilizers, heating fuel, electric grow lights, pumps, water purifiers, and computers. Like Dutch-style heated greenhouses, they appear to ignore the energy cost usually incurred when we attempt to replace free ecosystem services with human ingenuity. Although vertical farms can almost certainly produce high yields of hyper-local food, their ecological footprint would far exceed that of field-grown products transported to urban centers from land-based farms that depend on sun, rain, soil, and other gifts of nature.

Food processing, packaging, storage, and preparation account for most of the energy cost of most of our food.[13] If local food economies can reduce the need for these elements of the food system they will succeed in reducing our fossil-fuel dependence dramatically. Whole, unprocessed foods—often promoted for their health benefits—offer tremendous energy benefits too. If we're concerned about food-system energy, it's hard to beat whole grains, protein-rich beans (stored dry), and fresh produce, prepared simply. Yum!

In a society where less than 1 percent of the population grows most of the food for the other 99 percent, it's easy to feel removed from the food system, or disempowered by decisions that appear to be in the hands of others. The reality is that most of the power to wean the food system from fossil fuels rests with eaters, not farmers. The choices that we make in our homes and kitchens matter.

I work with many rural residents of Kentucky who have clear memories of getting their first fridge. Today almost everybody I know has a fridge (or two), and, chances are, it's a lot bigger than the one they had ten years ago. They probably also have a freezer, a microwave, a dishwasher, a food processor, a toaster, a coffee maker, a slow cooker, an electric kettle, a blender, and other electric kitchen appliances. Over the past thirty years our farms have reduced their energy consumption, but our kitchens demand ever more.

All of this kitchen technology should offer energy advantages. Microwaves are much more efficient than ovens; dishwashers can be more efficient than hand-washing; slow cookers and electric kettles can be more efficient than stove-tops. Advances in fridge, freezer, and stove technology generally make newer appliances more efficient than similarly sized older appliances. The problem is that we expect our new high-tech kitchens to do much more than replace the functionality of our old kitchens. Using the fridge as an example, we might replace a small, low-efficiency fridge with a bigger high-efficiency fridge, ultimately using more energy despite the efficiency gain. The unexpected result of efficiency gains leading to greater resource consumption is so common it has a name: the Jevons paradox.[14]

Weaning the food system off fossil fuels demands that we simplify our diets and kitchens instead of demanding an endless parade of bigger, better, and faster. It will be a difficult lesson.

Simplification does not mean an end to technological advances. On the contrary, it offers many opportunities for creative problem solving and new ideas. I think back to the freezer in my parents' basement in northern British Columbia. Why were we using energy to keep our food frozen in a heated basement when it was minus 40 degrees outside? Couldn't the freezer be outside of the house, with just an insulated door opening in? As we face the reality of higher energy prices, eaters—like farmers—will invent creative solutions that might have existed all along, but only become obvious when the bills come due.

We need only look to our own backyards—or apartment balconies, or community plots—to find one of the easiest, cheapest, and most enjoyable solutions: the garden. Stepping outside to harvest the evening meal is not only deeply satisfying, it eliminates most of the energy-intensive steps between farm and fork that contribute to our food system's dependence on fossil fuels. Provided that we can avoid the temptation to indulge in synthetic fertilizers, plastics, and pesticides, our gardens allow us to approach the ideal that most other animals realize as a matter of survival. We again become organisms fueled by photosynthesis.

TACKLING THE OLDEST
ENVIRONMENTAL PROBLEM

Agriculture and Its Impact on Soil

WES JACKSON

WES JACKSON *is one of the foremost figures in the international sustainable-agriculture movement. Founder and president of the Land Institute in Salina, Kansas, he has pioneered research in natural-systems agriculture for more than thirty years. He was a professor of biology at Kansas Wesleyan and later established the environmental studies program at California State University, Sacramento. He is the author of several books, including* Becoming Native to This Place *(1994),* Altars of Unhewn Stone *(1987), and* New Roots for Agriculture *(1980). Jackson is a Fellow of Post Carbon Institute.*

❖

I want to talk about the 10,000-year-old problem of agriculture and how it is both necessary and possible to solve it. Were it necessary but not possible this idea would be grandiose, and were it possible but not necessary it would be grandiose. But it has passed the test of grandiosity.

Figure 10.1 illustrates what most people think about when they talk about sustainable agriculture. This is part of an ad for a sustainable-agriculture conference in Chicago. Look at the diversity and think hard about how much that informs the sustainable-agriculture movement. There is not a single grain there. And what's wrong with that? The foods shown there represent fewer than 25 percent of the calories that humans eat, and I have a $100 bet that 70 percent of the calories eaten by the people in the most economically important agricultural state, California, come over the Sierra Nevada and up from Mexico in the form of grains.

In the background of all of us organisms on Earth is what I call the

This chapter is adapted from a presentation by Wes Jackson to the Cal Alumni Association at International House, University of California, Berkeley, on January 25, 2010.

FIGURE 10.1.
Typical illustration depicting sustainable agriculture.

3.45-billion-year imperative. We are a carbon-based planet. The carbon that enters so importantly into our bodies, we all now know, was cooked in the remote past of a dying star. But humans, with the big brain, have been around for only 150,000 to 200,000 years, and only some 11,000 to 13,000 years before the present we got to the first pool of energy-rich carbon, the young pulverized coal of the soil. And we mostly wasted it. With the opening of the North American continent, some soil scientists estimate the United States went from around 6 percent carbon to around 3 percent. I think that's when global warming began, with agriculture 10,000 years ago.

About 5,000 years ago, the second pool of energy-rich carbon, the forests, made it possible to smelt ore and brought on the Bronze Age and the Iron Age. The third pool, 250 years ago, was coal, which brought on the Industrial Revolution. Then in 1859 Edwin Drake drilled a well in western Pennsylvania and opened up the fourth pool, oil. And then came natural gas, the fifth pool, used not just for lighting and heating but also for fertilizer. These are the five pools of energy-rich carbon that stand behind civilization. I like to think what it would have been like had we not had, first of all, civilization that came from the soil. We wouldn't have had Plato, Aristotle, Jesus of Nazareth. And, of course, if it hadn't been for soil, forest, and coal, we would not have had Darwin—it took the slack that the British Empire had to send a naturalist around the world. I suspect that without oil we would not have had the Hubble Telescope

FIGURE 10.2. Pieter Bruegel, *The Harvesters* (1565).

and may not have known about how the elements have been cooked in dying stars. In other words, these five pools have given us knowledge of how the world is. What does this have to do with anything? Well, it gives us a perspective of where we come from and what kind of a thing we are.

Let's study figure 10.2. Is the wheat tall or are the people short? There is a pear tree, and in an apple tree off to the right, barely discernable in the image, someone upside down is picking an apple. Notice that they've limbed those trees up to let light through for the wheat. In this painting, nearly 100 percent of that agricultural landscape is devoted to grains, primarily because they don't have much juice in them, so they can be stored and not rot. Someone advanced the idea that societies that depend on root crops tend not to make war. They can't carry all that water around. I'd like to have someone do a PhD thesis on that—it would probably confuse us all.

Now let's jump to a new continent. We landed here in 1492. Think about how little changed from 1565, the year of Bruegel's painting, to 1665, and then to 1765 when the Industrial Revolution was just getting started. Now to the 1860s. In colonial times people wanted free land; our new nation wanted to charge for it because after the Revolutionary

FIGURE 10.3. Norman Rockwell, *The County Agent* (1948).

Reprinted by permission of the Norman Rockwell Family Foundation.

War we were broke, but Thomas Jefferson illegally made the Louisiana Purchase in 1803, and people clamored for free land. The South knew that if this were allowed, Northerners were likely to occupy that land. The Confederates fired on Fort Sumter in 1861 and the Civil War began. With the South no longer represented in Washington, in May 1862 the reduced Congress passed the Homestead Act and, within a few months, the Morrill Act, which established the land-grant colleges. Twenty-five years later, in 1887, Congress funded the agricultural experiment stations via the Hatch Act, and then in 1914 they passed the Smith-Lever Act establishing the extension services to connect the work of land-grant colleges to communities.

So here we are on a new continent, with the Louisiana Purchase, with legislation giving us free land, with colleges of agriculture, agricultural research, and extension—and away we go.

In figure 10.3, it is 1948 and the Depression and World War II are behind us. Here is the county agent, perhaps a product of Purdue University because this painting was made in Indiana by Norman Rockwell. There is the dutiful 4-H girl—you can bet her record book has big round letters in it—there's the brother with his poultry project, there's Sis with her sewing project, the dog is pleased with what's going on, Grandpa's intensely interested, Mom is interested, Dad's back there, at left, with a cat on his shoulder. Count the number of eyes focused on expertise and youth. Rockwell was painting not only what was, but also what got writ large. The year 1948 is important to keep in mind. Free land, education, and extension made expertise and youth central. Tradition and experience are peripheral.

Around 1948 we started using incredible amounts of nitrogen, phosphorus, and water; by the 1960s it was really taking off (figure 10.4). The most important invention of the twentieth century came from two Germans who learned how to take atmospheric nitrogen and turn it into ammonia using what's now known as the Haber-Bosch process. Vaclav Smil of the University of Manitoba says, "Without Haber-Bosch 40 percent of humanity wouldn't be here." So away we go applying tons of nitrogen to fields. Another thing that took off about 1948 is the production of pesticides, which, since the publication of Rachel Carson's *Silent Spring* in 1962, has doubled and doubled again. Also about this time, particularly in the early 1950s, farm consolidation began. And not too long after that, U.S. Secretary of Agriculture Ezra Taft Benson said, "Get big or get out." Later, Earl Butz, secretary of agriculture under Richard Nixon, told farmers to plow "fence row to fence row."

Once the loft of the barn was the fuel tank for the farm, dispersing sunlight in the form of hay. And the barn of 1948 was not too different from the barn in Bruegel's time, which had a hay mound. Below was the straw bedding for the animals, and it soaked up their urine and manure. Back to the question: Why was Bruegel's wheat so tall? To absorb the urine and the manure that would then go back to the fields. So, the fuel source (the hay mound) sat atop the nitrogen- and nutrient-management scheme (the bedding). Well, if you don't need that any more, then pretty soon you don't need the barn—you just need a diesel tank, with its dense energy, and an anhydrous ammonia tank.

There is something else that happened. If you look at an aerial view of farm country—at the fields and the county roads and farmsteads and the little towns—what you see are concentrators of sunlight. And, of course, if you've got a lot of energy and you can haul it around, then you don't need those houses, and you don't need the small towns, and you don't need the girl who can make her own dress. The cultural capacity goes down.

I found out the name of that county agent in the Rockwell painting

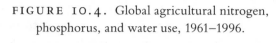

FIGURE 10.4. Global agricultural nitrogen, phosphorus, and water use, 1961–1996.

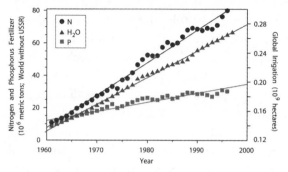

Source: David Tilman et al., "Agricultural Sustainability and Intensive Production Practices," Nature 418, no. 8 (August 2002).

and I called to the town in Indiana and asked for the name Rippey. The first person I got, it turned out, was a relative of the late county agent. From him I learned that the father in the painting, who stands off to the left in the shadows with the cat on his shoulder, farmed until he was killed by a registered bull on his farm. He gave me the name of the 4-H girl holding the calf, the one with her record book displayed, and I called her. She and her sister, the one with the sewing project, left the farm to marry. They never farmed. Their brother, the one with the poultry project, had farmed until he died in 1988. I asked if any of the children of the kids in the painting were farming. The answer was no.

I think there's a general law: High energy destroys information, of a cultural as well as a biological variety. There's a loss of cultural capacity. And from 1750, the beginning of the Industrial Revolution, the graphical curve for the use of high-energy fossil carbon is increasingly steep. A ten-year-old today has been alive for a quarter of all the oil ever burned. The twenty-two-year-old has been through 54 percent of all the oil ever burned.

Now let's come back to the 3.45-billion-year imperative. Bacteria on a petri dish with sugar simply go for it. Fruit flies in a flask with mashed-up bananas just go for it. Deer without a predator just breed and live and expand. I think what humans have is the powerful capacity to create abstractions—and one of the most important abstractions we ever invented was the one that allows us to ignore that our petri dish has a wall. It's called capitalism, growth. Even if you have twice the amount of oil that you think you have, you don't buy much time.

Now there's the reality of climate change. We've gone into overshoot and we are in economic trouble. We look to more economic growth, but once economics and population growth absorb all of the renewables and all of the efficiency, then what? The technological fundamentalist comes along and says, "We will solve the problem through technology." This is just another form of religion. We may get some technological substitutes for the fossil carbons, such as wind turbines, solar collectors, and so on, but I'd like somebody to help me come up with a technological substitute for soil and water. Let's get that on the inventory right away. Are we going to wait another thirty years while the soils of the planet decline? How are we going to keep ourselves fed while desecrating our agricultural lands worldwide and depending on fossil fuels?

I think we must recognize what the United Nations Millennium Ecosystem Assessment[1] said: that on a global basis, agriculture is the largest threat to biodiversity and ecosystem function of any single human activity. So let's look at those vegetables in figure 10.1. Let's look at the distribution of global agricultural acres. Cereals, oilseeds, and pulses (legumes' edible seeds) make up about 68 percent of the calories and about the same acreage. Upland rice is increasingly grown on steep hills in China and Indonesia, where erosion is a big problem. But even on flat land, agriculture can cause erosion, which happens after heavy rains in places like Iowa and Kansas.

What do we do?

I like to imagine the world before agriculture. And when we do, we see that essentially all of nature's ecosystems feature perennials in mixtures: alpine meadows, tropical rainforests, desert scrub, prairies, and more. All perennial mixes. Why is that? Well, one thing that is interesting about us organisms is that we use only a few atoms to make complex molecules. Chemists will use almost all the atoms to make simple molecules. That's one of the differences between us as chemists and nature's biota. And of the sixteen elements necessary to make organisms, only four are from the global atmospheric commons: hydrogen, carbon, nitrogen, and oxygen. The rest are in the soil.

Let's start at the beginning of our "fallen world." It all began in the Zagros Mountains of western Iran, some 10,000 to 12,000 years ago. Here one plant got civilization started: the wheat plant, an annual. When agriculture began, we reversed what nature's ecosystems do on a landscape. We started featuring annuals, and we grew them in monocultures much as we do today.

Figure 10.5 shows one of our perennial wheat relatives and annual wheat. It's hard to consistently remember that from the topsoil down are most of the elements that go into organisms. But when we do remember, doesn't it make sense that nature's ecosystems feature roots that are there year-round, holding the ecological capital as tenaciously as possible? And that banking everything on an annual crop is wrong-headed? The primary killers of soil on the continent are our top annual crops: wheat, corn, and soybeans. And then we promote a biofuels program, even though the energy balance is not good. We went from just over 70 million acres of corn to nearly 90 million acres in 2007. That's what *Homo* the homogenizer does.

Nebraska, Iowa, Minnesota, and North Dakota: Here we have the richest soils of the world, as the consequence of the glaciers scraping the nutrients off the Canadian Shield. And to reduce erosion and protect them, we say we will apply some human cleverness and come up with things like minimum-till or no-till agriculture. The water coming off a minimum-till or no-till field looks a lot better than the water coming off a conventional-till field. There's only one problem: The nitrogen level of the water from that no-till land is still three times above the acceptable level determined by the Environmental Protection Agency.

Annual systems leak; they are poor micromanagers of nutrients and water. So in the sea we have a dead zone because fertilizer runoff accumulates there and reduces the oxygen available for marine species. In fact, there are several dead zones worldwide. We had Gene Turner, from the Louisiana Universities Marine Consortium, come and talk to our graduate fellows one summer, and he said there were fifty dead zones. The next year Nancy Rabelais, his wife, came and showed a slide with 146 dead zones, and I said, "It's tripled in one year!" She replied, "Oh Wes, there are a thousand." So, here is one of the consequences of the Green Revolution, of human cleverness.

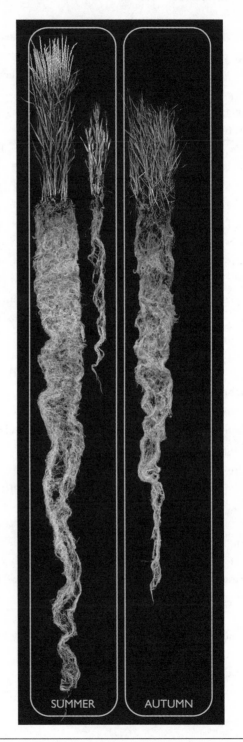

FIGURE IO.5.
Perennial wheat
(at left in the boxes)
and annual wheat
(at right in the boxes),
in summer and
in autumn.

Note: Unlike annual
crops, which must be
replanted every year,
the extensive root
system of perennial
crops retains nutrients
in the soil while
protecting against
soil erosion.

Photograph by
the Land Institute.

SUMMER   AUTUMN

What we are about at the Land Institute is perennializing the major crops, to be grown in mixtures. On our 600 acres we have about 160 acres of prairie, and most of it has never been plowed; on that prairie we have thirty bison. They remind us of the standard, something closer to the original relationship. We work with perennial wheat. We make the crosses in the greenhouse. We produce hybrids, and after we harvest, some of the wheat plants will shoot back up so we say we've got perennials. Maximilian sunflower is a perennial that we're crossing with an annual crop sunflower, and we're working on perennializing a winter-hardy sorghum. We had a good, hard freeze this year—thank goodness, because our breeders need to find out how much "antifreeze" we have in the plants' underground stems.

What is the hope for this? Many of us think that we need a fifty-year farm bill. Wendell Berry, Fred Kirschenmann of Iowa State University's Leopold Center, and I took a fifty-year farm bill to Washington, D.C., in 2009 and proposed the perennialization of the American farmscape, with the hope that this could catch on and go around the world. The idea is to use the current five-year farm bills as mileposts toward this goal. The five-year farm bills currently are devoted to exports, commodities, subsidies, some soil conservation, and the food programs. Our fifty-year farm bill would protect soil from erosion, cut wasteful use of water, cut fossil-fuel dependence, eliminate toxic chemicals, manage nitrogen, reduce dead zones, and restore an agrarian way of life. It would do this largely by shifting the makeup of U.S. agriculture from being 80 percent annuals, as it is today, to 80 percent perennials in fifty years. In the short run we need only to change the subsidies so that we increase the amount of perennials and rotations gradually, and then in about twenty years our perennial grains begin to be available.

Figure 10.6 shows what the fifty-year farm bill could accomplish. By steadily replacing annuals with perennials we can reestablish much—not all—of what we had in 1700.

The history of our country is one of permanent vegetation rather than denudation and soil erosion. In 1700 the nitrogen balance was there, rural community health was there, chemical health was there—there were no synthetics. Then we expanded westward, and on the way we scraped off the permanent vegetation. Wendell Berry said it very well in a letter he wrote to me: As we came across the continent cutting the forests and

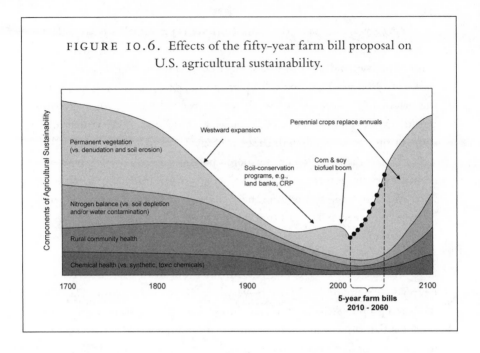

FIGURE 10.6. Effects of the fifty-year farm bill proposal on U.S. agricultural sustainability.

plowing the prairies, we never knew what we were doing, because we never knew what we were undoing. But what we were undoing were the benefits of those perennial roots.

Dan Luten also said, I think in his wonderful book *Progress against Growth*: We came as a poor people to a seemingly empty land that was rich in resources, and we built our institutions for that perception of reality. *Poor people, empty land, rich.* Our economic institutions, our educational institutions, and our political institutions are all predicated on *poor people, empty land, rich.* Then Luten said: We've become rich people in an increasingly poor land that's filling up, and those institutions don't hold.

Our challenge is to develop a whole different concept of how to live on the landscape. We have an abundance of knowledge about the way ecosystems work, but that knowledge is mostly gathering dust. This knowledge was accumulated by ecologists and evolutionary biologists out to understand how the world is, or how the world was; they have had the luxury to be descriptive. Agriculturists, on the other hand, have the burden to be prescriptive. So, we have to figure out a way to bring the agronomist who prescribes together with the ecologist who describes, and merge these two cultures. I have to say, it's harder than I thought it would be, because of the nature of our learning.

When we were gatherers and hunters we lived within the natural ecosystem, and then, 10,000 to 12,000 years ago, we got out of phase. And then industrial agriculture came along, and we struggled with sustainable agriculture until now, when we finally must face up to reality. We know we're not voluntarily going back to gathering and hunting or pre-industrial agriculture, so what do we do? I think we can have something close to what I propose here.

GROWING COMMUNITY FOOD SYSTEMS

ERIKA ALLEN

ERIKA ALLEN *is Chicago projects manager for Growing Power, a nationally acclaimed nonprofit organization and land trust providing equal access to healthy and affordable food, especially in disadvantaged communities. She is co-chair of the Chicago Food Policy Advisory Council and was appointed in 2008 to the Illinois Local and Organic Food and Farm Task Force. In 2009 she and her father, Growing Power founder Will Allen, were featured in the* New York Times Magazine. *She has a bachelor of fine arts from the School of the Art Institute of Chicago and a master of arts in art therapy from the University of Illinois at Chicago. Allen is a Fellow of Post Carbon Institute.*

❖

COMMUNITY FOOD SYSTEMS

The idea of a community food system is much larger than just urban farming. It deals with everything, all the components that are needed to establish, maintain, and perpetually sustain a civilization.

Urban farming is key in the reclamation of an Earth- and ecology-based value system, and it plays an important role: We need urban food production, communities growing food in an urban environment. But with a *community food system*, neighborhood stakeholders are the ones growing that food, moving it around, and in control of land tenure or wherever soil-, food-, and Earth-based materials are being grown. Basically we are talking about sovereignty, about having land and water rights.

This chapter is adapted from an interview with Erika Allen by Daniel Lerch on January 24, 2010.

This is not a new concept; indigenous communities globally struggle with powerful external entities that attempt to extract raw and refined resources from land that has traditionally been stewarded by families who understand the natural laws of replenishment and proper natural-resource management. In a locally operated food system we engage all members of the community, taking special care to engage the most marginalized members and those most impacted by food and land degradation. We begin with simple questions: "Where are you going to get water from, and how are you getting the water?" "Who makes the decision about how land—open space and commercial space—is being used?"

These simple questions activate civic and civil rights and account-ability with government, because there are always regulatory issues and agendas that (as is often revealed) community members are unaware of and have not been included in the conversations. So true sustainability in terms of community food systems means that disenfranchised people, especially youth and their families, are involved in the process not only as beneficiaries of "good (and carbon-neutral) food" but as central par-ticipants in the planning, development, and execution of the food system, including its interlocking parts: energy, housing, public transportation, economic development, and so on. You're building a whole infrastructure that supports local food systems.

This is how we differentiate it in our thinking at Growing Power, because we don't just do urban farming. We work with youth, go to mar-kets, do advocacy work around policy, write grants, give talks—and all those things are connected and part of reestablishing functional commu-nities and food systems. We have a food security program where people pay a basic weekly fee for year-round food security, and in return they get a bag of food with fresh fruits and vegetables both from local wholesalers and from stuff that we produce ourselves. This is the baseline and it forms the infrastructure for more sophisticated elements of the food system to "grow" into an infrastructure that supports community ownership and control of its own food system. We cannot stress enough that community food systems development and implementation are so much more than just "urban farming," and it's important because people don't typically think of food in that way. They think it's something that farmers do: "Let's support the farmers! Oh, they've got the farm bill; it's taken care of." Or worse, "Let's go buy 200 million acres and allow machines to grow commodities on it that indirectly may or may not be suitable for direct human consumption!"

It goes beyond community-supported agriculture (CSA), but CSA is important too. People think CSA is cute; well, it's a little beyond cute—it transforms communities. And it secures the community, because if something happens so that food cannot move from California to the Midwest or to the East Coast, what are people going to do? It's not going to be so cute anymore. Let's look at the basic "food-desert" neighborhood—it's usually a low-income neighborhood or ghetto. I live in a food desert; I chose to live there, but it is also what I could afford at the time I was purchasing my first home. I look around me every day and I think, "What would happen? I am the only one who's got food growing in my yard." And I have the privilege to know why it's important, and the capability to do something about it.

So yes, Growing Power does food—but it's food *plus*. Yes, I am an urban farmer, but I am also a community food systems planner. Many of us doing the hands-on implementation—farmers in the rural and urban environments—have always planned for the land, for the benefit of their family, community, and Earth. Community food systems provide a much needed reclamation of this tradition at a time in history where we are at a technological tipping point.

COMMUNITY DEVELOPMENT

We also work with healing, community reformation, and civic engagement. We work with people to develop, first, a vision of what they want their community to look like. This is not traditionally how community engagement happens; typically the community is the last to know what is being planned on its behalf. This is a backwards process. We advocate first identifying who needs to be involved: Who is not at the table, and needs to be? Who are the stakeholders most impacted? Who is going to operate this system? What are the ways that you can create food security within the city, and also create an opportunity for farmers? How do you connect the rural and the urban? We go through that process and start to form relationships. So it is a community-scale effort, and it dovetails with other efforts to build community resilience.

It is really about getting people in power to understand what's going on in the community—what is working, and how people are finding ways to survive under extraordinarily challenging conditions both here in the United States and abroad. It's about recognizing that it's going to be a long road for transformation and keeping the community connected to the resources and to the people who are doing the work, the visionary doers. It's about making sure all communities have equal access to culturally appropriate, environmentally responsible, affordable, nutritionally dense food—and to do that you have to address everything: housing, land, education, how you prevent and punish crime. So we are seeing that food systems can be a very powerful tool for resilience. In a revolutionary way, you can completely transform things without people realizing what's happening—they are aware, but it just makes intuitive sense this way. It's also not about just going out and fighting the proverbial "man," or continuing an academic dialogue about what could happen or should happen; you don't have time for this because you've got a lot to *do*. So instead of having people just being oppositional and trying to get someone else to make the changes, you have people who are assets to their community, who are making the transformation happen themselves (but being oppositional when they need to be).

TRANSFORMATION

This movement—the "good food/community food systems reclamation movement"—is so transformative because people have to go through a whole process within themselves and in partnership with others, because so few people have confidence in this area; so few of us have retained our agricultural legacies and knowledge. You can have ten Ph.D. degrees, but when you get a pitchfork in your hands you have to understand the fundamental principles of decomposition—you're dealing with basic concepts of life and death. It's actually really simple earth science; it's simple technology that many try to make overly complicated and end up confusing themselves and others in the process. But if you don't understand the basic principles of nature and don't have some degree of patience, you can't do anything to be truly self-sufficient without exploiting other people or the environment.

This is why farmers are geniuses—they do everything. They predict the weather, and they have to plan; it's a huge undertaking. Even a so-called dirt farmer, a poverty-stricken farmer, has to know so much just to survive. These farmers might not be literate in the Western-world sense, but they know everything and have humility and respect for Earth and her resources. Reclaiming that heritage and connecting people to that "understanding," whatever that may be for them, are very important.

We have our heritage as a family, Allen-Raiford-Bussler, and I have an unbroken line of agriculture people in my own lineage. I almost didn't carry on the tradition—I'm an artist. But I was always kind of a funky artist. I didn't want to be in galleries—instead I wanted to be a community-based artist. I wanted to do art in communities and work with communities and help others have a voice through art. And that led me all the way back to food. I became an art therapist because I was doing that kind of work already as a community-based artist. I had kids who could not even do art; they were out of their minds. I was thinking it was a psychiatric issue at the time. Then one day I realized that they didn't have any real food—they weren't eating foods with nutritional content, the food many of us from vegetable-farm backgrounds take for granted. With this epiphany I began to ask, How can I solve that? Well, artists are essentially problem solvers. So you have farming on one hand, which is essentially all about understanding natural systems, and artist problem solvers on the other hand—you put those two together, and all kinds of amazing solutions can happen. And you build on that principle. You bring these groups together, you start a facility where people can see natural systems working, and then they can learn those practical skills: They're learning how to farm and how to take care of themselves and others.

And then we see that the people we think don't know very much are really the ones who do. People come to our weekend-long "from-the-ground-up" workshops and are transformed. They go back to their community and they're going to do *something,* even if they're just putting in a compost bin or a backyard garden so their kids have that exposure. That makes a difference. It may not save the world, but it's going to save that microcosm of a family unit. They're going to have a different experience with the land. Maybe that will lead them to supporting a local farmer, or maybe that child will end up going into agricultural science or another meaningful profession.

There's no certainty about the future; things can change, and we can change. I've watched my dad work with some very scary people, some overtly bigoted, KKK-type people. He gets them on his side and they become his biggest fans and bring him farm implements, donate supplies and services; it's amazing. That ability to transform people by your own kindness or by your own ability to be who you are, that's something that you can learn how to do, but you have to be exposed to it and see it as a possibility. We are growing more of these possibilities.

SCALABILITY

Scalability is dependent on the community; we don't just go in and make something happen with a wave of a wand. We're scaling within our organization. We started off with 2.1 acres for our original facility in Milwaukee; Dad has acquired a couple of other properties, and it's spawning within the city of Milwaukee a bunch of other neighborhood projects, and those will spawn yet other neighborhood projects. The water and waste department has provided a long-term lease for fifty acres for us to be able to compost and build greenhouses. We also received a stimulus funding package for fifty youth—young adults who are going to be building greenhouses in Milwaukee and Chicago—and support for six full-time positions over two years. So by next year we will have a substantial year-round food-production operation underway that's low tech and community operated. In Milwaukee public schools we have a contract with their massive food provider; we're growing a sunflower-sprout snack that the fourth-graders have once a week.

People bring stuff to us—ideas, methods, tools, and technologies—and teach us how to use it, and then we amplify it and pass along the knowledge to others. Heifer Project brought us worms and got us started with a little vermicompost bin. We've amplified it to where we now have depositories five feet tall, millions of worms—and it's literally a depository from which we extract worms when we start a new project to distribute free of charge to anyone who takes the training.

KNOWLEDGE AND RESOURCE EXCHANGES

In addition to everything we're doing with our own infrastructure, a big part of our work is with other communities who are trying to replicate what we have. We've worked with communities in Africa and Eastern Europe—one had a Civil Society grant from the United Nations and in the last phases of it I went to project-plan for three days in Macedonia. It's very practical and grounded, and at the same time we're actually growing food and farming and developing those technologies. We're learning new things, and we're also helping communities do the same thing—and they're helping us because it's a reciprocal relationship. These kinds of knowledge and resource exchanges are natural for people who are connected to the earth.

REBUILDING DISADVANTAGED COMMUNITIES

One of the things that we try to do is demystify food systems and what food security truly is, empowering the powerless through sovereignty and an understanding of the importance of engaging *everyone* in the community in a responsible, equitable manner. But it's a challenge; many people are averse to the idea of farming. For people of color, especially, it's a huge taboo. Immigrants—really anyone who has been discriminated against—they don't want to do this work; they want to assimilate and reap the rewards that come from becoming a member of "white" society. There was a time when Jews, the Irish, Italians, and Poles were not considered white by the dominant culture when they immigrated to the United States. This continues today—we want to be professionals; lose our accents, cultures, and food traditions; be on Wall Street; and make cash. Why would you want to be poor? We left wherever we came from to come here for a better life—why would you go back? We were slaves; we were migrant workers; we were landless peoples. Why would we go back to that?

A lot of people look from the outside at what we're doing at Growing Power and see it as a way of empowering disadvantaged people: teaching them how to garden, teaching them job skills, giving that kind of uplift and inspiration through hands-on skill sets. We do that, but it's also bigger than that. We're not just teaching people how to grow food and how to make soil—we're rebuilding community food systems. We're creating space for a whole confluence of small to mighty things to happen. It's a big puzzle, and there are constantly new pieces being inserted. For example, the energy piece: That wasn't where we started because we just needed to get going, to get good food growing and into the community, but that piece gets plugged in. The peak-oil, community-resilience piece: We didn't start with microgreens right away, but now we do them because if you have the soil fertility (like a high-fertility vermicompost mix) you can grow sunflower seeds and have sprouts that are ready to harvest in seven to ten days. If there was some catastrophe but you had those materials at your disposal you could have sunflower sprouts growing in seven to ten days and there's 39 percent protein. Sunflowers have more protein as a green than they do as a seed, and fewer calories.

NEIGHBORS

I do not have a traditional yard; it's all garden—wood-chip-raised "living-biological-worm-system" beds growing greens, okra, tomatoes, legumes, callaloo, culinary and medicinal herbs, and African bowl gourds. My neighbors are down with it, and they know me. Historically, a lot more people used to grow food in my neighborhood. But they're older now and they're retired, or they are people who are completely disconnected from life, on crack and other abusively consumed drugs. As I work in my front yard garden I hear comments that range from "Go, girl!" to "No, no, I'm not going to grow a garden." I mean, in some ways, it's a privileged kind of thing to grow food; you need time, space, soil fertility, and water. People are trying to survive in my community and they don't see it as essential to survival. But this summer I am going to have a lot more people growing food.

Part of enabling those things to happen is having plants to distribute and having compost available. Another piece of it is that there is so much work to be done around regulatory issues. To do compost in Chicago there had to be a regulatory separation made at the state level between trash and food waste just to make it legal to dispose of food waste differently than trash—all waste was considered to be trash. Then we had to get a grant from the Department of Environment to set up a composter, get transfer stations, and get zoning permits. So I have to do all that and then work with the Illinois EPA just so I can legally compost at a scale that provides jobs for people?

THE FOOD SECURITY MOVEMENT

My introduction to the community food system movement and the food security movement was at a national conference in Boston. The Community Food Security Coalition (CFSC) was founded in southern California by Andy Fisher and other academics, and food security experts. It was groundbreaking work—they basically started the community food security movement nearly fifteen years ago. The founding leaders were able to motivate the USDA to start the Community Food Projects Competitive Grant Program. They specifically started talking about addressing food insecurity with people of color and disadvantaged communities nationally, and providing resources for those folks to transform their food systems. But for years very few people of color and people from low-income communities directly received grants, and so the whole movement was predominantly led by white folks coming into communities of color and "fixing the issues." Even though from the beginning there were people of color like Hank Herrera who confronted these concerns about the lack of diversity and outreach to develop more leaders of color, they were never really addressed as a high priority. It was clear that things had to change.

Then we and others came on board, and we began to compete for those grants and we started getting them, and we were able to start asking more questions, like: Why aren't more people of color getting these? We were able to get technical-assistance grants to be able to train more people of color to be more competitive and get funding from a program designed to fund them. So that's an example of how Growing Power works, in a larger sense. There are certain things in place to help people transform their communities, but they are not able to get to those resources because they don't have enough privilege to be able to be competitive. We help communities access those resources.

MONSANTO

In 2009 we had an interesting situation with Monsanto/Seminis (Monsanto purchased Seminis, a large, regional fruit-and-vegetable seed company, in 2005). They'd hired a communications firm in Chicago to find an urban agriculture group so they could fund a youth urban agriculture project. They just wanted to give us money, just do an urban farm so that youth could learn about what we do and also be introduced to other forms of agriculture; Monsanto's name wouldn't be on it. The people from the communications firm said, "This guy that we know at

Monsanto, he's really nice, and there are some really good people within the company." And I said, "I am sure there are." But I and we had to do some deep soul-searching about what we, as leaders, should do with this approach from Seminis—potentially gatekeepers of resources that could mean employment versus incarceration for some of our youth corps members. Do I *not* accept $200,000 to $500,000, which would build up infrastructure, provide adult mentors and social-service support, and supply stipends for pay for a few years? Could this be recompense for the global impacts of this company, but also a boon to their public relations efforts to spin their methods "to end hunger and to increase production"? I had to think about it. It's a real dilemma: What do you do when folks approach you and you're representing people who have very limited options and you're being offered all those resources to develop this infrastructure?

We turned it down because of the kind of work we do, the belief in our vision, and to show our solidarity with Via Campesina and the Department of Justice's antitrust hearings. We advocate seed saving and slow food, and potentially if we accepted the Monsanto/Seminis funds we would have legitimized their work.

On top of that, it would have been so hard for us, as one of the rare organizations led by people of color in this kind of work—work where we're doing something people can see, not just talking a good game. People, our youth most importantly, look to us as role models. You're no better than what you are trying to defeat if you do the same thing and get sucked into that system. Fortunately, we have reached a critical point in our development where we do have options.

INSPIRATION

We have to get people inspired, get them to understand basic principles like why agriculture is important. That's where I diverge somewhat with Wes Jackson, who talks about how the way humans have pursued agriculture has created so many huge ecological problems. I don't think agriculture is a bad idea—I think it's a really good idea; it just has to be managed well, and perhaps that is where Wes and I come full circle in understanding the importance of stewardship of the land and preservation of the soil and all of her inhabitants. It has to be managed by people who know what they're doing for a community, not for some abstract wealth-building scenario or commodities or craziness. I don't think agriculture is the end of ecology; I think it's the beginning of people having enough surpluses through balance and exploitive practices, so they can do the arts and they can develop to their full potential.

Part Six

POPULATION

POPULATION

The Multiplier of Everything Else

WILLIAM N. RYERSON

WILLIAM RYERSON *is founder and president of Population Media Center and president of the Population Institute. He has worked for nearly forty years in the field of reproductive health, including two decades of experience adapting the Sabido methodology for behavior change communications to various cultural settings worldwide. In 2006, he was awarded the Nafis Sadik Prize for Courage from the Rotarian Action Group on Population and Development. Ryerson is a Fellow of Post Carbon Institute.*

❖

When it comes to controversial issues, population is in a class by itself.

Advocates and activists working to reduce global population growth and size are attacked by the Left for supposedly ignoring human-rights issues, glossing over Western overconsumption, or even seeking to reduce the number of people of color. They are attacked by the Right for supposedly favoring widespread abortion, promoting promiscuity via sex education, or wanting to harm economic growth. Others think the problem has been solved, or believe that the real problem is that we have a *shortage* of people (the so-called birth dearth). Still others think the population problem will solve itself, or that technological innovations will make our numbers irrelevant.

One thing is certain: The planet and its resources are finite, and it cannot support an infinite population of humans or any other species. A second thing is also certain: The issue of population is too important to avoid just because it is controversial.

THE MAGNITUDE OF THE PROBLEM

The Big Picture of Growth Globally and in the United States

The world's population is growing by about 80 million people annually—the equivalent of adding a new Egypt every year. The total population is approaching 7 billion, seven times what it was in 1800. Every day approximately 156,000 people die, but 381,000 are born—a net daily growth of 225,000 human beings.

The cost in human suffering that results from unplanned and excessive childbearing is staggering: 500,000 women and girls die worldwide every year from pregnancy and childbirth[1]—a figure equal to all of the U.S. deaths in World War I, World War II, the Korean War, and the Vietnam War combined. Most of the women who die are in their teens and early twenties, forced by their societies into bearing children too young and far too frequently.

But the developing world is so capital starved owing to its high population growth rate that allocating some portion of government budgets to reproductive health care is often extremely difficult. For its part, the developed world as a whole has failed to come close to meeting the commitments for population assistance made at the International Conference on Population and Development in Cairo in 1994. To achieve the commitments made in Cairo, both developed and developing countries would need to triple their current contributions. The lives of billions of people are being rendered increasingly desperate by being denied access to family-planning information and services they want and need.

The top three countries for population growth are India, China, and the United States. India grows by about 17 million per year, China by about 7 million per year, and the United States by about 3 million per year. These three countries, plus Nigeria, the Democratic Republic of the Congo, Pakistan, Indonesia, Uganda, Ethiopia, Bangladesh, Brazil, and the Philippines, are poised to grow by 1.6 billion by 2050, representing 63 percent of the world's projected growth of 2.6 billion in the coming four decades. These projections are based on assumptions about reduced fertility rates in all twelve of these countries. If the expected fertility reductions do *not* occur, the world's population could double to 13.6 billion by 2067.

TABLE 12.1. Years Elapsed between Major Milestones
in Human Population Growth

Years Elapsed	Year	Approximate Population
3,000,000	10,000 BC (Agricultural Revolution)	5–10 million
10,000	AD 1	170 million
1,600	~1600	500 million
200	~1800 (Industrial Revolution)	1 billion
130	1930	2 billion
30	1960	3 billion
15	1975	4 billion
12	1987	5 billion
12	1999	6 billion
12	2011	7 billion

What Is Causing Population Growth?

Population growth of the magnitude we are experiencing now is a phenomenon that started in the twentieth century. As recently as 1925, India and many other developing countries were at zero population growth.[2] Table 12.1 and figure 12.1 give a quick historical look at world population growth rates.

The surge in population growth rates over the last half century is *not* the result of rising birth rates. Birth rates have dropped significantly on a worldwide basis since 1970. Instead, the very high rates of growth of the world's population result primarily from declining death rates—the result of widespread vaccination programs and other public health measures. Declining mortality has been the trend of the last two centuries, with especially rapid decline during the last six decades particularly among infants and children. Declines in mortality have been so much faster than declines in fertility that the result has been unprecedented net rates of population increase.

The only way population growth can stop is if the birth rate and death rate reach the same level. At some point, they will reach the same level, either because of rising death rates or reduced birth rates—or both.

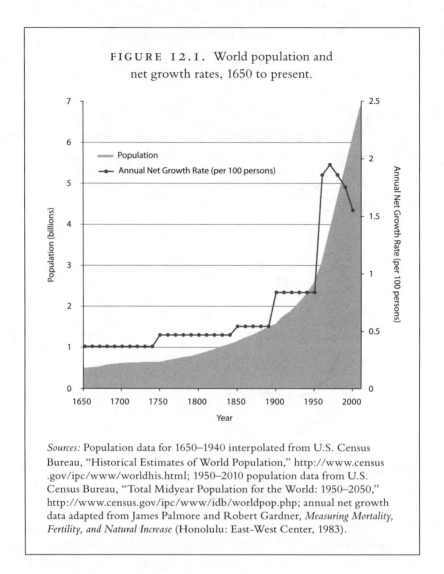

FIGURE 12.1. World population and
net growth rates, 1650 to present.

Sources: Population data for 1650–1940 interpolated from U.S. Census
Bureau, "Historical Estimates of World Population," http://www.census
.gov/ipc/www/worldhis.html; 1950–2010 population data from U.S.
Census Bureau, "Total Midyear Population for the World: 1950–2050,"
http://www.census.gov/ipc/www/idb/worldpop.php; annual net growth
data adapted from James Palmore and Robert Gardner, *Measuring Mortality,
Fertility, and Natural Increase* (Honolulu: East-West Center, 1983).

What We Know about the Carrying Capacity of
the United States and the World

Nobody knows what the exact long-term carrying capacity (the number
of humans—or any species—that can be sustained by natural resources) of
our planet is. In 1999, Cornell University biology professor David Pimentel estimated the planet's long-term carrying capacity at 2 billion people
and the carrying capacity for the United States at 200 million, assuming

people live at a standard of living similar to that in Western Europe.[3] At our current global lifestyle, the Global Footprint Network (GFN) estimates that humans have already outgrown the sustainable capacity of the planet by 40 percent. If GFN is right, the world is in population "overshoot," which will be followed by a die-off as critical resources become more and more scarce.[4]

In 1992, 1,700 of the world's leading scientists, including the majority of Nobel laureates in the sciences, signed a "Warning to Humanity," which said in part:

> Human beings and the natural world are on a collision course. . . .
> If not checked, many of our current practices put at serious risk the
> future that we wish for human society and the plant and animal
> kingdoms, and may so alter the living world that it will be unable
> to sustain life in the manner that we know.[5]

In 1994, fifty-eight of the world's scientific academies issued another warning, stating: "It is our collective judgement that continuing population growth poses a great risk to humanity."[6] Moreover, presidential commissions established by Richard Nixon and Bill Clinton both urged stopping population growth in the United States.

DIMENSIONS OF THE PROBLEM

Climate

Some environmentalists express doubts about the relevance of population trends to climate change. They rightly point out that high-consuming nations like the United States have the biggest per capita carbon footprints. They state that changing our lifestyles is more important than the growth in the number of Ethiopians, with their relatively small carbon footprints.

There is no doubt that changing Westerners' behavior with regard to energy efficiency and greenhouse gas emissions is critical to solving the climate crisis. However, per capita rates of carbon emissions leveled off in both Europe and the United States in the 1970s and have barely budged since then. On the other hand, total carbon emissions in both the United States and Europe have trended upward in a one-to-one ratio with rising populations. From 1975 to 2009, U.S. population and emissions both rose by 43 percent.

The importance of decisions about family size in developed countries was pointed out in a 2009 study, which concluded that, in the United States, the climate impact of not having an extra child is almost twenty times more important than that of many other environmentally sensitive practices people might employ in their lives: things like driving a hybrid vehicle, recycling, or using energy-efficient appliances and light bulbs.[7] The research also made it clear that potential carbon impacts vary dramatically across countries. The average long-term carbon impact of a child born in the United States—along with all of its descendants—is more than 160 times the impact of a child born in Bangladesh.

The United Nations' median projection of global population growth from 2010 to 2050 shows an addition of more than 2.5 billion people. Even in the low-consuming countries where much of that growth will occur, this is the carbon equivalent of adding two United States to the planet. Rising incomes in countries like China and India—and the desire of poor people worldwide to improve their lifestyles—are also driving per capita carbon emissions upward. Stabilizing population numbers at a sustainable level is the most cost-efficient way to reduce the growth in carbon emissions and to prevent the climate catastrophe that will otherwise occur.

University of Rhode Island biologist Fred Meyerson stated in a debate held by the *Bulletin of the Atomic Scientists* in 2008:

> Just stabilizing total emissions at current levels, while keeping pace with population growth, would require reducing global per-capita emissions by 1.2 percent each year. We haven't managed to decrease per-capita emissions by 1 percent in the last 38 years *combined*. The Intergovernmental Panel on Climate Change, former Vice President Al Gore, and many well-intentioned scientific, media, and activist campaigns haven't changed that fact.[8]

Funding for family-planning assistance in developing countries has been reduced since the Cairo conference in 1994. Yet the cost of full funding for family-planning information and services for everyone pales in comparison to the potential cost of climate change in the future.

Energy

Abundant and inexpensive energy has enabled the human population to grow sevenfold in just two hundred years. Cheap oil has provided the fuel for the Industrial Revolution and the Information Revolution; it has provided the pesticides and fertilizers used by farmers to increase crop yields, especially during and since the Green Revolution; and it has fueled the tractors and other equipment in developed countries that have driven crop yields even higher. All of these developments helped lower infant and child mortality rates around the world—and also helped produce, as an unintended by-product, the population explosion of the last half century.

Growth in demand for energy has outpaced population growth, as economies rich and poor have grown. The aspirations of the poorest countries for their share of economic wealth are dependent on continued availability of ever-growing amounts of cheap energy. The global community is only slowly waking up to the realization that shortages of energy and resulting price increases may make it impossible for economic growth to continue.

In 1973, John Holdren (now science adviser to President Barack Obama) wrote:

> Consider the true statement, "Total energy consumption in the United States increased 1,100 percent (12-fold) between 1880 and 1966, while population increased 300 percent (four-fold)." On a quick reading, one might infer from this statement that population growth was not the major contributing factor. Actually, the increase in energy consumption per capita in this period was only 200 percent (three-fold); the 12-fold increase in total energy use is the product, not the sum, of the four-fold increase in population and the three-fold increase in use per person.[9]

In the United States, where per capita energy demand is over ten times that of developing countries, the projected addition of 135 million to the U.S. population in the next four decades will likely increase energy demands by more than the total present energy consumption of Africa and Latin America combined.

Water and Food

Freshwater constitutes only 3 percent of all water on Earth, of which about a third is found in underground aquifers and about two-thirds in ice caps and glaciers. Only 0.3 percent of freshwater is found on Earth's surface in lakes, rivers, and wetlands. Massively increased water demand for agriculture and from growing cities and suburbs is rapidly depleting this precious resource. As Lester Brown and his colleagues stated in *Beyond Malthus*:

> There will be scarcely one fourth as much fresh water per person in 2050 as there was in 1950. With water availability per person projected to decline dramatically in many countries already facing shortages, the full social effects of future water scarcity are difficult even to imagine. Indeed, spreading water scarcity may be the most underrated resource issue in the world today.[10]

With water tables falling on every continent because of overpumping for agriculture, farmland is being lost as underground aquifers are depleted. This is particularly true of three major grain-producing countries: China, India, and the United States. Since 70 percent of water pumped from underground is used for irrigation, the depletion of aquifers, combined with loss of seasonal river flows as glaciers disappear, will likely lead to a serious decline in food availability in the next two decades. The twin forces of rising petroleum costs and inaccessible freshwater are likely to cause grain prices to increase dramatically, beyond the doubling and tripling of prices seen in recent years. The consequence will likely be starvation among the world's poorest people, who will be unable to afford to buy food in the marketplace.

In mid-2009, the World Economic Forum issued a report stating that in fewer than twenty years the world may face freshwater shortages so severe that "global food production could crater" because the world could "lose the equivalent of the entire grain production of the US and India combined." The report warned that half of the global population will be affected by water shortages, millions will die, and water wars will increase over diminishing supplies.

If land-based food becomes scarce, why not turn to the world's lakes and oceans for more fish to feed the growing human population? That is exactly what has been happening, with devastating effects on the world's fisheries. Study after study reveal that wild populations of fish are collapsing as a result of overfishing—in large part because the world's fishing fleet has a fishing capacity twice that of the sustainable yield of the world's wild fisheries. Fish farming is rapidly replacing wild-caught fish in its share of the world's fish market. However, as fish farming grows, fish are competing with poultry and livestock—and with humans themselves—for feedstuffs such as grain and fishmeal.

Biodiversity, Forests, and Protected Natural Areas

The concept of carrying capacity does not apply just to humans. It applies to all species competing for the same resources in any area. Growth in human numbers has greatly accelerated destruction of habitats, leading to a rapid increase in the rate of species extinction and rapid declines in the populations of other species. Despite efforts to protect and preserve various species, the last century has seen the greatest extinction of plant and animal life since the age of the dinosaurs 65 million years ago. Humans are responsible for this monumental tragedy, primarily through habitat destruction, but also through the introduction of "exotic" invasive species, pollution, overhunting, and overfishing.

Some of the destruction of the planet's biodiversity is the result of population-driven expansion of human activity, and some is the result of wasteful patterns of consumption and waste. As economies have expanded globally, the growth in human numbers has become even more destructive of biodiversity. Deforestation of rainforests like the Amazon has been driven both by a demand for lumber products and by the need for additional agricultural land. This deforestation is a major contributor to climate change, owing to the release of huge amounts of stored carbon and the elimination of the carbon-absorptive capacity of the forests.

Poverty and Economic Development

The assertion that rapid rates of population growth somehow stimulate economic growth has been made by economists for a long time, but it achieved prominence during the Reagan administration. As advocated by free-market economist Julian Simon and others, the contention was that rapid rates of population growth stimulate consumerism and that the added demand fuels economic growth.

The opposite is true. As explained by Ansley Coale of Princeton University, there is a direct relationship between rapid rates of population growth and declining economic conditions in underdeveloped countries.[11] The economies of many developing countries, such as those in Africa, are being damaged by the fact that a high percentage of personal and national income is spent on the immediate survival needs of food, housing, and clothing. There are simply too many people dependent on each working adult. This leaves little income at the personal or national level available to form investment capital, which in turn depresses industrial productivity growth and leads to high unemployment (which is exacerbated by rapid growth in the numbers seeking employment). Lack of capital also contributes to a country's inability to invest in education, government, infrastructure, environmental needs, and other areas that can contribute to the long-term productivity of the economy and living standards of the people. Indeed, in the twentieth century, no nation made much progress in the transition from "developing" to "developed" until it first brought its population growth under control.

Worldwide, according to a comprehensive report by American author Bruce Sundquist, developing nations spend about $13,000 in per capita public infrastructure costs over the lifetime of each resident.[12] Multiplying that figure by the 78 million in net growth of the population each year means that these countries now require about $1 trillion per year in new infrastructure development just to accommodate their population growth—a figure that is very far from being met and is effectively impossible for these countries to generate. This explains why the infrastructure of the developing world is sagging under the demands of the equivalent of a new Los Angeles County in additional population (9.5 million) every six weeks.

Health

In 2008, the world marked an unprecedented milestone: More than half the human population now lives in urbanized areas. The growth in human numbers—combined in many parts of the world with crowding, poor hygiene and health care, pollution, and close interaction of people and farm animals—has led to ideal conditions for pandemics. The World Health Organization has been warning for some years that it is not a question of *if* but *when* these conditions will lead to pandemic disease. Massive rural-to-urban migration in developing countries is making the situation in large urban centers increasingly desperate, with growing slums that lack basic sanitation and water—and it is likely that this migration will greatly increase in future years. At the same time, encroachment by people into previously wild habitats has led to the spread of new diseases to humans.

Ninety percent of all infectious diseases in Africa, Asia, and Latin America are waterborne, thanks to lack of sanitation and proper water treatment in many areas. The public health infrastructures of poor countries are unable to respond to new disease threats because they are already underfunded and overwhelmed by the existing disease burden. Rapid growth of the populations in these countries leads to stagnating economies that do not generate the funds needed to provide basic health care to those who need it most.

MYTHS AND REALITY

There is much misinformation about population, some of it intentionally planted by those who think continued population growth holds some benefit for them. Confusion also exists among journalists, who, in turn, misinform the public. The mathematics of exponential growth can also be confusing to those who have not studied math. Even the term "population" is emotionally laden for many people because of the associations it has had with various controversies over the years. Many population myths are based on faulty logic, and many population program policy-makers and funders have been reluctant to recognize overwhelming evidence that some of their beliefs are countered by impressive evidence.

The predominant myths about population include misconceptions about the nature of the problem, the belief that population growth poses no threat, the belief that we cannot do anything about population growth, and beliefs about interventions that are mistakenly thought to hold the promise of a quick fix to the population problem. Examples of these are discussed below.

The "Birth Dearth" Myth
The news media in recent years have been informing people in Europe and the United States that there is the possibility of a coming decline in

population numbers sometime in the next fifty to three hundred years because of a "birth dearth." The following headlines give the picture:

- "Birth Dearth; Remember the Population Bomb?," *Newsweek*, September 27, 2004
- "Population No Longer a Worry in Poor Countries," *Times of India*, January 26, 2005
- "Birthrate Decline Will Be Our Global Peril," *Philadelphia Inquirer*, July 9, 2006
- "A World Without Children," *Boston Globe*, June 22, 2008

These articles miss the bigger and more immediate picture of what is happening worldwide. Even though the current rate of global population growth at 1.2 percent is lower than the peak rate of about 2 percent that occurred in the 1960s, the world's population is still growing by about 78 million people each year. That's the equivalent of adding a new Ethiopia every year. Conservative demographic projections show the world's population growing by 2.5 billion people over the next four decades—a 40 percent increase. Many people are simply not aware of the scale and speed at which world population is expected to continue growing.

The Belief that Science and Technology Will Solve All Problems

The logical extension of the saying "Necessity is the mother of invention" is that deprivation is good because it stimulates innovation. On the other hand, population experts point out that solutions to some problems (such as high infant death rates and hunger) often cause new problems (such as overpopulation). Moreover, technological innovation doesn't always come to the rescue. People living in the fourteenth century were in desperate need of the medicines that weren't invented until after World War II. People living in Bangladesh and in the Gulf states in the United States are in great need of technology to control typhoons and hurricanes, but to say that their suffering is good because it might stimulate such development would not only be ludicrous but cruel.

Regions with severe overpopulation and related poverty and starvation do not have the relative luxuries of time and energy that are usually needed for invention. Indeed, technological growth may ease us through some of the potential crises of the future, but there is little about the current magnitude or nature of world population growth that can be expected to significantly accelerate technological progress—and in the meantime, many people are bound to suffer needlessly. Even if changing technologies allow for some expansion of population numbers in the future, the limits of social institutions and the needs of other species for habitat make it imperative that we question the desirability of adding more and more people to the population.

The Belief that There Is a Problem Only with Distribution of Food and Other Resources

During the discussion of the "new international economic order" that was prominent in the 1970s, the idea was put forward that enough food and other resources existed to support all the people currently on Earth. While there may indeed be enough food grown each year to feed all of the people who are currently alive, when it comes to population growth, trends are everything.

Even if we don't consider the global environmental consequences of population growth, some of the current trends in agriculture are disturbing. The per capita production of grain products, which comprise the bulk of the human diet, has been declining since 1984 despite continued conversion of forestland into crop production and the Green Revolution of high-yield grains. The simple reason for this change has been that population growth has outstripped growth in agricultural productivity. Since 1970, about 300 million people have died of hunger, and looking ten to twenty years down the road, many countries face massive starvation. Trends in overpumping of water for irrigation, climate change, and energy availability threaten to greatly reduce global grain production.

It is probably fanciful to imagine that the wealthy countries of the world will materially cut their standard of living to voluntarily give a major portion of their wealth and resources to the world's poor. If uneven distribution of resources is contributing to severe poverty in developing countries, is it responsible in the meantime to do little to help stop population growth? Of course, if population growth rates remain high, even redistribution of wealth and resources and changing power relationships among countries will not solve the problems of poverty and environmental degradation.

The Belief that Religious Barriers Will Prevent the Use of Family Planning

It is commonly believed that family planning is impossible in many countries in Latin America or the Middle East because of religious opposition to contraception. In fact, the mainstream denominations of Catholicism and Islam do not completely oppose family planning in their teachings. The Catholic Church supports broad-based sexuality education and encourages couples to limit the number of their offspring to those they can afford and nurture (it does, however, oppose the use of certain means to achieve those ends). The Koran teaches that women should breast-feed their infants for at least two years, which, according to some Islamic scholars, inherently favors child spacing.

Practically speaking, limiting family size and curbing population growth rates have already proved possible in Catholic and Islamic countries. Predominantly Catholic countries like Italy and Spain have achieved sub–replacement fertility, while predominantly Muslim nations like Indonesia, Iran, and Bangladesh have achieved remarkable progress in promoting family planning. The average woman in Indonesia has 2.5 children compared to a 2.7-child average in Asia outside of China.

The Myth that Economic Development Is Needed to Slow Population Growth

I personally attended the 1974 U.N. World Population Conference, and I heard many delegates there claim that "development is the best contraceptive." The example of the reduction in fertility rates in Europe and North America over the two previous centuries was proposed as evidence that improved economic welfare would lead automatically to such a demographic transition in the developing countries. The Demographic and Health Survey reports developed since 1984 for the U.S. Agency for International Development (USAID)[13] show that desired and actual levels of fertility are higher in countries with low levels of economic development and lower in countries with high levels of development.

But which is the cause, and which is the effect? It turns out there is strong reason to believe that lower fertility rates lead to improved economic development, and there is comparatively little evidence that improved economic conditions lead to lower fertility rates. Vanderbilt

University emeritus professor of psychiatry Virginia Abernethy points out a number of cases that cast doubt on the idea that economic development leads automatically to lower fertility:

> Land redistribution in Turkey [in the mid-twentieth century] promoted a doubling in family size (to six children) among formerly landless peasants. In the United States and much of Western Europe, a baby boom coincided with the broad-based prosperity of the 1950s. More water wells for the pastoralists of the African Sahel promoted larger herd size, earlier marriage and much higher fertility.[14]

Inversely, poverty can lead to lower fertility rates. For example, the United States had its lowest fertility rate in history prior to 1970 during the Great Depression of the 1930s.

These examples indicate that economic prosperity may lead to higher fertility levels and that economically depressed conditions may motivate people to limit family size. While there are examples of industrialization being associated with lower fertility levels, the nature of the relationship is not well understood. The point is that economic development by itself, without other measures that affect family-size desires or the ability to achieve those desires, is not necessarily a cure-all for the population problem.

The Myth that Providing Contraceptives Is All that Is Needed

There is a view among many population activists that the top priority in the population field should be to provide contraceptive services. This results from a belief that lack of access to these services is the major barrier to fertility reduction. Of the money spent by developing and developed countries for population-related work in the developing world, the largest share has gone to providing family-planning medical services to individuals and couples.

It is true that, over the last forty years, increasing access to contraceptive services has helped reduce fertility rates, but large-family norms and the cultural and informational barriers to use of contraception are now the major impediments to achieving replacement-level fertility. Changing this situation takes more than the provision of family planning. It requires helping people to understand the personal benefits in health and wealth for them and their children of limiting and spacing births. It also involves role-modeling family-planning practices and overcoming fears that contraceptives are dangerous or that planning one's family is unacceptable. And it requires getting husbands and wives to talk to each other about the use of family planning—a key step in the decision to use contraceptives. Delaying marriage and childbearing until adulthood and educating girls are also critical.

This does not mean that efforts to provide contraceptive services should be reduced; high-quality, low-cost reproductive health-care services are an essential element of family planning. But access to family-planning methods is not sufficient if men prevent their partners from using them, if women don't understand the relative safety of contraception compared with early and repeated childbearing, or if women feel they cannot take control of their own lives.

An estimated 100 million to 200 million women want to delay or limit childbearing but are not using a modern method of family planning. The top reasons for their nonuse are cultural and informational issues, namely fear of health effects, male opposition, religious opposition, and fatalism. A lot of effort has been focused on providing contraceptives to this group, but in reality less than 2 percent in most countries cite cost or lack of access to services as their reasons for nonuse. On the other hand, there are about 1.8 billion adults who don't use contraception specifically because they want additional children. Indeed, desired levels of fertility account for roughly 90 percent of the differences among countries in total fertility rates.[15]

WHAT'S NEEDED TO SOLVE THE POPULATION PROBLEM?

Universal access to family-planning services and information is one key to stabilizing population numbers. The freedom to choose how many children to have, and when to have them, has been recognized as a fundamental human right since the 1974 U.N. World Population Conference. When women have the resources to make informed, voluntary decisions about the number and spacing of their children, they often choose to have smaller families.

However, hundreds of millions of women today are not using any method of family planning, because of three main barriers: the desire for large families, lack of correct information, and social opposition. The gravity and complexity of the problem call for a holistic approach that not only improves information and access to family planning but also addresses social barriers such as the status of women—for example, by reducing violence against women and promoting the education of girls.

Provide Family-Planning Services

Reaching people with high-quality reproductive health services and information—including contraceptives and medical supplies at affordable prices—is important for preventing unintended pregnancies, reducing maternal deaths, fighting the spread of HIV, and stabilizing population numbers.

Between 1960 and 2009, the average number of births per woman globally fell from 4.9 to 2.6 as contraceptive use increased. Where family-planning services and related information have been made available, there have been reductions in both fertility rates and maternal mortality. According to the United Nations Population Fund, "The level of unintended pregnancy is lowest in countries with greatest access to effective methods of contraception and where women play a major role in family decision-making."[16] While significant improvements have been made globally, there are still large populations that lack access to services, particularly the more vulnerable groups such as the poor and those living in remote rural areas.

Ndola Prata of the Bixby Center for Population, Health, and Sustainability has found that the relationship between contraception use, income, and education can vary widely from country to country.[17] Globally, women from the richest segments of society have contraceptive-prevalence rates of two to seven times higher than their poorer counterparts. In countries where contraceptives methods are widely available and accessible, however, the disparity is less. For example, in Bangladesh, contraceptive use does not vary significantly according to level of education, whereas in the Philippines it does.[18] Bangladesh was able to address this variance by making family-planning services highly affordable and accessible, and by employing a vast force of female field workers to visit women in their homes and provide highly subsidized contraceptives. In contrast, the sale of contraceptives is outlawed in Manila, making it very difficult for people to obtain family-planning methods without traveling out of the city.

Role-Model a Small Family as the Norm

Family-planning education can reach large numbers of people very cost effectively through entertainment programs broadcast on radio and television. Serial dramas are especially well suited to this, allowing audiences to watch or listen along as their favorite characters change from holding traditional attitudes to holding modern attitudes regarding issues such as the role of women, family-size decisions, and the use of family planning.[19]

A growing body of evidence bears out the effectiveness of role modeling through entertainment. In 1977 Miguel Sabido, then vice president for research of the Mexican network Televisa, launched a prime-time weekday *telenovela* called *Acompañame* (*Accompany Me*) to educate viewers on family planning. *Acompañame* aired for nine months and dramatized the personal and familial benefits of planning one's family, focusing on the issue of family harmony. The results included a 33 percent increase in attendance at family-planning clinics and a 23 percent increase in the sale of contraceptives in pharmacies.[20] *Acompañame* was so successful that Televisa developed four additional family-planning soap operas with Sabido. During the nine years that the five family-planning programs were on the air, Mexico experienced a 34 percent decline in its population growth rate. In part through the efforts of the Population Media Center, Sabido's model has since been applied in numerous countries, and independent research has confirmed its effectiveness, even given the context of other economic and cultural factors.

In terms of births avoided per dollar spent, mass media communications are probably the most effective strategy for reducing fertility rates. Research on a Tanzanian radio serial drama showed that the cost of the program per new adopter of family planning was under $0.32 (U.S. currency).[21] News and information programs, comic books, and traditional media (such as traveling road shows) can also incorporate educational messages that people can relate to. Whatever the media, family-planning messages should not dwell on methods but on benefits. People will be much more motivated to use family planning to limit family size if they know that it can lead to happier marriages, improved family harmony, greater health and well-being, and material progress for them and the nation as a whole.

Elevation of Women's Status and Girls' Education

How well a society treats its women is one of the strongest indicators of the success and health of a society. Providing girls with an education, allowing women to have a voice in family decisions, and providing women with opportunities for economic freedom are key to creating an environment in which reduced fertility rates are possible.

Several factors affect demand for contraception. Women who cannot read or have limited education may know little about their own bodies, much less about family planning. Misconceptions and myths about pregnancy and contraceptive methods abound. Social norms surrounding fertility and virility, and the overall low status of women, keep many women and men from seeking family planning.

Girls' education is key. As economist Jeffrey Sachs has pointed out:

> Girls' education has time and again been shown to be one of the decisive entry points into the demographic transition. . . . There is the most direct effect: Girls in school, notably in secondary school, are likely to remain unmarried until a later age, and therefore are likely to begin child rearing much later than girls without schooling. . . . Perhaps most important for the long term, education empowers women in the labor market, raising the value of their time by imparting labor market skills.[22]

Worldwide, 62 million school-age girls are not enrolled in school. In many cases, schools are far away and going to school would take a child away for the entire day, robbing the family of her (or his) labor around the home. If they are enrolled at all, girls are usually taken out of school first, if needed, since boys' education is valued more highly. In most developing countries, a woman with the same education earns far less than a man, so there is more economic benefit in paying to educate a boy. Also, since in many societies it is the girl who leaves her parents' home to join her husband's household, there is little incentive for her family to educate her, as this "investment" will be lost to the household.

Girls' education and eliminating the gender disparity in primary and secondary education have a direct impact on the number of children a woman has. In Brazil, women with secondary education have an average of 2.5 children versus illiterate women who have an average of 6.5 children. Once women are aware of their options with regard to family planning and are empowered to seek out alternative opportunities in life, the desire for large families decreases. Having fewer children then allows families to invest more in the health and education of each child, thereby raising the productivity of future generations.

WHAT CAN BE DONE

We can begin solving the global population problem by providing family-planning information and services, role-modeling a small family as the norm, and elevating the status of women and girls. Because of the controversies surrounding population issues, it will take strong public support to give political leaders the courage to act. How can we best move forward with achieving these goals?

The governments of the world need to make policy and financial commitments to tackle overpopulation. It is critical that every country include reproductive-health issues in national budgets. Moreover, it is important to eliminate laws that require a woman to have her husband's permission to use contraceptive methods and laws requiring parental consent for adolescents under a certain age to obtain family planning.

There are many things individual citizens can do:

- Support domestic and international family-planning initiatives, both those providing services and those providing information and education to help bring about lower fertility rates and elevation of women's status.
- Support population organizations to educate people about population issues and to push for sound population-related policies.
- Contact elected representatives urging them to support comprehensive family-planning and reproductive-health services, both internationally and domestically, and to support women's rights and an end to abusive practices such as child marriages.
- Talk to family, friends, and co-workers about the pressing need for achieving gender equity and a sustainable population size.

It is also important that the United States take a leadership role; there are a number of actions the United States can take immediately:

- Issue a statement on the importance of addressing population growth and its relevance to all of the United Nations' Millennium Development Goals.
- Contribute a higher percentage of GDP to population assistance programs in developing countries.
- Establish a new Population Commission to set the agenda for population stabilization, using the recommendations of previous commissions as a starting point.
- Establish an Office of Special Assistant to the President for Population and Sustainability Issues, and similar offices elsewhere in the federal government, to elevate the discussion of the population issue and coordinate with relevant offices in other agencies.[23]

Finally, the philanthropic community and donor nations have important roles to play. Promotion of family planning has dropped steadily down the list of international development priorities since 1994. Between 1995 and 2003, donor support for family-planning commodities and service delivery fell from $560 million to $460 million.

GET INVOLVED IN THE SOLUTION

The goal of humanity should be to have a sustainable number of people living a comfortable lifestyle. Instead, we are recklessly pursuing an experiment to find out how many people can be supported in the short term without regard for the impact on future generations or the consequences for other species.

Finding a solution to the population problem will involve multiple strategies—and it will not be either simple or inexpensive. Much of the effort over the last forty years has focused on the development of governmental policies and the provision of family-planning medical services. We must add to this the development of social environments that motivate and empower people to use family planning and limit family size. Governments and the international donor community must get serious about providing ample funding to these and other highly effective strategies.

The world needs to focus major attention on stopping population growth. The planet is finite, and exponential growth is not sustainable. We can solve the population problem voluntarily if we apply what we know and mobilize the funds needed to provide all people with family-planning information and services.

Part Seven

CULTURE AND BEHAVIOR

DANGEROUSLY ADDICTIVE

Why We Are Biologically Ill-Suited to the Riches of Modern America

PETER C. WHYBROW, MD

PETER WHYBROW *is director of the Semel Institute for Neuroscience and Human Behavior and the Judson Braun Distinguished Professor of Psychiatry and Biobehavioral Science at UCLA. He is an international authority on depression and manic-depressive disease and the effects of thyroid hormone on brain and human behavior, and is the recipient of many awards. He has lectured widely across the United States and Europe, and is the author of* American Mania: When More Is Not Enough *(2006). Whybrow is a Fellow of Post Carbon Institute.*

❖

It's called the American dream," George Carlin lamented shortly before his death, "because you have to be asleep to believe it." Too bad for the rest of us that George and his signature satire haven't been around for the wake-up call of the current market meltdown. After all, George Carlin knew something about the dangers of addiction from firsthand experience. He understood earlier than most that the debt-fueled consumptive frenzy that has gripped the American psyche for the past two decades was a nightmare in the making—a seductive, twisted, and commercially conjured version of the American dream that now threatens our environmental, individual, and civic health.

The United States is the quintessential trading nation, and for the past quarter century we have worshiped the "free" market as an ideology rather than for what it is—a natural product of human social evolution and a set of economic tools with which to construct a just and equitable society. Under the spell of this ideology and the false promise of instant riches, America's immigrant values of thrift, prudence, and community concern—traditionally the foundation of the American dream—have been hijacked by an all-consuming self-interest. The astonishing appetite

of the American consumer now determines some 70 percent of all economic activity in the United States. And yet, in this land of opportunity
and material comfort—where we enjoy the 12-inch dinner plate, the
32-ounce soda, and the 64-inch TV screen—more and more citizens feel
time starved, overworked, and burdened by debt. Epidemic rates of obesity, anxiety, depression, and family dysfunction are accepted as the norm.

It is the paradox of modernity that as choice and material prosperity
increase, health and personal satisfaction decline. This is now an accepted
truth. And yet it is the rare American who manages to step back from the
hedonic treadmill long enough to savor his or her good fortune. Indeed,
for most of us, regardless of what we have, we want *more* and we want it
now. The roots of this conundrum—of this addictive striving—are to be
found in our evolutionary history. As creatures of the natural world, having evolved under conditions of danger and scarcity, we are by instinct
reward-seeking animals that discount the future in favor of the immediate
present. As a species we have no familiarity with the seductive prosperity
and material riches that exist in America today. A novel experience, it is
both compelling and confusing.

Brain systems of immediate reward were a vital survival adaptation
millennia ago when finding a fruit tree was a rare delight and dinner had
a habit of running away or flying out of reach. But living now in relative
abundance, when the whole world is a shopping mall and our appetites are
no longer constrained by limited resources, our craving for reward—be
that for money, the fat and sugar of fast food, or for the novel gadgetry
of modern technology—has become a liability and a hunger that has no
bounds. Our nature has no built-in braking system. More is never enough.

That the human animal is a curiosity-driven pleasure seeker easily seduced is of no surprise to the behavioral neuroscientist. It is clearly
established that "overloading" the brain's ancient reward circuits with
excessive stimulation—through drugs, novel experience, or unlimited
choice—will trigger craving and insatiable desire. Brain anatomy helps us
understand why this is so.

The human brain is a hybrid: an evolved hierarchy of three brains in
one. A primitive "lizard" brain, designed millennia ago for survival, lies
at its core and cradles the roots of the ancient dopamine reward pathways.
When the dinosaurs still roamed, around this reptilian pith there evolved
the limbic cortex—literally the "border crust"—of the early mamma-

lian brain, which is the root of kinship behavior and nurturance. The evolution of mammalian species is marked by a continuous expansion of this cortex, with the prefrontal lobes of the human brain—the powerful information-processing or "executive" brain that distinguishes *Homo sapiens* within the primate lineage—emerging only recently, within the last 200,000 years.

With the three brains working in harmony the human animal has extraordinary adaptive advantage, as is evident from the success we have achieved as a species. Through a process of continuous learning—orchestrated by the executive brain—the risks and rewards inherent in changing circumstance are carefully assessed and the personal and social consequence of what we do is remembered to future benefit. But there is a catch. Despite our superior intelligence, as in all animals, we remain driven by our ancient desires. Desire is as vital as breathing. Indeed, in human experience, when desire is lost we call it anhedonia—or depression—and consider it an illness. But, as George Carlin understood, the flip side of this is that when the brain's reward circuits are overloaded or unconstrained, desire can turn to craving and to an addictive greed that co-opts executive analysis and common sense.

All this is important when considering market behavior, for in the marketplace it is desire that fuels the vital engines of commerce—self-interest, novelty seeking, and social ambition. It was Adam Smith—the eighteenth-century Scottish philosopher and capitalism's patron saint—who first cogently argued the value of harnessing what he called "self-love" (instinctual self-interest) within the give-and-take of a market framework to create a self-regulating economic order. Although it was well recognized that the human creature left unchecked has a propensity for greed, Smith argued that in a free society overweening self-interest is constrained by the wish to be loved by others (the limbic brain's drive for attachment) and by the "social sentiment" (empathic and commonsense behavior) that is learned by living in community.

Therefore, with the adoption of a few rules—such as honesty in competition, respect for private property, and the ability to exchange goods for money—personal desire can be safely liberated to prime the engines of economic growth. Self-love will be simultaneously molded to the common good by the complex personal relationships and the social order in which the "free" market operates; self-interest will ultimately serve the common interest. And indeed, experience tells us that locally capitalized neighborhood markets do sustain their own rational order, founded as they are upon an interlocking system of self-interested exchange.

But Smith lived before the invention of the mega-corporation, before instant global communication, and before the double cheeseburger and hedge funds. Today the tethers that once bound self-interest and social concern into closely knit economic communities, and which gave us Adam Smith's enduring metaphor of an "invisible hand" balancing market behavior, have been weakened by an intrusive mercantilism that never sleeps.

Since the 1950s, rapidly advancing technologies have removed the physical limitations once placed upon human activity by darkness, sea, and distance, thus diminishing the natural barriers to free-market exchange. The United States, as a great trading nation, applauded these advances and sought to drive economic growth further by limiting government regulation of market practice as prescribed by economist Milton Friedman and the Chicago School. Thus beginning in the late 1980s, as the Soviet Union crumbled and the Internet was commercialized, Smith's engines of economic growth—self-interest, curiosity, and social ambition—were supercharged and placed in high gear with the conviction that *Homo economicus*, a presumed rational being, was capable of self-policing. Freed of constraint, markets would magically regulate themselves, delivering to the American people an ever-increasing prosperity. With a bright future ahead, credit laws were relaxed and borrowing was encouraged. The American dream was no longer a promise based upon old notions of toil and patience: It was immediate and material.

We had perfected the consumer-driven society. The idea was simple and irresistible. It tapped deep into the nation's mythology and for a brief moment, during the exuberant years of the dot-com bubble, the American dream was made material. Vast shopping malls proclaimed prosperity throughout the land. Horatio Alger's story was once again our story—the American story—but this time on steroids.[1] Temptation was everywhere. And true to our instinctual origins, we were soon focused on immediate gratification, ignoring future consequence. Shopping became the national pastime. Throwing caution to the wind, at all levels of our society we hungered for more—more money, more power, more food, and more stuff.

It was a dream dangerously addictive—and unsustainable. America's productivity per person per hour is comparable to that of most European nations but our material consumption per capita is greater by one-third. We finance the difference by working longer hours, sleeping less, cutting back on vacations, neglecting our families, and taking on debt—massive amounts of debt. Before 1985 American consumers saved on average about 9 percent of their disposable income but by 2005 the comparable savings rate was zero as mortgage, credit card, and other consumer debt rose to 127 percent of disposable income. With Uncle Sam similarly awash in red ink, America had transformed itself from the world's bank to a debtor nation. The "invisible hand" had lost its grip.

The financial meltdown that began as the "subprime" mortgage crisis has finally brought home the inherent dangers of our reward-driven, shortsighted behavior. As the post dot-com housing bubble inflated, both Wall Street financiers and ordinary Americans began to believe that real estate values could never fall. With prices skyrocketing at 20 percent each year, the family home was mistaken for a piggy bank—as just another asset to borrow against when struggling to finance an overstretched lifestyle. With zero down payment, adjustable interest rates, and deregulated borrowing practices, the challenge became, as historian George Dyson has puckishly observed, "whether you can live in a house you've paid nothing for and spend it at the same time."

But as we are now experiencing, the worst was yet to come. As part of the scramble toward "freeing" the market, in 2004 America's big investment banks had become exempt from Depression-era regulations that specified the capital reserves that must be held against losses. Instinctual desire, abetted by its wily cousin speculation, soon became greed. Avarice was rampant as the skill and analytic powers of the executive brain were placed in thrall to the lizard. Clever people were now manipulating money for money's sake. Mortgage-backed securities, credit derivatives, default obligations, and other mysterious financial instruments designed to limit risk were packaged and repackaged to create unknown trillions of imaginary wealth. *Homo economicus* had been too clever by half. In reality, when the meltdown began, few people—even the financial gurus—truly understood what was happening. Caught in a web of our own creation, we first had fooled ourselves about the risks involved, and then the instruments we had created had fooled us. With the nation's financial system at the brink of disaster we found ourselves rudely awakened.

The conflict between seeking fame and fortune and the corrupting power of money is a perennial source of fascination in America. As I write this, *Road Show*, the much-repackaged story by Sondheim and Weidman of the Mizner brothers and their get-rich-quick schemes, has opened in New York. The characters of Addison, the flapper-age dreamer who helped define the architectural vision of Florida's Palm Beach and Boca Raton, and Wilson, his manipulative huckster brother, together embody the striving that many Americans find irresistible—the urge to act out the dream in material representation.

But dreams are more than things material. Dreams cannot be packaged and placed on sale in the shopping mall. The American dream is not to be found in a new refrigerator, or a 64-inch TV screen, for as reward-driven creatures we quickly grow tired of such novelties. No, dreaming is a state of mind that binds the brain in harmony. For each of us, our dreams are an evolving work of the imagination, built upon an elusive inner reality that is shaped by emotion and experience—an intuitive sense of future possibility that binds instinct and hope with commonsense analysis. As a guiding metaphor, the dream holds a unique place in American culture and it will continue to do so. This is because while the U.S. Constitution is grounded in the Enlightenment and draws upon a faith in human reason, to dream is part of the émigré package, integral to our never-ending search for El Dorado.[2] In our self-selection, Americans are different: a migrant people defined by movement and change. By temperament we tend toward restlessness, optimism, curiosity, risk taking, and entrepreneurship—just as Alexis de Tocqueville described in *Democracy in America* in 1831. It is these same qualities of mind that kindled the *novus ordo seclorum*—the "new order of the ages"—that was the dream of the Founding Fathers and is proclaimed still on the back of each U.S. one-dollar bill.

Somewhere along the road to affluence—caught up in the excitement of global markets, a virtual world of electronic wizardry, and immediate material reward—America has lost sight of those founding hopes and dreams. What is the purpose of the journey in this land of opportunity when individual social mobility lags behind that of Europe, when 45 million souls are without health insurance, and when our educational system is badly broken? Now with reality challenging the laissez-faire ideology of recent decades we have the opportunity to take stock with a renewed self-awareness, to curb our addictive striving, and to reach beyond immediate reward to craft a vigorous, equitable, and sustainable market society—one where technology and profit serve as instruments in achieving the good life and are not confused with the good life itself. The dream that material markets will ultimately deliver social perfection and human happiness is an illusion. Perfection does not exist in nature. Nature is infinitely more pragmatic. In nature it's all a matter of dynamic fit—of living creatures striving for balance with their surroundings. Anaïs Nin put it well: "The dream is always running ahead . . . to catch up with it, to live for a moment in unison with it, that is the miracle." George Carlin would have agreed.

Reprinted with permission from Peter C. Whybrow, "Dangerously Addictive: Why We Are Biologically Ill-Suited to the Riches of Modern America," *Chronicle of Higher Education* 55, no. 27 (March 13, 2009), B11.

REMAPPING RELATIONSHIPS

Humans in Nature

GLORIA FLORA

GLORIA FLORA *is founder and director of Sustainable Obtainable Solutions, an organization dedicated to the sustainability of public lands and of the plants, animals, and communities that depend on them. In her twenty-two-year career with the U.S. Forest Service, she became nationally known for her leadership in ecosystem management and for her courageous principled stands: As supervisor of the Lewis and Clark National Forest in north-central Montana, she made a landmark decision to prohibit natural gas leasing along the 356,000-acre Rocky Mountain Front. Flora is a Fellow of Post Carbon Institute.*

❖

The depth and breadth of science in the disciplines of natural systems and ecology form an impressive knowledge base. And there's little dispute that natural systems and their resources provide fundamental human needs: air, water, food, shelter. Such clear understanding should allow for effective decisions and rapid response to threats to our environment. Yet, repeatedly, societies have enacted policies—and not only tolerated but encouraged actions and choices—that have directly and indirectly damaged ecosystems, the atmosphere, and, in turn, human health. Understanding why we act against our own best interests becomes more and more critical as the impacts of global climate change and unsustainable use of finite resources literally put the survival of millions of species at risk.

The mounting and interrelated calamities of a carbon-laden atmosphere and fossil-fuel depletion—chaotic temperatures and weather, melting ice fields and permafrost, rising sea levels, square miles of forest leveled to access and squeeze oil out of tar sands and shale—are well documented. The profound effects on people, plants, and landscapes are no longer speculative theory but reality. Proposals for mitigation and adaptation solutions and innovations abound as small factions scramble to protect the very systems that sustain life. But large-scale, definitive action and coordinated responses have yet to solidify. Even benign proposals are challenged and rebuffed. Our erstwhile leaders perfect their sound bites to play to their base—but do nothing of substance to avoid offense to their corporate sponsors.

Resolution of this impasse between science, knowledge, and action requires urgent attention. But little will change until we apprehend why humans, particularly in "advanced" societies, resist altering these practices that degrade our life-supporting natural systems. The disconnection between humans and their environment lies at the heart of the problem.

BACKCASTING FOR ANSWERS

There is no question that as humans evolved, the natural world provided for every physical need: water, food, clothing, shelter, medicine, and tools. But nature also satisfied deeper needs and desires. For millennia, the beauty and mystery of the land have drawn people, enticed them into its unknown corners, enchanted them, challenged them, and bestowed a sense of freedom. Whether by dint of necessity or by choice, people gravitated to particular landscapes. Once a community of people came to know and understand the plants, animals, resources, and seasons of a particular locale, a whole body of profound place-based knowledge and wisdom developed. That wisdom of place was passed to and enhanced by each successive generation. Those possessing the keenest knowledge of place were revered.

Aboriginal societies evolved complex ceremony, story, and social hierarchies based on natural features and phenomena and their understanding of them. Thus a spiritual dependency evolved along with their physical dependency on nature. A right relationship with the land was expected and honored, not only because it formed the basis of well-defined social mores, but also because it meant the difference between living and dying. Violations of moral code by transgressions against nature invited natural disaster and social disgrace.

Granted, the land's character, allure, and abundance fomented cultural attachment, but in addition, the meaning derived from events and experiences (their ancestors' and their own) that played across its vast canvas knit societies to place with interlocked stitches. Historically, landscapes called home have elicited in the human spirit an attachment so strong people will fight and die to protect them. The motherland, sandwiched right in there between God and family.

These utilitarian and spiritual relationships between place and people have profound, palpable outcomes on ecosystems and landscapes.

SENSE OF PLACE AND CULTURAL IDENTITY

The intrinsic connection people feel to the landscapes they love is rightly called sense of place. Sense of place encompasses one's holistic interpretation of a landscape. We synthesize this meaning from symbols, values, feelings, events, and our knowledge of the land. We layer aesthetics, personal experiences, and cultural activities—as well as social, political, and economic attributes—over the biological and physical setting. Sense of place then speaks to the unique sum of values that individuals, communities, and societies ascribe to their landscape and their relationship with it. And woe be it to anyone who attempts to violate or discount people's sense of place.

Recognition of sense of place may strike some like the proverbial thunderbolt; we fall in love with a place for inexplicable reasons but we know in our heart we belong. Or our sense of place can arise from long familiarity and the continuity of tradition; identification with a culture typically implies identification with place.

The details that allow us to know and recognize cultures are inextricably linked to landscapes because the formative norms of these cultures have all been deeply informed by place. For example, the subject matter and media of art reflect place—think sand paintings, tapa cloth, and Thomas Moran. Ethnic clothing expresses a practical, yet aesthetic, response to place in its material, style, and drape—Bedouin robes, Eskimo parkas, and grass skirts. Native housing, perhaps the most biomimetic response to landscape and climate, repeats locale in siting, design, and materials. Dynamically responsive to its surroundings, traditional architecture is a model of efficiency and elegance—thick adobe walls, steep thatched roofs, tipis, and igloos.

Daily activities resonate with seasons and landscape. The times to hunt, fish, gather, plant, rest, and travel for millennia have been syncopated with the rhythms of place—buffalo migration, salmon runs, snow for the dogsleds.

Ceremonies have grown from respect and gratitude for bounty of the land, the elements that define its character, and the processes that mark the passage of time in place, be it corn or kava, the solstice or rainy season.

Thus, throughout history, people aligned their lives, communities, and customs intimately and intensely with place: as the source of all sustenance and as the framework of their culture.

EVOLUTION AWAY FROM NATURE

It's baffling why, in so short a time, the value of human dependence on and relationship with landscapes has been dismissed in the formation of public policy, implementation of management activities, and societal choices. Of course, science has disabused us of such beliefs as that human malfeasance directly causes tornadoes or solar eclipses. But it remains immutable that our water, air, food, and the basis for most of our shelter and medicine still come directly from nature. Terrifyingly, policy-makers excise sense of place and respect for the environment from their decisions and scorn the small voices speaking for such values.

It seems that the more a society sees itself as cerebral, with clever technological and material innovations, the more its bonds with, and recognition of, the significance of natural processes and ecosystems recede. The ability to create artificial environments (air conditioning, heating, lighting) and chemically alter natural materials (processed food, plastic) perhaps gives the illusion that humans are capable of meeting their needs with minimal inputs from nature. The flawed logic suggests that if humans are only tangentially dependent on the natural world, functioning ecosystems lose importance.

This chasm between humans and nature has widened to the point, especially in developed countries, where ubiquitous pollution and extirpation of species are commonplace—accepted by the masses as a nominal required consequence of economic growth. The conveniences of a "modern" country insulate people; even the most basic needs of water, food, and energy are delivered from a supply chain so long and convoluted that consumers do not associate them with the natural world. Sadly, the deleterious effects on nature of those alienated societies spill into air and oceans that know no boundaries.

Indeed, nature and functioning ecosystems, when thought of at all, are seen as luxuries or impositions: Wilderness is a place for the elite to frolic while sporting expensive clothing and equipment, and open space is idle space. Likewise, protection of the quality and quantity of water in a stream can be accepted as long as it doesn't cost money or hinder the pursuit of money. And wildlife can be tolerated—with the exception of large predators—until it stands in the way of development, often called "progress" but more accurately, habitat demolition.

But progress, while bringing longer human lives and amazing technologies, has come at a very high price. Few want to see or talk about that itemized bill. Government, heavily influenced by industry through lobbying and campaign financing, is reticent to lead in the conservation of natural resources and landscapes, its official responsibility to sustain the values of public land and the commons of air and water. Elected officials do not want to alarm or upset the populace, or take an unpopular position that may compromise their reelection or subsequent careers as corporate lobbyists. Industry wants a steadily increasing cash flow sans environmental regulation. Values-based nongovernmental organizations, with limited resources, focus on a particular issue or campaign. Media chase market share with simplified controversy, infotainment, and a torrent of advertising. And consumers want low prices and wide variety with no impediments to unrestrained consumption.

A plethora of tools exists to shift, defer, extend, redefine, or obfuscate monetary debt. Yet the natural debt does not play by those rules and is going to be called in soon, in the form of rising prices for fossil energy, lack of water to share between all users, and collapse of ecosystems from shocks, such as massive die-off of forests, plankton, and coral.

Perhaps the only hope to find the will and way to implement meaningful solutions to these dilemmas like climate disruption—and the severe perturbations in natural systems it creates—is to reestablish, that is to say, rebalance, the relationship of humans with their landscapes. If we reunderstand humans as part of natural systems, physically and energetically, we then can hope that caring for and sustaining those systems will become a welcome imperative rather than a burdensome imposition. One place to begin is to remember that the rejuvenation and inspiration that nature provides to the human spirit are as important as what its material flows supply to the human body. Understanding where we are now is essential as we map where we need to go.

APPREHENDING APPREHENSION

The petroleum age has greased our feet (bottoms?) and slid us right into the age of apprehension. To apprehend means both "to understand" and "to anticipate with fear." By now, most people understand that we have a societal addiction to oil, especially cheap oil. We've built our American culture on and around inexpensive, high-quality energy.

Collectively, we fear what it's doing to our national security, the climate, and the land, yet that angst is subsumed by the fear of withdrawal from our oil addiction. There is no lack of consensus that we need to use less fossil fuel, but because it may mean changing habits and reducing consumption of all goods we fear doing it. So blame is cast out the front door, generally in the direction of corporations and Middle Eastern countries—and we continue, out the back door, to demand that those dealers feed our addiction.

And just as deftly, the petroleum age has slid us into increasingly severe global dichotomies: excess and scarcity, keen intellect and mass ignorance, high-tech comfort and knife-edge survival. And we apprehend the dichotomies. In journalism, news reports and data, formerly complementary, now compete. In discourse, the line between opinion and fact is blurry, with many people getting off the logic train when they find the station attractive—that is, compatible with their life-view—rather than riding the train to its conclusion. In politics, the gulf between stated intent and actual purpose gapes into a black maw. Who can forget the proposed "Clear Skies Act" designed to waive regulations on air pollution?

Likewise with the land, we find that our conveniently separate venues for organizing mass consumption—established dichotomies that used to provide such comfort and surety—have become murky. We live Here. We get our goods, like oil and cheap gadgets, from Over There, and Away is where things go when we don't want them anymore.

Like our addiction to oil, that stuff we accumulate so voraciously serves as metaphors for what we really want: freedom, comfort, happiness, beauty, security, respect, and love. But reality is clear. The degree to which we use these addictions as substitutes for what we really want is directly proportional to the loss of the same for others Over There. The more we indulge our drive to consume and thus to feel good Here, the more compromised are the land and its people Over There—even if Over There is just across a state line or a North American country's border.

We have learned hard lessons that there is no Away, that vast unseen place to dispose of unwanted or ignored consequences of consumption. Nothing in nature disappears or goes Away, it is just relocated, perhaps in a different form, but it will reappear again, fouling the air, water, food, soil, and shelter for all species, including humans.

This self-induced delusion of separate places on one planet has led to social schizophrenia and divisiveness. We want more and more stuff from Over There, while we try to throw more and more stuff Away. But that pesky junk keeps showing up Here. Unwanted stuff and pesky junk from Over There is coming Here, too, instead of staying Away where it's supposed to. People from Over There try to follow their good stuff Here because they're running out of it Over There and we seem to be pretty intent on getting all of it Here. But we clearly don't want the people from Over There Here. They should all just stay Away.

In our madness, we've failed to see that Here, Over There, and Away are simply one place with interchangeable names. Intellectually we know that the consequences of how we treat the atmosphere, the land, each other, and other species are inescapable; those consequences are all Here, it's all connected, and it's making us crazy.

Just two hundred years ago in the United States, if you couldn't identify sources for water, food, clothing, shelter, energy, and medicine from your immediate landscape, you died. Now, insulated by economics, technology, and social hierarchy, our contact with this chain of sustenance is infrequent and random. Almost none of us know exactly and precisely where our most basic needs come from. We've abrogated our personal responsibilities by delegating someone Over There to find, extract, and send our sustenance to us. At least now we argue that things should be harvested and produced sustainably. But if we know neither the source nor the producers, then how do we know if they are sustainable? Fossil fuels are a stunning example—we continue to use them as if they were cheap and abundant, when in reality they are priceless and diminishing fast.

And yet, no people called "Leaders" are telling us to stop doing this to ourselves and landscapes everywhere. Actually, they're encouraging our delusions by devising even more ways to wring something out of the people and environment Over There. No wonder we're crazy.

Resolution of these dichotomies and our addiction to consumption prompts some vital questions. Can we remap our understanding and appreciation of the world so that Here, Over There, and Away reveal themselves as one? Can we use the power of the land to knit dichotomies of polity and place into meaningful balance? Can conservation and restoration of place become a universal language between cultures and generations?

LAND AS TOUCHSTONE

The answers may well be found in exploring and rebuilding the human relationship to landscapes. As stated earlier, the rejuvenation and inspiration that nature provides to the human spirit are as important as what its physical dimensions supply to the human body. Land can become our touchstone; it's the place we understand, an anchor as we try to remain sane and connected in a maelstrom of change.

Perhaps if we can truly understand what we want and need from landscapes, we will treat them differently. These landscapes aren't just a picturesque backdrop for personal dramas and triumphs or something to buy and sell to finance lifestyles. Landscapes are not just the storehouse of goods and services to keep us happy. This way of thinking disconnects and dislocates us physically and psychologically.

Landscapes do provide the stuff of life—clean air, clean water, carbon sequestration—but what people really want from landscapes are the rejuvenation and inspiration from experience and relationship, food for the soul. This is particularly true of open spaces and undeveloped lands, where we can create memories and gather our stories. Landscapes allow us to experience history, the people and animals who walked this way before us, and to contribute to our collective legacy in walking those same paths.

We get to experience solitude in nature, scaling ourselves within the larger world, finding and exploring life's meaning through nature's metaphors and relationships between the land and its inhabitants. Nature stands as the original "house of worship" providing succor and spiritual sustenance as we contemplate our connectedness to and interdependence on the wonders and mysteries of the web of life.

We revel in the beauty of natural landscapes. Though protecting natural beauty has been routinely dismissed as softheaded or economically onerous, beauty has incalculable worth. Perhaps subtle aspects may be "in the eye of the beholder," but look at the value and power that we ascribe to place and people who are deemed beautiful. A home with a view demands a much higher price than one without. A person with a beautiful spouse or car raises their social standing simply through the acts of association with or possession of beauty. Works of art, deemed beautiful, can fetch millions and have elaborate buildings built to display and protect them. The resort towns of renown are in beautiful natural settings and you pay through the nose just to visit. Simply put, beauty translates to wealth and favor.

Natural beauty in and of itself attracts humans with irresistible force and inspires the spirit to incalculable heights. When one lists the artistic works inspired by nature, one lists the rich pinnacles of human accomplishment and the motives behind much landscape conservation: in this country alone, the paintings of Albert Bierstadt, the prose of Wallace Stegner, the photography of Ansel Adams, the poetry of Emily Dickinson, and the music of Paul Winter.

THE CHALLENGE

Regardless of culture or location, these themes—the value of nature for life-sustaining ecosystem services, inspiration, and identity—remain timeless and universal. We need to grasp this universality as a common point from which to launch serious discussions and negotiations on how we preserve this lifeline, these natural landscapes that sustain us.

But what does that require of us? Let's use Mexico as an example. We in the United States are a society that consumes five times more energy per capita than our neighbor to the south. We can demonstrate our concern for their landscapes if we stop exporting our demands, pollution, and water scarcity across the border and begin respecting our common resources. A simple step is reducing our consumption of energy, water, and products whose manufacture pollutes and compromises the health of people and ecosystems.

Despite an outcry that this will reduce their export revenues, this is a pay-me-now or pay-me-a-lot-more-later situation. For example, the precipitous decline in Mexican oil-field production suggests that what little fossil fuels Mexico has left might be better used to provide for its domestic energy needs for five times longer than it will fulfill ours. To run out of oil in Mexico would mean no income from exports and higher expenditures for imports just to meet domestic energy needs. In desperate situations like that, the quality of landscapes is a low priority. Conversely, a slow descent to less fossil energy, on both sides of the border, will allow communities to assess what they really need. And what we really need are thriving, functioning local landscapes that provide sustenance for physical and psychological comfort and security.

Indeed, remapping our relationship with our landscapes is key to responding to the serious calamities that confront us. Resilience in the face of social upheaval resulting from peaking supplies of traditional energy and climate disruption requires that we protect our landscapes and ensure that the services they provide are sustained. And this will lead to resolution of the deeper chaos of dichotomies, providing protection for the higher values engendered by the human relationship to landscapes—respect; thoughtful design; meaningful discourse; longevity of view; and sustainable, intentional action. We can do this and be better for it, come what may. And it's essential that we act now; the unraveling is well under way.

THE HUMAN NATURE
OF UNSUSTAINABILITY

WILLIAM E. REES, FRSC

WILLIAM REES *is a professor in the School of Community and Regional Planning
at the University of British Columbia. He is best known as the co-originator of
"ecological footprint analysis," a quantitative tool that estimates humanity's ecological impact in terms of appropriated ecosystem area. He is a founding Fellow of the
One Earth Initiative and a founding member and past president of the Canadian
Society for Ecological Economics. In 2006 he was elected to the Royal Society of
Canada. Rees is a Fellow of Post Carbon Institute.*

❖

THE (UN)SUSTAINABILITY CONUNDRUM

In 1992 the Union of Concerned Scientists (UCS) issued the following
gloomy assessment of the prospects for civilization:

> We the undersigned, senior members of the world's scientific
> community, hereby warn all humanity of what lies ahead. A great
> change in our stewardship of the earth and the life on it is required
> if vast human misery is to be avoided and our global home on this
> planet is not to be irretrievably mutilated.[1]

Thirteen years of continuing eco-degradation later, the Millennium Ecosystem Assessment, the most comprehensive assessment of the
state of the ecosphere ever undertaken, was moved to echo the UCS
sentiments:

> At the heart of this assessment is a stark warning. Human activity
> is putting such a strain on the natural functions of the Earth that
> the ability of the planet's ecosystems to sustain future generations
> can no longer be taken for granted.[2]

Just what is going on here? The world's top physicists, ecologists, and climatologists have warned the world repeatedly that current development strategies are undermining global life-support systems, that we have "overshot" long-term global carrying capacity, and that human-induced impacts on global systems threaten catastrophe for billions of people. Yet still the dismal data accumulate with the accelerating loss of ecosystem integrity around the world. Despite decades of rising rhetoric on the risks of global change, no national government, the United Nations, or any other official international organization has seriously begun to contemplate—let alone articulate publicly—the revolutionary policy responses evoked by the scientific evidence.

Humans may pride themselves as being the best evidence for intelligent life on Earth, but an alien observer would record that the (un)sustainability conundrum has the global community floundering in a swamp of cognitive dissonance and collective denial.[3] Indeed, our alien friend might go so far as to ask why our reasonably intelligent species seems unable to recognize the crisis for what it is and respond accordingly.

To begin answering this question, we need to look beyond conventional explanations—scientific uncertainty, societal inertia, lack of political will, resistance by vested interests, and so on—to what may well be the root cause of the conundrum: human nature itself.

UNSUSTAINABLE BY NATURE?

> Let's face it: *Homo economicus* is one hell of an over-achiever. He has invaded more than three-quarters of the globe's surface and monopolized nearly half of all plant life to help make dinner. He has netted most of the ocean's fish and will soon eat his way through the world's last great apes. For good measure, he has fouled most of the world's rivers. And his gluttonous appetites have started a wave of extinctions that could trigger the demise of 25 percent of the world's creatures within 50 years. The more godlike he becomes the less godly *Homo economicus* behaves.
>
> —ANDREW NIKIFORUK[4]

The Russian-born geneticist Theodosius Dobzhansky famously asserted in 1964 that "nothing in biology makes sense except in the light of evolution."[5] *Homo sapiens* is a product of evolution—it follows that the human brain and gene-based elements of individual and social behavior have been as much exposed to Darwinian natural selection as any other genetically influenced human qualities. It is therefore not much of a leap to assert that *nothing in human affairs—including much of economic and socio-political behavior—makes sense except in the light of evolution.*[6] In short, part of the explanation for the global ecological crisis must reside in humanity's genetic endowment.

What can our genes possibly have to do with whether we act sustainably or not? The connection is actually quite simple. There are certain behavioral adaptations that helped our distant ancestors survive—and thus those predilections were passed on to us. But those same (now ingrained) behaviors today are decidedly *not helpful* in solving our sustainability crisis—they have become maladaptive. Moreover, these natural predispositions are *reinforced* by modern humanity's technological prowess and addiction to continuous material growth.[7]

From a systems perspective, we might say that our current "unsustainability" is a product of the natural systems that led to the evolution of *Homo sapiens* together with the resource-intensive societal and economic systems *Homo sapiens* has gone on to create. Nature and nurture have combined to generate a perniciously intractable problem.

This perspective is not rooted in genetic determinism; it by no means denies that other factors contribute to humanity's sustainability dilemma. But unless we factor in the bioevolutionary contribution, our understanding of the modern human predicament will remain unintelligibly incomplete and any "solutions" hopelessly ineffective.

Humanity's Behavioral "Presets"

Humans share two behavioral traits with all other species that are critically important to (un)sustainability. Numerous experiments show that unless or until constrained by negative feedback (e.g., disease, starvation, self-pollution) the populations of all species:

· Expand to occupy all accessible habitats.
· Use all available resources.

Of course, different species use different reproductive strategies to achieve evolutionary success in different ecological settings.[8] Humans, for example, are what biologists call "K-strategists," a distinction we share with other mammals ranging from tapirs through elephants to blue whales. "K" stands for the long-term carrying capacity of an ecosystem; K-strategists are species that tend to have relatively stable populations approaching that carrying capacity. They are typically relatively large-bodied, long-lived, and late-maturing species that have evolved to persist in relatively predictable habitats. They have low reproductive and dispersal rates but also extended parental care and thus high survival rates to maturity and reproduction. Their individual survival and overall evolutionary success depend on competitive superiority at high population densities when resources are scarce.

Given the intense competition for habitat and resources characteristic of K-selected species, natural selection would favor those individuals who are most adept at satisfying their short-term selfish needs, whether by strictly competitive or by cooperative means.[9] Thus, a tendency for instant gratification may actually confer a selective advantage on its possessors compared to individuals with more conservative consumptive patterns. This suggests that humanity's inclination to discount the future—as incorporated into all economic planning models—has actually evolved by natural selection.

How do the well-honed competitive skills of *Homo sapiens* play out in the modern world? C. W. Fowler and L. Hobbs show that in terms of energy use (and therefore carbon dioxide emissions), biomass consumption, and various other ecologically significant indicators, humans' demands on their ecosystems dwarf those of similar species.[10] They find, for example, that the human consumption of biomass is hundreds of times greater than biomass consumption by virtually all the other ecologically similar mammals tested. These and related data show that *Homo sapiens* has become, directly or indirectly, the dominant macro-consumer in all major terrestrial and accessible marine ecosystems on the planet. Indeed, our species may well be the most voraciously successful predatory and herbivorous vertebrate ever to walk the earth.[11]

This very success is now the problem. Humans' competitive drive as K-strategists is relentless; we have no built-in "off" switch tripped by sufficiency. On the contrary, we habituate to any level of consumption (once a given level is attained, satisfaction diminishes) so the tendency to accumulate ratchets up. This is particularly so if we perceive that another social group—or country—is "getting ahead" faster than we are. Even within wealthy societies, widening income gaps lead to personal frustration and declining population health, so efforts to "keep up with the Joneses" continue unabated.[12] It complicates matters that humans' technological capacity to exploit nature now exceeds nature's reproductive capacity. As fish stocks decline, we both invent new fish-finding technologies to chase remaining schools farther and deeper and switch to alternative prey species lower in the food web.

To reiterate: Without powerful restraints, humans—like all other species—exploit all available resources; the difference is that, with people, what is "accessible" is defined by evolving technology.[13]

Sociocultural Reinforcement

Of course, humans are also social animals, so the quest for sustainability depends also on sociocultural factors. We can even discuss cultural "evolution" in terms of Richard Dawkins's concept of the meme.[14] A "meme" is a unit of cultural information (e.g., social norms, shared beliefs, common technologies) that, like a gene, can be passed between generations and influences the cultural phenotype—the outward appearance or expression—of the society concerned.

Memes are the basis of cultural inheritance but actually have an advantage over genes in that they can spread horizontally among living individuals in the *same* generation or population. Thus, cultural evolution is potentially much faster than genetic evolution—witness humanity's ever-accumulating technological tool kit.

What has all this to do with sustainability? The entire world today is in the thrall of a particularly powerful "meme complex" whose effect is to *reinforce* humanity's K-selected expansionist tendencies. The global community shares a socially constructed vision of global development and poverty alleviation centered on unlimited economic expansion fueled by open markets and more liberalized trade.[15] This growth-oriented mythic construct has shaped the lives of more people than any other cultural narrative in all of history.[16]

The concept of perpetual growth has actually taken hold in a remarkably short period of time. Only about eight generations of people have experienced sufficient economic growth or related technological change in their lifetimes to notice it. As an *influential* memetic construct, the growth imperative is actually just two generations old. Only in the 1950s did economic growth emerge from nowhere to become the "supreme overriding objective of policy" in many countries around the world.[17]

The problem for sustainability is that the infinite-growth myth knows no ecological bounds. Mainstream academic models of the economy make no *functional* reference to the ecosystems that contain it.[18] Thus we dismiss collateral damage to "the environment" as mere "negative externalities" that can be corrected by "getting the prices right" (e.g., through pollution charges or taxes). Resource shortages? No matter—we can relieve local shortages through trade, and should the problem be more widespread, we play the technology card—the expansionist myth asserts that human ingenuity will find a substitute for any depleting resource.[19]

Beyond Carrying Capacity: The Eco-footprints of Techno-exuberance

Humanity's unrivaled success as a culturally reinforced K-strategist is clearly revealed by ecological footprint analysis (EFA).[20] For any specified population, EFA estimates the area of productive land and water ecosystems (biocapacity) required to produce the resources that the population consumes and to assimilate some of its wastes.

Consumption varies with income. Thus, while the citizens of rich countries require *per capita* ecological footprints in the range of 4 to 10 global average hectares (10 to 25 acres) to support their lifestyles, the poor subsist on less than half a global average hectare (one acre).[21] EFA thus graphically translates socioeconomic inequity into biophysical terms.

A unique strength of the eco-footprint as a sustainability indicator is that, unlike monetary measures (e.g., GDP per capita) that have no theoretical limits, eco-footprint estimates (demand) can be compared to available supply. For example, EFA shows that densely populated rich countries such as the United Kingdom, the Netherlands, Germany, and Japan have eco-footprints several times larger than their domestic biocapacities.[22] All such countries are running large *ecological deficits* with the rest of the world.

More critically, the average world citizen has an eco-footprint of about 2.7 global average hectares while there are only 2.1 global average hectares of bioproductive land and water per capita on Earth.[23] This means that humanity has already overshot global biocapacity by 30 percent and now lives unsustainably by depleting stocks of "natural capital" (e.g., fish, forests, and soil) and eroding critical life-support functions. EFA also shows that the world's present growth-based approach to global "development" is fatally futile. For example, to extend North Americans' present consumer lifestyles (with an eco-footprint of 9.2 global average hectares) to the entire human family would require the equivalent of three or four additional Earth-like planets (and we have yet to account for the additional 2.5 billion people expected by midcentury).

HUMANITY'S "TRIUNE BRAIN": REASON, EMOTION, AND INSTINCT

The fact that human behavior is influenced by subconscious predispositions does not explain why the defining intelligence of *Homo sapiens* plays so small a role in our collective response to the (un)sustainability conundrum. Part of the reason is the incomplete evolution of human consciousness—*Homo sapiens* is very much a work in progress.

Consider an evolutionary vector that begins with totally subconscious, autonomic, or instinctive behavior and leads ultimately to actions based entirely on conscious intelligence, logical analysis, and free will. Humans like to think that we have arrived at the *free-will* end of this spectrum, but much of modern cognitive science suggests that this is largely illusion. Psychologist Robert Povine argues from the available evidence that the starting assumption in behavioral psychology should be "that consciousness doesn't play a role in human behaviour. This is the conservative position that makes the fewest assumptions."[24] The material basis for the gradient of consciousness is that most complex of evolved organs, the human brain. Neurologist Paul MacLean argued that the human brain has actually evolved in at least three broadly overlapping phases, each with its own anatomical subcomponent having distinct functions, memory, and "intelligence." MacLean referred to the three quasi-independent structures of the human brain as the reptilian or R–complex (the brainstem and cerebellum), the limbic or paleomammalian system, and the neocortex or neomammalian brain.[25] These three sub-brains are concerned with instincts for basic survival, emotions/value judgments, and conscious reasoning, respectively. While MacLean's compartmentalization of the brain may be somewhat simplistic, neurological research generally supports the behavioral implications of the theory.

Whatever the evolutionary details, the nominal sub-brains are intricately interconnected as an integrated whole. The emergent behavior and overall personality of the individual are therefore the blended product of reason, emotion, and instinct. Critically, however, there will be circumstances in which one of the sub-brains, with its distinct capacities and limitations, assumes dominance—*and the individual may not be fully aware of what part of the brain is in control.*

This last point is particularly important in the context of (un)sustainability. Humans "live" in consciousness as conferred by the human neocortex and therefore overestimate the role of mindful intelligence *even as our actions are being controlled by the lower brain centers.* In fact, much of expressed human behavior is shaped by emotions and subconscious mental processes including the innate propensities that qualify *Homo sapiens* as a dogged K-strategist. The problem for sustainability is that "biological drives . . . can be pernicious to rational decision-making in certain circumstances by creating an overriding bias against objective facts."[26] Everyone is aware from personal experience that passion will trump reason in shaping one's responses to emotionally charged or life-threatening encounters. The roles of reason and logic may actually be quite limited and their effect may be relatively trivial in the grand evolutionary context.

The key point for sustainability is that *humanity is a conflicted species.* We are torn on the one hand between what reason and moral judgment say we should do, and on the other hand by what pure emotion and baser instincts command us to do, particularly in stressful circumstances. We therefore cannot assume that *global* society will necessarily deal rationally with the data documenting accelerating global ecological change.

CAN HUMANITY BECOME SUSTAINABLE?

> [For humanity to survive the sustainability crisis] we must rely on highly-evolved genetically-based biological mechanisms, as well as on supra-instinctual survival strategies that have developed in society, are transmitted by culture, and require for their application consciousness, reasoned deliberation and willpower.
>
> —ANTONIO DAMASIO[27]

Homo sapiens is the highly successful product of millions of years of K-selection, but something has gone awry. Certain innate behavioral traits that assured the competitive supremacy, growth, and long-term survival of primitive peoples—for example, the tendencies to act on short-term individual (and tribal) self-interest, to discount the future, and to abide by unifying myths—have become maladaptive in the much changed circumstances on a finite planet *created by the expanding human enterprise itself*. If the world community fails to adapt to these "much changed circumstances" we may be forced to confront the harsh Darwinian reality that both bad genes and inappropriate memes may be *selected out* by an ecosphere in convulsion.

Scientific studies suggest that the only certain way to avoid "irretrievably mutilating" our planetary home may well be through global economic contraction combined with a world program for income/wealth redistribution. Fortunately, with the right policies and incentives, wealthy countries could make the necessary deep cuts in material and energy use in ways that would actually *enhance* their citizens' quality of life.[28] Even the material transition need not be painful—the technology exists today to enable a 75 percent reduction in energy and (some) material consumption without substantially affecting material standards of living.[29]

At this crucial juncture in human evolutionary history, long-term selective advantage may well have shifted from competitive to cooperative genetic predispositions. The question is whether the world community can muster the national and international political will to create the complementary memetic mutations necessary for collective survival in a resource-stressed world.

Improving the prospects for human civilization requires that we organize—globally and consciously—to override those behavioral propensities that have become maladaptive in the modern world. To reduce the human eco-footprint, the fetishistic emphasis in free-market capitalist societies on individualism, competition, greed, and accumulation must be replaced by a reinforced sense of community, generosity, and a sense of sufficiency. All these qualities are part of the human behavioral spectrum—the former reinforce the dumb instincts of primitive K-strategists but the latter must prevail in the interest of collective survival in a crowded world bristling with nuclear weaponry.[30]

It would be naive to think that the creation of a radically new cultural narrative would not be met by strenuous resistance. "Contraction" is not a narrative that resonates with the times. On the contrary, most people are psychologically committed to continuous economic growth, ever-increasing material prosperity, and the myth of progress.

Just how deeply committed we may become has only recently been revealed. Cognitive scientists have determined that cultural norms, beliefs, and values are effectively imprinted on the human brain. In the normal course of a person's development and maturation, repeated social, cultural, and sensory experiences actually help to *shape* the individual's synaptic circuitry in a neural "image" of those experiences. Once entrenched, these neural structures alter the individual's perception of subsequent experiences and information. People seek out experiences that reinforce their preset neural circuitry and select information from their environment that matches these structures. Conversely, "when faced with information that does not agree with their internal structures, they deny, discredit, reinterpret or forget that information."[31]

The lesson here is that any attempt to create a cultural transformation must confront the fact that humans are naturally behaviorally conservative. We are indeed creatures of habit. To reestablish cognitive consonance between ingrained perceptions and new environmental realities requires that affected parties engage in *the willful restructuring of their belief systems and associated neural pathways*. These efforts require conscious effort and will not always be successful: "There are indeed potions in our own bodies and brains capable of forcing on us behaviours that we may or may not be able to suppress by strong resolution."[32] Even when people accept that such a change in their beliefs and their thinking is necessary, the process can be lengthy, difficult, and unpredictable.[33]

It boils down to this: Modern society has been paralyzed by cognitive dissonance, collective denial, and political inertia in dealing with the sustainability conundrum. However, assuming international agreement on the nature of the problem, a global solution is at least theoretically possible. All the world community needs is commitment to a collective solution, unprecedented political will, and the creative engagement of modern communication technologies! These are the minimal cultural tools needed to socially reengineer ourselves, and to educate the next generation from scratch, in a whole new sociocultural paradigm for survival.

Part Eight

ENERGY

MAKING SENSE OF PEAK OIL
AND ENERGY UNCERTAINTY

DANIEL LERCH

DANIEL LERCH *is program director of Post Carbon Institute and the author of* Post Carbon Cities: Planning for Energy and Climate Uncertainty *(2007), the first major guidebook for local governments on peak oil and global warming. He has delivered presentations and workshops on local responses to peak oil to elected officials, planners, and other audiences across the United States, as well as in Canada, the British Isles, and Spain.*

❖

For more than sixty-five years we have designed our communities for oil. We've built nearly 47,000 miles of high-speed interstate highways, a vast continental network for fueling and servicing gasoline-powered vehicles, and millions upon millions of acres of car-dependent suburbs. This gargantuan legacy of long-term investments has all been made with the assumption that the petroleum fuels that make the whole system work will be available and affordable for the foreseeable future.

But global trends of oil supply and demand are changing to such a degree that this assumption is no longer realistic. Far more than a problem of higher prices at the pump, the quickly emerging new energy reality has enormous implications for just about every aspect of our lives. Forward-thinking households, businesses, and governments are now rushing to plan for an unprecedented energy crisis, the first phases of which we are already experiencing.

What lies behind this twenty-first-century energy crisis? Why can't we rely on the market to fix a problem that is ultimately about supply and demand? To make sense of what's going on, we first need to understand some of the basics of how we harness and use energy and the limitations of the various energy resources available to us.

SUPPLY AND DEMAND

Our supply of cheap, easy-to-extract "conventional" oil, from places like the flat plains of Texas and the deserts of Saudi Arabia, is at or near permanent decline[1]; the remaining "unconventional" oil, from places like the tar sands of Canada and the depths of the Gulf of Mexico, is increasingly difficult to find, extract, and refine. At the same time, global demand for petroleum is sky-high at 85 million barrels per day—twice as much as in 1969. That's a lot of oil to keep pouring in to the pipelines to meet "business-as-usual" needs, let alone to meet new demand from growing countries like China and India.

With the conventional oil dwindling and the unconventional oil that's replacing it increasingly problematic, there will inevitably come a point at which the flow of oil from the wells and the refineries will simply be unable to keep up with global demand. The point at which total global oil production cannot grow any further and begins its permanent decline is known as "peak oil," a term that was hardly known outside the petroleum geology field as recently as 2004 but is rapidly attracting attention and concern. A growing number of analysts and government agencies are acknowledging that we will have reached peak oil by 2015, if we haven't reached it already.[2]

A BIG PROBLEM

None of this would be a real concern if the product in question were a market commodity like soybeans or pork bellies: Demand and supply would find a new equilibrium without fundamentally threatening the global economy. Oil, however, is unlike any other commodity in four important ways.

First, oil is absolutely essential to the most basic functions of the industrialized world. Oil is the key raw material for gasoline, diesel, jet fuel, home heating oil, industrial oils, many chemicals, and most plastics. Many key industries are wholly dependent on oil in multiple forms; for example, the modern global system for producing and distributing food uses oil as a fuel for farming and transportation and as a raw material for agrochemicals. Instability in oil supply and price has serious potential consequences for virtually all sectors of the global economy, particularly transportation, agriculture, and manufacturing.

Second, there are currently no viable substitutes for oil at current rates of consumption. Although alternatives to oil do exist for many of its uses, they are generally vastly inferior to oil in their energy content and in the ease with which they can be extracted, transported, and turned into a commercially usable fuel. "Net energy" or "energy returned on (energy) invested" (EROI) refers to the ratio between the energy expended to harvest an energy source and the amount of energy gained from that harvest. All alternative fuels have worse EROIs than conventional oil, and some have such poor net energy that they are practically useless to manufacture (see chapter 18). Even other conventional energy sources—especially coal, natural gas, hydropower, and uranium—face serious constraints as potential replacements for oil as our dominant fuel.[3]

Third, the modern world's complex interfirm and intergovernmental economic relationships, made up of movements of raw materials and goods across the globe, very much depend on the price and availability of oil being relatively predictable. If the price of oil becomes very high or very volatile, or both, the globalized economy as a whole will face fundamental challenges.[4] Indeed, the threat of peak oil is already creating change and uncertainty in diverse sectors of the global economy: As oil prices surged above fifteen-year highs after 2004, beef prices rose rapidly in part because the high energy prices (together with new federal subsidies) spurred farmers to sell more corn to ethanol producers and less to cattle feedlots—a chain of events that few predicted.[5] More worryingly, during the oil price spike of 2008 it became apparent that much of the airline industry simply can't survive in a world where oil costs $110 or more per barrel.[6]

Finally—and in part a result of the previous three qualities—oil is such an intrinsic part of how our world works that Adam Smith's "invisible hand" of the market is simply unable to deal adequately with the threats posed by peak oil. As a 2005 report on peak oil for the U.S. Department of Energy observed:

> Mitigation will require a minimum of a decade of intense, expensive effort, because the scale of liquid fuels mitigation is inherently extremely large. . . . Intervention by governments will be required, because the economic and social implications of oil peaking would otherwise be chaotic.[7]

Modern oil projects take a lot of money (billions) and a lot of time (years) to get from exploration to oil heading to the refinery. As oil prices go up, markets (and oil-producing countries) respond by putting more money into exploration and production. But the combination of the exploration-to-production lag time, the enormous financial risks on big unconventional-oil projects, imperfect information on international oil reserves, and other factors means that the private sector has not yet seen the incentives (and, indeed, may never see them) to respond at a sufficient scale to the multifaceted threats posed by peak oil.[8]

Clearly, peak oil is much, much more than a problem of higher fuel prices. In *Post Carbon Cities*, I used the term "energy uncertainty" to collectively describe the wide and growing range of economic and social uncertainties that are being driven by peak oil. In a similar way, global warming is driving a wide and growing range of economic, social, and of course environmental uncertainties, which I collectively termed "climate uncertainty." "Energy and climate uncertainty" is an important joint frame for understanding and approaching these two crises because our responses to one inevitably affect the other.

WHAT CAN BE DONE?

The private sector is limited in the degree to which it can respond to energy uncertainty. Governments have been slow to recognize the problem and will be unlikely to respond decisively until economic conditions worsen severely. Although energy uncertainty is difficult to address even at the scale of our largest governments and businesses, it is essential that public- and private-sector decision-makers be educated rapidly about the realities of peak oil and what the possible responses are. The other chapters in Part eight of this book provide a basic overview of this information: chapter 17 on the remaining fossil-fuel resources in North America, chapter 18 on the many challenges of developing alternative energy sources, and chapter 19 on the ramifications of peak oil for the economy.

Portions of this chapter originally appeared in Daniel Lerch, *Post Carbon Cities: Planning for Energy and Climate Uncertainty* (Sebastopol, CA: Post Carbon Press, 2007).

HYDROCARBONS IN NORTH AMERICA

J. DAVID HUGHES

DAVID HUGHES *is a geoscientist who has studied the energy resources of Canada for nearly four decades, including thirty-two years with the Geological Survey of Canada as a scientist and research manager. Over the past decade he has researched, published, and lectured widely on global energy and sustainability issues within North America and internationally. He has been interviewed extensively on radio and television, and his work has been featured in* Canadian Business, Walrus *magazine, and Thomas Homer-Dixon's book* Carbon Shift *(2009). Hughes is a Fellow of Post Carbon Institute.*

❖

North America is at the top of the food chain when it comes to consuming energy: Its inhabitants have nearly four times the average global per capita energy consumption.[1] Although Mexicans consume less than the global average, Americans consume 4.5 times and Canadians nearly 6 times as much. In absolute numbers, we in North America consume one-quarter of the world's primary energy production, even though we make up less than 7 percent of the world's population.

North America's massive energy diet is largely made up of hydrocarbons—a full 83 percent comes from oil, gas, and coal, and if we include nuclear energy, 91 percent comes from nonrenewable fuel sources. In 2008, North America consumed 27 percent of the world's oil production, 25 percent of natural gas production, and 18 percent of coal production. Most of the rest of our energy consumption was derived from nuclear power and large hydropower, with renewable energy sources such as biomass, wind, photovoltaics, and geothermal making up less than 2 percent of our total. Moreover, despite a several-fold growth in non–hydropower renewable energy sources,[2] nonrenewable sources are still forecast to supply 88 percent of our primary energy consumption by 2030 (figure 17.1).

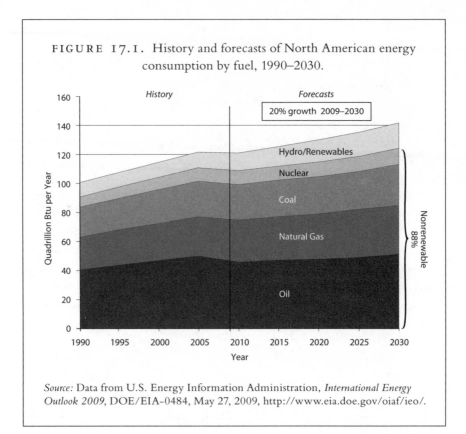

FIGURE 17.1. History and forecasts of North American energy consumption by fuel, 1990–2030.

Source: Data from U.S. Energy Information Administration, *International Energy Outlook 2009*, DOE/EIA-0484, May 27, 2009, http://www.eia.doe.gov/oiaf/ieo/.

The sheer scale of our dependency on nonrenewable, energy-dense "fossilized sunshine" is often lost on those who believe that renewable energy sources can supplant hydrocarbons at anything like today's level of energy consumption. Thus it is prudent to examine the prognosis for fossil fuels within North America, as they will make up the bulk of our energy consumption for many decades to come.[3] The North American fossil-fuel story is largely driven by consumption in the United States, the biggest user of energy in the world and, until China overtook it in 2006, the biggest carbon dioxide emitter. Also critical to this story is the vulnerability of the U.S. economy given its addiction to hydrocarbons. It is highly dependent on imported oil and may soon be dependent on imported natural gas. For these reasons, this chapter will focus primarily on the future availability and vulnerability of supplies of hydrocarbons to the United States, and will look in detail at oil, natural gas, and coal.

OIL

Oil is a globally traded and priced commodity. Nonetheless, oil produced at home is much preferable from the point of view of one's national trade balance, and imported oil from secure and reliable sources is much preferable to that from less reliable and potentially hostile sources. Oil consumption in the United States grew by 69 percent from 1965 through 2008, with notable drops following the oil embargo in the late 1970s and during the recession that started in 2008. Domestic oil production peaked in 1970, however, and in 2008 about 65 percent of U.S. oil consumption was imported.[4]

New U.S. oil discoveries, such as "deep-water" offshore oil in the Gulf of Mexico and shale oil in the Bakken Formation of Montana and North Dakota, are sometimes touted as panaceas to offset declines in domestic production. In reality, however, these discoveries will add relatively little supply compared to the country's massive annual consumption of 7 billion barrels, as the Gulf of Mexico is very expensive and time consuming to develop, and the Bakken Formation oil is produced at low rates and has been estimated to contain only 4.3 billion barrels or less of recoverable oil.[5] Oil shales in Colorado and Wyoming, although purported to have massive in-place resources, are expensive and logistically challenging to extract and process, and are expected to have limited flow rates and a very low net-energy profit, should they ever be proved to be commercially viable.[6] Ultimately, the potential flow rate of a resource is more important than its purported size—and the reality is that the flow rates of North American unconventional-oil sources and oil in difficult locations (such as deep water offshore) cannot be scaled up rapidly enough to significantly compensate for declines in the flow rate of conventional oil.

There are geopolitical and economic risks to being dependent on imports for two-thirds of consumption. The Organization of the Petroleum Exporting Countries (OPEC) cartel provided 46 percent of U.S. oil imports in 2008 (table 17.1). Of the major non-OPEC exporters, only Canada and Brazil—comprising 21.3 percent of 2008 imports—likely have the ability to increase exports significantly. Although non-OPEC exporter Mexico is the third-ranked source of U.S. imports, it is in steep decline as its Cantarell field (formerly the second-largest producer in the world) has plunged from more than 2 million barrels per day (bpd) in 2005 to half a million bpd at present.[7]

TABLE 17.1. Top Crude Oil and Petroleum
Product Exporters to the United States, 2008

(OPEC countries denoted by asterisk)

Country	Exports to U.S. in 2008 (thousand barrels per day)
Canada	2,499
Saudi Arabia*	1,534
Mexico	1,305
Venezuela*	1,192
Nigeria*	991
Iraq*	628
Algeria*	550
Angola*	514
Russia	466
Virgin Islands	321
Brazil	259
United Kingdom	237
Ecuador*	221
Kuwait*	211
Colombia	201
Other (80 countries)	1,821
Total	12,951

Source: Data from U.S. Energy Information Administration, "U.S. Imports by Country of Origin," June 29,
2009, http://tonto.eia.doe.gov/dnav/pet/pet_move
_impcus_a2_nus_ep00_im0_mbbl_a.htm.

Canada is the largest oil supplier to the United States.[8] Canadian
conventional-oil production peaked back in the 1970s, but Canadian oil
production is still big business, and its future is focused on the tar sands of
Alberta. As recently as 2007, Canada's National Energy Board (NEB) was
highly optimistic about the tar sands, forecasting a near *tripling* of production from 1.4 million bpd at present to 4.15 million bpd by 2030.[9] But in
July 2009, owing to the suspension of several projects due to the 2008
economic downturn, NEB forecast a comparatively restrained doubling
of tar-sands output by 2020.[10] The Canadian Association of Petroleum
Producers, noted for its bullish forecasts, is similarly now more restrained
and forecasting an increase to 3.2 million bpd by 2025.[11] Given some of
the new environmental regulations being implemented for the tar sands,

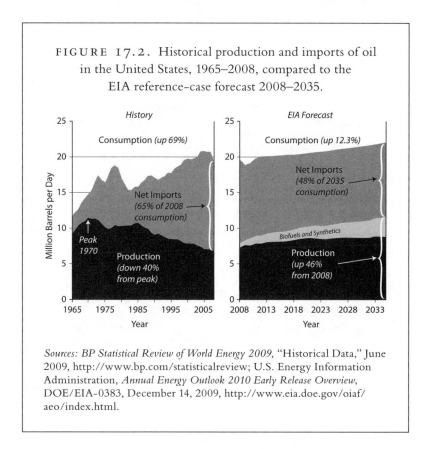

FIGURE 17.2. Historical production and imports of oil in the United States, 1965–2008, compared to the EIA reference-case forecast 2008–2035.

Sources: BP Statistical Review of World Energy 2009, "Historical Data," June 2009, http://www.bp.com/statisticalreview; U.S. Energy Information Administration, Annual Energy Outlook 2010 Early Release Overview, DOE/EIA-0383, December 14, 2009, http://www.eia.doe.gov/oiaf/aeo/index.html.

including tailings and carbon management (which will increase cost and make this poor net-energy source of liquids even worse), these forecasts are still highly optimistic.

Forecasts of future energy supply that merely extrapolate consumption trends from the past, with the assumption that new supplies will somehow miraculously be available, are trademarks of government energy reports such as those from the International Energy Agency (IEA) of the Organisation for Economic Co-operation and Development (OECD), the United States' Energy Information Administration (EIA), and Canada's NEB. One example is illustrated in figure 17.2, which is the EIA's reference case for liquids supply (i.e., all liquid petroleum and natural gas liquid products) in the United States through 2035 compared to actual supply for the previous four decades. The EIA apparently assumes that the geology of the United States' oil provinces, with production long in decline, will miraculously heal itself, and production will go up through 2035. This, coupled with a forecast rapid growth in biofuels (mainly ethanol of dubious net-energy content), serves to decrease imports in the forecast from 65 percent of consumption at present to 48 percent in 2035, even though consumption rises by 12.3 percent over this period. The old adage "if it seems too good to be true then it probably is" comes to mind.

The EIA's forecasts are used to inform government and the general public on future energy-supply issues. In light of what we know of global peak-oil issues (i.e., the increasing cost and diminishing quality and deliverability of the world's oil sources), these reports unfortunately promote complacency and hence squander valuable time to mitigate the impacts of declining supply in the belief that all is well on the energy front. Kjell Aleklett, leader of the Global Energy Systems research group at Uppsala University in Sweden, has stated that the head of the EIA is "one of the world's most dangerous people."[12] A clear view of the realities of future oil supply is crucial—rosy forecasts may serve the immediate needs of bureaucrats and politicians but are a travesty when considering the consequences of the lost opportunity of time and capital in managing a transition to a more sustainable future.

NATURAL GAS

The United States consumed 22 percent of global natural gas production in 2008. Unlike oil, natural gas is not a globally priced commodity but rather is continentally priced because of the expense and logistical difficulty of moving it across oceans as liquefied natural gas (LNG). LNG accounted for about 8 percent of global gas consumption and less than 2 percent of U.S. consumption in 2008. Thus most natural gas consumption in the United States is from domestic production and pipeline imports from Canada. Gas consumption in the United States reached a recent peak of 23.3 trillion cubic feet in 2000. Consumption has declined in all sectors except electricity generation since then, although its use has been rising again recently. The industrial sector, comprising petrochemical, fertilizer, and other industries, declined the most as volatile and often high gas prices pushed factories offshore.

Gas production in the United States hit an all-time high in 1973 and then declined, but has been rising to near 1973 levels recently owing to the development of unconventional gas (i.e., shale gas) and unprecedented amounts of drilling. This does not imply a long-term solution to production declines, however. Depletion rates of gas wells are much higher than those of oil wells—overall decline rates averaged 32 percent per year for the lower forty-eight states in 2006.[13] This means that one-third of gas production must be replaced each year by more drilling, and that 60 percent of current lower-forty-eight gas production comes from wells drilled and connected in the previous four years. Unconventional production from shale-gas wells has much higher decline rates than conventional-gas wells, typically in the range of 65 to 80 percent in their first year of production, suggesting that the increased reliance on shale gas going forward is likely to accelerate the overall rate of U.S. gas depletion.[14]

This has contributed to what I refer to as the "exploration treadmill": more and more drilling to keep production flat, let alone growing (figure 17.3). The number of successful gas wells drilled each year has tripled since 1999, yet production has grown by only 15 percent. Active-rig counts (the number of rigs drilling for gas) peaked in late August 2008 and had collapsed by 56 percent by the fall of 2009 (the drop in successful gas wells is just visible in the left-hand chart), a dip that will likely show up in declining U.S. gas production by mid-2010. This exploration treadmill is just as pronounced in Canada, which is the main source of gas imports to the United States. Even though Canadian successful gas-well completions are nearly triple what they were in 1996, and were at one point in 2004 nearly quadruple, Canadian gas production is now declining at 7.5 percent per year, and Canada's ability to export any gas by 2030 is seriously in doubt.[15]

Nonetheless, there is a wave of hype promoting natural gas as a panacea to offset the United States' extreme vulnerability to imported oil. The natural gas industry has established a new lobbying group in Washington called America's Natural Gas Alliance, in addition to the existing American Clean Skies Foundation, which was chaired by Chesapeake Energy's CEO Aubrey McClendon until December 2009.[16] This hype on the ability of natural gas to fuel business as usual for a very long time, including replacing imported oil, is based on shale gas, a resource made accessible by new technology involving horizontal drilling and multiple hydraulic fracture treatments. Chesapeake is a major shale-gas producer, and the ultimate natural gas optimist is McClendon himself, who testified to Congress on July 30, 2008:

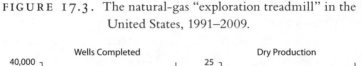

FIGURE 17.3. The natural-gas "exploration treadmill" in the United States, 1991–2009.

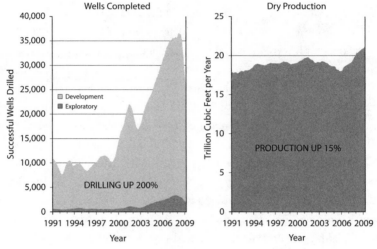

Note: The level of effort quantified by the number of wells drilled has tripled, yet production has risen by only 15 percent.

Sources: Drilling data from U.S. Energy Information Administration, "Crude Oil and Natural Gas Exploratory and Development Wells," http://tonto.eia .doe.gov/dnav/pet/pet_crd_wellend_s1_m.htm; production data through October 2009 from U.S. Energy Information Administration, "Natural Gas Monthly," http://www.eia.doe.gov/natural_gas/data_publications/natural _gas_monthly/ngm.html.

I believe natural gas can and should be the driving force for how this Congress can take bold action to free our country from the death grip of high prices for imported oil, thereby improving our economy, enhancing national security and helping the environ- ment. It's a trifecta, triple play and hat trick all rolled into one. . . . I believe U.S. natural gas producers can increase supplies by 5% per year for at least the next decade and that assumes there is no more access to public lands and waters than there is today.[17]

The hype on shale gas as a silver bullet is pervasive. T. Boone Pickens and McClendon have promoted the natural gas panacea in ads on CNN and elsewhere for the Pickens Plan.[18] Actor Tommy Lee Jones was even brought into the fray in 2008 promoting shale gas, and Shale TV, a station dedicated to promoting shale gas in Texas and funded by Chesapeake, was about to be launched until the economy rolled over in the fall of 2008. In Canada, even though gas production is dropping at 7.5 percent per year, Pacific Trail Pipelines is planning on building a 463-kilometer pipeline to connect to a proposed liquefaction facility on the West Coast to export gas it envisages coming from shale gas in northeastern British Columbia (which has little production at present).[19]

So what are the realities behind shale gas, which now accounts for 14 percent of U.S. production? As of mid-2009 the Barnett shale-gas play (i.e., the production operation), which in part underlies the Dallas–Fort Worth metro area in Texas, accounted for 64 percent of U.S. shale-gas production, a significant part of the remainder being Antrim shale gas in Michigan, which has been in decline for many years. The Barnett play peaked, as predicted, in the first quarter of 2009, by which time more than 12,000 wells had been drilled at a cost of $2 million to $4 million each. Decline rates in the Barnett are typically 65 percent in the first year but initial production rates are high. Other shale plays throughout the United States are having similar experiences of high initial productivities, but also high decline rates and challenging economics. The Haynesville play of east Texas and Louisiana, for example, experienced decline rates of over 80 percent in the first year, and a sky-high cost of up to $10 million per well.[20] In addition, the environmental impacts of shale-gas drilling are coming under increasing scrutiny: Two to five million gallons of water are required *per well* in the Barnett, a third of which is recovered and must be disposed of, with potential impacts on aquifers.

Arthur Berman, a geological analyst formerly with *World Oil* magazine, has done some very insightful analyses of shale-gas potential in the Barnett, Haynesville, and other plays. He has found that decline rates, well lifetimes, and ultimate recoverable reserves for shale-gas wells in these plays have been optimistically assessed, to say the least.[21] Assumptions of production profiles over well life, compared to actual measurements, suggest ultimate recoverable reserves per well are a *third* of what is commonly quoted, and well life spans could average eight years, not forty years as is commonly assumed. Berman has stated, among other things:

> I am disturbed that public companies and investment analysts make
> fantastic claims about the rates and reserves for new shale plays with-

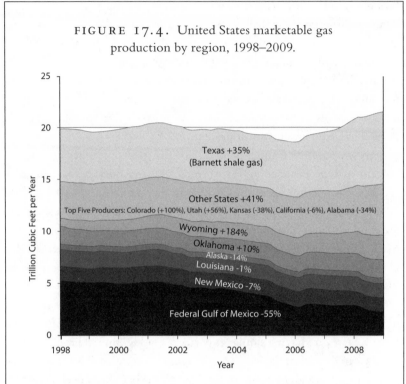

FIGURE 17.4. United States marketable gas production by region, 1998–2009.

Source: U.S. Energy Information Administration, data through October 2009 from "Natural Gas Monthly," http://www.eia.doe.gov/natural_gas/data_publications/natural_gas_monthly/ngm.html.

out calibrating them to the only play that has significant production history. . . . Almost every assumption used by the industry to support predictions about the Haynesville or Marcellus shale plays is questionable based on well performance in the Barnett shale.

Berman was a contributing editor for *World Oil* magazine until November 2009 when he resigned after his column was canceled over protests from shale-gas producers, whose stock price and stock issues for raising capital depend on a gung-ho worldview of shale-gas potential. Berman's editor was subsequently fired over the issue.[22] Stifling analysis and debate on such a crucial issue is disturbing considering its importance for planning future energy security. Much more will be known about the

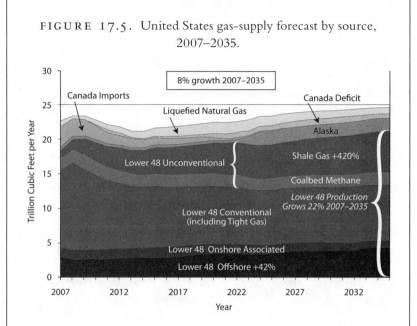

FIGURE 17.5. United States gas-supply forecast by source, 2007–2035.

Sources: U.S. Energy Information Administration, *Annual Energy Outlook 2010 Early Release Overview*, DOE/EIA-0383, December 14, 2009, http://www.eia.doe.gov/oiaf/aeo/index.html; Canada deficits based on projections of the Canada National Energy Board, *Energy Outlook*, November 2007, http://www.neb-one.gc.ca/clf-nsi/rnrgynfmtn/nrgyrprt/nrgyftr/nrgy ftr-eng.html#s4.

true potential of shale gas in plays outside of the Barnett in two to four years.

When it comes to the forecasts our leaders use to assess what lies ahead in terms of natural gas supply, the situation is very similar to that previously described for oil. Figure 17.4 illustrates what has actually happened with natural gas in the United States over the past decade. Production (both conventional and unconventional) in Colorado, Wyoming, and Texas has been increasing, whereas production in Kansas, Alabama, Louisiana, and New Mexico has been declining, and Gulf of Mexico production fell by more than 50 percent. But looking forward, the EIA provides basically another no-worries forecast (figure 17.5) through 2035, with shale gas growing more than fivefold, a miraculous reversal in the geological fortunes of the Gulf of Mexico, and an overall growth in lower-forty-eight production of 22 percent by 2035.

This forecast is based on the following premises, which may prove to be unwarranted:

1. Drilling rates after a decline due to the current economic recession will be ramped up to equal and higher levels than those at their all-time peak (more than 36,000 successful gas wells per year in 2008), resulting in nearly *one million* new gas wells drilled by 2035.

2. The observed "exploration treadmill" of declining average well productivity will cease to operate and in fact will reverse itself, as yet more wells are crowded into available prospects.

3. Shale gas will live up to the hype, despite high decline rates, high costs, and significant associated environmental issues.

Such forecasts do not reflect the underlying uncertainties controlling future gas supply and, in my view, are unhelpful in putting together a coherent plan for a sustainable energy future as they lull policy-makers into a false sense of security.

In the likely event that EIA forecasts of gas supply do not materialize, imports of LNG will be needed. Much new LNG receiving capacity has been built in the United States over the past few years and at present is highly underutilized. The real story of LNG, however, is global liquefaction capacity, which is much less than global re-gasification capacity. As well as adding geopolitical complications to the gas trade (complications that have long been a fact of life with oil but so far have not been a serious issue for gas), LNG will very likely be a higher-cost supply source because a spot market is developing and the gas will be sold to the highest bidder. LNG is also an unfriendly source of gas from the point of view of net energy and greenhouse gas emissions, as 15 to 30 percent of the energy in the gas is consumed in the liquefaction, transportation, and re-gasification process.

COAL

The United States could be said to be a Saudi Arabia of coal as it controls some 29 percent of world resources. The United States produces over a billion metric tons of coal per year, a distant second only to China, which produces more than 2.7 billion metric tons per year. Half of the electricity generated in the United States is fueled by coal, much of it in older plants with less than optimal controls on emissions. In addition, the United States produces more than 60 million metric tons of high-quality metallurgical coal each year, which is used in steel making. Metallurgical coal is indispensable in the steel industry, and hence underlies much of the infrastructure of modern society.

In the United States, much of the higher-energy-content coal is mined in Appalachia, which produces bituminous thermal- and metallurgical-grade coals from underground mines and by "mountaintop-removal" surface operations that have major environmental impacts.[23] Declining Appalachian production is being made up from very large-scale and mainly surface mining operations in the West, in particular the Powder River Basin of Wyoming, which produces more than 400 million metric tons per year from very thick seams of low-sulfur, sub-bituminous coal. Owing to the decline in production of the high-heating-value coals of Appalachia and their replacement with the lower-heating-value coals of Wyoming and other regions, the United States experienced a recent peak in the *energy content* of extracted coal in 1998 even though the total amount of coal extracted increased through 2008 (although it dropped significantly in 2009).

Several studies have recently been published on "peak coal," the point at which global coal deliverability will begin an inexorable decline, likely in the 2020–2030 time frame. These studies are nicely summarized in Richard Heinberg's book *Blackout* and hence will not be dealt with further here, except to say that the conventional wisdom of coal being a fuel for the long haul has been found severely wanting.[24] Another excellent in-depth review of U.S. coal resources and other coal issues has been written by Leslie Glustrom.[25]

The United States has been a major coal exporter in the past (over 12 percent of total production in the early 1980s), but more recently it has been importing ever-larger quantities of mostly thermal coal (for power generation), mainly from Colombia and Indonesia, although it is still a minor net exporter (59 million tons in 2009). When it comes to future forecasts of coal production in the United States, the EIA provides, as with oil and natural gas, yet another no-worries forecast.[26] Figure 17.6

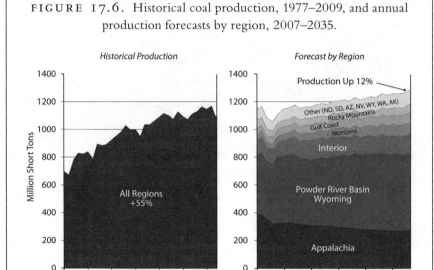

FIGURE 17.6. Historical coal production, 1977–2009, and annual production forecasts by region, 2007–2035.

Sources: U.S. Energy Information Administration, "Monthly Energy Report: Coal," February 26, 2010, http://www.eia.doe.gov/emeu/mer/coal.html; U.S. Energy Information Administration, supplementary tables 120 and 121 in *Annual Energy Outlook 2010 Early Release Overview*, DOE/EIA-0383, December 14, 2009, http://www.eia.doe.gov/oiaf/aeo/index.html.

illustrates the EIA's reference-case forecasts for coal production by region compared to historical production. Coal production is forecast to grow from the lower-quality deposits in the West and decline in the mature mining region of Appalachia.

Whether U.S. coal production can be ramped up by 12 percent, as in the EIA forecast, or even maintained is questionable. It would certainly require major new investments in mines and transportation infrastructure as the infrastructure for moving coal from the Powder River Basin, for example, is at maximum capacity. Given the issues with supply of natural gas discussed earlier, and challenges with the scaling up of renewables, there will clearly be a role for coal in the transition to a more sustainable energy future. However, the current focus on carbon capture and storage (CCS) with its parasitic energy losses and high capital costs is, in my opinion, the wrong way to go. Energy losses for CCS amount to 30 percent of the energy produced in a typical coal plant, requiring an increased burn rate for the same amount of electricity, which accelerates the consumption of a nonrenewable resource. Moreover, the capital costs for CCS infrastructure can be 50 percent of the cost of a plant—money that could be better invested in infrastructure to provide an alternative to high-energy throughput lifestyles.[27]

Coal is a low-value fuel compared to natural gas or oil because it is less versatile in its potential applications without significant energy-conversion losses and costs. High-efficiency configurations of coal-fired generation with heat capture ("combined heat and power," or CHP) have the potential to double the efficiency of coal plants and eliminate the consumption of hydrocarbons that would otherwise be required to generate that heat (thereby also radically reducing emissions). The issue of coal use is often fraught with emotion. However, considering the scale of its contribution to U.S. energy supply, and the lack of scalable alternatives, it is unlikely that it can be completely phased out in the foreseeable future. Coal must therefore be used in its highest-efficiency and lowest-emitting configurations.

THE SCALING DILEMMA

Hydrocarbons have a role in every aspect of modern life, including building materials, transportation, food, communication, electricity, and so forth. The scale at which hydrocarbons are consumed to fuel the global economy as currently structured makes it impossible to conceive of alternatives to replace them at that scale; clearly a more sustainable future necessitates a radical reduction in the amount of energy consumed. Renewable sources of energy, which must contribute to a solution, are still dependent on hydrocarbons for their manufacture.

Then there is the issue of energy quality. Renewable sources of energy such as wind or photovoltaics are intermittent and unpredictable—their actual generation is typically a third or less of their rated capacity, and hence they require backup by reliable generation sources, usually fueled by hydrocarbons. Our electricity infrastructure is tasked to provide uninterrupted service at all hours to all users, no matter how high the demand—it is highly unlikely that it can be converted to renew-

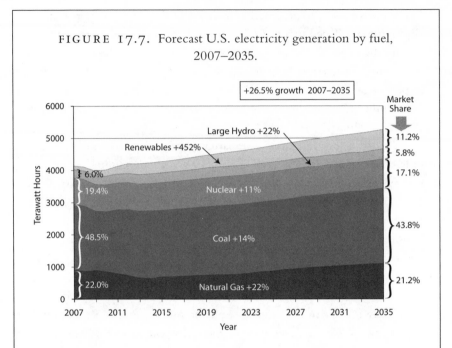

FIGURE 17.7. Forecast U.S. electricity generation by fuel, 2007–2035.

Source: U.S. Energy Information Administration, supplementary table 85 in *Annual Energy Outlook 2010 Early Release Overview*, DOE/EIA-0383, December 14, 2009, http://www.eia.doe.gov/oiaf/aeo/index.html.

able energy at anything like the scale of electricity consumption we enjoy today because of the intrinsic limitations of renewables and the massive scale required. The concept that we can maintain our current massive transportation infrastructure by converting from vehicles that run on liquid petroleum products to those that use electricity or natural gas is likely doomed to failure—we need to rethink our transportation requirements to have a much lower energy footprint.

Although electricity generation is only a fraction of the work hydrocarbons perform for us, it is particularly instructive to examine the role of hydrocarbons in electricity generation to appreciate the daunting scale of replacing them with alternatives at present consumption levels going forward. The EIA forecasts U.S. electricity generation to increase by nearly 27 percent from 2007 to 2035 (figure 17.7). Hydrocarbons account for 71 percent of electricity generation at present, with coal being nearly half—

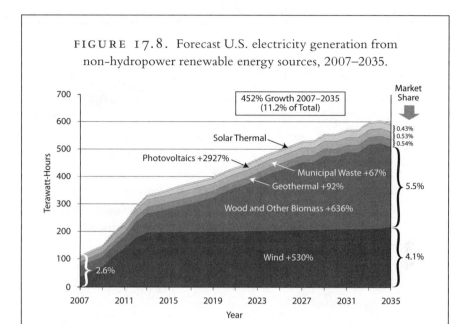

FIGURE 17.8. Forecast U.S. electricity generation from non-hydropower renewable energy sources, 2007–2035.

Source: U.S. Energy Information Administration, supplementary table 101 in *Annual Energy Outlook 2010 Early Release Overview*, DOE/EIA-0383, December 14, 2009, http://www.eia.doe.gov/oiaf/aeo/index.html.

and by 2035 they are expected to still be the main power source, at 65 percent of total generation and with coal comprising 44 percent. A massive 452 percent increase in the capacity of non-hydro renewables, if achieved, would make up only just over 11 percent of total electricity-generation market share. Large hydropower is also forecast to grow but lose market share owing to a lack of remaining developable sites, as is nuclear due to the enormous challenges and expense of refurbishing and/or replacing the aging U.S. nuclear fleet.

The prognosis for non-hydropower renewable sources is particularly at odds with the popular vision of our future economy being powered by wind turbines and solar panels (figure 17.8). The largest single source of renewable energy is actually forecast to be wood and other biomass, growing more than sevenfold to serve 5.5 percent of total market share, followed by a sixfold growth in wind to 4.1 percent of market share. Solar photovoltaics are forecast to grow by thirty times, but even then they would contribute only less than half a percent of forecast generation.

This illustrates the scaling dilemma society faces in replacing hydrocarbons in our current business-as-usual mode of energy consumption. Even with a radical scale-up, non-hydropower renewables are forecast to make up less than 12 percent of electricity generation in 2035, and a much smaller proportion of total energy consumption. The fossilized sunshine that hydrocarbons represent is an extremely convenient, dense form of energy for which there are no alternatives at the scale of energy throughput we enjoy at this point in humanity's existence. Forecasts of continuing availability of hydrocarbons for the next couple of decades for business-as-usual levels of consumption are tenuous at best and wishful thinking at worst. Solutions to the pending decline in the availability of hydrocarbons rest on rethinking and radically reducing our levels of energy consumption and developing the infrastructure for alternatives to lifestyles now based on cheap energy.

NINE CHALLENGES OF
ALTERNATIVE ENERGY

DAVID FRIDLEY

DAVID FRIDLEY *has been a staff scientist at the Energy Analysis Program at the Lawrence Berkeley National Laboratory in California since 1995. He has nearly thirty years of experience working and living in China in the energy sector and is a fluent Mandarin speaker. He spent twelve years working in the petroleum industry both as a consultant on downstream oil markets and as business development manager for Caltex China. He has written and spoken extensively on the energy and ecological limits of biofuels. Fridley is a Fellow of Post Carbon Institute.*

❖

The scramble for alternatives is on. High oil prices, growing concerns over energy security, and the threat of climate change have all stimulated investment in the development of alternatives to conventional oil. "Alternative energy" generally falls into two categories:

- Substitutes for existing petroleum liquids (ethanol, biodiesel, biobutanol, dimethyl ether, coal-to-liquids, tar sands, oil shale), both from biomass and fossil feedstocks.
- Alternatives for the generation of electric power, including power-storage technologies (wind, solar photovoltaics, solar thermal, tidal, biomass, fuel cells, batteries).

The technology pathways to these alternatives vary widely, from distillation and gasification to bioreactors of algae and high-tech manufacturing of photon-absorbing silicon panels. Many are considered "green" or "clean," although some, such as coal-to-liquids and tar sands, are "dirtier" than the petroleum they are replacing. Others, such as biofuels, have concomitant environmental impacts that offset potential carbon savings.

Unlike conventional fossil fuels, where nature provided energy over millions of years to convert biomass into energy-dense solids, liquids, and gases—requiring only extraction and transportation technology for us to mobilize them—alternative energy depends heavily on specially engineered equipment and infrastructure for capture or conversion, essentially making it a high-tech manufacturing process. However, the full supply chain for alternative energy, from raw materials to manufacturing, is still very dependent on fossil-fuel energy for mining, transport, and materials production. Alternative energy faces the challenge of how to supplant a fossil-fuel-based supply chain with one driven by alternative energy forms themselves in order to break their reliance on a fossil-fuel foundation.

The public discussion about alternative energy is often reduced to an assessment of its monetary costs versus those of traditional fossil fuels, often in comparison to their carbon footprints. This kind of reductionism to a simple monetary metric obscures the complex issues surrounding the potential viability, scalability, feasibility, and suitability of pursuing specific alternative technology paths. Although money is necessary to develop alternative energy, money is simply a token for mobilizing a range of resources used to produce energy. At the level of physical requirements, assessing the potential for alternative energy development becomes much more complex since it involves issues of end-use energy requirements, resource-use trade-offs (including water and land), and material scarcity.

Similarly, it is often assumed that alternative energy will seamlessly substitute for the oil, gas, or coal it is designed to supplant—but this is rarely the case. Integration of alternatives into our current energy system will require enormous investment in both new equipment and new infrastructure—along with the resource consumption required for their manufacture—at a time when capital to make such investments has become harder to secure. This raises the question of the suitability of moving toward an alternative energy future with an assumption that the structure of our current large-scale, centralized energy system should be maintained. Since alternative energy resources vary greatly by location, it may be necessary to consider different forms of energy for different localities.

It is not possible to single out one metric by which to assess the promise of a particular alternative energy form. The issue is complex and multifaceted, and its discussion is complicated by political biases, ignorance of basic science, and a lack of appreciation of the magnitude of the problem. Many factors come into play, of which nine are discussed here.

I. SCALABILITY AND TIMING

For the promise of an alternative energy source to be achieved, it must be supplied in the time frame needed, in the volume needed, and at a reasonable cost. Many alternatives have been successfully demonstrated at the small scale (algae-based diesel, cellulosic ethanol, biobutanol, thin-film solar) but demonstration scale does not provide an indication of the potential for large-scale production. Similarly, because alternative energy relies on engineering and construction of equipment and manufacturing processes for its production, output grows in a stepwise function only as new capacity comes online, which in turn is reliant on timely procurement of the input energy and other required input materials. This difference between "production" of alternative energy and "extraction" of fossil fuels can result in marked constraints on the ability to increase the production of an alternative energy source as it is needed.

For example, the tar sands of Canada (although often excluded as an "alternative" energy, tar sands are subject to the same constraints because the production of oil from the tar-sands deposits is essentially a mining and manufacturing operation) have already achieved a fully commercial scale of production, and because of the immense reserves indicated in Alberta, tar sands are looked to be a backstop to declining conventional crude oil production. In 2008, production of oil from the tar sands reached 1.2 million barrels per day (bpd), less than 2 percent of global production of conventional crude oil. By 2020, the Canadian Association of Petroleum Producers projects that production will increase by 2.1 million bpd to a total of 3.3 million bpd.[1] But the International Energy Agency (IEA) estimates that the global decline rate from conventional-oil fields is 6.4 percent, or about 4.8 million bpd per year.[2] Thus by 2020, the new oil coming from tar-sands production will not even make up half of what is being lost from ongoing depletion of existing conventional-oil fields. Even with a "crash" production program, it is estimated that tar-sands production in 2020 could not exceed 4.0 million bpd, an increase still less than the annual rate of conventional crude oil depletion.[3]

Scale also matters in comparing projected production of an alternative energy form against expected demand growth. In 2007, the U.S. Energy Policy Act established a target for the production of ethanol in 2022 at 36 billion gallons, of which 15 billion gallons were to be sourced from corn and the remainder from cellulosic sources. In terms of gasoline equivalency, this target is equal to 890,000 bpd of additional supply. In 2008, however, the U.S. Department of Energy, in its *Annual Energy Outlook*, forecast demand for gasoline would grow by 930,000 bpd by 2022,[4] more than offsetting projected supply growth from ethanol and leaving gross oil dependency unchanged.

This lack of the kind of scalability needed given the magnitude and time frame of conventional-oil depletion and in the face of continued demand growth is found as well in other biofuels, coal-to-liquids, and alternative liquids for transportation. Also of concern is the difficulty of scaling up alternative energy quickly enough to meet greenhouse gas emissions targets.

2. COMMERCIALIZATION

Closely related to the issue of scalability and timing is commercialization, or the question of how far away a proposed alternative energy source stands from being fully commercialized. Often, newspaper reports of a scientific laboratory breakthrough are accompanied by suggestions that such a breakthrough represents a possible "solution" to our energy challenges. In reality, the average time frame between laboratory demonstration of feasibility and full large-scale commercialization is twenty to twenty-five years. Processes need to be perfected and optimized, patents developed, demonstration tests performed, pilot plants built and evaluated, environmental impacts assessed, and engineering, design, siting, financing, economic, and other studies undertaken. In other words, technologies that are proved feasible on the benchtop today will likely have little impact until the 2030s. This reality is reflected in the key message of the now-famous Hirsch Report, which noted that to properly mitigate the economic impacts of peak oil, we would have needed to start fundamentally redesigning our national energy infrastructure *twenty years* in advance of the peak.[5]

3. SUBSTITUTABILITY

Ideally, an alternative energy form would integrate directly into the current energy system as a "drop-in" substitute for an existing form without requiring further infrastructure changes. This is rarely the case, and the lack of substitutability is particularly pronounced in the case of the electrification of transportation, such as with electric vehicles. Although it is possible to generate the electricity needed for electrified transportation from wind or solar power, the prerequisites to achieving this are extensive. Electric-car development would require extensive infrastructure changes, including:

· Retooling of factories to produce the vehicles
· Development of a large-scale battery industry
· Development of recharging facilities
· Deployment of instruments for the maintenance and repair of such vehicles
· A spare-parts industry
· "Smart-grid" monitoring and control software and equipment
· Even more generation and transmission facilities to supply the additional electricity demand

The development of wind and solar-power electricity also requires additional infrastructure; wind and solar electricity must be generated where the best resources exist, which is often far from population centers. Thus, extensive investment in transmission infrastructure to bring it to consumption centers is required. Today, ethanol can be blended with gasoline and used directly, but its propensity to absorb water and its high oxygen content make it unsuitable for transport in existing pipeline systems,[6] and an alternative pipeline system to enable its widespread use would be materially and financially intensive. While alternative energy forms may provide the same energy services as another form, they rarely substitute directly, and these additional material costs need to be considered.

4. MATERIAL INPUT REQUIREMENTS

Unlike what is generally assumed, the input to an alternative energy process is not money per se: It is resources and energy, and the type and volume of the resources and energy needed may in turn limit the scalability and affect the cost and feasibility of an alternative. This is particularly notable in processes that rely on advanced technologies manufactured with rare-earth elements. Fuel cells, for example, require platinum, palladium, and rare-earth elements. Solar-photovoltaic technology requires gallium, and in some forms, indium. Advanced batteries rely on lithium. Even technology designed to save energy, such as light-emitting diode (LED) or organic LED (OLED) lighting, requires rare earths, indium, and gallium. Expressing the costs of alternative energy only in monetary terms obscures potential limits arising from the requirements for resources and energy inputs.

Because alternative energy today constitutes only a small fraction of total energy production, the volume of resources and energy demanded for its production has so far been easily accommodated. This will not necessarily be the case with large-scale expansion. For example, thin-film solar has been promoted as a much lower-cost, more flexible, and more widely applicable solar-conversion technology compared to traditional silicon panels. Thin-film solar currently uses indium because of its versatile properties, but indium is also widely used as a component of flat-screen monitors. Reserves of indium are limited, and a 2007 study found that at current rates of consumption, known reserves of indium would last just thirteen years.[7]

Can greatly increased demand for these resources be accommodated? As shown in table 18.1, successful deployment to 2030 of a range of new energy technologies (and some non-energy advanced technologies) would substantially raise demand for a range of metals beyond the level of world production today. In the case of gallium, demand from emerging technologies would be expected to reach six times today's total global production by 2030; for indium, more than three times today's production—compared to just fractional increases in the demand for ruthenium and selenium.

Although alternative metals and materials exist for certain technologies (albeit often with performance trade-offs), embarking on a particular technology deployment path without consideration of long-term availability of material inputs can substantially raise risks. These risks are not limited to physical availability and price; they include potential supply disruptions as a consequence of the uneven geographical distribution of production and reserves. Currently, China is the dominant world source (over 95 percent) of the rare-earth element neodymium, a key input in the production of permanent magnets used in hybrid-vehicle motors and windmill turbines. In 2009, the Chinese government announced restric-

TABLE 18.1. Global Demand on Raw Materials
from Emerging Technologies

Raw Material	Fraction of Today's Total World Production		Emerging Technologies (selected)
	2006	2030	
Gallium	0.28	6.09	Thin-layer photovoltaics, integrated circuits, white LEDs
Neodymium	0.55	3.82	Permanent magnets, laser technology
Indium	0.40	3.29	Displays, thin-layer photovoltaics
Germanium	0.31	2.44	Fiber-optic cable, infrared optical technologies
Scandium	Low	2.28	Solid oxide fuel cells, aluminum alloying element
Platinum	Low	1.56	Fuel cells, catalysts
Tantalum	0.39	1.01	Microcapacitors, medical technology
Silver	0.26	0.78	Radio-frequency ID tags, lead-free soft solder
Tin	0.62	0.77	Lead-free soft solder, transparent electrodes
Cobalt	0.19	0.40	Lithium-ion batteries, synthetic fuels
Palladium	0.10	0.34	Catalysts, seawater desalination
Titanium	0.08	0.29	Seawater desalination, implants
Copper	0.09	0.24	Efficient electric motors, radio-frequency ID tags
Selenium	Low	0.11	Thin-layer photovoltaics, alloying element
Niobium	0.01	0.03	Microcapacitors, ferroalloys
Ruthenium	0.00	0.03	Dye-sensitized solar cells, Ti-alloying element
Yttrium	Low	0.01	Superconduction, laser technology
Antimony	Low	Low	Antimony-tin-oxides, microcapacitors
Chromium	Low	Low	Seawater desalination, marine technologies

Source: Gerhard Angerer et al., "Raw Materials for Emerging Technologies," (Karlsruhe: Fraunhofer Institute for Systems and Innovation Research ISI; Berlin: Institute for Futures Studies and Technology Assessment IZT, February 2, 2009).

tions on the export of rare earths, ostensibly to encourage investment within China of industries using the metals. Whether for the rare earths themselves or for final products made from them, import dependency in the face of such a high concentration of production would do little to alleviate energy security concerns now seen in terms of import dependency on the Middle East for oil.

Alternative energy production is reliant not only on a range of resource inputs, but also on fossil fuels for the mining of raw materials, transport, manufacturing, construction, maintenance, and decommissioning. Currently, no alternative energy exists without fossil-fuel inputs, and no alternative energy process can reproduce itself—that is, manufacture the equipment needed for its own production—without the use of fossil fuels. In this regard, alternative energy serves as a supplement to the fossil-fuel base, and its input requirements may constrain its development in cases of either material or energy scarcity.

5. INTERMITTENCY

Modern societies expect that electrons will flow when a switch is flipped, that gas will flow when a knob is turned, and that liquids will flow when the pump handle is squeezed. This system of continuous supply is possible because of our exploitation of large stores of fossil fuels, which are the result of millions of years of intermittent sunlight concentrated into a continuously extractable source of energy. Alternative energies such as solar and wind power, in contrast, produce only intermittently as the wind blows or the sun shines, and even biomass-based fuels depend on seasonal harvests of crops. Integration of these energy forms into our current system creates challenges of balancing availability and demand, and it remains doubtful that these intermittent energy forms can provide a majority of our future energy needs in the same way that we expect energy to be available today.

One indication of intermittency challenges in electric power generation is the capacity factor, or the average percentage of time in a year that a power plant is producing at full rated capacity. As shown in table 18.2, photovoltaic systems produce at full capacity only 12 to 19 percent of the time over the course of a year, compared to an average of 30 percent for

TABLE 18.2. Common Capacity Factors
for Power Generation

Generation Type	Capacity Factor
Photovoltaics	12–19%
Thermal solar	~15%
Thermal solar with storage	70–75%
Wind	20–40%
Hydropower	30–80%
Geothermal	70–90%
Nuclear power	60–100%
Natural gas combined cycle (non-peaker)	~60%
Coal thermal	70–90%

Sources: Renewable Energy Research Laboratory, University of Massachusetts at Amherst, *Wind Power: Capacity Factor, Intermittency*; National Renewable Energy Laboratory, *Assessment of Parabolic Trough and Power Tower Solar Technology Cost and Performance Forecasts*, NREL/SR-550-34440 (Golden, CO: NREL, 2003).

wind systems. In contrast, a coal-thermal plant will typically run at full capacity 70 to 90 percent of the time, while nuclear power operates at over a 90 percent capacity factor in the United States.

Our current electricity system is dominated by large baseload coal- and nuclear-power generation. The integration of intermittent energy forms such as solar and wind is increasingly seen as a matter of expanding transmission capacity and grid interconnections to extend the area over which these variations are felt, as well as implementing more complex operations controls. This approach in effect relies on strengthening and expanding the large centralized energy production and distribution model that has characterized the fossil-fuel era, but may not necessarily be suitable for a future of renewable energy generation.

The key to evening out the impact of intermittency is storage; that is, the development of technologies and approaches that can store energy generated during periods of good wind and sun for use at other times. Many approaches have been proposed and tested, including compressed-air storage, batteries, and the use of molten salts in solar-thermal plants.

The major drawbacks of all these approaches include the losses involved in energy storage and release, and the limited energy density that these storage technologies can achieve.

6. ENERGY DENSITY

Energy density refers to the amount of energy that is contained in a unit of an energy form. It can be expressed in the amount of energy per unit of mass (weight) or in the amount of energy per unit of volume. In everyday life, it is common to consider energy density when considering food choices. Food labeling in the United States requires that both numbers needed for calculating energy density be provided: the number of food calories per serving and the weight or volume of the serving (expressed in grams or liters, respectively). Potatoes, for example, have an energy density of 200 food calories per 100 grams, or, expressed in units common in energy discussions, 8.4 megajoules[8] (MJ) per kilogram (about 2.2 pounds). Cheese is more energy dense than potatoes, containing about 13 MJ per kilogram.

Energy density has also influenced our choice of fuels. Aside from alleviating a growing wood shortage, the conversion to the use of coal in the seventeenth and eighteenth centuries was welcomed because coal provided twice as much energy as wood for the same weight of material. Similarly, the shift from coal- to petroleum-powered ships in the early-twentieth century was driven by the fact that petroleum possesses nearly twice the energy density of coal, allowing ships to go farther without having to stop for refueling. Even when used in a motor vehicle's inefficient internal combustion engine, a kilogram of highly energy-dense gasoline—about 6 cups—allows us to move 3,000 pounds of metal about 11 miles.

The consequence of low energy density is that larger amounts of material or resources are needed to provide the same amount of energy as a denser material or fuel. Many alternative energies and storage technologies are characterized by low energy densities, and their deployment will result in higher levels of resource consumption. As shown in figure 18.1, the main alternatives under development to supplant gasoline use in cars are dramatically lower in energy density than gasoline itself. Lithium-ion batteries—the focus of current research for electric vehicles—contain only

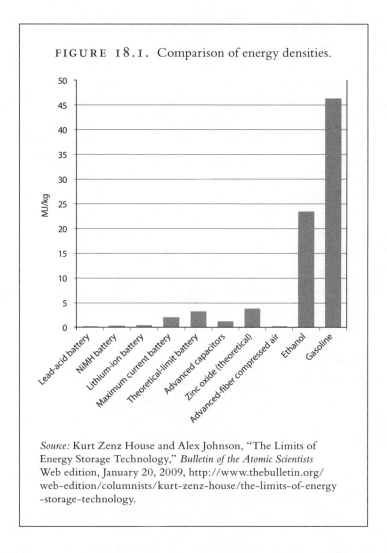

FIGURE 18.1. Comparison of energy densities.

Source: Kurt Zenz House and Alex Johnson, "The Limits of Energy Storage Technology," *Bulletin of the Atomic Scientists* Web edition, January 20, 2009, http://www.thebulletin.org/web-edition/columnists/kurt-zenz-house/the-limits-of-energy-storage-technology.

0.5 MJ per kilogram of battery compared to 46 MJ per kilogram for gasoline. Advances in battery technology are being announced regularly, but they all come up against the theoretical limit of battery density of only 3 MJ per kilogram. Low energy density will present a significant challenge to the electrification of the car fleet and will raise challenges of adequate material supply: Today, the advanced Tesla Roadster has a lithium-ion battery pack weighing 900 pounds, which delivers just 190 MJ of energy. In contrast, a 10-gallon tank of gasoline weighs 62 pounds and delivers

1,200 MJ of energy. To provide the equivalent energy to a typical gasoline car, an electric-car battery pack would need to consume resources weighing 5,700 pounds, nearly the weight of the last Hummer model.

The more dense an energy form is, the less land is needed for its deployment. Because many alternative energies are far less energy dense than fossil fuels, large-scale deployment will incur considerable land costs. For example, a single 1,000-megawatt coal-fired power plant requires 1 to 4 square kilometers (km^2) of land, not counting the land required to mine and transport the coal. In contrast, 20–50 km^2, or the size of a small city, would be required to generate the equivalent amount of energy from a photovoltaic array or from a solar-thermal system. For wind, 50–150 km^2 would be needed; for biomass, 4,000–6,000 km^2 of land would be needed. The sprawling city of Los Angeles, in comparison, covers 1,200 km^2. The land-use issue is thus a problem not only of biofuels production; siting of alternative energy projects will likely be a constant challenge because of the inherent high land footprint.

7. WATER

Water ranks with energy as a potential source of conflict among peoples and nations, but a number of alternative energy sources, primarily biomass-based energy, are large water consumers critically dependent on a dependable water supply. As seen in figure 18.2, the "full-cycle" water requirement (including water for growing and processing biofuels) for key ethanol and biodiesel feedstocks is in some cases hundreds or even many thousand times higher than for the refining of gasoline. In well-watered regions with regular and adequate rainfall, much of this water can be provided through rain; in a region such as California, where no rain falls during the summer growing season because of its Mediterranean climate, irrigation is an absolute necessity for growing commercial biomass feedstocks. However, all of California's water resources have already been allocated, so existing uses for other crops would have to be reallocated to support biomass farming—raising the issue of "food versus fuel" from yet a different angle. The water problems, however, promise only to intensify with global warming as California's winter snowpack fades and runoff to support summer agriculture declines.

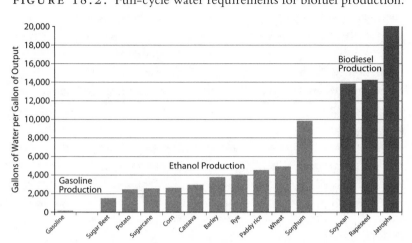

FIGURE 18.2. Full-cycle water requirements for biofuel production.

Source: Winnie Gerbens-Leenes et al., "The Water Footprint of Bioenergy," *Proceedings of the National Academy of Sciences* 106, no. 25 (June 23, 2009), 10219–10223.

Considering just the processing stage, biomass and unconventional fossil-fuel energy also often require much greater water usage than the 2.5 gallons of water required per gallon of gasoline produced. Coal-to-liquids production consumes 8 to 11 gallons of water per gallon of output, corn ethanol requires 4 to 6 gallons, and cellulosic ethanol needs 11 gallons. In the United States, Montana has looked into becoming a leader in coal-to-liquids production, yet Montana's dry climate suggests that water could be a limiting factor.

8. THE LAW OF RECEDING HORIZONS[9]

An often-cited metric of the viability of alternatives is the expected break-even cost of the alternative with oil, or the price that crude oil would have to be to make the alternative cost competitive. Underlying this calculation, however, is an assumption that the input costs to alternative energy production would remain static as oil prices rise, thereby providing the economic incentive to development. This assumption, however, has not always proved to be the case, particularly for those alternatives for which energy itself is a major input. Because of price linkages in the energy (and now energy and biomass) markets, rising oil prices tend to push up the price of natural gas as well as coal; for processes that are heavily dependent on these fuels, higher oil prices also bring higher production costs.

A good example of this phenomenon is the assessment of the economics of production from oil shale (kerogen-rich marlstone), found in vast quantities in Colorado, Utah, and Wyoming. In the early 1970s, shale oil was expected to flood the market if the price of crude oil were to rise above $2 per barrel. When world oil prices had shot up to $35 per barrel by 1979, oil-shale production still required federal government assistance, and when oil prices fell in the mid-1980s, development and production were abandoned. Fast-forward to 2008 when oil prices moved above $100 per barrel—oil shale was then expected to be economic at $80 to $90 per barrel, and the U.S. government again provided incentives to explore production in the area. This ratcheting up of oil-shale economics with the price of oil reflects in part the high energy-input requirement to the production process.

Similarly, the corn ethanol industry has recently been subject to the same dynamic step-up in costs as the price of oil has risen. Two major input costs to the industry are the processing fuel (usually natural gas) and the corn feedstock itself. Rising oil prices after 2004 pulled natural gas prices up as well, increasing the processing energy costs for ethanol. At the same time, higher fuel prices made cultivating corn more expensive because of higher costs for operating farm machinery; this, together with the additional demand for corn created by the growing ethanol industry, helped push corn prices up even further. So, although the record-high oil prices of 2008 increased demand for ethanol, some ethanol producers were operating with minimal or no profit because they had to pay more for both their processing fuel and their corn feedstock.

Ultimately, the "law of receding horizons" is a phenomenon reflective of the general orientation toward financial and economic accounting to gauge project viability and prospects. Physical accounting—that is, analyzing the material and energy inputs to a process—would help in better understanding the degree to which an alternative energy production process is vulnerable to the rise in energy costs.

9. ENERGY RETURN ON INVESTMENT[10]

The complexity of our economy and society is a function of the amount of net energy we have available. "Net energy" is, simply, the amount of energy remaining after we consume energy to produce energy. Consuming energy to produce energy is unavoidable, but only that which is not consumed to produce energy is available to sustain our industrial, transport, residential, commercial, agricultural, and military activities. The ratio of the amount of energy we put into energy production and the amount of energy we produce is called "energy return on investment" (EROI).

This concept differs from "conversion efficiency," which compares the amount of energy provided as a feedstock to a conversion process (such as an electric power plant or petroleum refinery) with the amount remaining after conversion. Physics dictates that this figure is always less than 100 percent. In contrast, EROI can be very high (e.g., 100:1, or 100 units of energy produced for every 1 unit used to produce it—an "energy source") or low (0.8:1, or only 0.8 unit of energy produced for every 1 unit used in production—an "energy sink"). Society requires energy sources, not energy sinks, and the magnitude of EROI for an energy source is a key indicator of its contribution to maintenance of social and economic complexity.

Net-energy availability has varied tremendously over time and in different societies. In the last advanced societies that relied only on solar power (sun, water power, biomass, and the animals that depended on biomass), in the seventeenth and early-eighteenth centuries, the amount of net energy available was low and dependent largely on the food surpluses provided by farmers. At that time, only 10 to 15 percent of the population was *not* involved in energy production. As extraction of coal, oil, and natural gas increased in the nineteenth and twentieth centuries, society was increasingly able to substitute the energy from fossil fuels for manual or animal labor, thereby freeing an even larger proportion of society from direct involvement in energy production. In 1870, 70 percent of the U.S. population were farmers; today the figure is less than 2 percent, and every aspect of agricultural production now relies heavily on petroleum or natural gas. The same is true in other energy sectors: Currently, less than 0.5 percent of the U.S. labor force (about 710,000 people) is directly involved

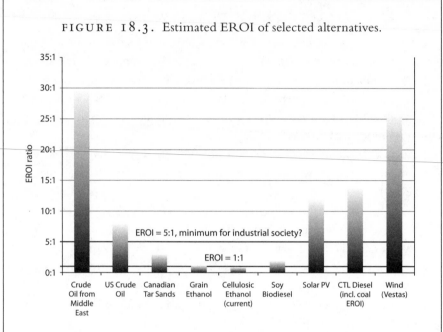

FIGURE 18.3. Estimated EROI of selected alternatives.

Note: EROI measurements are not standardized; the shading indicates ranges from various studies. PV = photovoltaic; CTL = coal-to-liquids; Vestas = Vestas Wind Systems.

Sources: P. J. Meier and G. L. Kulcinski, *Life-Cycle Energy Requirements and Greenhouse Gas Emissions for Building-Integrated Photovoltaics,* Fusion Technology Institute (2002); National Renewable Energy Laboratory, *What Is the Energy Payback for PV?* DOE/ GO-102004-1847 (2004); Vasilis Fthenakis and Erik Alsema, "Photovoltaics Energy Payback Times, Greenhouse Gas Emissions and External Costs," *Progress in Photovoltaics* 14, no. 3 (May 2006), 275–280; Luc Gagnon, "Civilisation and Energy Payback," *Energy Policy* 36, no. 9 (September 2008), 3317–3322; Cutler Cleveland, "Net Energy from the Extraction of Oil and Gas in the United States, 1954–1997," *Energy* 30 (2005), 769–782; Charles A. S. Hall et al., "Peak Oil, EROI, Investments and the Economy in an Uncertain Future," in *Biofuels, Solar and Wind as Renewable Energy Systems,* David Pimentel, ed. (Springer Science, 2008); Vestas Wind Systems, *Life Cycle Assessment of Offshore and Onshore Sited Wind Power Plants Based on Vestas V90-3.0 MW Turbines* (Denmark, 2005); Alexander E. Farrell et al., "Ethanol Can Contribute to Energy and Environmental Goals," *Science* 311 (January 27, 2006).

in coal mining, oil and gas extraction, petroleum refining, pipeline transport, and power generation, transmission, and distribution.

The challenge of a transition to alternative energy, then, is whether such energy surpluses can be sustained, and thus whether the type of social and economic specialization we enjoy today can be maintained. Indeed, one study estimates that the minimum EROI for the maintenance of industrial society is 5:1, suggesting that no more than 20 percent of social and economic resources can be dedicated to the production of energy without undermining the structure of industrial society.[11]

In general, most alternative energy sources have low EROI values (see figure 18.3). Because of their high energy-input requirements, biofuels produce very little or no energy surplus.[12] Similarly, tar sands provide less than 3 units of energy for each unit consumed. In contrast, wind energy shows a high return on energy investment, but it is subject to the problems of intermittency and siting issues.

A high EROI is not sufficient to ensure that the structure of modern society and economies can be maintained, but it is a prerequisite. Unfortunately, EROI is not well understood or routinely used in energy analyses by government or industry, despite the insights it can provide. Because of the enormous investment in resources and energy that any alternative energy pathway will require, it is important that we look beyond simple financial payback, particularly in a future of rising energy prices, declining fossil-fuel resources, and increasing danger of climate catastrophe.

HOW WILL SOCIETY EVOLVE IN A POST-CARBON WORLD?

Alternative energy forms are crucial for a global transition away from fossil fuels, despite the myriad challenges of their development, scaling, and integration. In face of the peaking of global oil production—to be followed by peaks in natural gas and coal extraction—and of the need to reverse trajectory in carbon emissions, alternative energy sources will need to form the backbone of a future energy system.

That system, however, will not be a facsimile of the system we have today based on continuous uninterrupted supply growing to meet whatever demand is placed on it. As we move away from the energy bounty provided by fossil fuels, we will become increasingly reliant on tapping the current flow of energy from the sun (wind, solar) and on new energy manufacturing processes that will require ever larger consumption of resources (biofuels, other manufactured liquids, batteries). What kind of society we can build on this foundation is unclear, but it will most likely require us to pay more attention to controls on energy demand to accommodate the limitations of our future energy supply. Moreover, the modern focus on centralized production and distribution may be hard to maintain, since local conditions will become increasingly important in determining the feasibility of alternative energy production.

PEAK OIL AND THE GREAT RECESSION

TOM WHIPPLE

TOM WHIPPLE *is one of the most highly respected analysts of peak-oil issues in the United States. A retired thirty-year CIA analyst who has been following the peak-oil story since 1999, he is the editor of the daily* Peak Oil News, *published by the Association for the Study of Peak Oil–USA, and a weekly columnist for the* Falls Church News Press. *He has degrees from Rice University and the London School of Economics. Whipple is a Fellow of Post Carbon Institute.*

❖

When in the late 1990s it was recognized that world oil production was likely to start declining early in the twenty-first century, petroleum geologists and other industry observers started talking and writing about the economic damage this event would cause. Serious economic consequences were a virtual certainty because, since the beginning of the industrial age, economic growth had required increasing quantities of fossil fuels. During most of the twentieth century economic growth increased the demand for oil, which had come to serve as our primary transportation fuel, the source of energy for many production processes, and the raw material for an ever-increasing range of industrial products. Unless satisfactory substitutes could be found quickly, economic growth was likely to stop. And without alternatives, economic decline—if not a collapse—was likely.

This chapter explores the relationship—as it is understood thus far—between the peaking of oil production, which started around 2005, and the current global recession, which officially started in late 2007. In the long run, global warming may turn out to be of more significance than the peaking of fossil-fuel supplies. However, it is clear that the peaking of global oil production has already had economic consequences, which will become increasingly serious as time goes on, and that the global economic recession is due at least partially to the lack of significant growth in world oil supplies since 2005.

Although concerns about the amount of crude oil that can ultimately be produced go back many decades, modern interest in the topic was revived in March 1998 by an article published in *Scientific American* written by two senior European geologists, Colin Campbell and Jean Laherrère. The article warned that, from the perspective of geology alone, world oil production would likely reach an all-time peak sometime around 2010. Worldwide production of crude oil and various liquid substitutes[1] in 1998 was roughly 75 million barrels per day (bpd), and oil was selling for $10 a barrel. Over the next seven years production grew rapidly, reaching a multi-year plateau of 85 million to 86 million bpd starting in 2005. Prices then started climbing rapidly, peaking at over $130 per barrel for the month of July 2008 (see figure 19.1).

Over those ten years, public and media awareness of the issue grew slowly while organizations,[2] books, and Web sites appeared, tracking and discussing the various implications of worldwide oil peaking. The revival of the idea that global oil production would soon peak also brought forth many detractors, some of whom remain highly vocal to this day. The most important doubters were the two major organizations charged with tracking the world's oil supply and making forecasts as to what was likely to happen in the decades ahead—the International Energy Agency of the Organisation for Economic Co-operation and Development (OECD), based in Paris, and the U.S. Department of Energy's Energy Information Administration in Washington, D.C.

Until very recently, neither of these agencies had ever examined in depth the question of whether there was going to be enough oil available in the future to satisfy rapidly growing world GDP.[3] It was simply assumed, based on general estimates by the U.S. Geological Survey, that there was sufficient oil underground to supply humanity's needs for the foreseeable future. Therefore, oil-production levels were forecast on the basis that the oil industry would be able to supply however much oil was required by economic growth, with little if any consideration of the geologic, economic, and political constraints on producing ever-greater amounts of oil.

However, the global oil market has changed in very significant ways since 1998. The real price of oil has increased several-fold as demand has

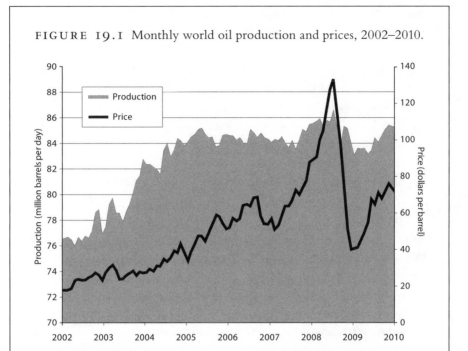

FIGURE 19.1 Monthly world oil production and prices, 2002–2010.

Sources: Production data from U.S. Energy Information Administration, "February 2010 International Petroleum Monthly," March 10, 2010, http://www.eia.doe.gov/ipm/supply.html; price data from U.S. Energy Information Administration, "World Crude Oil Prices," accessed April 7, 2010, http://tonto.eia.doe.gov/dnav/pet/pet_pri_wco_k_w.htm.

continued to increase. Demand has been shifting away from the developed OECD countries and toward the rapidly growing economies of Asia (primarily China and India) as well as the oil-exporting nations that can easily afford to subsidize domestic prices. Finally, world production—which has been growing steadily for nearly 150 years—has flattened out (or, as some say, "plateaued") in the vicinity of 85 million to 86 million bpd, suggesting to many that all-time peak-oil production has already occurred.

A GREAT RECESSION

While the current economic difficulties can be traced back to events and policy decisions over the past century, the proximate causes of the current crisis, at least from the point of view of the United States, stem from the 1970s when real wages[4] in the United States stopped growing.

For the thirty years following World War II the United States, having emerged virtually unscathed from the war, held a monopoly on much of the world's industrial production. By the 1970s, however, much of the devastation of World War II elsewhere—as well as the consequent political and social turmoil—had been overcome. Soon a significant share of the world's industrial production was shifting to Asia, where cheaper labor (and in some cases, better-quality products) coupled with cheap overseas shipping and digital communications left the United States largely as a service and consumer economy.

Also in the 1970s, millions of foreigners had immigrated to the United States to work for wages that were lower than what Americans expected but higher than what they could earn in their home countries. Just as important, millions of emancipated women joined the U.S. workforce. These demographic developments, coupled with the globalization of manufacturing and the new labor-saving efficiencies of digital computers and industrial automation, combined to freeze real wages for the first time in American history.

Stagnant real wages along with increasing worker productivity resulted in massive increases in corporate profits, unprecedented growth in the equity markets, and the expansion of the "financial-services" industry to an important position in the U.S. and global economy. The availability of massive amounts of corporate money led not only to increasing inequality of wages between workers and management but also to major efforts to achieve perceived corporate goals through manipulation of the political system. Corporate lobbying and public relations became industries unto themselves, and corporate political contributions skyrocketed. Today the power of very well-financed "special interests" to influence the political response to major issues such as tobacco, global warming, and peak oil is a well-established part of the American political scene.

With real wages frozen, the only way Americans could keep increasing their consumption was to work longer hours and borrow. Working more hours has limitations, but borrowing can continue as long as someone is willing to lend. Borrowing by Americans in every conceivable form began in earnest in the 1970s, leading to the greatest credit bubble the world has ever known. As long as the U.S. and world economy grew and the value of major assets such as investments and houses kept increasing, it all worked. But then the growth stopped and much of the world, particularly the United States, had a very big problem on its hands. By 2007–2008 it was obvious that a major economic crisis was under way, with falling real estate values, increasing unemployment, sagging economies, and unstable, overleveraged financial markets.

Mindful of what had happened nearly eighty years earlier when economic crisis turned into the Great Depression, governments around the world (at least, those that were in trouble and could afford to spend or borrow the money) launched massive multitrillion-dollar bailout and stimulus programs to stabilize the situation. While it was generally recognized that too much borrowing, overleveraging, and inadequate regulation of financial markets were the fundamental reasons the global economy got out of hand, the role of oil in deepening and spreading the global recession has only recently begun to be appreciated.

OIL AND THE RECESSION

Before the peaking of world oil production began in earnest in 2005, it was expected to be a rather straightforward phenomenon:

- The global economy would continue to grow, consuming more and more oil each year.
- At some not-too-distant point in the future, a combination of geological constraints, geopolitical problems, and insufficient investment in new production would cause the flow of oil to global markets to start shrinking.
- The inability to continue increasing oil production to support continued economic growth would lead to much higher prices for oil, which in turn would stifle both economic growth and the demand for oil. It would be a period during which oil prices would cycle up and down, first stifling and then permitting some economic growth.
- At some point the constraints on oil production would simply overwhelm demand and the depletion of existing oil fields would send global production downward.
- Very hard economic times would ensue as the world rushed to keep functioning with falling oil supplies and scrambled for alternative forms of energy.

It was all rather simple, if unpleasant.

Between 2003 and 2007, the world's real GDP[5] grew between 9 and 10 percent a year. World oil production, however, stopped growing significantly after 2005. With demand still increasing, spectacular increases in oil prices ensued. Oil, which was trading for as low as $20 a barrel in 2002, reached $70 a barrel in 2006, increased to $80 a barrel in late 2007, and topped $100 at the beginning of 2008. During the price rise, there were many predictions that oil was approaching a point at which its price would damage the economy, but as the months rolled on and nothing particularly untoward seemed to happen, the warnings were forgotten.

But the price rise had a huge impact on real GDP: With world oil consumption running at about 85 million bpd and U.S. consumption at about 20 million bpd, a dollar-a-barrel increase in the price of oil is a lot of money and places a major burden on an economy. The $60-per-barrel increase in oil prices between 2002 and late 2007 meant that $1.2 billion additional each day—or $36 billion each month—was being spent in the United States solely to pay for the increased cost of oil.

The year 2008 will be remembered as a major turning point in industrial history, for it was the first year when the world got a taste of the unpredictable price spikes that come from inadequate oil supplies. The first half of the year was marked by a steady increase in the weighted average price of oil, which started the year at about $90 a barrel and finally peaked in July just shy of $150 a barrel. At the same time, the global economy was contracting rapidly with falling industrial production, falling exports, and rising unemployment. By July 1, 2008, many industries that are dependent on oil, especially the airline and trucking industries, were desperate and in danger of being forced out of business. With the average price of gasoline above $4 a gallon in the United States (above $5 in California), car sales plummeted, leading to bankruptcy for much of the U.S. automobile industry and eventually massive government bailouts.

Two major lessons from the first half of 2008 were that oil prices can indeed increase rapidly to unanticipated levels and that very high prices will cause serious economic damage in short order. Although by early 2008 oil consumption in the United States and other OECD countries had started to drop owing to high prices and faltering economies, this was more than offset by continued growth of oil consumption in the heavily subsidized economies of the Organization of the Petroleum Exporting Countries (OPEC), in India, and particularly in China, which increased its oil imports by nearly 1.5 million bpd in the first part of 2008 to ensure there would be no shortages during the Beijing Olympics.

While the 2008 oil and gasoline price spike can be explained by conventional economic theory, this was not a satisfactory answer for politicians facing reelection with gasoline at $4 to $5 a gallon. A search for scapegoats, so that the U.S. Congress could look as if it were doing something about the crisis, began in earnest. The usual suspects—Arabs, OPEC governments, speculators, and environmentalists—all became targets for proposed legislation, some of which, such as suing OPEC for price fixing, were totally bizarre.

With the start of the 2008 Olympics in August, however, Chinese demand for oil dropped by 2 million bpd and the great oil price spike of 2008 melted like an ice cube in the sun. To nearly everyone's surprise, the weighted price of oil fell from more than $130 a barrel to less than $40 a barrel by the end of the year. U.S. consumers were soon spending roughly $1.7 billion a day less for the same amount of oil products as they were in July. Thus, in six months, falling oil prices gave back to the consumer much of the spending power that had been taken away in the previous few years. This economic "stimulus" for a while was in a class with anything the government could do.

The collapse of oil prices in the second half of 2008 was good for hard-pressed, unsubsidized consumers in oil-consuming countries. But it was a disaster for oil-producing countries and the international oil companies, which now no longer had the revenue to cover state and investment budgets that were predicated on much higher oil prices. Starting in the late fall of 2008 OPEC (mainly the Saudis and their Persian Gulf brethren) cut oil production by roughly 3 million bpd and the price of oil began a steady climb, reaching $80 a barrel in the fall of 2009.

The steep decline in oil prices to the vicinity of $40 a barrel in late 2008 triggered yet another set of forces. Most new oil production is now coming from deep-water wells or deposits of heavy oil in Canada and Venezuela, which require very large investments to exploit. Most published estimates say it takes a market price of $70 to $90 a barrel for these projects to be viable. Thus, in the winter of 2008–2009 some $150 billion worth of new oil-production projects were canceled or delayed until prices became more favorable.

Given that some 3 million to 4 million bpd of new oil production has to be brought online each year simply to offset depletion from currently producing oil fields, this sharp decline in investment has the potential to cause, a few years from now, steeper declines in production than had been anticipated. The rapid contraction of commercial credit during 2008 and 2009 compounded the problem, for it meant that small oil companies could no longer get sufficient credit to continue or to expand drilling operations. Thus, another important lesson of 2008 was a reminder that new oil sources are becoming so expensive to find—and new oil production is becoming so expensive to develop—that it will take relatively high prices to keep exploration and new production projects viable.

As 2009 unfolded, various U.S., Chinese, and European economic stimulus packages began to take hold. In most countries the stimulus packages only checked the precipitous fall in economic activity that took place in 2008. In China's largely command economy, the stimulus was more effective so Beijing increased its oil consumption by some 2 million bpd during the first half of 2009. This, coupled with OPEC's production cut, was enough to offset a 3 million bpd drop in consumption among the OECD nations (due to lower industrial activity).

During 2009, with the prospect of higher oil prices brought on by an economic recovery, the question arose as to just how high oil prices can rise before they start damaging economic development. As gasoline in a motorized society—North America, parts of Europe, and scattered cities around the world—is nearly as essential as food, the demand for personal transportation will fall very slowly as prices increase. Oil for commercial use, however, will not be consumed unless someone can make money or at least not suffer unbearable losses from its use. Every increase in the price of oil keeps money from being spent for some other purpose, and in that sense harms the economy. Although there is disagreement, economists looking into the issue believe that, based on the record of the last forty years, there will be a major decline in economic activity when the cost of oil reaches about 4 percent of GDP.[6]

There are psychological as well as economic barriers to spending caused by high oil prices. Surveys taken during the 2008 gasoline price spike suggest that U.S. consumers were far less interested in purchasing large, high-fuel-consumption cars when gasoline was above $3 a gallon.

There are only a limited number of ways that the current economic recession and the looming prospects of a final decline in oil production can play out. None of these will permit much of an economic revival. The global financial crisis as presently understood is clearly too firmly rooted to be fixed by government bailouts and stimulus packages. The recession will only deepen for the foreseeable future, and the massive deficit financing by the United States and many other countries cannot go on much longer. Although China, with its large reserves of foreign currency, may be able to continue underwriting stimulus packages longer than other countries, it too will succumb to the lack of exports, the need to import energy, and other looming problems.

It seems reasonable to conclude the following concerning the peaking of world oil production and economic recession:

1. Although oil shortages and higher prices would have eventually caused major economic troubles, overextension of credit and over-leveraging by financial institutions started the economic troubles a year or two earlier than was expected.

2. The substantial increase in the price of oil during the last eight or nine years, coupled with the 2008 oil price spike, certainly made a United States/European Union recession global and much worse.

3. Global oil production has probably reached as high as it ever will. Any increases beyond 86 million to 87 million bpd are likely to be insignificant.

4. The global reduction in the demand for oil caused by falling economic activity and high oil prices has delayed significant declines in world oil production by two to three years.

5. The decline in oil industry investment caused by the current recession and low oil prices in the winter of 2008–2009 will lead to an even steeper decline in oil production than would have been the case.

6. Any increase in the demand for oil caused by improving economic conditions will cause much higher prices, which in turn will choke off the economic upturn.

7. It is unlikely that there will ever be an economic recovery in the conventional sense; the economic downturn is likely to continue in one form or another for many years, perhaps overlapping the economic calamities wrought by global warming.

Part Nine

ECONOMY

ECOLOGICAL ECONOMICS

JOSHUA FARLEY

JOSHUA FARLEY *is a Fellow of the Gund Institute for Ecological Economics and a professor in the Community Development and Applied Economics department at the University of Vermont. With economist Herman Daly, he co-authored the foundation textbook* Ecological Economics: Principles and Applications *(2003). He has received several fellowships and has spent considerable time abroad, including several years at the School for Field Studies' Centre for Rainforest Studies in Far North Queensland, Australia. Farley is a Fellow of Post Carbon Institute.*

❖

Market economies—in which the prices of goods and services are determined by the interplay of supply and demand in voluntary exchanges—play a critical role in the modern world. Market forces determine the quantity of oil pumped, minerals mined, forests cut, and fish caught. They determine the industries to which these resources are allocated, how much labor and capital are employed to convert them to market products, and who gets to consume those products.

In theory, competitive markets[1] allocate factors of production—resources like energy, raw materials, land, labor, and capital—toward the most profitable goods and services and, in turn, allocate the goods and services toward those who value them the most, as measured by their willingness to pay. The competitive markets described in textbooks in theory maximize monetary value while ensuring that consumers are able to purchase market products as cheaply as they can be produced. What's more, competitive markets achieve all this through a process based on free choice and decentralized knowledge, without centralized coordination.

The Great Depression, however, revealed huge flaws in market economic theory. Markets sometimes left vast numbers of skilled laborers unemployed, left machinery idle, and left food to rot on farms while the poor went hungry. The Great Depression helped economists understand that sometimes markets required government intervention to function well and to allocate resources appropriately. Confronted with this crisis, economists developed the field of macroeconomics, which explained how governments could use monetary and fiscal policies[2] to keep economies healthy and growing.

When macroeconomics emerged, however, practically no one was aware of the coming challenges of global climate change, peak oil, biodiversity loss, resource depletion, or overpopulation. Economists focused on the problem of how to convert seemingly abundant natural resources into apparently scarcer economic goods and services. Since then, production of economic goods and services has increased more than eighteenfold in the United States,[3] and nearly as much in the world as a whole. We have learned that intact ecosystems provide vital life-support functions upon which we, like all other species, depend for our survival, and that human activities threaten the planet's ecosystems.

Unfortunately, market systems largely fail to account for the impacts of ecosystem degradation on human welfare. The ecological and resource crises we currently face are orders of magnitude more serious than the Great Depression, as they threaten not only the economic system but also human survival. We must develop a new type of economics that addresses these shortcomings (see box 20.1 for a glossary of selected terms).

WHAT IS ECONOMICS?

Adapting our economic system to the twenty-first century's interconnected sustainability crises demands that we understand precisely what economic systems are meant to achieve. One widely used definition of economics is "the allocation of scarce resources among competing desirable ends."[4] We use what we have to create what we want.

A series of questions flows from this definition:

· First, what are the desirable ends of economic activity? Until we decide what we want, we can't possibly figure out how to get it.
· Second, what resources do we have at our disposal?
· Third, what are the physical and institutional characteristics of those resources relevant to their allocation?

BOX 20.1 Glossary

Ecosystem goods and services *Ecosystem goods* are biotic (living) and abiotic (nonliving) raw materials provided by nature that alternatively serve as elements of ecosystem structure. They are stock-flow resources (see below). *Ecosystem services* are ecosystem functions of value to humans. They are fund-flux resources (see below).

Excludability A resource is *excludable* when one person or group can prevent others from using the resource and is *nonexcludable* when this is not possible.

Feedback loop (negative and positive) A causal path through which the outcome of an event has an impact on future occurrences of that event. *Negative-feedback loops* have a dampening or stabilizing impact (i.e., they reduce the likelihood or impact of the event in the future), whereas *positive-feedback loops* have an augmenting or destabilizing impact (i.e., they increase the likelihood or impact of the event in the future).

Fund-flux resource A fund is a specific configuration of stock-flow resources (see below) that generates a flux of services at a given rate over time. The fund is not transformed into the services it provides, and the services cannot be stockpiled.

Market economy A system of allocation in which the prices of goods and services are determined by the interplay of supply and demand in voluntary exchanges.

Market firms Businesses that produce market products.

Market products Goods and services that are bought and sold in markets.

Open-access resource A good or service for which no property rights exist.

Rivalry A resource is *rival* when use by one person leaves less available for others to use and is *nonrival* when this does not occur.

Stock-flow resource A resource that is physically transformed into whatever it is used to produce, can be stockpiled, and the rate of use of which can be controlled.

We must answer these questions before deciding what types of mechanisms for allocating resources will help us achieve our economic goals.

What Are the Desirable Ends of Economic Activity?

Many people would agree that the central desirable end of economic activity is a high quality of life for this and future generations. Conventional economists argue that humans are insatiable, and therefore economics should focus on endless economic growth and ever-increasing consumption. Considerable evidence, however, suggests that humans are in fact satiable—there is a point beyond which increasing consumption does not make us better off. For 90 percent of human history, we were nomadic hunter-gatherer tribes and faced starvation if we accumulated more than we could carry in our search for food; insatiability was maladaptive.[5] Indeed, quality of life depends on the satisfaction of a wide variety of human needs, which include subsistence, reproduction, security, affection, understanding, participation, leisure, spirituality, creativity, identity, and freedom, very few of which are closely related to market goods and services.[6] Advertising leads us to believe that we can satisfy these needs through material consumption, and when we fail to satisfy them, we mistakenly believe it is because we are not consuming enough.[7]

An economic system designed to sustain a high quality of life across generations must satisfy at least three requirements:

1. *An ecologically sustainable scale.* The economic system is sustained and contained by the finite planetary ecosystem, so continuous exponential growth of physical economic production is impossible. A sustainable economy cannot extract renewable resources faster than they can regenerate, use up critical nonrenewable resources faster than renewable substitutes are developed, or emit wastes faster than they can be absorbed. Given the current extent of human impacts on the environment, sustainability also demands that we maintain and restore ecological resilience—the ability of ecosystems to recover from disturbances.

2. *Just distribution.* Numerous studies show that people care about fairness and justice; injustice makes us feel bad.[8] Furthermore, those without enough to eat will sacrifice a sustainable future to feed themselves and their children today, while the wealthy consume

more than their fair share of limited planetary resources. Justice is necessary for sustainability.

3. *Efficient allocation, because there exist finite resources and unmet human needs.* Intact ecosystems provide a flow of goods and services that contribute to quality of life. They can also be converted into *economic* goods and services, but only at the cost of ecological degradation. Efficiency demands that we stop this conversion process before the additional costs of continued conversion exceed the additional benefits. Beyond this point, continued growth in human-made goods and services is uneconomic. Efficiency also demands that we allocate available ecosystem resources toward those products that most enhance quality of life, and those products to those who derive the greatest benefit from them.

What Are the Scarce Resources?

The first law of thermodynamics states that matter-energy can be neither created nor destroyed—it is only transformed. All economic production therefore requires the transformation of raw material provided by our finite planet, which irrevocably limits the physical size of our economy.

A more binding constraint on resource availability comes from the second law of thermodynamics, which states that entropy—the dissolution of order—always increases. In economic terms, this means that things break down, wear out, fall apart, and become less useful over time, and the production process ultimately and unavoidably increases total disorder. A corollary of the second law is that it is impossible to do work without energy, and that energy cannot be recycled. The ultimate scarce resource is therefore low-entropy matter-energy. The only sustainable source of low-entropy energy is the sun. A sustainable economic system cannot convert raw materials to economic products and then to waste faster than solar energy flows can replenish the order lost in the process. Ecosystems have evolved over millennia to capture solar energy and build up "order" in the form of increasingly complex plants, animals, and relationships. As we degrade ecosystems, we reduce the capacity of solar energy to replenish order.

We depend on ecosystems not only for the regeneration of usable raw materials ("ecosystem goods"), but also for the generation of ecosystem functions of value to humans ("ecosystem services"). Most of the raw materials—plants, animals, water, minerals, and so on—transformed into economic products alternatively serve as elements of ecosystem structure (i.e., the building blocks of ecosystems). When we remove ecosystem structure, we also lose ecosystem functions, including vital life-support functions. Human survival requires healthy ecosystems capable of converting low-entropy solar energy and available raw materials into essential ecosystem goods and services.

Two other nonphysical resources deserve mention. One is the institution of money, which, along with financial systems, has enormous influence on how resources are allocated. The other is knowledge, or information, which is essential to all economic activity. We live in an information economy, and new knowledge will play a critical role in solving our current problems.

Unfortunately, conventional economists frequently argue that there are no binding resource constraints on economic production other than human ingenuity (i.e., knowledge), which they claim is essentially limitless.[9] Through the magic of market forces, as a resource becomes scarcer, its price increases, creating incentives to use the resource more efficiently or to develop substitutes. For example, as wood became scarce as an energy source, we developed coal as a substitute, followed by oil and natural gas. We are now developing heavy crude, oil shale, and tar sand. From this perspective, our ingenuity, guided by market forces, eliminates the problem of absolute scarcity.

However, it is no coincidence that both the market economy and the carbon economy emerged together during the eighteenth century. Market production has increased in tandem with the use of fossil fuels. It takes an estimated 25,000 hours of human labor to generate the energy found in one barrel of oil.[10] Many examples of innovation induced by growing scarcity and rising prices are actually examples of increased reliance on fossil fuels. For example, as we ran short of land to meet the global demand for food, we learned to convert natural gas into biologically active nitrogen and petrochemicals into an array of pesticides, herbicides, and fungicides. By shifting from animal-powered to fossil-fuel-powered traction and transport, we freed up land previously used to feed draft animals. The magic of fossil fuels is more responsible for economic production than the magic of the market.

Unfortunately, our capacity to continually increase fossil-fuel use to power ever-increasing economic production has ended. Fossil-fuel stocks are finite and we have already used up the most accessible supplies with the highest net-energy gains. Fossil-fuel emissions threaten climate stability, hence agriculture and civilization. The age of the carbon economy is coming to an end.

What Are the Physical and Institutional Characteristics of the Resources?

To design a sustainable economy, we must understand key characteristics of the resources at our disposal. To begin, we distinguish between ecosystem goods and ecosystem services, which have fundamentally different physical characteristics.

Ecosystem goods are the raw materials provided by nature that are essential to all economic products. These include food, fiber, fuels, water, minerals, and so on, and alternatively serve as elements of ecosystem structure. *Ecosystem services* are those ecological functions that contribute to human quality of life. These include:

- Regulation of climate, water, disturbances, and atmospheric gases (regulating services).
- The capacity of ecosystems to reproduce food, fiber, fuels, and water (provisioning services).
- Habitat, nutrient cycling, and pollination (supporting services).
- Recreation, genetic information, and spiritual values (cultural services).

When ecosystems provide raw materials, they act as stocks that are physically transformed into other products; they are used up, not worn out. Think of forests being converted into timber, or fossil fuels being transformed into carbon dioxide and waste heat. Ecosystem goods are "stock-flow" resources. Stock-flow resources can be used up at the rate we choose and can also be stockpiled.

When ecosystems provide services, in contrast, they act as funds, agents of transformation that are not themselves physically transformed in the act of production. A fund is a particular configuration of stock-flow resources capable of generating a flux of valuable services. Ecosystem services are "fund-flux" resources. When a forest regulates water flows, it remains a forest. Fund-flux resources are provided at a given rate over time, and cannot be stockpiled. Ecosystems can transform oxygen, carbon, minerals, and sunlight into a given amount of ecosystem goods and services per day, and human-made capital and labor can transform these into a given amount of economic product per day. While fund-flux resources such as labor and capital are worn out over time, ecosystem fund-flux resources are spontaneously renewed by solar energy.

Another critical characteristic is excludability. A resource is "excludable" when one person or group can prevent others from using the resource. Excludability is not an inherent characteristic of a resource, but rather the result of institutions protecting private or common property rights. Most ecosystem goods have been made excludable; for example, trees, land, oil fields, and mineral deposits typically have owners. Some ecosystem services can also be made excludable; for example, Earth's waste absorption capacity for greenhouse gases is now a tradable commodity resource in Europe, as established by the European Union Emission Trading System.[11] A resource is "nonexcludable" when one cannot prevent others from using it, in which case markets provide no incentives to pay for its use, production, or protection, threatening overconsumption and underprovision. Many ecosystem services, such as climate regulation, protection from ultraviolet light, flood regulation, solar photons, and pollination, are inherently nonexcludable as a physical characteristic. Markets are only feasible for excludable resources.

A final critical characteristic is "rivalry." A resource is rival when one person's use of the resource leaves less available for others to use. A resource is "congestible" when it is rival but fluctuates between scarce and abundant ("abundant" means enough is available for all desired uses, and no competition is necessary). All stock-flow resources and hence all ecosystem goods are rival, but so are many ecosystem services. When a rival resource is scarce, there is competition for use. If use is not rationed, the resource is likely to be overused, like the waste absorption capacity for carbon dioxide (e.g., if carbon dioxide is emitted faster than the ecosystem can sustainably absorb it) or oceanic fisheries (e.g., if a fishery is depleted faster than it can replenish itself). The market price mechanism is one form of rationing because it allocates use of a resource to whoever is willing to pay the most.

A resource is nonrival when one person's use does not leave less for others to use. Examples include streetlights, climate stability, and many other ecosystem services. Knowledge has the special property that it often improves through use—for example, James Watt developed a better steam engine by taking apart and understanding an older, inferior one. Because nonrival resources are not depleted through use (though they can be destroyed by abuse) and hence are not scarce, once they exist it is inefficient to ration them. Take as an example a clean, cheap solar alternative to fossil fuels. A patent makes the knowledge behind the technology excludable, allowing it to be sold at a price. While this creates incentives for markets to produce the knowledge, it also rations use to those willing to pay, thus reducing use. If the price is high enough, countries may continue to burn coal, worsening global climate change. Paradoxically, the economic value of knowledge is highest at a price of zero, in which case markets will not produce it.[12] There appears to be no market solution to this dilemma.

Allocation

Resource allocation is too important to be left to any one ideology, whether capitalist, socialist, or communist. Rather, appropriate allocative mechanisms for production and consumption should be determined by existing institutions and the physical characteristics of resources. Institutions can be changed, but rivalry and inherent nonexcludability are innate physical characteristics, not policy variables.

When rival resources are scarce, different users must compete for their use—therefore, consumption should be restrained in some way. Market economies do this by "price rationing," which simply means that consumption is limited to those who are able to pay. Price rationing provides an incentive for market production, but other rationing mechanisms or cooperative supply are also possible. In contrast, rationing abundant or nonrival resources via prices or other mechanisms creates artificial scarcity and is inefficient. Open access, which means that there are no rules, regulations, or property rights that limit use, is efficient for nonrival resources and unavoidable for inherently nonexcludable resources. In this case, some form of cooperative or public provision[13] (i.e., production, maintenance, and/or protection) is required.

Excludability is the result of institutions, and hence a policy variable. Rationing is only possible for excludable resources and only desirable for scarce resources. Some form of cooperative provision or protection is required for nonexcludable resources. An approach suitable for potentially

TABLE 20.1. Resource Allocation Matrix: Possible Combinations of Rivalness, Scarcity, and Excludability

	Excludable	Nonexcludable
Rival and Scarce	**Potential Market Goods** Consumption: Rationing required Production: Price rationing creates incentives for private sector production	***Open-Access Regimes*** Consumption: Rationing desirable, but not possible Production: Cooperative or public institutions required to regulate use (i.e., make resource excludable) so that rationing is possible.
Congestible (rival, on the border between scarce and abundant)	**Club or Toll Goods** Consumption: Rationing required to avoid scarcity Production: Price rationing creates incentives for private sector production	Like ***open-access*** regimes when scarce Like **public goods** when abundant
Nonrival or Abundant	***Artificial Scarcity Regimes*** Consumption: Rationing creates artificial scarcity and is inefficient Production: Price rationing creates incentives for private sector production	**Public Goods** Consumption: Open access is efficient and generally unavoidable Production: Cooperative or public institutions required

excludable resources is to cooperatively make them excludable—for example, a cooperative global effort to limit greenhouse gas emissions would make the absorption capacity for greenhouse gases excludable. Cooperation should be on the scale of the benefits produced—local cooperation for local benefits, global cooperation for global ones.

Table 20.1 shows the possible combinations of rivalness, excludability, and scarcity, along with relevant allocation mechanisms, which are explained below. The regimes in italics are inherently inefficient at increasing human welfare.

Potential Market Goods

Market competition can work reasonably well for the production and consumption of resources that are both rival and excludable, but can also fail catastrophically. There are several problems with conventional markets that must be addressed in a post-carbon world.

Markets allocate resources among products, and products among consumers, in a way that maximizes monetary value. The question, however, is whether monetary value is actually what we want to maximize. If an American is willing to pay more for corn to make ethanol for her over-sized sport utility vehicle (SUV) than a malnourished Mexican can afford to pay for tortillas, then converting corn to ethanol maximizes monetary value. Markets allocate resources based on the principle of one dollar, one vote, and future generations have no vote. Markets are guided by the preferences of living individuals weighted by their purchasing power.

Furthermore, markets rely on negative-feedback loops: As resource scarcity increases, prices rise, signaling consumers to consume less and suppliers to supply more or develop substitutes. Prices balance supply with demand. However, the supply of low-entropy matter-energy and land is fixed. When the price of nonrenewable resources like fossil fuels or minerals increases, we may extract in-ground stocks more rapidly to temporarily increase current supply, but at the expense of future supply. If we extract renewable resources like timber or fish more rapidly in response to a price increase, we may actually decrease their capacity to reproduce, again reducing future supply. It is also extremely difficult to develop substitutes for fossil fuels, land, or critical ecosystem services.

Price signals could still balance supply and demand through their effect on consumption. However, as oil, land, or resource prices increase in response to scarcity, speculative demand may also increase, leading to further price increases in a positive-feedback loop. The result is a speculative bubble. Eventually, the bubble pops, and falling prices decrease speculative demand in another positive-feedback loop. The more wealth that concentrates in the hands of a few and the more the financial sector finances speculation, the more money is available for speculation and the worse the resulting instability. In the past decade, speculative bubbles in information technology, real estate, oil, food, and financial instruments have destabilized the global economy. Without extensive regulations on speculation and the financial sector, destabilizing positive-feedback loops can overwhelm the stabilizing function of market price signals.

Finally, when markets allocate ecosystem goods toward the production of market goods and services, this degrades the capacity of the ecosystem to generate nonpriced ecosystem services. There is no price change to signal rising scarcity. While markets can allocate ecosystem structure among different market goods to maximize their monetary value, they are unable to determine how much of that structure should be conserved to provide vital, nonmarketed ecosystem services. Our economic system requires mechanisms, ideally cooperative and democratic, that limit ecosystem conversion, resource extraction, and waste emissions to an ecologically sustainable scale before permitting market allocation.

Open-Access Regimes

The most serious problem with open-access regimes we currently face is waste absorption capacity, particularly for carbon dioxide. While there is no inherent limit to the stock of carbon dioxide that the atmosphere can hold, the natural rate at which geological and biological processes remove carbon dioxide from the atmosphere—that is, the waste absorption capacity (WAC) of carbon dioxide—appears to be about 20 percent of current emission rates.[14] We must therefore reduce current emissions by 80 percent to stabilize atmospheric carbon dioxide stocks, and how fast we do so determines whether the atmospheric stock will finally stabilize at 350 parts per million (ppm), posing little risk of catastrophic climate change, or 550 ppm or more, posing a substantial risk. If we fail to eventually reduce emissions by 80 percent, atmospheric stocks will simply continue to increase, and with them the risk of catastrophic change. The WAC for carbon dioxide is a rival resource: When one nation spews carbon dioxide into the atmosphere, less absorption capacity remains available to absorb another nation's carbon dioxide. Since few countries currently regulate emissions, the WAC for carbon dioxide is also nonexcludable (i.e., the atmosphere is an open-access regime) at the relevant planetary scale. As a general principle, regulation of open-access regimes must be carried out by cooperative institutions at the scale of the problem and must limit use to a sustainable scale determined by physical and ecological limits, erring on the side of caution. Institutions must also determine a just distribution: Which nations will have the right to emit carbon dioxide, and which firms and individuals within those nations?

Once cooperative institutions have determined both sustainable scale and just distribution, WAC should be efficiently allocated. Economists generally favor tradable emission permits or carbon taxes, which are theoretically efficient in maximizing monetary value. Emission permits can be auctioned off, with revenue spent for the public good, or awarded to specific users. In practice, permits have typically been awarded to the polluters, ignoring the criterion of social justice. Alternatively, if carbon taxes are used, the state retains property rights to WAC and charges a fixed fee for use. In the "cap, distribute, and trade" approach, supply determines price, whereas with carbon taxes, price determines supply. Because prices adjust quite quickly to supply constraints and ecosystems adjust quite slowly to human activities, caps determined by ecological constraints that are then justly distributed are likely superior to taxes.[15]

Public Goods and Artificial-Scarcity Regimes

Nonrival resources have the wonderful property that no matter how much we use them, just as much remains. It is therefore inefficient to ration use, via prices or other mechanisms, in which case markets will not provide them. For resources that are also inherently nonexcludable—such as climate stability, protection from the ozone layer, and the ecological resilience provided by biodiversity—open access is the only option. If there is no way to limit use, there is no way to charge for use and no way to create purely market mechanisms for provision. Public goods must be provided or protected cooperatively.

Potential solutions to climate change and peak oil illustrate the economics of nonrival resources. Society currently faces two critical and conflicting thresholds. The first is an economic threshold. Without fossil fuels, existing technologies could not satisfy the basic needs of 7 billion humans. If we reduce fossil-energy consumption below some minimum level, perhaps 40 percent of current use, our economy is likely to collapse. The second is an ecological threshold. If we fail to reduce carbon emissions by at least 80 percent, runaway climate change may cause agriculture and hence civilization to collapse. Bridging the gap between these two critical thresholds requires new, more environmentally benign technologies, including solar energy.

Solar energy itself is inherently nonexcludable and nonrival[16] at the global level, as the capture of photons by one nation leaves no fewer for others. Since photon flows from the sun are fixed, applied knowledge in the form of new technologies largely determines how much we can capture and how cost effectively we can do so.[17] Knowledge actually improves with use. One policy option, patents, makes knowledge an excludable market good, in which case prices create an incentive for producing knowledge but simultaneously ration its use and create artificial scarcity. A more efficient alternative, for at least five reasons, is cooperative production of knowledge (e.g., through public funding and open-access use):

1. The most serious problems we face today include threats to climate stability and other critical ecosystem services, most of which are public goods. Markets provide no direct incentives to invest in technologies that provide or protect public goods.

2. In spite of the peak-oil threat, energy companies are reluctant to invest in alternate technologies that will substitute for fossil fuels and drive down the value of their existing investments.

3. Though every dollar spent on meeting the needs of the poor is likely to have a greater net impact on welfare than a dollar spent satisfying the wants of the rich, the latter is more profitable.

4. Information improves through sharing. However, scientific teams competing to be the first to patent efficient solar technologies are unlikely to share information with their competitors. Patents on other products and processes essential to developing the new technology further slow down research.[18]

5. Patents on knowledge ration access, and carbon-neutral energy technologies must be widely adopted if they are to prove effective. The challenges we confront are too serious for such inefficiencies.

With the same resources, publicly funded scientists would work cooperatively toward producing technologies that provide and protect public goods and meet the needs of the poor, sharing knowledge to speed the rate of advance. Once developed, technologies would be open access, leaving others free to use and improve the product without worrying about patent infringement. Open-access technologies would be more widely adopted and more quickly improved upon without worries of patent infringement and thus far more likely to address global problems. Cooperation would appear to be inherently more efficient than competition in developing the new knowledge required to solve society's most pressing problems.

A central objection to cooperative supply of open-access knowledge is the problem of funding. However, whether through market prices or taxes, citizens will ultimately pay the costs of new technologies, as well as the costs of climate change, and both are likely to be lower with public funding of research. Unfortunately, the ideological assumption that markets are always more efficient than government undermines the political will required for adequate public funding. Another objection is that, at the international level, we lack the institutions necessary to force countries to contribute, leading to the threat of some countries "free-riding" on the efforts of others. However, when countries free-ride by using carbon-free energy technologies, the country that supplied that technology also benefits. Given the nature of knowledge, the free-rider is likely to develop improvements, which would then be available to the original supplier.

Money and the Financial Sector

Finally, though not a true physical resource, money plays a critical role in determining how resources are allocated—and the existing financial system is not sustainable, just, or efficient. A growing economy requires more money to chase more goods and services. Most money is created when the financial sector simply loans it into existence. The money is destroyed when the loans are repaid, but borrowers must also pay interest. If the economy is not growing, then interest payments are a zero-sum game: a transfer of resources to the financial sector, creating intense pressures for economic growth requiring yet more money creation, which is unsustainable on a finite planet. Furthermore, money that must be repaid with interest can only be loaned for profit-generating market activities, and thus will not be used to finance the provision of public goods no mat-

ter how critically important they might be. If, in addition to lending by
the financial sector, governments create money to finance the provision of
public goods, there is a growing risk of too much money chasing too few
goods and services, leading to inflation. Lending money into existence for
speculation enhances speculative bubbles. When such bubbles collapse,
financial-sector lending freezes up, aggravating the resulting collapse. The
current system of money creation is highly pro-cyclical, enhancing inherent economic instabilities.[19]

SOLUTIONS

Given the financial and ecological crises faced by our complex ecological economic system, how do we proceed? Based on extensive research,
systems theorist Donella Meadows identified several places to intervene
in complex systems, and three are discussed here: changing the paradigm,
changing the goals, and changing the rules.[20]

Changing the Paradigm: What Is Biophysically Possible?

A paradigm is a worldview, a philosophical framework that provides
the underlying support to our actions and institutions. The dominant
economic paradigm of our civilization sees economic activity as largely
separate from physical and ecological realities. Several elements of this
paradigm must change:

1. We must recognize that the economy is not whole unto itself, capable
   of endless expansion. Rather, it is part of something larger—specifically, it is a subsystem of the sustaining and containing global ecosystem. The degradation of the planetary ecosystem is an unavoidable
   cost of physical economic growth. Once it becomes obvious that
   infinite economic growth is impossible, the key allocation question
   is how much economic structure can be converted into economic
   production and waste, and how much must be conserved to provide
   vital life-support functions.

2. We must recognize that the economy is not just a complicated system that can be managed by the single feedback signal of prices;
   rather, it is a complex system characterized by nonlinear change,
   emergent properties, surprises, and both positive- and negative-
   feedback loops. In such a complex system, we must actively seek to

weaken positive-feedback loops, strengthen negative-feedback loops to cope with the scale of impacts, and create new feedback signals where necessary.

3. We must recognize that competitive markets are not suitable for allocating all resources and that humans are social animals capable of both competition and cooperation. Different institutions can elicit different degrees of cooperation and competition.

Changing the Goals: What Is Socially, Psychologically, and Ethically Desirable?

The goals of an economic paradigm define the desirable ends toward which economic production should be allocated. Our dominant economic goal for well over a century has been simple: increased consumption. But consumption is only one of many human needs contributing to quality of life. Moreover, endless economic growth is not only impossible, it is not even ultimately desirable. Per capita consumption in the United States as measured by gross national product (GNP) has more than doubled since 1969, with little detectable change in people's self-expressed levels of happiness and satisfaction with life as a whole.[21] A recent study commissioned by French president Nicolas Sarkozy concluded that GNP is not an adequate measure of economic well-being.[22] Recent studies of the Canadian and English economies conclude that economic growth is not required to improve quality of life.[23]

We must rethink our goals and ask ourselves, "What, ultimately, is socially, psychologically, and ethically desirable?" To create a sustainable post-carbon economy, we must create a new shared vision of a sustainable and desirable future emphasizing healthy ecosystems, communities, and people over ever-increasing consumption.

Changing the Rules: Institutions for a Sustainable, Just, and Desirable Economy in a Post-Carbon World

The solutions to our most serious problems will require cooperation. But economists have long maintained that humans are by nature purely self-interested. They have argued that institutions based on cooperation are not feasible and have championed more "realistic" market solutions to channel unavoidable self-interest into socially optimal outcomes.

However, numerous studies in evolutionary biology have convincingly established that, while selection within a group leads to the evolution of self-interested behavior, selection *between* groups favors cooperative behavior—the success of the human species actually results from cooperation.[24] Indeed, most human cultures have evolved mechanisms that punish purely self-interested behavior, thus promoting cooperation.[25] Behavioral economists have firmly established that people care about others and about fair outcomes and, together with institutional and political economists, have shown that certain institutions promote cooperative behavior that can lead to effective solutions to the types of problems we now confront.[26] One common element of such institutions is social punishment of selfish behavior.[27] Competitive markets appear to be a rare example within human cultures of an institution that *rewards* selfish behavior.

Some specific institutional changes are necessary to bring our economic systems back in line with both our biologically inherited values and our long-term sustainability needs:

1. We must create institutions that protect, enhance, and declare common ownership of those resources created by nature or by the shared efforts of society. One option here is to specifically assign property rights to common-asset trusts that manage common assets for this and future generations. The scale of institutions should be determined by the natural distribution of asset benefits, from the local watershed level for water regulations to the global scale for management of carbon emissions. For rival common assets, such as waste absorption capacity and fisheries production, the annual increment could be rationed through use of market mechanisms in a cap-and-auction system, with the resulting revenue accruing to the trust.[28] Nonrival assets such as information would not be rationed, but the trust would invest in their provision and protection.

2. The right to create and destroy money must be removed from the financial sector and restored to the public sector, which should then use it to enhance the public good. Specifically, this would require 100 percent reserve requirements for the private financial sector, which would no longer be able to loan money into existence. The goals of the public financial sector would be ecological sustainability, just distribution, and the efficient allocation of resources toward maximizing quality of life. Money could be spent into existence

for the production of public goods during economic downturns to stimulate the economy and could be loaned into existence at zero interest for the production of important market goods as necessary. No loans would be available for speculative investments, thus dampening a pernicious positive-feedback loop. A steady-state, no-growth economy would favor a steady-state money supply, in which case money spent into existence should later be recaptured in taxes in a countercyclical, stabilizing system.[29]

3. We need a new Bretton Woods-type agreement for the international economy. The first Bretton Woods agreement was created in 1944 to rebuild the international economic system after the Great Depression and World War II. It established global institutions like the International Monetary Fund and the International Bank for Reconstruction and Development (which later became a part of the World Bank Group) to promote stable growth of the global market economy. A new agreement must be created in response to the current ecological and resource crises, and it must promote the cooperative provision of nonrival and nonexcludable resources, the stable contraction of the market economy, the convergence of global consumption levels, and the improvement of global quality of life. As a simple example, the new Bretton Woods could create the infrastructure for investing revenues from a global carbon-commons trust in open-access, renewable energy technologies.[30]

NEXT STEPS

The challenges of developing a post-carbon economy are formidable, but so are the resources available. Per capita GNP in the United States has more than doubled since 1969,[31] which suggests that if the United States dedicated half its GNP to solving the problem, its citizens could still sustain a 1969 standard of living. Straightforward solutions exist, but they require fundamental changes to the existing system. How can individuals help create such massive changes? Donella Meadows's leverage points still apply:

- *Change the paradigm—spread the word.* We must understand and disseminate a new economic paradigm recognizing that the human economy is sustained and contained by the global ecosystem, and together they form a single complex system subject to the laws of physics and ecology.

- *Change the goals—set the example.* We must show that it is possible to live within the planet's biophysical limits while improving our quality of life by relocalizing our communities and adjusting our lifestyles for the realities of the post-carbon world.
- *Change the rules—speak up for change.* We must push for the reform of our political and economic institutions so that they once again act for the public good. From local government policies to international agreements, the structures that define how our world works are ultimately products of political consent, and thus can be changed with sufficient political will.

MONEY AND ENERGY

RICHARD DOUTHWAITE

RICHARD DOUTHWAITE *is co-founder of Feasta, an Irish economic think tank focused on the economics of sustainability. He was instrumental in the development of the "contraction and convergence" approach to dealing with greenhouse gas emissions, which has since been backed by many countries. He is the author of two books, including* The Growth Illusion *(1999) and* Short Circuit *(1996). Douthwaite is a Fellow of Post Carbon Institute.*

❖

Money and energy have always been linked. For example, a gold currency was essentially an energy currency because the amount of gold produced in a year was determined by the cost of the energy it took to extract it. If energy (perhaps in the form of slaves or horses rather than fossil fuel) was cheap and abundant, gold mining would prove profitable and a lot of gold would go into circulation, enabling more trading to be done. If the increased level of activity then drove the price of slaves or coal up, the flow of gold would decline, slowing the rate at which the economy grew. It was a neat, natural balancing mechanism that worked rather well. In fact, the only time it broke down seriously was when the Spanish conquistadors got gold for very little energy—by stealing it from the Aztecs and the Incas. That caused a massive inflation and damaged the Spanish economy for many years.

Gold rushes were all about the conversion of human energy into money, as the thousands of ordinary people mining in the Amazon Basin show. Obviously, if supplies of food, clothing, and shelter were precarious, a society would never devote its energies to finding something that its members could neither eat nor live in, and which would not keep them warm. In other words, gold supplies swelled in the past whenever a culture had the energy to produce a surplus. Once there was more gold available, using the precious metal as money made more trading possible—enabling the conversion of whatever surpluses arose in future years into buildings, clothes, and other needs.

Lots of other ways of converting human energy into money have been used as well. For example, the inhabitants of Yap, a cluster of ten small islands in the Pacific Ocean, converted their energy into carved stones to use as money. They quarried the stones on Palau, some 260 miles away, and ferried them back on rafts pulled by canoes. But once on Yap, the heavy stones were rarely moved, just as lots of gold never leaves Fort Knox.[1]

The last fixed, formal link between money and gold was broken on August 15, 1971, when President Richard Nixon ordered the U.S. Treasury to abandon the gold exchange standard and stop delivering one ounce of gold for every $35 that other countries paid in return. Some people think that this link between the dollar and energy was replaced by an agreement that the United States then made with the Organization of the Petroleum Exporting Countries (OPEC) that "backed" the dollar with oil. Supposedly, OPEC agreed to quote the global oil price in dollars and, in return, the United States promised to protect the oil-rich kingdoms in the Persian Gulf against threat of invasion or domestic coups. If it exists, this arrangement is currently breaking down.

A more important current link between energy and "official" money is the consumer price index. The central banks of every country in the world keep a close eye on how much their currency is worth in terms of the prices of the things the users of that currency purchase. Energy bills, interest payments, and labor costs are the key components of those prices. If a currency shows signs of losing its purchasing power, the central bank responsible for managing it will reduce the amount in circulation by restricting the lending the commercial banks are able to do.

Almost all the money we use is created as a debt. If a bank gives someone a loan to buy a car, the moment the purchaser's check is deposited in the car dealer's account, more money—the price of the car—has come into existence, an amount balanced by the extra debt in the purchaser's bank account. In the current monetary system, the amount of money and the amount of debt are equal and opposite.

Until recently, if the banks gave out more loans and the amount of money in circulation increased, more energy could be produced from fossil-fuel sources to give value to that money. Between 1949 and 1969—the heyday of the gold exchange standard—the price of oil was remarkably stable in dollar terms. But then the energy supply was suddenly restricted by OPEC in 1973 and 1979, and the price of energy went up—not just because users were competing for less oil, but also because there was too much money in circulation for the amount of oil available. And so money's exchange rate with energy fell.

Looked at another way, besides there being too much money in 1973 and 1979, there was also too much debt. A country's income is largely determined by its direct and indirect energy use—thus, whenever less energy becomes available, incomes fall and debt becomes harder to service. This is exactly what happened in the 1970s.

This simple analysis helps explain why the "credit crunch" of recent years came about. Because of resource constraints, world oil output was almost flat between September 2004 and July 2008 and its price went up and up. The rich world's central bankers were blasé about this price increase because the overall cost of living was stable thanks to lots of cheap imports from China and elsewhere. They allowed the banks to go on lending and the money supply—and debt—to increase and increase. The only inflation to result was in the price of assets such as shares and real estate, and most people felt good about that. They were getting richer, on paper at least.

A lot of the money the banks created left the energy-importing economies and went to the energy-producing ones, which took in more than they could spend. So the producing countries lent huge sums back to banks in the countries from which the money had come, and those banks in turn lent it out rather too easily, in ways that included subprime mortgages. The trouble was, as energy prices continued their climb, more and more of those who took out the easy loans were unable to service them and—weighed down by bad debts—the banking system collapsed.

The debt-based money system just described cannot work if there is less and less energy available. We only borrow if we think we're going to have more money in the future with which to repay, and a society as a whole cannot expect to have more money unless there is economic growth, or inflation, or a combination of the two. Moreover, we can't expect to have growth without more energy. Historically, the link between growth and energy use has been very close.

So if we don't borrow (or the banks won't lend) the money supply will contract as previous years' debts are paid off, destroying the money the debts created when they were issued. This makes it progressively harder for businesses to trade and to pay employees. They also have more problems paying taxes and servicing their debts.

This is exactly the situation at present. Now that the effects of the federal stimulus package are running out, a terrifying downward spiral is developing. Profits and incomes are shrinking, making people very reluctant to borrow. Of course, the question remains, what would they borrow *for*? Is there any part of the economy in which people can invest borrowed money and be sure of being able to pay it back? What economists call a liquidity trap has developed.

THE COMPETITIVENESS OF
LOCAL LIVING ECONOMIES

MICHAEL H. SHUMAN, JD

MICHAEL SHUMAN *is director of research and public policy at the Business Alliance for Local Living Economies (BALLE). He holds an AB with distinction in economics and international relations from Stanford University and a JD from Stanford Law School. He has authored, co-authored, or edited seven books, including* The Small Mart Revolution: How Local Businesses Are Beating the Global Competition *(2006) and* Going Local: Creating Self-Reliant Communities in the Global Age *(1998). Shuman is a Fellow of Post Carbon Institute.*

❖

Economic localization ("localization" in the rest of this chapter) offers the key to solving a growing number of global problems, including peak oil, climate disruption, and financial meltdowns. Yet the perception remains that this solution is very costly, because local goods and services supposedly are more expensive than their global alternatives. American consumers are convinced that "big-box" stores and bigger businesses mean lower prices—"always," in the Wal-Mart vernacular. And not a few localization activists concur, arguing that consumers should nevertheless be prepared to pay more to responsibly avert the calamities of a carbon-dependent world.

In fact, local goods and services are already competing remarkably well in the marketplace—and they are likely to do better in the near future. This chapter lays out why cost-effectiveness actually is a reason to *embrace* localization and argues that the only thing standing in the way of localization flourishing is, oddly, policy-makers committed to propping up increasingly noncompetitive global corporations.

A LOCAL LIVING ECONOMY

Ever since 2001, when the Business Alliance for Local Living Economies (BALLE) was founded, the term "local living economy" has become shorthand for a pragmatic approach to localization. Two principles lie at its core:

1. The wealthiest communities are those with the highest percentage of jobs in businesses that are locally owned. A growing body of evidence suggests that local ownership in businesses pumps up the multiplier effect of every local dollar spent, which increases local income, wealth, jobs, taxes, charitable contributions, economic development, tourism, and entrepreneurship.

2. The wealthiest communities are those that maximize local self-reliance. This doesn't mean that they cut themselves off from global trade. But they rely on trade only for the diminishing universe of goods and services that they cannot competitively provide for themselves.

Both principles would be very difficult to vindicate, if not impossible, were global businesses ultimately more competitive than local ones. If the scale of business has to be large for them to compete, then it would be difficult for communities to embrace locally owned firms, because larger-scale businesses require global pools of owners. Nor could communities possibly achieve greater self-reliance, because larger-scale businesses imply greater reliance on trade. Fortunately, there's powerful evidence that local businesses in the United States are *already* quite competitive—and likely to become more so in the years ahead.

THE CURRENT ECONOMY

The U.S. economy turns out to be remarkably local already. A good sense of the U.S. economy can be gleaned from the 2010 edition of the *Statistical Abstract*, an annual publication of the U.S. Census Bureau[1] (unless noted otherwise, the figures below are all for 2006, the most recent year for which most data are available in the report).

Table 744, on "Employer Firms," shows that in 2006, firms with fewer than 500 employees (which is how the U.S. government officially defines "small businesses") accounted for 50 percent of all private-sector jobs. Since smaller businesses pay employees slightly less than larger businesses, they account for 44 percent of payrolls. Roughly speaking, then, small businesses make up about half the private economy. Probably 99 percent of these small businesses are locally owned sole proprietorships, partnerships, and small corporations.

Add both government entities and nonprofits to small businesses and one finds that nearly 60 percent of the economy is rooted in place. That's the national average. Any decent accounting of unpaid labor, like stay-at-home parents, family care of the elderly, and volunteerism generally—all items economists don't know how to count and therefore assign a value of zero to—would conclude that perhaps 80 percent of the economic activities in a typical community are done by resident entrepreneurs and firms. *In other words, the world's most powerful industrial nation is largely made up of locally owned businesses today.*

But isn't globalization upending this? Haven't Wal-Marts, Home Depots, Borders bookstores, and thousands of other chains taken over our communities and destroyed local businesses? Well, yes, they have, but keep in mind that every business listed in the previous sentence is a retailer. The Census Bureau abstract's table 654, which breaks down gross domestic product (GDP) by industrial sectors, shows that retail accounts for about 7 percent of the economy. In much of the other 93 percent of the economy, in everything from manufacturing to finance, local businesses have been experiencing a renaissance.

If global companies were really beating local companies, their "market share" of GDP would be growing. Table 744 in the abstract shows that in 2006, the global-local breakdown was practically identical to what it was in 2000, and that small businesses accounted for 3 percent less of the economy than in 1990.[2] So, in sixteen years of globalization, small businesses lost only 3 percent "market share." Big deal. In fact, even that loss may not have occurred.

The Census Bureau's table 741 provides figures on "Nonemployer Establishments," businesses (many informal and home based) with no employees at all. These entrepreneurs are not included in the small-business figures just discussed. It turns out that in 2006, more than 20 million Americans generated $970 billion of business with no employees at all—or more than 7 percent of the U.S. economy (GDP that year was a bit over

$13 trillion). Comparable nonemployer data go back only to 1997, when 15 million Americans generated $586 billion of business. Extrapolating backwards, there were perhaps 10 million self-employed individuals generating $300 billion of business in 1990. The 3 percent of market share supposedly lost by small businesses since then was actually more than made up for by growth in smaller, home-based businesses.

So, despite nearly two decades of globalization and public policies (elaborated below) tilted like a double-diamond ski slope against small business, local businesses have steadily maintained their share of the economy. This fact underscores how competitive the sector is. And if we retooled public policies to remove their big-business bias, local businesses could be expected to substantially increase their market share.

But surely these local businesses, even if they survive from year to year, are not as profitable as global businesses. In fact, table 728 in the abstract, on "Number of Tax Returns, Receipts, and Net Income by Type of Business," shows that nonfarm proprietorships generate three times more after-tax income, for every dollar of sales, than corporations. Partnerships fall in between. Because the profits of corporations are effectively taxed twice—through corporate taxes and then individual taxes on dividends and stock gains—their relative profit rates are even less attractive to investors.

So are local businesses profitable in every sector? Let's look at the 1,100 categories of the North American Industrial Classification System (NAICS), which is effectively the inventory of all firms in the United States.[3] Of all 1,100 categories, only *four* showed the number of large firms exceeding the number of small firms in 2006. Topping the list of industries hard to localize is nuclear power (yet another reason to oppose that economically and environmentally dangerous energy alternative). The other three least localizable industries are sugar beet manufacturing, potash mining, and pipeline manufacturing. In every other part of the economy, we have many more examples of successful small, local businesses than we do of large, global businesses.

A mistake that economic developers commonly make is that they look at the average business size in a given industry. From a community perspective, this is irrelevant. A community should be looking at just the right size firm consistent with local resources and regional markets. And any community trying to become self-reliant can find myriad examples of small-scale business success in nearly every category of the economy.

Another feature of the U.S. economy is that, as a country, we are surprisingly self-reliant. Table 651 in the Census Bureau's *Statistical Abstract* shows that in 2008, the country imported $2.5 trillion worth of goods and services into our $14 trillion economy. That is, imports represented about 17 percent of the economy. When the Chinese stop artificially keeping their currency low and other foreigners begin unloading their shrinking American dollars, both of which seem inevitable, this import percentage will drop. We are destined to become more self-reliant very soon. The only question is how fast.

LOWEST PRICES

But what about prices? Aren't the Wal-Marts of the world always going to charge lower prices than their local competitors? What is not well appreciated is how nonsensical this question is. The U.S. economy is made up of literally millions of products. Studies that claim that this or that chain store is cheaper—and many of these studies have been commissioned by said stores and still call themselves "independent" surveys—do little more than cherry-pick a tiny sampling.

If you believe that price is the primary driver of consumer demand, then you've never been to Starbucks. There may be many reasons to buy your mocha latte with a shot of vanilla, but price is not one of them. What really matters to consumers is *value*, which considers price alongside many other factors: What's the quality of the product? How trustworthy is the producer? What's the after-purchase service package look like? How rewarding is the shopping experience? What's the chance I'm going to be overcharged or ripped off? How well does the company treat its workers and the environment? Does it contribute to local charities and sponsor the local Little League? These turn out to be the very categories in which local businesses naturally excel.

If local businesses provided goods and services with low value, then consumers—given the real facts about more expensive and shoddy local alternatives—would flock to the chain stores. In fact, buy-local campaigns always move consumers in the opposite direction. The more information consumers have, the more they buy local. One compelling explanation is that most consumers today know relatively little about great deals locally and instead have been influenced by billions of dollars of advertising pumping the virtues of buying globally.

Back to the Census Bureau's *Statistical Abstract*. Table 651 breaks down consumer spending in the United States into three categories: durable goods, nondurable goods, and services. In 1970 services made up 45 percent of spending. By 2008, it grew to 60 percent. This trend is mirrored in every industrialized country in the world. As people make more money, they get saturated with "stuff." Once you have your third car, your fourth computer, and your fifth television set, you begin to see the virtue in spending your next available dollar on more education or better health care. This trend is great news for localization, because most services are inherently local and depend on face-to-face relationships with people we know and trust.

But what about outsourcing to global service providers? Thomas Friedman's book, *The World Is Flat*, is filled with anecdotes about American firms turning to low-wage workers in India and China to do taxes or patent filings.[4] But all his colorful stories turn out to have little statistical significance. Table 1250 in the Census Bureau's *Statistical Abstract* shows that the U.S. trade balance in services has been in surplus and steadily growing over the past decade to $144 billion in 2008. Imports of outside services have been fairly inconsequential.

Yes, the U.S. trade deficit has ballooned in recent years, but it's all been because of our imports of foreign *goods*. Table 651 in the abstract shows that only about a quarter of our goods consumption is of "durables." Cars, appliances, gadgets, DVDs, computers, toys, housewares—all the stuff increasingly manufactured in China—constitute only about a tenth of our overall spending. The "nondurables" tend to include food, building materials, wood, textiles, clothing, office supplies, and paper products. And the greater importance of nondurable goods in consumer spending provides yet another opening for localization.

An important characteristic of many of the nondurables is that their weight-to-value ratio is much greater than that of durables. When energy prices and shipping costs rise, nondurable imports will be the first casualties. This means that local production of food and clothing coupled with local distribution, for example, will once again be competitive against Wal-Mart's importing of these goods 10,000 miles from China—even if the Chinese wages were zero. A paradoxical implication of distant, low-wage manufacturing is that distribution costs are becoming more important. The less that labor is valued, the more that rising shipping costs can threaten the competitiveness of the model.

Other trends, of course, also are likely to make global goods more expensive. Carbon taxes, which will proliferate as the evidence of climate disruption becomes clearer, will further pump up the costs of global shipping. Fears of terrorists cutting off or sabotaging long-distance supplies will put a new premium on local production of food, energy, and other necessities. The Internet is giving more and more people the opportunity to choose to live in places they love, irrespective of the community's size or natural resources, and to participate in their professions of choice from their own homes. As noted earlier, home-based businesses constitute one of the fastest-growing parts of the U.S. economy.

Meanwhile, local businesses in every industrial sector are learning how to compete more effectively. Through community-based networks, local businesses are sharing best practices—in service, in technology, in business design, in marketing, in finance. These businesses are learning the competitive value of working together. For years, True Value Hardware stores—all locally owned—have successfully competed against Home Depots through a producer cooperative. Tucson Originals is a group of independently operated restaurants in Arizona that collectively buys foodstuffs, kitchen equipment, and dishes to bring down their costs. There is no economy of scale that local businesses cannot plausibly realize through collaboration.

Thanks to the work of groups like the Business Alliance for Local Living Economies and the Transition Network, local business innovations are now spreading globally. Community food enterprises are increasingly collaborating through sister restaurants and technical exchanges. Global conferences are passing along innovations in small-scale energy systems, credit unions, and local currencies. While the Lilliputian businesses have been slow to find their footing, they finally are learning that by working together they can restrain the Gullivers of globalization.

POSTGLOBALIZATION POLITICS

If the analysis above is correct, globalization is fast approaching a cliff— one that much of the world is not anticipating. Global corporations will not disappear, of course, but their role will shrink and many will go out of business. They will be forced to focus on the diminishing number of highly specialized goods and services that communities cannot cost effectively provide for themselves.

All of this assumes naively, however, that economics trumps politics. In fact, wobbly global corporations can be expected to convince politicians everywhere to save them. After the major U.S. banks and financial institutions began to fail spectacularly in late 2008, a progressive president and Congress stepped in to bail them out with Troubled Asset Relief Program (TARP) legislation. If this happens every time other inefficient global enterprises are about to go out of business, then of course localization will fail—not because it can't compete, but because policy-makers can't tolerate its winning.

Many do not appreciate the extent to which U.S. policy-makers have rigged the economy against local business:

- If you're a local business in most U.S. states, you must assess a sales tax. If you're online retailer Amazon.com, you don't.
- If you're a global business, you can afford a battalion of attorneys that work the rest of the tax system so that your obligation is close to zero. If you're a local business, you can't.
- A generation ago, the way that Wal-Mart strong-arms its suppliers would have been illegal under antitrust laws. Today, the behemoth gets a pass.
- Securities laws are so ridiculously expensive for small businesses who wish to have small (unaccredited) investors that virtually no pension funds are invested in the local half of private economy. Given the greater profitability of local businesses, this is a huge and inexcusable market failure.
- The World Trade Organization and other trade regimes, by prohibiting communities from identifying which goods are locally made, essentially give placeless companies an unfair advantage while denying consumers information that could help them make more informed market choices.
- A recent study of forty-five economic development programs in fifteen states found that 90 percent were spending most of their funds to attract or retain nonlocal business. Given this, the estimated $50 billion spent each year by state and local economic developers—not to mention federal supports for big oil, big farming, big coal, big defense contractors—primarily accomplishes one result: to make local businesses less competitive.

These inequities in public subsidies, regulations, laws, and economic development practices are so extreme, so uniformly tilted against local business, that they cannot be regarded as a mere accident. They reflect years of lobbying, favor buying, and campaign contributing by global businesses. As the economic plight of global companies deteriorates, these political manipulations will intensify. And thanks to a January 2010 decision by the U.S. Supreme Court overturning a 103-year ban on direct corporate spending to influence elections,[5] corporations are now free to spend unlimited amounts on "political free speech." Localization, therefore, could still be thwarted, along with its ability to deliver a new era of prosperity to communities across the country.

Increasingly, those supporting local living economies must be prepared to expose and block this coming political backlash. Whether the country's landing in a post-carbon future is harsh or gentle, exorbitant or affordable, ultimately turns on whether our politicians will just allow local goods and services to win.

Part Ten

CITIES, TOWNS, AND SUBURBS

THE DEATH OF SPRAWL

Designing Urban Resilience for the Twenty-First-Century Resource and Climate Crises

WARREN KARLENZIG

WARREN KARLENZIG *is president of Common Current. He has developed urban sustainability frameworks, recommendations, and metrics with agencies of all sizes around the world; his clients have included the United Nations, the U.S. Department of State, the White House Office of Science and Technology, the State of California, and the Asian Institute for Energy, Environment, and Sustainability. Warren is the author of* How Green Is Your City? The SustainLane US City Rankings *(2007) and* Blueprint for Greening Affordable Housing *(1999). Karlenzig is a Fellow of Post Carbon Institute.*

❖

In April 2009—just when people thought things couldn't get worse in San Bernardino County, California—bulldozers demolished four perfectly good new houses and a dozen others still under construction in Victorville, 100 miles northeast of downtown Los Angeles.

The structures' granite countertops and Jacuzzis had been removed first. Then the walls came down and the remains were unceremoniously scrapped. A woman named Candy Sweet came by the site looking for wood and bartered a six-pack of cold Coronas for some of the splintered two-by-fours.[1]

For a boomtown in one of the fastest-growing counties in the United States, things were suddenly looking pretty bleak.

The adobe-colored two-story houses had been built by speculators in a desert region dubbed the "Inland Empire" by developers. The unsold homes faced vandalism and legal liabilities when the town's average home sales prices dropped from well over $300,000 in 2007 to $120,000 in

2009. These plummeting prices pushed Victorville over the edge, making the city one of the nation's foreclosure capitals.[2]

After people began to ransack fixtures from the vacant homes, Victorville town officials warned the bank owning the sixteen-home development that it would be on the hook for security and fire calls. The bank, which had inherited the mess from the defaulted developer, assessed the hemorrhaging local real estate market and decided to cut its losses. A work crew was dispatched to rip the houses down and get what they could—money, beer, whatever—for the remains.[3]

BOOM AND BUST

Why did this town boom and then bust so spectacularly? After all, it followed a seemingly tried-and-true model of suburban growth that was replicated across the United States for decades.

To begin with, gasoline prices had risen from under $2 in the boom years to over $4 by 2008. Thanks to such massively increased personal transportation costs, Victorville by 2009 had an extremely thin margin between what people *thought* they could afford and what they now *actually* could afford. By one estimate, Americans as a whole spend $1.25 billion less on consumer goods for each one-cent increase in the price of gasoline.[4] Thus by 2008, compared to 2005, consumers nationwide had $250 billion *less* to spend on cars, furniture, appliances, and all the other items families typically purchase when moving into a growing area like Victorville. To the alarm of real estate developers, city officials, and investors, the true total costs of living in Victorville (including gasoline and time spent commuting) also weighed heavily against market valuation.

Victorville's residents are mostly dependent on private cars to get to work—or anywhere else. The town has a few seldom-used local bus routes (less than 1 percent commute ridership) and, statistically in 2007, close to *zero* percent of people in town walked or rode bikes to get to work. Lacking other viable options, private cars are economic necessities in Victorville, as they are for millions of people living in similar exurban boomtowns across the U.S. Sun Belt.[5]

Mandatory car ownership is more than a financial burden—it constantly drains people's time and health as well as community and family involvement. Making matters worse, because San Bernardino County has only seven jobs for every ten working-age adults, many residents must become supercommuters to where there are more employment opportunities—such as Los Angeles County, which has nearly nine jobs for every ten working-age adults living in the county.[6] In 2007, almost a quarter of the people in Victorville spent more than two hours driving to and from work each day, and 10 percent wasted more than three hours in their daily work commute. At least partially because of traffic jams on the 80-mile route into Greater Los Angeles, 15 percent of commuters in Victorville in 2007 left home before 5 a.m.[7]

Victorville illustrates a story that became all too familiar over the past two decades in the United States, particularly in the West. The town's explosive growth—from 64,000 people in 2000 to 107,000 in 2007—was in part the result of lax land-use policies combined with a deregulated, no-holds-barred mortgage industry that approved loans for almost any live body that walked in the door. Home buyers and real estate investors also implicitly assumed that there would always be unlimited supplies of inexpensive water and, of course, cheap gasoline.

The rapid ascent of exurbia created conditions for steady nationwide growth in private-car ownership and driving (measured in "vehicle miles traveled"). By 2005, Americans on average were driving about 35 percent more than they were in 1980, and private-vehicle ownership had almost doubled since 1960.[8] Car ownership costs—at an average of $5,783 per vehicle—take an even greater toll on personal finances than fuel costs, which averaged $1,514 per vehicle in 2009.[9] In addition, the exurbs brought a flood of massive single-family homes built for size as symbols of affluence—but not for energy efficiency. In 2004 the average new house was 40 percent bigger than in 1970,[10] requiring additional energy to heat, cool, and maintain.

Even if cars are made to be more fuel efficient or eventually run on more renewable energy sources (e.g., solar-powered electric), the growth of large car-dependent communities will contribute to continued climate and environmental damage beyond tailpipe emissions. A significant amount of the carbon footprint produced by cars comes from their manufacturing, shipping, and eventual disposal. Indirect carbon impacts are also caused by constructing and maintaining parking spaces, roads, and other infrastructure.[11] The slurry of discharged auto fluids (oil, antifreeze, transmission fluids) that combines with particulates from engines and brake pads is a key source of water pollution in the United States, causing an estimated $29 billion a year in damages.[12]

Ultimately, the car-dominant model of urban and suburban development is not sustainable. Recognizing the limitations of this outmoded model is the first step in planning for our future of economic, energy, and environmental uncertainty.

EXURBAN SUNSET: FAILING THE MILK TEST

The least environmentally and economically sustainable form of urbanization over the past twenty years has been the exurb. Defined as smaller cities located outside of—yet dependent upon—major cities, exurbs usually are more than 50 miles from the original city center. Typically built on "greenfields" (a category that can include agricultural land as well as undeveloped wetlands, deserts, forests, or other biologically sensitive natural habitat), they leapfrog existing communities, jobs, and infrastructure. Even more than established suburbs, exurbs are designed almost exclusively for cars, needing massive supporting highway and parking infrastructure. A relatively new kind of exurb is the "boomburb," with populations over 100,000 and boasting double-digit percentage population growth within an average ten-year period.[13]

A quintessential boomburb, Victorville grew from 64,000 residents in 2000 to 107,000 in 2007, similar to the fast-growing population gains in other U.S. boomburbs during this time period. Relatively cheap real estate, flat land, and single-purpose zoning meant big profits for real estate developers and construction companies. Builders could easily and quickly build vast residential neighborhoods without thinking about where residents would work or how they would get there. Relaxed federal regulations on the financial industry meant first-time home buyers could "own" their home without a down payment, and sit back while home prices climbed.

And for a few years, climb they did. When home prices were rising in the region in the early 2000s, Victorville seemed like a sound investment. But by 2006 the price of gasoline began its steady ascent above $2 a gallon and a burst bubble in Victorville and other exurban housing markets created the first wave of foreclosures that helped set off a national economic crisis.

A complex and devastating chain of events began with people losing confidence in the seemingly ever-upward growth of exurban economies. Across the country, home foreclosures began to appear overnight in exurban hyper-growth markets, most notably inland central and southern California, Las Vegas, Phoenix, and much of Florida. The house of cards that had been built on cheap energy, imported water, easy lending terms, and massive speculation tumbled down like a tar-paper shack in a windstorm.

The nationwide exurban decline that has ensued may prove to be the last gasp of the Sun Belt's decades-long development frenzy. We will be absorbing or trying to erase the unwanted surplus of this end-of-the-twentieth-century building spree for years, if not decades. A recent report by the Urban Land Institute and PricewaterhouseCoopers, "Emerging Trends in Real Estate 2010," cautioned commercial and institutional investors against spending a penny in exurban and outer-suburban markets: "Avoid neighborhoods wracked by foreclosures, especially in outer suburbs—these places may have no staying power." And "shy away from fringe places in the exurbs and places with long car commutes or where getting a quart of milk takes a 15-minute drive."[14]

Californian exurbs like Victorville will have to contend not only with dismal real estate outlooks but also with the ramifications of a statewide (and global) push to fight carbon emissions. In 2007 California successfully sued San Bernardino County, charging that its out-of-control growth endangered the state's air quality and its goals for greenhouse gas reduction.[15] San Bernardino and other California counties will now have to forecast the greenhouse gas emissions of future development and provide detailed actions for how they will keep total emissions within state limits—a major change in how communities are allowed or are not allowed to grow, and a precedent that other states may ultimately follow.[16]

REMAINING FUNCTIONAL

Exurban communities will need to do more than adapt to changing economics and regulations. In the long term, the biggest challenge of the exurbs will be keeping them *functional* after the global peaking of oil production.[17] Many exurbs—especially in the Sun Belt—will also need to contend with the regional peaking of freshwater availability. Again, Victorville illustrates this monumental challenge: Substantial amounts of electricity are needed to power the city's ubiquitous air conditioning (the average late-July high temperature is 100 degrees), while the city's water comes from arsenic-contaminated groundwater supplies that are diminishing.[18] Moreover, like much of the rest of the nation, Victorville's food supply has become utterly dependent on a global corporate supply chain fueled by cheap oil. Even if the Inland Empire wanted to grow more of its own food, the lack of rainfall (less than 4 inches a year) makes agriculture without constant irrigation highly challenging.

The speculative model that came to a grinding halt in Victorville and at the fringes of dozens of other Sun Belt cities was largely predicated on the underlying assumption that energy (whether for vehicles or for houses) would always be cheap and readily available, which led to high per capita community energy use and greenhouse gas emissions. But the world has changed. With climate change now an almost universally recognized challenge, and top analysts in government and industry warning of a global "oil crunch" by 2014–2015,[19] communities have little choice but to make better use of energy—through smarter practices in land use, transportation, and food production, and in the use of resources, particularly water.

VOTING WITH THEIR TIRES

It is worth recalling that during the latter part of the twentieth century, urban living in the United States was widely viewed as an outmoded way of life, with high taxes, crime, blight, and vanishing manufacturing jobs. America's formerly urban middle class had been fleeing to the suburbs since the end of World War II, decimating inner-city economies while fueling near-continuous development in the suburbs and, by the 1980s, in the exurbs. Well into the twenty-first century, some experts went so far as to predict that the exurban development model was the key to the nation's economic future. Harvard economist Edward Glaeser, for example, argued that most boomburbs had two key ingredients necessary to drive economic growth: sun and sprawl. He even argued that the more cars a community had per person, the more likely that community would succeed economically.[20]

For a time, it seemed like Glaeser was right.[21] Not coincidentally, this was also the point when gas prices reached their lowest relative cost in U.S. history (see figure 23.1). But far from heralding the next era of the

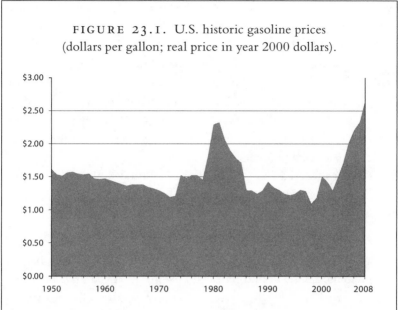

FIGURE 23.1. U.S. historic gasoline prices (dollars per gallon; real price in year 2000 dollars).

Source: U.S. Energy Information Administration, table 5.24, "Retail Motor Gasoline and On-Highway Diesel Fuel Prices, 1949–2008," in *Annual Energy Review 2008*, http://www.eia.doe.gov/emeu/aer/.

nation's suburban ascendency, boomburbs have proved instead to be the final expression of the unsustainable sixty-year development model driven largely by cheap oil.

Modern suburbia got its start in the 1950s when construction began on the federal Interstate Highway System.[22] Much of the system was in place by the mid-1960s, and vast areas of suburban and rural land were suddenly easily accessible from cities. Meanwhile, innovations in the mass production of tract housing and consumer goods made the cost of owning a new suburban home affordable to tens of millions of people. Together with the dominance of the United States in world oil production (which lasted until the late 1960s) and federal policies supporting both suburban house financing and road construction, the stage was set for the country's rapid suburbanization and concurrent deurbanization.

By the late 1980s and throughout the 1990s, ultra-cheap energy prices fueled the perfect conditions for the next phase of suburban development. Multiple "beltways" now ringed both large and medium-sized cities, while automobile manufacturers morphed the family car into the minivan and the oversized sport utility vehicle (SUV). Ever-larger gated communities of "McMansions"—served by malls designed not just for shopping but also for entertainment—sprouted beyond the farthest suburban edges and in between existing suburbs. New exurbs acted as petri dishes for different configurations of "big-box" retail centers and horizontal office campuses. Car ownership and vehicle miles traveled per person spiked dramatically upward, while once-vibrant downtown Main Streets were boarded up and left to fester.

Glaeser observed and condoned these cultural shifts in his foreword to Robert Lang and Jennifer LeFurgy's *Boomburbs: The Rise of America's Accidental Cities* (2007):

> Shopping malls increasingly play the role of downtowns. Lang and LeFurgy emphasize correctly that there is plenty of walking in boomburbs, but it takes place in the mall that you drive to. The boomburbs are able to deliver some sort of facsimile of a pedestrian experience, where people mix with each other and experience street life. The experience is, however, planned by developers rather than delivered by the chaotic functioning of the market. While traditional urbanists may find these malls no substitute for the market of the Ponte Vecchio, people do seem to be voting with their feet or at least their tires. It may make more sense to put effort into humanizing the mall than into reinvigorating many older downtowns.[23]

It wasn't just the physical appearance of the metro landscape that was transformed during the 1990s: Our own bodies began to change as well, despite all that walking in malls. The number of older adults (ages forty to seventy) not engaging in any regular physical activity increased from 15 percent in 1988–1996 to 35 percent in 2001–2006.[24] The main causes for this disturbing trend were attributed to longer commutes and more time spent on the computer.[25] Children began to have less physical activity because they were being driven more, and childhood obesity began to increase. In 1969 just over 40 percent of all children walked or bicycled to school; by 2001 this number had fallen to about 15 percent, and about half of all children were being driven to school in private vehicles.[26]

Cheap gasoline continued to drive runaway suburban and exurban growth into the twenty-first century. But in the middle of this century's first decade, around the same time that the term "peak oil" entered the public lexicon, oil prices began climbing, and quickly.[27] By the summer of 2008, when gasoline was more than $4 a gallon (over $5 in California) and oil hit an all-time record of $147 a barrel, the long era of gasoline-powered suburban expansion went into paralysis. As for future exurban development potential, the "Emerging Trends in Real Estate 2010" report summarized the inherent investment risks: "Road congestion, higher energy costs, and climate change concerns combine to alter people's thinking about where they live and work."[28]

FROM GREEN TO RESILIENT CITIES

As the U.S. exurban era was experiencing a (final?) rise and fall in the twenty-first century's first decade, the "green" urban movement was coalescing in North America.

Before this watershed decade, "green buildings," downtown street-cars, urban farms, carsharing companies, high-quality bicycle infrastructure, and other physical features now associated with urban sustainability were found in only a handful of North American cities. Today, these hallmarks of green cities are popping up *everywhere*. Big cities like New York, Los Angeles, Vancouver, Toronto, and Chicago are actively trying to "out-green" each other, while suburbs like Boulder, Colorado, and Alexandria, Virginia, are rolling out their own localized sustainability solutions. Some communities have taken pioneering steps toward protecting their surrounding agricultural lands, or "foodsheds,"[29] from well-established regional plans and policies in Portland, Oregon, to a comprehensive local food policy in San Francisco.[30]

This multifaceted movement is spreading nationally and internationally as cities recognize that they can't just "grow smarter"—they have to fundamentally remake themselves to be resilient for the unprecedented economic, social, and environmental challenges of the twenty-first century. In the United States, existing metropolitan areas can be retrofitted to take advantage of breakthroughs in sustainability and efficiency technologies, as well as new financial incentives. The American Recovery and Reinvestment Act of 2009 provided some funding for the energy-efficient redesign of buildings and transportation infrastructure.

Growing a green economy will be a fundamental facet of urban resilience. Key areas of future job growth are in green building and landscaping, water-conservation technologies, low-carbon materials design, advanced low-carbon transportation, green information and communications technologies, and smart-grid development. Some metro areas are already becoming home to "clean-tech" centers with significantly high job growth rates.[31] Clean-tech clusters are emerging in the San Francisco Bay Area, Boston, and Austin, as well as in some less-obvious locations. In Toledo, Ohio, for instance, more than 4 percent of all jobs are now in research, development, and manufacturing for solar energy.[32]

Multiple, concurrent steps need to be taken to prepare our cities, towns, and suburbs for the future. When analyzing the early adopters of sustainability planning, seven overall strategies stand out. These strategies can be expanded from sustainability planning to *resilience planning*:

1. *Planning:* Enable the development of vibrant mixed-use communities and higher-density regional centers that create a sense of place, allow for transportation choices (other than private automobiles), and protect regional agricultural, watershed, and wildlife-habitat lands.

2. *Mobility:* Invest in high-quality pedestrian, bicycle, and public transit infrastructure with easy access, shared connectivity, and rich information sources, from signage to cell-phone alerts.

3. *Built Environment:* Design new buildings and associated landscaping—and retrofit existing buildings—for state-of-the-art energy efficiency (e.g., smart-grid applications) and resource efficiency, integrated with mobility options.

4. *Economy:* Support businesses to provide quality local jobs and meet the needs of the new economy with renewable energy and other green technologies and services. Support local and regional economic decision-makers in adapting to the new world of rising prices, volatile energy supplies, and national demographic shifts.

5. *Food:* Develop regional organic food-production, food-processing, and metro-area food-distribution networks.

6. *Resources:* Drastically cut the use of water, the production of waste, and the use of materials, reusing them whenever possible.

7. *Management:* Engage government, businesses, and citizens together in resilience planning and implementation; track and communicate the successes, failures, and opportunities of this community-wide effort.

UNEXPECTED BEHAVIOR CHANGES

As examples in transportation, food consumption, and energy use demonstrate, citizen behavior changes are proving to be a major factor in the growth of green urbanism.

By 2008, high energy costs and the slowing national economy made U.S. citizens do something few economists predicted: They began to drive less and take public transit more. They surprised economists again by continuing to drive less even *after* gas prices plummeted in 2009. Nationally, vehicle miles traveled decreased 3.6 percent between 2007 and 2008, one of the largest yearly decreases on record. In U.S. metropolitan areas, public transit ridership swelled in 2008—4 percent more than in 2007, setting a fifty-two-year record of 10.7 billion trips by public transit in one year.[33]

Cities that had already developed and maintained alternatives to private automobile travel saw nonautomotive commute rates rise as fast as pump prices. While most commuting U.S. citizens were behind the wheel in 2007, half of all commuters in Washington, D.C., San Francisco, and Boston went without cars, making use of their regions' already-existing and extensive transit infrastructure. In New York City, a full two-thirds of commuters went to work car free. It wasn't only big cities experiencing this freedom of mobility: Residents of small cities and suburbs—like Cambridge, Massachusetts; Berkeley, California; and Evanston, Illinois—used transit, walking, or biking to get to work almost as much as they used cars to commute. Bicycling in particular became a viable form of transit: New York City's commute bicycle ridership increased 35 percent from 2007 to 2008, while Portland, Oregon, saw its already-impressive cycling trip rates double from 1997 to 2007, and then increase again by a third from 2007 to 2008.[34]

The quest for reduced fossil-fuel dependency and increased self-sufficiency has also begun to impact other sectors, especially food. Farmers' markets featuring locally grown and organic produce (which does not require fossil-fuel-based fertilizers and pesticides) have sprouted up like fresh shoots, first in downtown urban districts, then in outer-city neighborhoods, suburbs, and small towns around the country. The evocative concepts of foodsheds, "locavorism" (preferring local food), and even backyard chickens are taking root—or roost!

A few U.S. cities have made significant strides in developing opt-in renewable energy choices for their citizens and businesses, while also producing renewable energy and alternative fuels for local government's own needs. Austin, Texas, has one of the largest residential and business renewable energy programs in the country, providing nearly 800 million kilowatt-hours in wind energy from western Texas in a voluntary program through the city-owned utility.[35] San Francisco generates more than 2 megawatts of solar power from eight major projects on city buildings, funded by a voter-approved bond measure.[36] Many other western and midwestern cities are converting public vehicles to less carbon-intensive alternative fuels.[37]

Portland, Seattle, and Austin are leading the national drive to create energy- and resource-conserving green building ordinances, which started with city-owned buildings and then expanded to office buildings, condominiums, and houses. Early on, Portland and Seattle created privately funded cash incentives for developers to build to greener standards, supporting hundreds of projects and making the Northwest the leading U.S. region for energy- and resource-efficient building.

Thousands of miles of lanes and trails for pedestrians, cyclists, runners, and skaters are being created in cities and suburbs across the country. In New York City, bicycle lanes have appeared on major thoroughfares in every borough, and a world-class cycling/skating/walking trail now rings much of Manhattan Island. San Francisco began a program in 2009 to restrict private auto traffic on its busiest downtown bicycle thoroughfare.[38] Even suburban and exurban developments have begun to include "must-have" pedestrian and cycling features like wide sidewalks, human-scale building facades, and dedicated bike parking—together with mixed-use zoning—so people can shop, eat out, play, work, and sleep in the same neighborhood without needing to drive so much. As significant as these efforts may be, however, they represent only an initial step in the long, complex task of systemically building the resilience of our communities for future energy and climate constraints.

Of the many differences between cities building for resilience and cities stuck in the unsustainable "boomburb" model, two stand out: transportation choices and regional planning. If Victorville and San Bernardino County represent the consequences of little or no planning, Portland, Oregon, represents a model of collaborative foresight.

Portland has been a national leader in transportation choices and regional planning since the 1970s, when an unlikely combination of state land-conservation legislation, regional waste management needs, federal highway expansion plans, and local community activism led to the creation of:

- An urban growth boundary separating land for development from land for agricultural preservation.
- An elected regional government to coordinate and manage regional issues such as waste management, land-use planning, and transportation planning.
- One of the nation's first light-rail transit lines, built as an alternative to a new interstate highway extension.

Portland metro-area stakeholders drew a line between land for development and land for agriculture, and then invested heavily in public transit, bicycle infrastructure, and pedestrian infrastructure to make urban living as attractive and convenient as possible. The region has become one of the few metropolitan areas in the United States that can claim reduced vehicle miles traveled per household over the past fifteen years.[39] Today it is hard to believe that the Portland region once had declining property values and poor air quality. Many other metropolitan areas have recently noticed these obvious changes and have since followed Portland's forward-looking example, almost always with a primary focus on providing new multimodal alternatives to private car travel, largely through public transit.

For metro regions across the country, transit systems might well become the difference between a functioning regional economy and an economy in chaotic free fall when gasoline once again becomes extremely high priced, scarce, or unavailable. Fuel-delivery disruptions in the Southeast provide a cautionary tale. The Southeast depends on two major pipelines to deliver petroleum products like gasoline and diesel from refineries on the Gulf Coast. But in September 2008, these pipelines were shut down when Hurricane Ike struck Texas and refineries across the region were forced to reduce or halt production. While U.S. oil reserves fell to their lowest level in more than forty years, Atlanta, Nashville, Knoxville, Charlotte, and many other southeastern cities suffered intermittent fuel shortages for weeks.[40] In most of these cities, few alternatives to private vehicles exist to move people and goods around, and outraged residents, businesses, and city officials were left stranded.

In addition to being at risk for energy-supply disruptions, either from natural disasters or from other threats, urban areas have another large-scale consideration: the need to reduce their greenhouse gas contributions while adapting to the already unavoidable effects of climate change. Climate change mitigation will be a serious challenge for all communities, but will be especially difficult and costly for car-dependent, sprawling suburbs and towns. Large freestanding houses and one-story office campuses with manicured lawns need far more energy and resources to heat, cool, clean, and water than smaller houses, row houses, apartments, and multistory offices landscaped with native plants.

In contrast, compact developments in cities and suburbs save energy beginning with physical proximities: Shared walls mean shared heating, cooling, and insulation. Accommodating growing populations and expanding businesses with repurposed existing buildings—rather than constructing new buildings—is another energy saver; rehabilitating and retrofitting areas that have already been built means that new streets, curbs, sidewalks, and utility lines often do not need to be installed. Compared to exurban sprawl, where all amenities have to be created with each new development, the infrastructure of denser preexisting urban environments saves energy and water and reduces waste because of shorter and more efficient electric, sewage, and water distribution lines.[41]

Building for energy and climate resilience represents a safer investment, as evidenced during times of high instability in energy prices. From 2006 to 2008, a period of unprecedented exurban real estate collapse, many exurban communities experienced 30 to 50 percent year-to-year property value decreases.[42] In contrast, property values in communities served by public transit, bicycling, and walking held up very well, and some of these areas actually *increased* in value during this tumultuous period. According to "Emerging Trends in Real Estate 2010":

> The lifestyle cost-of-living equation starts to swing away more dramatically from bigger houses on bigger lots at the suburban edge to greater convenience and efficiencies gained from infill housing closer to work. These homes may be more expensive on a price-per-pound basis, but reduced driving costs and lower heating/cooling bills provide offsets . . . near-in suburbs will do well especially if they link to business cores by mass transportation.[43]

GETTING TO THE RESILIENT CITY

If the "Great Recession" that began in late 2007 taught us anything, it is that allowing the unrestrained sprawl of energy-inefficient communities and infrastructure is a bankrupt economic development strategy and constitutes a recipe for continued disaster on every level. Twentieth-century-style sprawl has destroyed valuable farmland, sensitive wildlife habitat, and irreplaceable drinking-water systems at great environmental, economic, and social cost. We can no longer manage and develop our communities with no regard for the limits of natural resources and ecological systems that provide our most basic needs.

What lessons emerge from metropolitan areas that have begun to plan for the future by building their resilience with economic, energy, and environmental uncertainty in mind?

Build and Rebuild Denser and Smarter

Most suburban and urban population densities need to be increased so that energy-efficient transportation choices like public transit, bicycling, and walking can flourish. Multimodal mobility cannot succeed at the densities found in most American suburban communities today.[44] Increasing density doesn't have to mean building massive high-rises: Adding just a few stories on existing or new mixed-use buildings can double population density—and well-designed, increased density can also improve community quality of life and economic vitality.[45] Resource-efficient building technologies, as rated and certified by the U.S. Green Building Council's Leadership in Energy and Environmental Design (LEED) green building program or the U.S. Environmental Protection Agency's Energy Star rating, can be retrofitted onto existing building stock and mandated for all new construction.

Track and Measure Progress and Consider Standards

As communities increasingly come under the stresses of extreme weather induced by climate change—more frequent heat emergencies, smog alerts, floods, water shortages, and power outages—planning for resilience will be seen as an act of survival, not ingenuity or trendiness. But without implementation of large-scale resilience planning based on standards and measures, individual programs will have isolated impacts. Promising ways to measure the resilience of urban systems are being devised and refined, such as LEED for Neighborhood Development (LEED-ND), which gives credit for mixed real estate uses and access to public transit for neighborhoods or developments. On the citywide level, sustainability standards and measures are emerging from organizations like ICLEI–Local Governments for Sustainability and the Global Footprint Network.[46]

Focus on Water-Use Efficiency and Conservation

Our freshwater supply is one of our most vulnerable resources in the United States. Drought is no longer just a problem for southwestern desert cities—communities in places like Texas, Georgia, and even New Jersey have recently had to contend with water shortages. As precipitation patterns become less reliable and underground aquifers dry up, more communities will need to significantly reduce water demand through efficiency, conservation, restrictions, and "tiered pricing" (which means a basic amount of water is available at a lower price while above-average use becomes increasingly more expensive).

Global climate change is already known to be melting mountain snowpack much earlier than average in the spring, causing summer and fall water shortages. This has serious planning and design implications for many metro areas. For example, Lake Mead, which provides 90 percent of the water used by Las Vegas and is a major water source for Phoenix and other cities, has a projected 50 percent chance of drying up for water storage by 2021.[47] The days are likely numbered for having one's own swimming pool and a large, lush, ornamental lawn in the desert Southwest, unless new developments and urban growth are planned with water conservation having the highest design priority.

Focus on Food

Urban areas need to think much bigger and plan systemically for significantly increased regional and local food production. Growing and processing more food for local consumption bolsters regional food security and provides jobs while generally reducing the energy, packaging, and storage needed to transport food to metro regions. In Asia and Latin America—even in big cities like Shanghai, China; Havana, Cuba; and Seoul, South Korea—there are thriving small farms interspersed within metro areas.[48] Gardens—whether in backyards, community parks, or in and on top of buildings—may supplement people's diets with fresh local produce. Suburbs around Denver, for instance, have organized to preserve and cultivate unsold tract-home lots for community garden food production.[49]

Think in Terms of Combined Risks

The costs of energy from systems overly or solely dependent on fossil fuels, particularly coal-fired power plants, will be severely impacted by carbon-reduction regulations as well as the global decline of economically viable fossil-fuel resources. Petroleum supplies for transportation will also be at great risk of supply disruptions, whether natural (hurricanes) or man-made (terrorism, warfare, political acts).

Communities and regions should decide for themselves which initiatives reduce their economic risks and provide the greatest "bang for the buck." As we learned with Wall Street's financial-derivatives crisis in 2007, we can't rely on government or conventional wisdom to identify all the big risks to our economy—and what we don't know *can* hurt us. Imagine if Las Vegas informed its residents and tourists on one 120-degree summer day that they would not be able to wash the dishes or take a shower, let alone golf, because there simply wasn't any water left. Whole regional economies will be threatened if we continue making decisions about how we use resources and energy without considering the risks of future energy and climate constraints.

Think in Terms of Interrelated Systems

If we think of our urban areas as living, breathing entities—each with a set of basic and more specialized requirements—we can better understand how to transform our communities from near-random configurations into dynamic, high-performance systems. In the same way that food, water, and oxygen make our own bodies run, we can think about the flows of resources that make urban systems run, and then consider what we might do to improve the "metabolism" of that system.[50]

For example: More people living in southern California means more people wanting scarcer water. The conventional response might be to build more infrastructure to capture and pump more water from the Sierra Nevada to the cities and suburbs. A systems analysis, however, would note that water procurement over long distances and treatment can account for as much as 20 percent of electric power use (as is the case in California),[51] and that energy prices and supplies are only going to be more volatile in the future. Another energy-water nexus can be found in the solar-thermal power plants in the desert, which happen to require large amounts of water for cooling, thus competing for scarce drinking-water supplies.[52] These accelerating system dependencies complicate management approaches for communities across the region.

By thinking of urban areas as interrelated systems economically dependent on water, energy, food, and vital material resources, communities can begin to prepare for a more secure future. Merely developing a list of topics that need to be addressed—the "sustainability checklist" approach—will not prepare regional economies for the complexity of new dynamics, such as energy- or water-supply shortages, rising population, extreme volatility in energy prices, and accelerating changes in regional climate influenced by global climate change.

CHALLENGE AND OPPORTUNITY

In the wake of global climate change, fossil-fuel depletion, water scarcity, and the worst economic crisis since the Great Depression, there is unprecedented opportunity to challenge and overcome the bankrupt status quo. Globally and nationally, large-scale research, planning, and management practices are just beginning to be mobilized in response to these threats to our civilization. Preparations at the regional to local level, however, are often more effective than national actions because they have the ability to be more nimble as they are based on local climate, cultural, and economic conditions and needs. The era of peak oil and climate change requires that communities determine how they can best prioritize building their own resilience for an uncertain future.

The world has moved rapidly toward an urban existence. We must immediately transform the way we plan and build our cities and suburbs so that resilience is an integral part of every community's design. We need to synthesize often fractured and specialized knowledge. Citizens, businesses, and elected officials will need to contribute their skills, creativity, leadership, and expertise to this massive effort. It is imperative that "know-how" and state-of-the-art management and cultural practices are shared among our existing cities and even faster-urbanizing regions such as Asia.

Cities and suburbs have long been thought of as separate entities from nature or "the environment." That false dichotomy has come and gone: Both impact nature and are supported by it. The way we—and the rest of the world—redesign our communities for the energy and climate constraints of the twenty-first century will determine the fate not only of our nations but also of Earth's climate and the well-being of every species, humans included.

SMART DECLINE IN
POST-CARBON CITIES

The Buffalo Commons Meets Buffalo, New York

DEBORAH E. POPPER AND FRANK J. POPPER

DEBORAH POPPER *teaches geography at the College of Staten Island/City University of New York and is a member of its graduate faculty.* FRANK POPPER *teaches land-use planning at Rutgers University. They teach together at Princeton University. She is a vice president of the American Geographical Society. He chairs the board of the Great Plains Restoration Council. They are members of the board of the National Center for Frontier Communities. In 1987 they originated the Buffalo Commons concept, which has stimulated a national debate about the future of the Great Plains. In 2002 they devised the influential smart-decline concept.*

❖

Cities have always gained or lost population because of economic shifts, immigration, war, and environmental blessings or disasters. Settlements can dwindle and even disappear, as American western (and eastern) ghost towns and archaeological sites the world over show. Yet the United States has typically considered long-term urban population decline unusual—an anomaly that, should it occur in one place, has less significance than growth there and elsewhere.

Many American cities—mostly in the Midwest and Northeast—have, however, seen serious continuing shrinkage in recent decades and are now beginning to face up to it. A few have tentatively tried to craft measures that accept the persistence, even permanence, of their smaller size. As these cities search for answers, one of the few models they can turn to comes from, of all places, the buffalo country of the Great Plains states. There, communities that fought population decline for decades are now preparing for the realities of a smaller, but not necessarily worse, future. Through our work with these communities over many years, we believe that they have experience that can help guide shrinking cities in what we have called "smart decline."[1]

HISTORICAL BACKGROUND

Americans, as late-model products of the Protestant ethic and inheritors of Western culture generally, have had a bias toward growth and expansion. Large American cities first appeared in the late-nineteenth and early-twentieth centuries, a time of high industrialization and rapid external and internal immigration. Chicago had 30,000 people in 1850 and grew to nearly 300,000 in 1870. It endured the 1871 Great Chicago Fire and kept ballooning anyway, rising to more than 500,000 by 1880 and doubling again by 1900 as it became a center for railroads, meat processing, timber brokering, and finance. Midsized cities, too, like those in northeast Pennsylvania such as Bethlehem, Scranton, and Wilkes-Barre, flourished as coal and steel processors. Their overall boundaries expanded, with affluent neighborhoods for the local elites and ethnic enclaves for the working classes. Their downtowns and main streets prospered. Many cities and neighborhoods in this high industrial era grew at least as rapidly as their present-day, less industrial Sun Belt counterparts.

American city planning emerged to deal with the consequences. Sir Peter Hall's canonical history of planning shows the field forming to deal with the large new urban slums of late-nineteenth-century industrializing America (and Europe): unhealthy, congested, dangerous, ugly, vice ridden, and aggrieved, but growing fast—what he calls "The City of Dreadful Night."[2]

As the twentieth century unfolded, American city and regional planning tried to manage the pressures of rising urban and later suburban populations, as well as the effects of industrial growth. Local zoning ordinances, state land-use regulations, federal antipollution laws, and environmental reviews appeared, whose proponents expected them to uphold property values—which, under good regulatory management (i.e., theirs), would inevitably rise.

As land-use and environmental mechanisms for cities burgeoned, population and economic growth provided both the norm and the ideal— the standard template—to guide development. Thus in the 1950s and 1960s American planning devices focused on "growth control," in the

1970s and 1980s on "growth management," and in the 1990s and 2000s on "smart growth." No zoning ordinance, still the most frequent tool of American local land-use planning, explicitly anticipates that the locality or its neighborhoods will lose population.[3]

THE RECENT PAST

By the late-twentieth century vast national and global locational/industrial shifts undid the American fable of all-but-permanent urban and economic growth. Cheaper manufacturing centers arose outside the old Northeast and Midwest, first elsewhere in the United States and then abroad. White- and blue-collar workers had already used their postwar rising wages and the new federal home loans (essentially a mortgage subsidy) to flee the cities for the suburbs in huge numbers, leaving behind the poor and many minorities. Large public sewer and road-building programs further subsidized American suburbanization. Most older cities, especially in the Rust Belt, found themselves increasingly left behind: No large cohort of upwardly mobile urban newcomers moved in to replace the former residents. "The City of Dreadful Night" became "The City of the Permanent Underclass."[4]

The Big Three American carmakers, once national symbols and the country's most visible group of corporations, began their initially shallow, then steep descent into two-thirds complete bankruptcy and federal bailout by 2009. Their suppliers in the steel, coal, tire, glass, machinery, and utility industries suffered with them. The same pattern recurred in the electronics and aircraft sectors, among many others. American manufacturing could often no longer compete with its new rivals around the world.

The urban effects were predictable, though few wanted to admit to them. Long-established cities like St. Louis, which in 1900 had been the fourth-largest American city, and Buffalo, the eighth largest, dropped out of the nation's top twenty by 1980. Their smaller counterparts like Flint, Scranton, and Trenton lost population decade after late-twentieth-century decade. By the 1990s many new immigrants—for instance, Russians and South Asians in the Northeast—moved directly to the suburbs rather than undergoing the previous typical newcomer rites of passage in big cities.

Ohio, Michigan, and Pennsylvania cities, in particular, dwindled significantly. Frequently even their suburbs shrank. In 2000–2009 "the failed state of Ohio" contributed four of the ten metro areas that lost the largest absolute numbers of people.[5] Behind New Orleans and Pittsburgh, Cleveland was in third place, Youngstown-Warren fifth, Dayton eighth, and Toledo tenth.[6] About half of Detroit's surrounding cities and towns lost population in the decade.

Youngstown emerged as a clear example of a shrinking city trying hard to adapt.[7] In 1950 the city was a vibrant steel town with 170,000 people, the fifty-seventh-largest U.S. city. Then suburbanization hit, the steel mills began to close in 1977, and by 2000 it had 82,000 inhabitants, less than half its size two generations earlier. Its decrepit neighborhoods had typical signs of shrinkage: abandoned or underused buildings, empty overgrown lots, high crime, and aging and heavily minority populations.

In 2002, after decades of trying to restart economic development like most other Rust Belt cities, Youngstown made a radical change in approach. The city began devising a transformative plan to encourage some neighborhoods to keep emptying and their vegetation to return.[8] The plan, still early in its implementation as we write (March 2010), would raze underoccupied structures, streets, and alleys to form larger land parcels and home lots, more green space, and new parks. At the heart of the plan is Youngstown's acceptance of decline and attempt to use it to improve the remaining buildings, infrastructure, and services by strategically concentrating them.

A perverse measure of the nation's (and the environmental professions') neglect of shrinkage possibilities showed up in the media reception of Youngstown's 2005 plan. Accepting shrinkage seemed so unusual that within two years the city's approach appeared on the front pages of *USA Today* and the *Wall Street Journal*, on National Public Radio's *Morning Edition*, on the Voice of America, and on the *New York Times Magazine*'s list of 2006's most interesting ideas.[9] The shrinkage policies of Braddock, Pennsylvania, a small town near Pittsburgh, won its mayor, John Fetterman, the cover of the November 2009 *Atlantic*'s "100 Brave Thinkers" issue.[10] The town's population losses—90 percent, according to the *Atlantic*—call for extreme approaches, and Fetterman has emphasized art, turning eyesores into murals and bidding for artists to relocate there.

Buffalo's decline has left it with the threadbare assets of a much larger place, a size-40 city in a size-60 suit. It retains the architectural treasures, theaters, hospitals, schools, and government buildings (including an always-outsized City Hall) to anchor a major region, but now, at less than half its population at its height, it has too few people to fully occupy them. The city's "5 in 5" plan calls for razing five thousand buildings in five years by evaluating vacant buildings and putting them up for bids.[11] Razing occurs if there are no takers.[12] The city promotes historical preservation, trying to weed out the excess but keeping the design gems. As elsewhere, vacant land is used for community gardens. Flint, too, draws on these strategies and emphasizes greening vacant land in its master plan.[13]

Detroit, with more than a third of its residential lots already vacant or derelict, has seen smart-decline efforts by nonprofits like the Detroit Vacant Property Campaign, which advocates land banking and improving foreclosure procedures and works with neighborhoods to devise approaches to vacancies.[14] The Detroit City Council approved the Detroit Land Bank in July 2008. Urban agriculture is growing. Most telling, shrinkage strategies figure as the mayor's top priority. In March 2010, in his first State of the City address, Mayor Dave Bing announced his plan to demolish three thousand buildings in 2010 and ten thousand overall by 2014. The program draws on considerable federal support and is described as a way to strengthen neighborhoods and improve land use.[15] Detroit, the poster child of urban shrinkage, has become the site of some of the nation's liveliest discussions about where to go next in smart decline.

All of these places—still a minority among shrinking cities—are struggling to grasp their next steps: how to respond to lost revenue and political power, and how to salvage their obsolete land uses and unexpectedly open spaces. They seem to lack useful models to help them adapt to their new size. But models of decline do exist—in rural America.

A GREAT PLAINS APPROACH

While the Detroits and Youngstowns grew in the late-nineteenth and early-twentieth centuries, rural regions and communities shrank. By the late-twentieth century, rural growth had become unusual unless based on exurbia, amenities, or (typically short-term) resource strikes. In fact, generations-long population declines in the Corn Belt, upper Midwest, and lower Mississippi Delta fit a clearly standard pattern of the early phases of the Industrial Revolution globally.[16] American rural regions, like shrinking cities later, at first thought (quite understandably) that their old sources of growth would return or sought new ones. Mostly fruitless decades passed before some came to creative solutions to their problems of shrinking populations.

Our own experience points to the rural Great Plains as a useful source of smart-decline strategies. The region, a seventh of the lower forty-eight United States stretching over large parts of Montana and North Dakota in the north through equally big chunks of New Mexico and Texas in the south, historically produces wheat, cattle, fossil fuels, and (in the south) cotton. It has seen three cycles of short booms and long busts since the arrival of white settlers. The first boom began with homesteading after the Civil War and ended with many of the settlers headed back east in the late 1880s and early 1890s—driven out by blizzard, drought, and economic crises. The two later cycles ended first with the 1930s Dust Bowl and then the modern decades-long, slow-leak shrinkage.[17]

The third long bust was well under way by the mid-1980s, when we began writing about the region.[18] We suggested that Manifest Destiny-style growth visions for the region had proved self-defeating, largely because of excessive resource exploitation. We argued that the rural Plains, especially its most depopulating parts, should pursue paths of ecological restoration, with large land preserves: federal, tribal, state, non-profit, and private holdings that would emphasize ecological restoration and research and mesh well with ecotourism. Traditional farming, ranching, and energy extraction could also profit by adopting lighter approaches to land that minimized inputs and disruptive landscape changes. We had no wish to displace existing secure owners or communities, or their land uses, but rather to shift the region's way of thinking about its future.[19] We called our approach the Buffalo Commons, an open-ended metaphor that evokes native species and shared land and futures.

Most Plainspeople at first dismissed the Buffalo Commons as near lunatic: a foolish and unnecessary acceptance of shrinkage. Or perhaps it was predatory—we, big eastern or West Coast interests, or the federal government, had designs on their land.[20] But over the next two decades, the old approaches continued to fail. By 2005 two more censuses had documented the continuing outmigration and the economic stress it brought. Gradually Plainspeople undertook more and more Buffalo Commons approaches.

Farmers and ranchers started shifting from cattle to buffalo. Plains banks began lending for buffalo. Plains states' agricultural extension offices offered advice on how to raise buffalo. Encouraged by the newly formed InterTribal Bison Cooperative, Sioux and other Plains tribes took steps to recover buffalo herds and restore their buffalo culture. The Nature Conservancy, the country's largest land-conservation group, began to buy and preserve Plains land, along with the Montana-based American Prairie Foundation, the Nebraska-based Grassland Foundation, and the Texas-based Great Plains Restoration Council.[21]

In late 2009 Kansas's two largest newspapers ran editorials endorsing the Buffalo Commons, suggesting that it become a national park in the western part of the state and proposing two counties as its core.[22] The two papers quoted the state's former governor and sitting secretary of wildlife and parks—a Republican and in the 1980s a critic of the Buffalo Commons—who said that it "makes more sense every year."

The term "Buffalo Commons" itself generated a wealth of possibilities. It stimulated creative assessments of the Plains' long-term assets, ecologically sensible land uses, and community-building strengths.[23] The region's still-unfolding adaptation suggests that large stretches of it are successfully moving toward the Buffalo Commons, which situates it better for the realities of the climate-changing, post-fossil-fuel era.[24]

POLICY MESSAGES

The Great Plains and the Buffalo Commons offer useful lessons for shrinking cities in the Rust Belt and elsewhere. As in the Plains, many shrinking cities' politicians and people recoil from measures that accept the ongoing decline. The initiatives feel un-American, suggest that past approaches (or one's ancestors) were inadequate, force admission that much of local destiny lies beyond local control, present political risks, and provoke other discomforts. So the cities' first responses to shrinkage continue previous "Hail Mary" approaches, hoping that only a new employer, industry, or tax policy is needed to return to growth. For most cities, this approach is misguided and ultimately useless. It misses the window these cities have to redefine themselves, basing their future on tapping the creativity of their citizens and ecosystems.

In such tasks, shrinking cities have some advantages over the Plains and other shrinking rural regions. Old cities first built for compactness, high population density, and neighborhood walkability have suddenly useful post-carbon assets such as centralized amenities and short-distance transportation. Their unintended open space offers sites for food production. They can experiment with renewable energy options that do not rely on long-distance transmission. New groups such as the National Vacant Properties Campaign ("Creating Opportunity from Abandonment") are emerging to deal with the issues urban shrinkage raises. The Obama administration may yet redeem its urban promises, especially since big states like Ohio, Pennsylvania, and Michigan, whose urban counties often have larger populations than entire Plains states, remain crucial in national elections.[25] The cities' governments, however ragged or corrupt, have precise boundaries and duties that many rural regions lack. For all their problems, Buffalo and Cleveland run their own governments in a way western Kansas, much less the Plains as a whole, does not.

The experiences of Youngstown, Flint, Braddock, Detroit, and Buffalo amount to early attempts to act on the new reality. These cities stand about where the Plains states stood in the mid-1990s and show that the search for adaptive urban shrinkage has only begun. The Buffalo Commons experience suggests specific tasks for cities that embrace rather than deny shrinkage: Reorganize space; remove unneeded infrastructure; rethink transportation, energy, and food options; encourage industrial and other heritage tourism; and, above all, rightsize themselves in authentic, resilient ways that shun past magical thinking and face the realities of the post-carbon world.

TOWARD ZERO-CARBON BUILDINGS

HILLARY BROWN, FAIA

HILLARY BROWN *is principal of the firm New Civic Works. As a professor at the City College of New York, she directs the architecture track for the interdisciplinary master of science program in urban sustainability. While assistant commissioner with the City of New York she founded the Office of Sustainable Design and co-authored the city's internationally recognized* High Performance Building Guidelines. *She has authored several publications on green building and infrastructure, and is a former board director of the U.S. Green Building Council. Brown is a Fellow of Post Carbon Institute.*

❖

The Empire State Building, its luster dimmed and its epic height overtaken during the building boom of the last several decades, is getting a timely makeover. Led by the Clinton Climate Initiative's team of experts, this iconic American skyscraper is embracing energy efficiency and carbon-emissions reduction. When completed, the 2.8-million-square-foot landmark will serve as a beacon for the real estate industry gearing up for the reality of a post-carbon future.

In a city where buildings account for 80 percent of all greenhouse gas emissions, the Empire State Building presents a highly replicable model of an environmentally progressive retrofit, in three basic steps.[1]

1. Sixty-five hundred existing windows will be reglazed to reduce the building's winter heat loss and summer heat gain. As daylight better illuminates the interior, electric lighting may be reduced, eliminating tons of waste heat.

2. The building will downsize its climate-control systems to meet its remaining heating and cooling needs more efficiently. With reduced

need for cooling, downsized air-handling systems will support comfort and good air quality with lower energy expenditure.

3. A new computerized system will give building tenants feedback on their energy use, encouraging further energy savings.

An anticipated 38 percent reduction in energy use will rank the project in the 90th percentile of the U.S. Department of Energy's Energy Star benchmark system against comparable office buildings.[2] With $4.4 million in projected annual savings, it may repay the $13.2 million cost in just over three years. Co-owner Anthony Malkin contends that this model process "will inform lawmakers, property owners, and lenders on actions to take, laws and codes to write, and new financing programs to support, ultimately yielding reduced energy consumption, reduced carbon output, higher quality workspaces, and green local jobs."[3]

As he achieves these goals, Malkin is in stride with a leading generation of forward-thinking building owners, architects, engineers, developers, contractors, and product manufacturers intent on reengineering how buildings perform. This burgeoning green building movement, now in its second decade, strives to holistically reduce (and eventually eliminate) the negative impacts buildings have on local and global ecosystems. While energy effectiveness is a leading driver, the movement also encompasses other "best practices," including locational efficiency and compact design, site restoration, stormwater and urban heat-island management, scaling back raw material and potable water use, and focusing on the quality of the indoor environment. Practiced together and done well, these strategies combine to yield operating savings in a short time, as well as a range of tenant health and productivity benefits.

BUILDINGS AND CLIMATE CHANGE: DEFINING THE PROBLEM

Viewed through a green building lens, conventionally built buildings are rather poor performers. They generate enormous material and water waste as well as indoor and outdoor air pollution (see box 25.1). As large containers and collection points of human activity, buildings are especially prodigious consumers of energy. They depend on both electricity and

BOX 25.1 The Impacts of Buildings

- *Materials:* Construction materials—including buildings, roads, and infrastructure supplies—make up 60 percent of the total flow of materials (excluding food and fuel) through the U.S. economy.[1]
- *Solid Waste:* Building construction and demolition waste accounts for 60 percent of all nonindustrial waste and more than 30 percent of the mercury in landfills in the United States.
- *Water:* Over 12 percent of U.S. water consumption—about 50 billion gallons per day—is from building occupants. The amount of water used to support municipal, agricultural, and industrial activities has more than tripled since 1950.[2]
- *Health:* Indoor levels of air pollutants in buildings can be two to five times higher than outdoor levels. Improved air quality (and fewer sick days) could potentially reduce U.S. health-care costs on the order of $17 billion to $37 billion.[3]

---

1. Wagner, L. *Materials in the Economy: Materials Flow, Scarcity, and the Environment*, U.S. Geological Survey Circular 1221, February 2002 (Denver: U.S. Department of the Interior, U.S. Geological Survey Information Services).

2. National Science and Technology Council, *Federal Research and Development Agenda for Net-Zero Energy, High-Performance Green Buildings*, October 28, 2008, http://www.bfrl.nist.gov/buildingtechnology/documents/FederalRD AgendaforNetZeroEnergyHighPerformanceGreenBuildings.pdf.

3. William J. Fisk, "How IEQ Affects Health, Productivity," *ASHRAE Journal* 44, no. 5 (2002), 56–58, available at http://doas.psu.edu/fisk.pdf.

on-site fossil-fuel use to support myriad transactions: transporting and exchanging water, air, heat, material, people, and information.

Compared to the transportation and industrial sectors, buildings account for the lion's share of U.S. energy use: 41 percent and growing, likely to over 50 percent by 2050.[4] Distributed equally between residential and commercial users, buildings consume more than 70 percent of all electricity produced.[5] With overall demand increasing at a rate of about 1.5 to 2 percent a year, buildings are the largest single source (43 percent) of carbon dioxide emissions in the United States.[6] It is thus through this very local, everyday activity of powering our facilities that building occupants unwittingly participate in global resource depletion and climate change.

MARKET TRANSFORMATION SO FAR

Initially a self-organized effort of builders and architects, the green building movement today is a rapidly growing force in urban planning and real estate development, spanning the commercial, nonprofit, government, and institutional sectors. Over the last decade, professionals and organizations within the movement have developed countless guidance documents, design tools, and policy models, essentially "training wheels" that help to demystify the complex process of rethinking a conventional development project to be truly green. One of the most widely used tools is the Leadership in Energy and Environmental Design (LEED) rating and certification system, a suite of guidelines and metrics for improving existing and new building performance, which has been in continuous development since 1998 by the U.S. Green Building Council (USGBC). The federal Energy Star program (a joint venture of the U.S. Department of Energy and the U.S. Environmental Protection Agency) has also proved to be a tremendously effective benchmarking system, identifying best energy efficiency practices for close to 100,000 businesses and 200,000 homes.[7]

The reliability of rating systems such as LEED, Green Globes, and the National Association of Home Builders Green Building Standards has led to their adoption by federal, state, and local government for public works and publicly funded projects.[8] In an increasing number of locales, rating systems are being used as regulatory measures or incentives—both pushing and pulling the market. By 2010, LEED or "LEED-equivalent" rating systems had been adopted by thirteen federal departments and agencies, thirty-four state governments, and nearly two hundred local governments. Other institutional sectors have followed suit: Fifty-six public school jurisdictions and institutions of higher education are requiring LEED standards for individual school buildings and campuses.[9]

The private sector has also adopted green building with gusto. In the commercial real estate sector, LEED-certified projects already account for 6 percent of *new* commercial/institutional construction and are expected to climb sevenfold over the next three decades, with the 70 percent anticipated growth in new building stock.[10] Today's green buildings sell themselves, surpassing conventional buildings in indicators such as sales value, rental rates, and occupancy.[11] The spillover to the residential sector is only just now beginning. The year 2005 saw a 30 percent jump in the number of green home builders, pushed by a proliferation of programs offering developers and other home building professionals a variety of rating systems, guidelines, training, and other services to help advance the market in green housing. The building manufacturing sector has responded vigorously to these trends. Since 2006, markets for green products and building materials have grown at an annual rate of 23 percent.[12]

In many ways, the green building movement represents a broad urge among builders, designers, and citizens alike to proactively respond to climate change and other environmental issues without waiting for governmental action. There's a fierce energy at work that is harnessing market forces and industry's collective intelligence to drive change. It may further evidence a deeper cultural change in attitudes about architecture, moving away from celebrating buildings as commodities—often as signature objects of art—and rebalancing the design dialogue from one that is object oriented to one that is much more *outcome oriented.*

SHORTCOMINGS AND BARRIERS

Despite its persuasive momentum, the green building movement signifies a mere initial advance toward a low-carbon future. Even as we acknowledge that green facilities must be the building blocks of the resilient cities of tomorrow, we face significant barriers to a wholesale shift in the industry. Several challenges dominate. One is the fragmented makeup of the building sector, which is composed of a vast number of small units, quite diverse.[13] There are no simple mechanisms to influence the wide range of decision-makers involved, including owners, tenants, investors, insurers, regulators, manufacturers, contractors, and real estate agents. The building sector in 2002 included more than 223,000 businesses alone.[14]

A second obstacle is cost, both real and perceived. Done right, most cost premiums for building green today can be eliminated or otherwise recouped in the short term—but few investors and developers are willing to make decisions on anything other than a first-cost basis.[15] Compounding this drawback is the fact that incentives to build green are often "split," unfairly disadvantaging the developer who pays for better-performing systems versus the tenants who reap the advantages. For publicly owned facilities, this divide is manifested in the disconnect between capital and operating budgets, normally separately appropriated, where future operational savings cannot be used to help finance the premium costs of efficiency measures.

Alongside such structural obstacles, other forces impede the momentum of the green building movement. To date, the relatively low cost U.S. consumers pay for energy (compared to consumers in Europe) inappropriately lengthens the payback on energy efficiency improvements beyond what's considered a tolerable return on investment for many stakeholders (i.e., three to five years). On the implementation side, regulatory barriers hinder the uptake of many renewable technologies (photovoltaics, fuel cells, microturbines) owing to grid connection and net-metering permitting issues. Finally, research-and-development funding for new building technologies is disproportionately low in the United States compared to other developed countries, estimated at a minuscule 0.02 percent of the estimated annual value of U.S. building construction.[16]

TWO BOLD PATHS FORWARD

Despite the significant successes of the green building movement, its efforts will not significantly lessen the building sector's contribution to energy overconsumption and climate instability for many years to come. Over the next twenty-five years, total energy consumption is expected to grow by almost 19 percent; it is still the dominant driver of our economy.[17] During that same period, the amount of building stock is expected to increase by as much as 46 percent.[18] Given these increases, it's imperative that we start to decouple economic health from energy consumption—by reducing demand while raising the energy "productivity" of our buildings. This basically means providing more service while consuming less power.

Many energy economists, policy-makers, and progressive design thinkers are optimistic on this front. Their extrapolations indicate that substantial efficiency investments not only may take us halfway toward major greenhouse gas reduction goals, but also may ultimately generate a net-savings stream that could finance other climate protection measures.[19] They foresee that the roll-out of energy-efficient buildings will be composed of two major thrusts: harnessing wholesale the carbon-savings potential of existing building retrofits, and radically reducing the carbon intensity of new structures with "zero-energy buildings."

Opportunities for Increasing Energy Efficiency in Existing Buildings

Given the fact that new construction constitutes a mere 2 to 3 percent of our total building stock in a given year, it is not surprising that more than 86 percent of building-related construction expenditures relate to renovation.[20] Today, there are more than 45 million structures in the United States (representing billions of occupied square feet), the majority of which will still be in use by midcentury. This points to the scale of the near-term opportunity for cutbacks in greenhouse gas emissions that may be obtained from retrofits and upgrading of energy-consuming systems. In a downturned economy, such actions are much more likely to be undertaken than new building ventures.[21]

In fact, market predictions suggest burgeoning green building activity over the next five years, with expenditures growing from just $2.1 billion to $3.7 billion in 2010 to $10.1 billion to $15.1 billion by 2014.[22] This prediction is corroborated by green building trend tracker Jerry Yudelson, who found that "the fastest growing LEED rating system in 2008 was the LEED program for existing buildings."[23]

For impressive results today, commercial building owners can pursue the same three-step sequence modeled by owner Anthony Malkin at the Empire State Building: Reduce external energy loads by upgrading the building enclosure, diminish internal loads with daylight-responsive lighting controls and maximized equipment efficiency, and install smaller heating and cooling systems, computer controlled, that minimize consumption while increasing comfort.

Technology has radically advanced in all these areas. Today, building envelopes may be retrofitted with high-performance windows (with interior films and gas fill), external solar-shading devices, extra insulation, insulating films, heat mirrors, crack sealing, and other techniques. Considerable savings can be captured by replacing conventional lighting with high-efficiency fluorescent or LED (light-emitting diode) fixtures, using adjustable artificial lighting to make better use of daylight, and upgrading to Energy Star office equipment and appliances. Then, after integrating all of these efficiency measures, boilers, chillers, fans, pumps, and motors can each be "downsized" to scales appropriate to the newly reduced loads.[24] Such synergies pay off handsomely, with performance-based retrofits earning operational savings of anywhere from 40 to 75 percent.[25]

While efficiency measures with the greatest potential return often require substantial up-front investment that is not easily recoverable within the preferred three to five years, financing vehicles are becoming more and more plentiful. These include federal, state, and local tax-credit programs, utility rebates, low-interest loans, and even direct-installation programs operated by third-party organizations.

Still, much more needs to be done in terms of regulation to accelerate the transition to an energy-smart reality. Upgrading building energy codes, promoting equipment efficiency, and establishing clean-energy portfolio standards can hasten this shift. One recent study found that upgrading residential and commercial equipment standards could cumulatively save 31 quadrillion Btu of energy nationwide in the next decade—between $48 billion and $103 billion in net present value.[26]

Quicker routes to carbon reduction may include legislative actions. With the implementation of its "Greener, Greater Buildings Plan," New York City will embark on an aggressive campaign to reduce greenhouse gas emissions by targeting its 22,000 largest commercial and residential buildings. Recently enacted legislation closes loopholes in existing energy efficiency codes, requires ongoing benchmarking and regular auditing, and encourages lighting upgrades and other easily achievable retrofits. Building owners will be able to finance upgrades through revolving-fund loans. Accompanied by a green skills training program for 19,000 workers, this legislative effort presents a full range of mechanisms to transform New York's building stock over time while raising the bar for other cities nationwide.[27]

"Power Down": How Zero-Energy Buildings Will Lead the Transition

While building retrofits and renovations offer the largest carbon-reduction potential over the next twenty-five years, new construction plays a key role in advancing the technologies required to make the products of the building industry truly resilient for our energy-uncertain future.[28] Environmentalists, policy-makers, and professionals alike foresee that only an accelerated "powering down" of all new commercial and residential facilities will allow us to achieve the necessary swift contraction in global carbon emissions. Many of these technological leaps have been demonstrated by a new class of structures called "zero-energy buildings."

A zero-energy building (ZEB) is designed to be optimally energy efficient and to satisfy remaining energy demands to the greatest extent with on-site renewable sources. Even if energy is occasionally purchased from the grid (e.g., on cloudy, windless days when on-site wind and solar generators can't meet regular demand), it may be offset on an annual basis by returning surplus energy to the grid at a different time (specifically, by on-site sources producing more energy than consumed by the building). Thus most zero-energy buildings are, technically speaking, actually *net* zero energy. In addition, ZEBs that purchase *renewably sourced* power off the grid may also be designated "zero-carbon buildings."

Getting to net zero energy cannot be achieved using conventional building and operating methods alone. For example, while today's off-the-shelf technologies may economically achieve a 30 to 50 percent energy savings for a typical office building, closer to a *70 percent reduction* must be reached for the remaining demands to be feasibly satisfied by on-site renewable energy.[29] Here, conventional technologies and best-practice efficiencies must be coupled with more far-reaching design measures:

- Minimize heating and cooling needs. Integrate comprehensive passive-design strategies by orienting buildings for maximum winter sun exposure and/or summer heat rejection and designing windows and openings for controlled daylight. Use active-facade systems with operable windows, movable shading, spectrally selective triple glazing, and considerably improved insulation and radiative barriers.
- Meet residual energy demand with on-site renewable sources managed with high-performance mechanical systems such as ground-source heat pumps, heat recovery, radiant heating, and under-floor air distribution.

Challenges lie ahead for getting to net zero energy. Not all buildings are candidates. Given the high operating loads in facilities such as hospitals and laboratories, sufficient energy reductions may be impractical. Buildings in urban locales may have inadequate solar exposure owing to shading by adjacent buildings and may not be able to achieve net zero energy. Also, medium- to high-rise buildings—or even unusually wide buildings—will be problematic candidates given the high ratio of solar-panel surface to total floor area required for ZEBs. According to the U.S. Department of Energy, however, although merely 22 percent of buildings today have the potential to be ZEBs, as technology advances this may triple by 2025.[30]

Various enterprises are in place to accelerate this trend. The Department of Energy has set the goal of making zero-energy buildings fully marketable by 2025. The 2030 Challenge, a voluntary program backed by the American Institute of Architects, the U.S. Conference of Mayors, and twenty-five other organizations, has set aggressive national schedules and benchmarks to push all new buildings and major renovations to be net zero carbon by 2030.[31] The Living Building Challenge, a rapidly spreading initiative of the U.S. Green Building Council's Cascadia chapter, has called for a next generation of self-sufficient buildings with net-zero-energy and net-zero-water goals, coupled with further stringent resource- and land-use requirements.[32]

Legislative measures may soon follow these initiatives. The European Parliament recently called for all new construction to be zero energy by 2019. In 2007 California energy regulators set a goal for all new homes to be built to net-zero-energy standards starting in 2020. Many other states and cities will, in all likelihood, follow suit.

THE AGENDA AHEAD

If we implement all of these measures at the needed scale across our nationwide building stock, we will quickly reap benefits of enormous proportion. Dramatic drops in overall grid-based power demand, coupled with widespread flattening of peak-demand curves, will reduce power price and volatility for the consumer. This will also reduce the need for investment in new generation and transmission capacity, allowing our most polluting power plants to be taken offline sooner.[33]

In contrast, the consequences of inaction are frightening. The current 2 percent annual rise in U.S. buildings' energy use means that by 2030 we would need to supply 23 percent more energy to residential buildings and 36 percent more energy to commercial building sectors—on top of already near-unsupportable energy demands.[34] The uncertainties we face in a future of increasingly expensive energy—not to mention the potentially catastrophic consequences of steadily worsening climate change—mean that we can't simply build more power plants to meet ever-rising demand. Unprecedented industry and governmental leadership, plus a concerted response by American consumers, will be required to seriously reduce energy demand overall and meet remaining demand from renewable resources. A mix of mutually reinforcing public and private measures must achieve the following:

- *Create a sense of urgency:* Americans must grasp that powering down buildings today is a necessary and urgent first move toward future-proofing our communities. Focused demonstration, education, and outreach campaigns must prepare the public and the industry for the order-of-magnitude shifts required ahead: swift advancements in efficiency *based on full integration of passive and active building measures,* and rapid scaling up of distributed solar and other renewable energy technologies.

- *Standardize overall targets:* Governments—if not federal, then state and local—must take the next step and mandate realistic but aggressive targets for major retrofits and net-zero-carbon buildings, not only for public projects but for private properties as well. That said, such ambitious and far-reaching mandates are likely to succeed only in concert with the following measures listed here.

- *Step up energy codes:* Building codes must be brought into alignment with green building rating systems, the best of which are themselves under constant revision. One example is American Society of Heating, Refrigerating, and Air-Conditioning Engineers (ASHRAE) Standard 189.1, which is aligned with LEED and will shortly be available for adoption by local jurisdictions as a code-enforceable standard for green buildings.[35] Leveling the playing field for building owners and tenants through such regulation is a crucial step.

- *Ratchet up equipment standards:* Successful federal efforts to standardize minimum performance levels for all energy-consuming equipment—from appliances and electronics to mechanical systems—must continually be enhanced. In the past, these measures have provided the highest levels of returns.

- *Use carbon metrics:* While operational efficiency savings may motivate and reward owners and investors, we cannot depend on these direct inducements, even coupled with many of today's available tax incentives, government grants, loans, and other creative financing vehicles. Additional market drivers are needed and may include carbon-based price signals and valuations of external costs that make efficiency investments compelling.

- *Create implementation capacity:* Further market measures can relieve building owners of the burden of tackling specific improvements themselves. Third-party entities—companies, governmental agencies, nongovernmental organizations, and utilities—are increasingly available to undertake efficiency upgrades, repaying themselves through a share in operating savings.

- *Address key barriers:* Creativity at all government levels is required to remove deep-rooted market barriers and disincentives. We must substitute *life-cycle costing* methods for today's unilateral *first-cost* decisionmaking. New mechanisms are needed in leases and purchase agreements to overcome the disconnect between those who pay and those who benefit. We also need to solve technical and administrative barriers to interconnecting distributed energy systems with the grid.

- *Invest in research and development:* Research funding levels for green building technologies are sadly disproportionate to today's carbon-reduction imperative. We must promote industry development of the most promising technologies, such as complex active facades (e.g., automated shades, switchable electrochromic/thermochromic window glass), next-generation radiant heating/cooling systems, and small-scale combined heat and power systems.

- *Shift basic paradigms:* Zoning codes that ensure solar access, for example, can promote more universal use of passive solar design. We might also begin to question and discourage, or disincentivize, the architecture and building industry's fixation with vision-glass curtain walls (building facades that are predominantly glass, seen especially on modern office buildings), the most profligate consumers of energy next to artificial lighting. We need to recognize as well that *building size* matters—square footage directly drives energy and resource consumption. We need new mental models that decouple spatial size from status—no more 10,000-square-foot "green" homes.

- *Change behavior:* The future of buildings also depends on thoughtful designs that enlist occupants as crucial actors in the low-carbon world. Appealing stairways can get people to relinquish elevator habits. Operable windows, flexible settings for workstation lighting and thermal comfort, and in-building displays of real-time energy consumption all coach occupants in more energy-smart behavior.

A wide array of devices—user prompts, instant feedback, modeling alternatives, and even peer pressure—will sensitize us to a new energy reality. Initiating behavior change and driving an accompanying shift in values are primary keys to a sustainable future.

A full suite of policy initiatives as outlined above is essential for the shift to a national building stock appropriate to the low-carbon future. To transform the sociological systems shaping our built environment and capable of reducing its impacts, we must work to integrate these measures across time and scale. The full flowering of today's green momentum can be realized. But it will require a broad base of civic intelligence and strong political will.

LOCAL GOVERNMENT IN A TIME OF PEAK OIL AND CLIMATE CHANGE

JOHN KAUFMANN

JOHN KAUFMANN *was lead staff for the City of Portland's groundbreaking Peak Oil Task Force. He worked with the Oregon Department of Energy for twenty-nine years, helping to make Oregon a national leader. He received the Professional Achievement Award from the American Planning Association's Oregon Chapter for getting twenty-six jurisdictions in the Portland metro area to jointly adopt solar orientation and solar rights ordinances, and received the 2009 Energy Manager of the Year Award from the Association of Professional Energy Managers–Oregon. He currently is senior buildings energy manager for the Pacific Northwest National Laboratory. Kaufmann is a Fellow of Post Carbon Institute.*

❖

Government is an orphan—few people, it seems, support it. Over the past few decades Americans have become increasingly cynical and jaded about their government. They complain about taxes. They complain about poor service and government waste. They want government off their backs and out of their lives.

And yet, they still expect government to be there when it's a service they want or need. Many responses to peak oil urge individual and community solutions, ignoring government. They argue that since government hasn't done anything to address the problem, citizens and businesses must take matters into their own hands. Some even argue that government is part of the problem, particularly federal and state governments.

This attitude is shortsighted. While it may be true that government has been slow to respond to peak oil and climate change, it nevertheless has a vital role to play. There are many things a government can do that an individual or community cannot do. As Abraham Lincoln said:

The legitimate object of government is to do for a community of people whatever they need to have done, but cannot do at all, or cannot so well do, for themselves, in their separate and individual capacities.[1]

There will always be a need for the things government does. Rather than walk away from government, we should work toward ensuring that it serves our needs.

THE ROLE OF GOVERNMENT

In U.S. democracy, authority is divided among several levels of government. The three main levels are the federal government, fifty state governments, and tens of thousands of local (primarily municipal and county) governments. In addition, there are special districts—such as school districts, housing authorities, port authorities, transit districts, and water and irrigation districts—many of which have elected governing structures and the authority to raise revenues.

There are things that can and should be done to address peak oil and climate change at all these levels of government. Moreover, there are things one level of government may be able to do that the other levels can't do. The transportation system is a great example of a service that is, by necessity, implemented at different levels. From pedestrian crosswalks to international airports, local, state, and federal agencies are all involved in some aspect of transportation planning, design, funding, construction, and maintenance.

There are also many things that can be done at the community level by local grassroots organizations, including religious organizations, charitable organizations, affinity and advocacy groups, the Transition Towns movement, and others. These groups help prepare people at the individual and neighborhood level, and promise to help keep crucial social support networks in place. But while they are necessary pieces of the puzzle, they are not sufficient. They can complement government, but they will not replace it.

What are those things that the people "cannot do at all, or cannot so well do, for themselves" and thus need government's attention? The main functions of modern government now include:

- Provide *security* and protect *public order*. At the local level this includes primarily police and fire services.
- Administer *justice and fairness*. This includes not just the courts, but the authority to set rules protecting basic rights and opportunities in such things as employment, housing, education, and health.
- Provide *essential services and infrastructure* that are best done in common, such as roads, water, wastewater treatment, public health, parks, and education.
- Provide for the *public welfare*. Ensure that citizens' minimum needs are met, such as water, food, shelter, transportation, and economic opportunity.
- Provide an environment conducive to *economic prosperity*. There is considerable disagreement about how this might be accomplished, but there is broad agreement on the goal.
- Protect the *commons*. There is general acceptance about government's responsibility to protect and manage that which is of necessity shared, although there is considerable disagreement over the means, and how far that responsibility extends. The commons includes natural resources like air and water, cultural resources like historically important monuments and documents, and even intangible resources like the electromagnetic spectrum (for wireless communications).

Failure to provide these services at some level will ultimately lead to myriad social problems—crime, unemployment, homelessness, hunger, disease, environmental degradation.

THE CHALLENGES FACING GOVERNMENTS

The two main challenges governments will face in the post-carbon future are:

1. How to maintain order and basic services during a time of economic contraction, when demand for services is rising and revenues are shrinking.

2. How to use governmental powers to enable, foster, support, and lead the transition to a more resilient world.

The impacts of peak oil and climate change will vary from region to region, state to state, and city to city. Specific impacts will depend on location, geography, natural resources, population size, and many other factors, but all have one thing in common—they will all be manifest in the local economy.

Peak oil and climate change are energy problems: Both are driven by our high use of fossil fuels. Society as a whole must reduce its use of these fuels; unfortunately, at this time, all alternatives are less energy dense and less productive than fossil fuels.[2] Unless and until that changes, it will cost more to make and move things. We will be spending more of our individual and national incomes on energy, and less on other goods. The result will be a decline in economic activity, possibly accompanied by inflation or even stagflation, where recession and inflation occur simultaneously, as they did during the energy crisis in the 1970s.

How does this affect local government? During economic recessions and depressions, people have less money for food, housing, utilities, health care, and transportation. Demand for government services increases, but at the same time, government tax revenues typically decline. This exact scenario played out during the 2008–2010 national economic downturn as states from coast to coast faced massive budget shortfalls, causing many to cut services and even—in the case of California—to issue IOUs to creditors.

There are many things governments at all levels can do to meet these challenges. But perhaps even more important, there are several things that will be limited or ineffective in addressing the magnitude of the problem:

- *Preserving the status quo.* We know the status quo won't work. Revenues to do things will be shrinking at a time when demand for services will be increasing.
- *Increasing taxes.* Raising taxes to provide increased public services is difficult even in the best of economic times. It will be virtually impossible during a time of economic contraction, when people are struggling to pay their mortgages, heat their homes, pay for medical care, and put food on the table and gas in their tanks.
- *Focusing only on reducing energy waste, improving internal operations, and providing services more efficiently.* State and local government accounts for about 5 to 10 percent of energy use in this country, and energy

represents only a small part of governmental expenses. Governments must do everything they can to reduce their energy use and operate more efficiently, but the improvements likely will not be enough to offset both rising energy costs *and* shrinking revenues.

· *Focusing only on increasing energy supplies.* We need to find alternatives to fossil fuels, but we cannot focus exclusively on supply—we must also significantly reduce how much we use. Alternative energy sources, despite recent advances, are in general less productive and more costly than fossil fuels. More important, they will not be able to be scaled up fast enough to replace fossil fuels in the time frame needed.

· *Relying on markets or technology to rescue us.* It is highly unlikely that renewable energy sources will ever achieve the high energy return on energy invested that fossil fuels have historically afforded; thus they are likely to be more expensive. Moreover, as energy costs rise, economic difficulties will reduce the ability of markets to respond.

WHAT GOVERNMENTS CAN DO

Principles

In *Post Carbon Cities*,[3] Daniel Lerch lists five principles to help guide local government planning efforts in the face of peak oil and climate change:

· *Deal with transportation and land use (or you may as well stop now).* Incorporate peak-oil and climate change considerations into all transportation and land-use aspects of policy-making and infrastructure investment decisions.

· *Tackle private energy consumption.* Improving government operations is insufficient to address the magnitude of the problem. Create strong incentives and support for innovation, and aggressively engage the business community.

· *Attack the problems piece by piece and from many angles.* Meet goals with multiple, proven solutions, and enlist the entire community in the effort.

· *Plan for fundamental changes—and make fundamental changes happen.* Change internalized assumptions about the future availability and affordability of energy.

- *Build a sense of community.* Strengthen community resilience by encouraging relationship building among citizens, businesses, and government agencies.

To these can be added five principles to guide local government management efforts:

- *Don't expect to find one grand solution.* There are no solutions, just intelligent responses—and there will be many little responses that will help communities adapt and muddle through.
- *Don't try to do everything all at once.* Focus on a few big issues requiring several years of lead time and issues that are immediate problems. Other issues can be dealt with as they become ripe.
- *Consider how energy affects everything and everybody.* Government needs to consider how businesses, institutions, and households are affected by high energy prices and energy-supply shortfalls, not just how its own operations are affected. These impacts are significant to the community and the local economy, and will shape what the government needs to do and what it *can* do.
- *Connect the issues.* Climate change, peak oil, diminishing water supplies, topsoil loss, biodiversity loss, and most all major challenges of the twenty-first century are ultimately intertwined. Worsening conditions in one area could affect the ability of society to respond in another area. Conversely, there are synergies to be gained by dealing with these challenges in an integrated fashion.
- *Expect the unexpected.* We must avoid making irreversible commitments based on past experience or current projections, expecting the future to be more of the same. We are entering a period of what is likely to be rapid and nonlinear change. We must reconcile ourselves to the idea that there will be no business as usual anymore. We must be able to adapt and reverse direction as conditions change.

Planning for Crisis

In developing strategies and actions to address these challenges, governments should ask four basic questions:

1. How will peak oil and climate change affect the community? What are the expected impacts, and when will they set in?

2. What can government do to cushion the community against the long-term negative consequences of those impacts?

3. What should government be prepared to do in the case of emergencies (e.g., fuel shortage, fuel price spike, prolonged heat wave, drought, wildfires, flooding, etc.), some of which are inevitable?

4. How will future government activities be funded as economic volatility and prolonged recession keep tax revenues from rising as quickly as in the past?

In the last five years, several communities have studied how to prepare for some of these challenges. One of the first was the City of Portland, Oregon, which released a report on peak oil in 2007 that has since served as a model for many other cities because of the depth of its strategic analysis.[4] The Portland report looked at four main areas—the local economy, transportation and land use, food and agriculture, and public and social services—and recommended eleven high-level strategies, with specific steps identified under each strategy (see box 26.1).

Several other communities have prepared reports of various depth and usefulness, from the tiny Town of Franklin, New York, to the regional coordinating agency of the Los Angeles metropolitan area.

Local responses to climate change have a much longer history, with some of the first major climate action plans appearing in the early 1990s; today, more than six hundred communities in the United States are planning for climate change.[5] However, there are no good examples of tying peak oil and climate change together. Most climate action plans have been generic and do not specifically address how to adapt to local impacts. Moreover, they have primarily looked at strategies to replace fossil fuels with renewable resources. As discussed earlier, it is questionable whether that is a reasonable assumption. See box 26.2 for a list of resources on both issues.

Framework

The first step for any government body planning for peak oil and climate change is to identify the expected and potential impacts so that recommendations can be tailored for maximum effect. Impacts can be prioritized by how critical they are, and a broad strategy can be developed that addresses the major impacts and identifies the key needs and goals within

BOX 26.1 Portland (Oregon) Peak Oil Task Force:
Recommended Strategies

1. Reduce total oil and natural gas consumption by 50 percent over
   the next twenty-five years.

2. Inform citizens about peak oil and foster community and
   community-based solutions.

3. Engage business, government, and community leaders to initiate
   planning and policy change.

4. Support land-use patterns that reduce transportation needs, promote walkability, and provide easy access to services and transportation options.

5. Design infrastructure to promote transportation options and
   facilitate efficient movement of freight, and prevent investments
   in infrastructure that would not be prudent given fuel shortages
   and higher prices.

6. Encourage energy-efficient and renewable energy transportation
   choices.

7. Dramatically expand building energy efficiency programs and
   incentives for all new and existing structures.

8. Preserve farmland and expand local food production and
   processing.

9. Identify and promote sustainable business opportunities.

10. Redesign the safety net and protect vulnerable and marginal
    populations.

11. Prepare emergency plans for sudden and severe shortages.

Source: City of Portland Peak Oil Task Force, *Descending the Oil Peak: Navigating
the Transition from Oil and Natural Gas*, Final Report, March 2007, available at
http://www.portlandonline.com/bps/index.cfm?c=42894.

those areas. Individual agencies should then be charged with developing
specific plans and actions to mitigate and adapt to the expected impacts.
The lead government body (e.g., the city council) should establish benchmarks and continually monitor how peak oil and climate change are
unfolding and affecting the community, to see what adjustments to the
plan are warranted.

In developing plans, governments should focus initially on issues that
need several years' lead time. These tend to be issues that involve infra-

BOX 26.2 Resources for Local Government Responses to
Peak Oil and Climate Change

- Amy Snover et al., *Preparing for Climate Change: A Guidebook for Local, Regional and State Governments* (Oakland, CA: ICLEI, 2007), http://cses.washington.edu/db/pdf/snoveretalgb574.pdf.
- Daniel Lerch, *Post Carbon Cities: Planning for Energy and Climate Uncertainty* (Sebastopol, CA: Post Carbon Press, 2007).
- Post Carbon Institute database of local government responses to peak oil (including task forces, policies, and studies): http://post carboncities.net/peakoilactions.
- C40 Cities Climate Leadership Group database of city climate change action plans: http://www.c40cities.org/ccap/.
- Center for Climate Strategies database of state reports: http://www .climatestrategies.us/State_Reports_Summaries.cfm.

structure and are not quickly changed, such as transportation, land-use patterns, and housing. Governments should not only look at developing public transit and other land-use and infrastructure changes that may be needed for reducing fossil-fuel use, but should also carefully evaluate large investments in roads, airports, and other infrastructure dependent on fossil fuels. At a minimum, governments need to consider scenarios with much higher fuel prices than exist today when running models to determine demand for various options.

However, while necessary, long-range plans are not sufficient. Local and state governments also need to develop emergency plans for the kinds of events more likely to occur thanks to peak oil and climate change. Fuel spikes, fuel shortages, lingering droughts, and torrential floods are no longer threats only in the developing world—in just the last few years, each of these emergencies has challenged well-funded and highly skilled government agencies and first responders in the United States, Europe, and elsewhere.

During such events, how will essential community needs be met? How will we ensure adequate fuel for police, fire, and medical services? How will we ensure that food gets out of the fields and to market? How will we ensure that people get to their jobs so they can earn an income and so provision of goods and services continues? Higher prices will induce some voluntary response, but the responses may be inequitable and not necessarily reflect social priorities.

Where possible, plans should address both peak oil and climate change. Because they are both energy issues at their root, there is considerable overlap in the response to each. However, there are also some responses to each issue that could undermine government's ability to respond to the other if they are not coordinated. For example, certain responses to peak oil—such as the development of biofuels and increased use of hydro-electricity—may by curtailed by the effects of climate change.

Any plans should also consider government revenues. As the economy contracts, so too will tax revenues, while at the same time demand for services will increase. Governments will need to determine (1) which services are most critical, and which can be left to charity and other community solutions, and (2) how to raise revenues to provide some level of certainty, stability, and equity, while minimizing the burden on the taxpaying public.

WHAT YOU CAN DO

Government has a major role to play in helping to ensure a smooth transition through peak oil and climate change to a post-carbon world. Government, by itself, is not the solution—but individuals working alone aren't the solution either. There is a role for everybody: the individual, family and neighborhood support networks, volunteer community service groups, business and industry, local government, state government, and the federal government. Ideally, all would cooperate with one another while fulfilling their unique roles and responsibilities.

If government is not responding as we would like it to, we cannot tear it down or abandon it. We must make it work. Government, after all, is us. Government officials are elected by us, to serve our needs. They are people like us—friends, neighbors, and fellow citizens—and are answerable to us. If you don't like what they're doing, get engaged. Call or write your elected officials. Attend city council or county commission meetings, submit ideas, and testify on issues. Or better yet, run for office yourself. That's what makes democracy vibrant.

Part Eleven

TRANSPORTATION

TRANSPORTATION IN
THE POST-CARBON WORLD

RICHARD GILBERT AND ANTHONY PERL

RICHARD GILBERT *is a consultant on transportation and energy issues, with clients in North America, Europe, and Asia in the private sector and in government. He has produced fourteen books and several hundred book chapters, research reports, and academic and popular articles. He served as a municipal councillor in Toronto for many years and was the first president and CEO of the Canadian Urban Institute. Gilbert is an adviser to Post Carbon Institute. He is co-author, with Anthony Perl, of* Transport Revolutions: Moving People and Freight without Oil *(2008).*

ANTHONY PERL *is director of the Urban Studies Program at Simon Fraser University and one of the world's leading experts on passenger rail policy. He chairs the Intercity Passenger Rail Committee of the U.S. Transportation Research Board and is a board director at VIA Rail. He has authored or co-authored five books and has published in numerous scholarly journals. Perl is a Fellow of Post Carbon Institute.*

❖

REVOLUTIONARY CHANGE

One aspect of modern life that will change dramatically during the post-carbon adjustments examined in this volume is our approach to developing and delivering mobility, as well as our expectations from the resulting transport options. The carbon-fueled motor vehicles, aircraft, and marine vessels we now rely on have offered ongoing improvements in their economy, convenience, and reliability over a long enough time that all but a few transport professionals have come to take their smooth functioning for granted. As in other domains, cheap and abundant carbon fuels have made it easy to expand the quantity of mobility, without stimulating major efforts to make that mobility more energy efficient. But, with some

94 percent of transport currently fueled by a derivative of crude oil, our mobility modes are positioned to be on the leading edge of the change that will be driven by the need to shift energy sources.[1]

In this chapter, we present the concept of a "transport revolution" as a way to guide thinking about the mobility changes that lie ahead. Transport revolutions will differ significantly from the incremental changes in mobility that have been the norm over the past twenty-five years, and indeed over most of history. Appreciating the differences between revolutionary change and incremental adjustments will be useful in pursuing transition strategies that can move more people and freight without oil before it is too late to avoid a global energy crisis.

TRANSPORT REVOLUTIONS: THE FAST TRACK TO POST–CARBON MOBILITY

Successful post-carbon transitions will benefit from understanding the dynamics of transport revolutions. We define a transport revolution as being a substantial change in a society's transport activity—moving people or freight, or both—that occurs in less than twenty-five years. "Substantial change" means one or both of the following: an ongoing transport activity increases or decreases dramatically, say by 50 percent, or a new means of transport becomes prevalent to the extent that it is made use of by 10 percent or more of the society's population. By our definition, a breakthrough in transport technology is not a transport revolution. If the breakthrough changes the way in which people or freight move, it could make a revolution possible. Most but not all transport revolutions depend on major technological improvements.

For much of history, people have advanced their capacity for mobility through a long line of modest improvements in their ways of moving about. Tinkering with wheels, sails, and engines has accumulated to produce significant transport advances. But more than such fine-tuning will be required to enable the rapid adjustment of transport systems to impending energy challenges. Transport revolutions, such as those analyzed in our book of the same name, will be needed to keep ahead of oil depletion.[2] The changes will have to be far-reaching enough to break entrenched organizational structures and user expectations.

In *Transport Revolutions*, we examine five episodes of rapid change in mobility. They include the inauguration of modern railway operations in England in the 1830s and the introduction of the overnight package delivery service in the United States during the 1980s. Each one of the five, and others we could have focused on (e.g., the introduction of containers into American freight transport in the 1950s), illuminates differences between radical shift and incremental adjustment that will be relevant for transitions to post–carbon mobility.

Transport revolutions over the next twenty-five years could have two predominant features. Some revolutions will involve maintaining the same or even higher levels of transport activity but in different ways from the present. An example could be continuation of the current level of freight movement between cities but with very much more of it performed by rail than by road. Some revolutions will involve large declines in transport activity. An example would be travel between continents, which could fall steeply because of economic decline or because no reasonable substitute for oil-fueled aviation emerges.

Economic decline could characterize what might be regarded as a "hard landing" into oil depletion. Rising demand for oil constrained by supply could push up prices to a level that reduces overall economic activity. As we discussed in the second edition of *Transport Revolutions*, such a process was a feature of the recession that began in late 2007, during which much transport activity fell.[3] Even before the dramatic spike in oil prices and the economic crisis of 2008, there was a growing preoccupation with looming economic decline and societal collapse that could follow such a hard landing.[4] These dark visions posited, among other problems, a failure to keep society mobile in an era of energy constraints. We have argued that trying to adapt oil-based transport systems incrementally during such an era of oil depletion—that is, falling oil production—would likely yield a repeating vicious cycle of high oil prices, economic recession, declining oil prices, modest economic recovery, and newly rising oil prices. Such grim outcomes would be the most likely path to a hard landing of widespread deprivation and intensified conflict.

The alternative route, which we characterize as a "soft landing," would arise from transport revolutions that refashion the current tight linkages between mobility and oil-based energy sources. In a soft landing, new transport systems would introduce growing capacity to move people and goods without oil such that demand for oil falls ahead of constrained supply. High oil prices and consequent economic turmoil—and even intense geopolitical conflict—could thus be avoided. We believe that such a soft landing is possible. Its key requirements are transport revolutions that, without oil or with very much less oil, allow continuation of humanity's gains in comfort, convenience, productivity, and freedom from want.

GRID-CONNECTED VEHICLES: PROVEN TECHNOLOGY THAT CAN LEAD A SHIFT TO ELECTRIC MOBILITY

Over the next two or three decades motorized land transport will become mostly propelled by electric motors (EMs) rather than by the internal combustion engines (ICEs) that propel most of today's land transport. This shift of motive power would bring many benefits. Electric vehicles are quiet and energy efficient, require little maintenance, have good acceleration at low speeds, and emit essentially no pollution at the vehicle. The challenge inhibiting such a shift has always been that of delivering sufficient quantities of electricity to the motor or motors.

Most electric vehicle research-and-development efforts in the United States, Europe, and Asia have pursued advances in storing electricity on board vehicles, in batteries and other storage devices, or generating electricity on board vehicles, using fuel cells or ICEs. Work on storage devices and fuel cells has so far not brought electric traction near the low cost and high effectiveness of ICE-propelled vehicles. Work on on-board generation using ICE-based generators has been fruitful—the Toyota Prius is the most widely used such automobile—but such hybrid ICE-electric vehicles are as dependent on oil as pure ICE vehicles and use only a little less oil-based fuel in typical driving.

The surest path to expanding the share of trade and travel met by electric mobility would be to expand the use of grid-connected vehicles (GCVs). For GCVs, electricity is generated remotely and delivered directly by wire or rail to the motor as the vehicle moves. GCVs are responsible for the most movement of people and freight by electric vehicles today. In a transport revolution that features a soft landing, we would expect this lead to continue, even as many more electric vehicles come into use, because of GCVs' especially high energy efficiency.

GCVs' advantages over battery-electric vehicles (BEVs) would justify their primacy in the transition away from carbon-based energy sources.

No matter how good BEVs might become, they will still need to carry a large weight of batteries, which can amount to several hundred kilograms (in pounds, more than double that number). These batteries take up space and their weight increases the vehicle's energy consumption. A GCV needs no battery, or a relatively small one for limited "off-wire" travel. A GCV is subject only to energy distribution losses in moving the electricity from its source (e.g., a wind turbine) to the motor. For a BEV, as well as these distribution losses there are losses when charging and discharging the battery that can amount to several times the distribution losses.[5]

Unlike pure BEVs, which disappeared early in the automobile's evolution and which have proved challenging to reintroduce, GCVs have been in use for at least as long as vehicles using ICEs. Electric streetcars and trains were operating in many cities at the end of the nineteenth century. Today, about 150 cities around the world have or are developing electric heavy-rail (e.g., "metro" and "commuter" rail) systems running at the surface, elevated, or, most often, underground. Some 550 cities have streetcar or light-rail systems, including 72 cities in Russia and 70 in Germany, and about 350 have trolleybus systems.[6]

Electrification of intercity railroads began early in the twentieth century, although most of it has occurred after 1950. Now most routes in Japan and Europe are electrified. Russia has the most extensive system of electrified rail, approximately half of the total of 85,000 kilometers, including the whole of the 9,258-kilometer Trans-Siberian Railway, for which electrification was begun in 1928 and completed in 2002. China's rail system is being rapidly electrified and now boasts the second most extensive electrified system: 49 lines totaling about 24,000 kilometers. In these countries and elsewhere, these are mostly main routes and thus carry a disproportionately large share of passengers and freight. The revolution caused by introducing high-speed electrified passenger rail has transformed the way that people move between major cities in Japan and Western Europe.[7]

As well as freight trains, other types of GCVs have been and are used to move goods. These include diesel trucks with trolley assist such as were used in the Quebec Cartier iron ore mine from 1970 until the mine was worked out in 1977. These trucks were in effect hybrid vehicles with electric motors powered from overhead wires that provided additional traction when heavy loads were carried up steep slopes. A diesel generator provided the electricity. The reported result was an 87 percent decrease in diesel fuel consumption and a 23 percent increase in productivity.[8]

Several direct comparisons of energy consumption by GCVs and comparable vehicles with diesel-engine drives confirm that energy use *at the vehicle* is invariably lower. For example, in 2008 San Francisco electric trolleybuses used an average of 0.72 megajoule of energy per passenger-kilometer; in contrast, the average for diesel buses in the same city was 2.67 megajoules per passenger-kilometer.[9] If the electricity for the trolleybuses were produced by a diesel generator operating at 35 percent efficiency, with a 10 percent distribution loss, the trolleybuses would still use less energy overall than diesel buses. When electricity is produced renewably, what counts is energy use at the vehicle.

Electricity is the ideal transport fuel for an uncertain future. Unlike other alternative energy transition paths for transport, only electric mobility can move people and goods using a wide range of energy sources. Electric vehicles can use electricity produced from hydroelectric sources, wind turbines, and photovoltaic panels, and from steam-turbine generating stations fueled by coal, natural gas, oil, enriched uranium, wood waste, solar energy, or any combination of these sources. Thus, whatever the exact paths of the transitions toward renewable generation of electricity, transport systems based on these vehicles can readily adapt. They will not have to be changed each time a primary energy source changes. The energy requirements of transport systems will not limit innovation in energy production systems, either. The challenge will be moving to electric mobility fast enough to keep ahead of oil depletion. Electric traction's flexibility with respect to its ultimate energy sources is an important reason for favoring GCVs as the leading edge of such a transition.

HOW TO ANTICIPATE TRANSPORT'S POST-CARBON REDESIGN

In this section, we illustrate a scenario for redesigning the movement of people in the United States to reduce oil consumption by 44 percent in 2025 and maintain a stable level of total mobility. The analytical effort supporting this scenario includes five steps:

1. Set the desired energy use and transport activity parameters for the system redesign. In our scenario, we have sought a 44 percent

reduction in U.S. use of liquid fuels between 2007 and 2025 and essentially no change in motorized transport activity (actually a 1 percent increase in passenger-kilometers).[10]

2. Estimate current transport activity and energy use.

3. Anticipate what the available modes will be in 2025 and their unit energy use.

4. Develop a plausible balance of modes that matches the levels of transport activity and energy use in 2025 to the established parameters.

5. Continually improve energy-use estimates and expectations of future transport activity.

The particular values for transport activity and unit energy consumption for 2025 set forth in table 27.1 are less important than the process of developing and making use of such a table. Readers may well want to use different values, which may in turn require different balances among the modes. Our point is not that we have found the most appropriate values (although we have tried to identify them) but that the specification of a scenario such as that presented in table 27.1 is an essential part of transport redesign.

We chose 2025 as the target year for several reasons. It is near enough to provide a meaningfully close target date that could motivate action— as opposed to simply planning for action—by incumbent government and corporate leaders. If we had chosen 2050, there could be a strong temptation to put off action until 2025 or later, or at least until the next generation of leaders will be in a position to deal with these challenges. Moreover, 2025 will be a decade or so after we expect the occurrence of the world peak in petroleum production to have become evident. If we had set the target year even five years later, in 2030, the required cuts in oil consumption would have been larger and more likely to appear intimidating and engender defeatism.

The key factor in establishing our redesign scenario is the extent of the reductions in oil consumption that would be required by 2025. For this, we have estimated that world oil production—and consumption—in 2025 will be on the order of 26.3 billion barrels.[11] This is only 15 percent below production in 2007 and it is actually 7 percent *above* production in 1990. However, *the most important difference is that anticipated oil production*

TABLE 27.1. Motorized Movement of U.S. Residents in
2007 (Estimated) and 2025 (Proposed)

| Mode | 2007 | | | |
	pkm (billions)[a]	Fuel Use per pkm (MJ)	Total Liquid Fuel Use (EJ)	Total Electricity Use (EJ)
Personal vehicle (ICE)	7,700	2.6	20.4	
Personal vehicle (electric)				
Future transport				
Local public transport (ICE)	50	2.8	0.1	
Local public transport (electric)	40	0.6		0.0
Bus (intercity, ICE)	200	0.7	0.1	
Bus (intercity, electric)				
Rail (intercity, ICE)	6	0.9	0.0	
Rail (intercity, electric)	3	0.3		0.0
Aircraft (domestic)	950	2.0	1.9	
Aircraft (international)	330	2.3	0.8	
Airship (dom. and intl.)				
Marine (dom. and intl.)				
Totals	9,300		23.4	0.0
Per capita	30,500		76.5[b]	0.1[b]

[a]Except per capita

[b]Measurements in GJ for per capita

Note: Values and totals are rounded to aid comprehension. Electric modes are
in italics. ICE = internal combustion engine; pkm = passenger-kilometer(s);
MJ = megajoule; EJ = exajoule; GJ = gigajoule.

			2025			
Local pkm (billions)[a]	Nonlocal pkm (billions)[a]	Fuel Use per pkm (MJ)	Total Liquid Fuel Use (EJ)	Total Electricity Use (EJ)	Liquid Fuel Powered pkm	Electrically Powered pkm
2,500	2,500	2.1	10.5		5,000	
1,000		1.0		1.0		1,000
200		0.5		0.1		200
100		2.0	0.2		100	
400		0.5		0.2		400
	500	0.5	0.3		500	
	500	0.4		0.2		500
	100	0.6	0.1		100	
	400	0.2		0.1		400
	600	1.8	1.1		600	
	400	2.1	0.8		400	
	100	1.2	0.1		100	
	100	0.7	0.1		100	
4,200	5,200		13.1	1.6	6,900	2,500
26,500			37.0[b]	4.5[b]		

Sources: Passenger-kilometers (pkm) for 2007 are extrapolated from data for 1995–2004 in table 4.21M (aviation) and table 1.37M (other modes) of Bureau of Transportation Statistics, *National Transportation Statistics 2006* (Washington DC: U.S. Department of Transportation, 2007), http://www.bts.gov/publications/national_transportation _statistics. The split between ICE and electric intercity rail was estimated from the energy use data in table 4.6M of the same source and an assumption that electric loco-motives use about one-third of the energy used by diesel-electric locomotives. The rates of energy use in 2007 are those in table 4.15 (and derived from the sources noted there) of Richard Gilbert and Anthony Perl, *Transport Revolutions: Moving People and Freight Without Oil*, 2nd ed. (Gabriola Island, BC: New Society, 2010), 240.

of 26.3 billion barrels in 2025 would be 30 percent below the projected "business-
as-usual" consumption of 37.6 billion barrels in 2025. We propose that about
two-thirds of the shortfall be borne by the richer countries, roughly corresponding to their share of total consumption in 1990.[12]

We suggest that the cuts in oil used by transport should be propor-
tionately larger than the overall reduction in oil use. This would allow
for smaller cuts in, or even temporary maintenance of, consumption of
currently essential uses of oil. These include the oil used as feedstock in
chemical industries, particularly the production of fertilizers, pesticides,
and pharmaceuticals. In 2005 in the United States, these and other nonfuel uses of oil comprised about 13.5 percent of total oil use.[13] Such uses
should be protected or even allowed to grow in proportion to population.

On the other hand, there will also be some replacement of petroleum
oil for transport by liquid biofuels and by liquid fuels derived from coal.
We do not expect more than a few percent of total transport fuels to be
replaced by such liquids. Biofuels could be constrained by land availability and soil depletion. Coal-to-liquids could be constrained by concerns
about climate change and local and regional pollution. Production of both
could be limited by their inherent energy requirements, which may well
be unacceptable when global oil production is declining. We assume here
that the yield of other liquid fuels will offset the greater cuts to be required
of oil for transport. Thus, the net result would be a cut of about 30 percent
in the use of oil and other liquid fuels.

Taking all these considerations into account, and allowing for a margin of error in the form of underestimation of the rate of production after
the peak, we conclude that by 2025 richer countries should plan to reduce
their use of liquid fuels for transport—almost all oil—by about 40 percent
below 2007 levels.

This oil-reduction parameter is a key driver in our proposal for the
revolution in moving people around the United States by 2025, detailed in
table 27.1, which provides comparisons with the likely transport activity
and energy use for each mode in 2007. A key underlying feature of table
27.1 is that the U.S. population is projected to grow by 16 percent across
this period, from 306 million to 355 million.[14] Accordingly, in some cases
we have shown both total and per capita values.

We are not proposing that the motorized movement of people decline
in direct proportion to the reduction in oil used by transport. Indeed,

motorized passenger-kilometers would increase very slightly between 2007 and 2025 (by 1 percent) but decrease per capita (by 13 percent). This would be achieved in two ways: by using oil more efficiently and by a substantial shift to electricity generated from other energy sources. Overall in 2025 compared with 2007, each liter of oil products would fuel about a third more passenger-kilometers. Electricity would fuel 27 percent of the motorized movement of people in 2025 compared with about 0.5 percent in 2007.

In our scenario, ICE-based personal vehicles (cars) will be providing just over half of the movement of people in the United States in 2025, much less than today's share, which is more than 80 percent. Their average energy consumption in megajoules per passenger-kilometer will be about 20 percent lower because of technical improvements and higher occupancies. Electric personal vehicles in 2025 will include cars and two-wheelers that have only electric motors and a declining number of "plug-in hybrids," which can use a built-in ICE but do so rarely.[15]

Future transport may also include the availability of new local transport options that encompass electric jitneys and various kinds of on-demand transport, including what is known as personal rapid transport (PRT).[16] By 2025, local public transport would have expanded substantially and become largely electrified. Electrified service would comprise a mix of modes: trolleybuses, light rail (trams), and heavy rail (metro). A considerable reduction in megajoules per passenger-kilometer is anticipated in ICE-based transport, chiefly through higher occupancies, but less in electrified transport, which already operates with high efficiency and, as it expands, will encounter capacity challenges.

Intercity bus services would also expand. About half would be powered by more efficient versions of today's diesel engines and half would be electric buses, drawing power from overhead wires installed for bus and truck use along some major highways. Intercity rail undergoes one of the largest increases by 2025, taking up some of the reduction in car travel and replacing many short-haul flights under 500 kilometers. Most of the expansion would be by electrified rail, much of it providing high-speed service—more than 200 kilometers per hour (125 miles per hour). Unit energy use by ICE and electrified trains is expected to fall by a third, largely owing to higher occupancies. In the period until 2025, there would also be expansion of diesel-powered passenger rail service, over tracks not yet electrified, although eventually just about all rail—passenger and freight—will be powered by electricity.

Domestic aviation would have contracted substantially by 2025. A trend will be under way to use larger aircraft (because they are more fuel efficient) flying over fewer routes—that is, those that can generate the high occupancies that will also be required to attain low levels of fuel use per passenger-kilometer. Modest reductions in unit fuel use are expected by 2025, chiefly because of higher occupancies. Further reductions can be expected after 2025 as more of the fleet comprises large, efficient aircraft. International aviation would have expanded a little by 2025, although remaining about the same per capita. Its character would be changing toward movement of larger, more fuel-efficient aircraft flying over fewer routes, to be a much more prominent feature after 2025, when even international aviation will decline. By 2025 there would be some use of fuel-efficient, partially solar-powered airships for moving people over distances, particularly to remote locations for which service by rail or road is impracticable.[17]

There would be more use of water-based modes by 2025, particularly domestically in the form of coastal, lake, and river ferries, but also by transoceanic vessels. The latter especially could make considerable use of wind power through use of kites or solid sails.[18]

THREE PILLARS OF POST–CARBON MOBILITY AND THE VISION BEHIND THEM

Launching a transport revolution in the United States along the lines described above will require three pillars to support efforts at steering change away from chaos and conflict. First would be establishment of an agency that can develop a detailed post-carbon mobility plan and facilitate its effective implementation. Second would be termination of existing programs and plans that expand airport and highway capacity for more oil-fueled mobility, and a corresponding redeployment of human and financial resources toward introducing grid-connected vehicles. Third would be imposition of an escalating tax on oil used for transport—perhaps reaching $0.50 per liter (about $1.90 per U.S. gallon) within a few years. The proceeds would be used in part to induce individuals and businesses to retire what could soon be "stranded assets." These would include jet aircraft and motor vehicles that can be fueled only by petroleum. The proceeds of the tax would also be used to stimulate private, state, and local investment in electric mobility infrastructure in much the way that motor fuel and airline ticket taxes are used now for expanding aviation and road infrastructure.

These first steps away from the status quo would be among the most difficult moves made during the course of America's impending transport revolutions. Interests vested in today's oil-powered mobility would highlight and fiercely oppose the costs and disruption of change. The more numerous eventual beneficiaries of electric traction would be less motivated to support redesign, not least because its advantages could arrive further into the future. Most Americans would be unfamiliar with the transport alternatives being developed and thus uneasy at the prospect of such radical change. Communicating the risks of inaction in the face of oil depletion will require strong, effective leadership. The key to success in communicating the benefits of transport revolutions will be articulating a vision of the future in which the quality of mobility can be seen to improve at the same time that the growth of travel slows down.

We close with a brief vignette of what such a vision could look like, in the hope that it will convince future leaders to advance it while inspiring most people to embrace it. For intercity trips up to 500 kilometers, grid-connected vehicles should require no more total travel time than today's aviation system and highways. Planned and run well, new intercity mobility options could do away with much of the "hurry up and wait" that adds time and stress to flying and driving. This includes waiting for increasingly invasive security procedures at airports, waiting in traffic jams of road vehicles (gridlock) and aircraft queues for takeoff (winglock), waiting for connections through air hubs, and waiting to claim luggage that must be checked to keep a growing number of items that could be weaponized out of passenger cabins (e.g., liquids and gels). A well-run train and bus system will reduce the time and the discomfort of these travel experiences. Passengers on Japan's Shinkansen (the original "bullet train") routinely arrive at their originating station just a minute or two before departure because there are no ticketing, luggage, and security formalities to contend with. The Eurostar service linking London with

Brussels, Paris, and elsewhere has more elaborate predeparture screening, with identity and luggage checks, but even there passengers are accepted up to twenty minutes before departure.

Trains and buses can distribute travel time differently, with the longer journey offset by shorter waits to board, connect, and collect one's belongings. The speed of the vehicle in motion will be slower than an aircraft, but travelers will reclaim minutes or hours that are consumed by today's unpleasant aspects of air travel. More time spent aboard the vehicle will create greater opportunity for undisturbed work and rest, as well as for taking meals and for the social interactions that are largely missing from contemporary flying and driving.

Even when the total journey time increases by many hours for land travel in the thousands of kilometers, and by days for voyages by sea, the experience will offer compensation. Wireless network connectivity, comfortable accommodations, and appealing food and drink could offer the chance to work and play in motion that is today reserved for those who can afford first-class flying and luxury cruise ships.

Just as gourmets celebrate the emphasis on quality found in the "slow food" movement, so too could post–peak-oil travelers appreciate the quality gained by slower motion. Taking the time to savor a relaxing, productive, and enjoyable trip while it is happening could seem natural to future travelers. When they think about what came before, they may well look back on the twilight of the "jet set" era—when passengers brought along their own food and drink, pillows, blankets, and other creature comforts to survive no-frills flights—with the kind of bemusement with which their parents regarded photos of passengers packed into steerage accommodation on early-twentieth-century ocean liners.

If post-carbon transitions are successfully managed, Americans in the 2030s will be incredulous at the ways in which Americans in the 2000s endured the waste and discomfort of cramming onto planes and jamming roads with huge motor vehicles most often occupied by a lone driver. The revolutionary mode of disruptive change will have enabled electric mobility to become a mainstay of future transportation. Once the new technology and organizational arrangements have been put in place, transportation management will revert to incrementally improving our new ways of moving people and freight without oil.

Part Twelve

WASTE

CLIMATE CHANGE, PEAK OIL, AND THE END OF WASTE

BILL SHEEHAN AND HELEN SPIEGELMAN

BILL SHEEHAN *is executive director and co-founder of the Product Policy Institute. He has worked with local governments, communities, and nongovernmental organizations to bring extended producer responsibility (EPR) policies to a growing number of communities across the United States. He was co-founder and executive director of the GrassRoots Recycling Network from 1995 to 2003 and a board member of the National Recycling Coalition in the late 1990s. Sheehan is a Fellow of Post Carbon Institute.*

HELEN SPIEGELMAN *is board president and co-founder of the Product Policy Institute. She has worked on waste and EPR issues in British Columbia for over a decade, including as director of communications for the Recycling Council of British Columbia, and most recently with Zero Waste Vancouver.*

❖

Household waste is often overlooked in discussions of big issues like climate change and peak oil. Even dedicated environmentalists sometimes share the prevailing view that waste "will always be with us." In fact, waste as we know it today is not an inevitability but an indicator of massive failure in both markets and market regulation. Worse, we are poised to compound that failure by building costly energy infrastructure that relies on waste as a substitute for declining fossil fuels.

THE NORMALIZATION OF WASTE

It's important at the outset to recognize a paradox about waste. Our culture holds generally negative attitudes toward wastefulness, yet waste is supported with community services that are more universal, more affordable, and more accessible than health care, housing, or education. Consider the ubiquitous street litter bins provided and maintained at public expense. These community amenities make wasting easy and convenient. Similarly, household garbage containers lined up at the curb every week communicate unabashedly that *wasting is a publicly sanctioned behavior in our society.*

How did wasting become socially normalized to this extent? The answer lies in a well-intentioned effort a century ago to take public action to protect human health and safety.

In the booming industrial cities of the late-nineteenth century "heaps of garbage, rubbish and manure cluttered the streets and alleys," writes waste historian Martin Melosi.[1] Imagine teeming cities where horses were the main mode of local transportation. Pigs and fowl were kept in basements of the crowded tenement buildings that housed the growing numbers of the new laboring class. In such conditions, yellow fever, typhoid, cholera, and other diseases emerged quickly and spread rapidly, affecting neighborhoods both rich and poor.

The only waste collection services were informal arrangements with itinerant entrepreneurs such as rag collectors. As time went by and things got worse, Melosi writes, the traditional notion of individual responsibility for refuse disposal gave way to an acceptance of community responsibility. A broad-based civic reform movement demanded that cities provide "municipal housekeeping" to keep the streets clean. In this way, *waste management* became a core function of our local governments. The streets and alleys were cleansed and, best of all, citizens had the assurance that their waste was safely in the hands of competent professional engineers and public servants.

No one could have predicted what would happen over the next hundred years (figure 28.1). When local governments assumed responsibility for solid waste (box 28.1) a century ago, household and commercial waste consisted mainly of inorganics, in the form of coal ash and wood ash from furnaces and stoves.[2] Beyond that, waste was mostly food scraps, with a smaller quantity of simple manufactured products made with paper, cloth, and leather. By 1960, the ash had been almost completely eliminated by the introduction of other forms of space heating and cooking appliances, biodegradable wastes had doubled because of suburbanization, and there was already striking evidence of the advent of the throwaway economy.

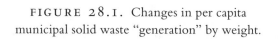

FIGURE 28.1. Changes in per capita
municipal solid waste "generation" by weight.

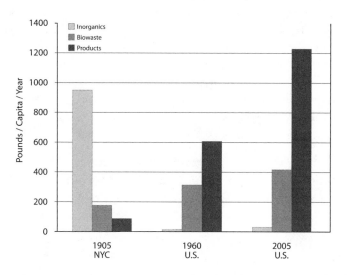

Note: Inorganics = "ashes" (1905), "miscellaneous inorganic wastes"
(1960, 2005); Biowaste = "garbage" (1905), "food scraps" plus "yard
trimmings" (1960, 2005); Products = "rubbish" (1905), "products"
(1960, 2005).

Sources: Helen Spiegelman and Bill Sheehan, *Unintended Con-
sequences: Municipal Waste Management in the Throwaway Society*
(Athens, GA: Product Policy Institute, 2005). 1905 data are from
Martin V. Melosi, *Garbage in the Cities* (College Station, TX: Texas
A&M University, 1981). 1960 and 2005 data are from United
States Environmental Protection Agency, "Municipal Solid Waste
in the United States: 2005 Facts and Figures," EPA530-R-06-011
(Washington DC, October 2006), 64; http://www.epa.gov/wastes/
nonhaz/municipal/pubs/msw2005.pdf.

By the year 2005, products and packaging made up 74 percent of our
waste and reflected a thirteenfold increase in per capita consumption from
one hundred years earlier. The growth in production and consumption is
driving waste growth.

Throwaway products and packaging have become a hallmark of
modern industrialized economies, eagerly emulated by less industrialized
economies. Constant demand for "new" products is actively encour-

---

BOX 28.1 What Is "Solid Waste"?

The U.S. Environmental Protection Agency (EPA) defines *municipal solid waste* as the materials traditionally managed by municipalities, whether by burning, burying, recycling, or composting.[1] This material is actually a small fraction of the far larger universe of waste created "upstream" of the consumer in the course of extracting raw materials, processing and manufacturing products, and packaging. These industrial-process wastes are called *industrial hazardous waste* and *industrial nonhazardous waste*.

There are three major components of municipal solid waste:

1. Inorganics (inert material such as ashes, rocks, bricks, etc.).
2. Food scraps and yard trimmings and other biodegradable wastes.
3. Manufactured products and their associated packaging.

The EPA uses the term *waste* to refer to all materials managed by municipalities, and the term *discards* is the subset that is buried or burned. To acknowledge the resource value of unwanted materials, we prefer the opposite usage: *Discards* refers to all materials set out, whereas *waste* refers to discards destroyed by burning or burying.

---

1. U.S. Environmental Protection Agency, *Municipal Solid Waste Generation, Recycling and Disposal in the United States: Facts and Figures for 2007*, EPA-530-R-08-0 1 0 (Washington DC: Government Printing Office, 2008).

---

aged, spurred by advertising and planned obsolescence in product design. Historian Susan Strasser has noted that the mass-marketing of consumer goods started as long ago as catalog sales in the nineteenth century, and that advertising campaigns had to be developed to replace established values of thrift with new values of conspicuous consumption.[3] Consumerism and planned obsolescence became even more entrenched after World War II when the development of the national highway system increased the mobility of people and goods, encouraging the proliferation of convenient disposable products and packaging. Note in figure 28.1 that between 1960 and 2005 per capita product and packaging discards doubled while the per capita generation of organic discards like food scraps and yard trimmings remained relatively constant (yards and stomachs have natural limits, while desire for new stuff is seemingly limitless). Today we think nothing of consuming and discarding thirteen times more manufactured goods than our great-grandparents did.

Product and packaging waste grew not only in quantity but also in toxicity. As petroleum production expanded in the twentieth century to power a growing fleet of motor vehicles, cheap petrochemical by-products became the building blocks for whole new classes of products and packaging. Plastics were novelties in the 1930s but their use virtually exploded after World War II and has experienced continued growth ever since. Moreover, whole new classes of other synthetic chemicals based on petroleum—the vast majority untested for toxic effects on human health and the environment—proliferated during this period, and they continue to be invented and used in products and packaging at an ever-increasing rate. While much has been done to reduce and regulate releases of chemicals during industrial production, many of the more than 80,000 synthetic chemicals produced in commercial quantities wind up in products and packaging and are released during the use and disposal of the products containing them, posing risk not only to public health and safety but to the global ecosystem.[4]

THE THROWAWAY ECONOMY AND CLIMATE CHANGE

The stuff we buy, use, and discard has a long and complicated life story. The waste we discard at the curb is only a fraction of the total waste produced along the way. Annie Leonard sums it all up in a fast-paced, twenty-minute blockbuster Web film called *The Story of Stuff*.[5] Raw materials are gouged from nature, manufactured into packaged products by underpaid workers, shipped halfway around the world to rich countries, sold in "big-box" stores, and, more often than not, deposited in huge industrial-scale landfills and incinerators. The average life span of the materials used in manufactured goods and packaging, according to Leonard's sources, is six months.

The greatest impacts from our consumption happen to someone else, somewhere else. We don't see the pollution, depleted resources, and social ills in the distant communities that supply our stuff. And because our waste is increasingly hauled longer and longer distances to massive disposal facilities, we don't see the impacts where our waste ends up. In short, the "distancing" of the pleasurable consumption experience from both production and wasting insulates us from the consequences of our actions.[6] But new analytical tools are making it possible to quantify the upstream and downstream impacts of the products we buy and use.

Ecological footprint analysis, developed by Canadian researchers William Rees and Mathis Wackernagel in the 1990s,[7] provides a measure of the global scale of our resource consumption. It shows us that North American consumption requires resources from an area four times greater than what our actual land-based biological carrying capacity can support. We are able to enjoy this extra consumption (temporarily) because we *appropriate the carrying capacity* of other parts of the world. We are, every day, throwing away other people's shares of limited global resources to supply our wants and needs. Furthermore, global per capita consumption of some commodities has grown eight to twelve times faster than population over the past four decades.[8]

We have yet to come to grips with our own vulnerability in this global supply system. We in rich countries have almost lost the ability to supply our own needs through local manufacturing and agriculture—or even to extend the life of products through reuse, repair, and repurposing. We rely on others, and on a system lubricated by cheap oil, to meet our needs as well as our wants. In the post-peak-oil period, inevitable interruptions in the flow of the goods we rely on every day will be profoundly destabilizing.

It turns out that our throwaway economy is also a major contributor to climate change. The U.S. Environmental Protection Agency (EPA) released a report in September 2009 that shines new light on the greenhouse gas impacts of "stuff" bought and thrown away by Americans.[9] Conventional greenhouse gas analysis apportions emissions based on industrial sectors—electricity, transportation, and so on. This EPA report instead used life-cycle analysis to incorporate all of the emissions associated with end-user materials and energy that are consumed, in the economists' sense, by households and governments. In this new systems-based analysis (also known as consumption-based analysis),[10] we can quantify the greenhouse gas emissions that are embodied in the goods we buy and use.[11] These include the energy used at all stages of the product life cycle: to extract and process the resources, to manufacture and transport the

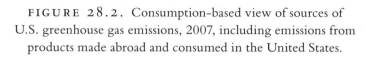

FIGURE 28.2. Consumption-based view of sources of U.S. greenhouse gas emissions, 2007, including emissions from products made abroad and consumed in the United States.

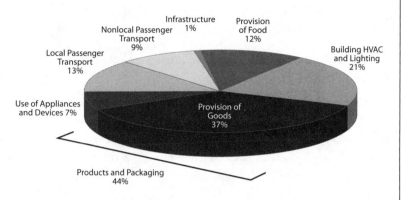

Source: Joshuah Stolaroff, "Products, Packaging and U.S. Greenhouse Gas" Emissions (Athens, GA: Product Policy Institute, September 2009).

products, to operate the retail outlets, to use the products themselves, and then to dispose of them by recycling, burying in landfills, or burning in incinerators.

The EPA report concluded that the provision of goods and materials is responsible for the largest share, by far, of *direct* U.S. greenhouse gas emissions. The Product Policy Institute commissioned a supplementary white paper by the technical author who wrote the EPA report to factor in *indirect global* emissions—that is, the emissions from products produced abroad and consumed in the United States minus products produced here and shipped abroad.[12] The white paper showed that 44 percent of total U.S. greenhouse gas impacts are due to the provision, use, and disposal of products and packaging (figure 28.2). That's more than the emissions from the energy used in buildings, passenger transportation, or the provision of food—activities that get the lion's share of attention in government and business efforts to reduce greenhouse gas emissions.

We cannot address climate change or prepare for the post-peak-oil period without changing the way we manage products and packaging throughout their life cycles. And since previous research has shown that most impacts occur in the production stage[13]—and thus are determined at the design phase—policies are needed that address how products are designed and marketed to encourage conservation and recycling. These policies should be a part of every state and local government's climate action plan. But our waste management policies are having the exact opposite effect.

MARKET FAILURE

Many of the social and environmental problems we face today can be traced to market failure, often occurring as an unintended consequence of well-intentioned public policy. This is the case with waste. Much of the stuff we throw away cannot be recycled, reused, or repaired because it was designed to be wasted. The waste management system supports planned obsolescence by providing the convenient removal and disposal of all those poorly designed products and their associated packaging.

Because of our waste policy, it is local communities—not the producers of throwaway products and packaging—that bear the cost of cleaning up after the throwaway economy. Over the course of the twentieth century, taxpayers and ratepayers have faced higher and higher costs to manage more and more waste.

On top of the direct financial costs, we must also factor in the *opportunity costs* of allocating more and more public dollars to waste management instead of to other essential community services like public safety, schools, libraries, and parks. And then there are the hidden social, economic, and environmental costs imposed on the communities (usually poor) and ecosystems where our stuff is produced and where our waste is sent. Economists call these *externalized costs*, because they fall on someone other than the producers and consumers who directly benefit from the products.

The externalization of costs leads to what economists call *market failure*. The market's "invisible hand" pushes us toward choices that are underpriced because they don't factor in the externalized costs. If the market had been working correctly, the real costs of wasteful products would long ago have given producers and consumers clear feedback telling them to produce less waste. But because our cities and towns provided the programs to clean up after the throwaway economy at taxpayer or ratepayer expense, this critical feedback loop was broken. In this way, our communities have become unwitting enablers of the market's turn to massive scales of excess production and consumption.

SUPERSIZING MUNICIPAL WASTE MANAGEMENT

As waste grew over time, so did the waste management system. From its humble beginnings of horse-drawn carts and dumps at the edge of town, waste management has grown into a multibillion-dollar, multinational industry that hauls local garbage to huge disposal facilities that are sometimes hundreds or even thousands of miles away.[14] The municipal waste management system is made up of both public entities (municipal waste authorities) and private-sector waste management companies. This complex waste management system has evolved its own regulatory, administrative, technological, market, and social components, which operate largely out of the view of ordinary citizens and with loose oversight by local elected officials, who generally defer to the expertise of their professional staff when it comes to decisions about waste.[15]

By the middle of the twentieth century, impacts arising from the growing volume and toxicity of municipal waste had begun to rouse public concern. State and federal governments started to intervene in municipal waste management, forcing the cleanup of former landfill sites (one-fifth of all the federal-designated "Superfund" hazardous waste sites in the United States are old municipal landfills) and imposing new guidelines on the operation of landfills and incinerators.[16] By the late 1980s government regulations were forcing the closure of hundreds of municipal landfills across North America—resulting in further unintended consequences.

The closure of local dumps, along with the ever-rising quantities of waste (the amount of waste flowing to U.S. landfills grew by more than 70 percent between 1960 and 1990[17]), created a perceived "landfill crisis," which in turn created a growth opportunity for the private waste management industry. The waste industry consolidated, with a handful of publicly traded waste corporations buying up thousands of small companies that used to serve their local communities. During this period, the corporate "Giants of Garbage" built huge regional landfills serving many municipalities.[18] This eliminated the landfill shortage and indeed created an abundant supply of disposal capacity that kept disposal costs relatively low, despite the extra cost of long-distance hauling.[19]

The period between 1980 and 1990 also saw hundreds of proposals to solve the landfill "crisis" by building waste incinerators, and these received strong encouragement from the federal government.[20] A new movement of citizen reformers sprang up and battled proposals for waste incinerators in their communities. The citizens called instead for municipal recycling programs to conserve the valuable resources in the waste stream. Like their Progressive Era predecessors, these activists left a lasting mark on municipal waste management. Almost three hundred incinerator proposals were shelved and the waste industry was forced to adapt to the changing political climate.

The response was a new waste management policy called integrated waste management (IWM). IWM is based on a hierarchy of preferred management strategies: reduce, reuse, recycle, and, last, bury or burn. This policy approach was sanctioned by senior levels of government including the EPA.[21] To reinforce the hierarchy, more than two dozen U.S. states and several Canadian provinces required local governments to meet recycling or waste "diversion" targets, diverting waste from landfills and incinerators into local recycling or composting programs. The State of California passed legislation in 1989 requiring cities to divert half of their waste by the year 2000 or face stiff fines.[22]

In practice, IWM settled for what was deemed to be an "optimal mix" of traditional disposal in landfills and incinerators operating alongside recycling and composting programs. After three decades of effort and a huge public investment in recycling infrastructure, the national diversion rate for municipal solid waste reached barely 33 percent in the United States and 22 percent in Canada.[23] In other words, despite the hierarchy of preferred options, the large majority of discards are still being entombed and destroyed in landfills and incinerators. The lion's share of solid waste department budgets and waste industry profits are in waste disposal, rather than in the "three Rs" (reduction, reuse, and recycling).[24] Most important, in the broader context of global material flows, waste continues to grow. New York University writer Samantha MacBride comments:

> Using metrics of tons flowing globally and ending in waste, rather than the vibrancy of the recycling industry or the popularity of recycling, it is fair to say that solid waste solutions practiced in the U.S. today are not achieving outcomes in a materially meaningful way.[25]

IWM has had no discernible effect on production and consumption because these occur outside the scope of the end-of-pipe waste management system. Indeed, gains achieved by municipal recycling programs have been offset by continuing growth in both consumption and population. Even with recycling programs in place, cities in the United States and Canada are sending more waste to landfills and incinerators today than they did in 1990.[26] Municipal waste managers do their planning around the assumption that waste will continue to grow over time; thus they tend to favor continued expansion of waste facility infrastructure to accommodate that growth.[27]

GARBAGE REBRANDED AS FUEL: WASTED ENERGY

Conceding that IWM is incapable of significant further progress on waste reduction, the waste industry is now shifting its focus to brand garbage as a renewable energy source.

Incinerators—Burning the Furniture to Heat the House

The incineration industry is exploiting concern about the declining supply of fossil fuels to create a growth opportunity for waste incineration. Co-opting the language of the citizen reformers who battled incinerators in the 1980s, incinerator salespeople tell municipal officials that waste is a "resource." A ton of garbage, says global incineration giant Covanta Energy, contains the energy equivalent of a barrel of oil or a quarter ton of coal.[28]

Municipal officials desperate for a positive solution have been convinced. The chair of Metro Vancouver's waste committee tells his constituents that sending a million tons of garbage to landfills is like "burying a million barrels of oil in the ground every year."[29]

Less attention is paid by busy politicians to the counterargument posed by economist Jeffrey Morris. Using systems-based life-cycle analysis like that of the U.S. EPA report cited above, Morris points out that one ton of garbage actually represents the equivalent of *eight barrels of oil* that were used during the manufacture, distribution, sale, use, and disposal of the products and packaging in the waste.[30] Thus, burning mixed garbage in waste-to-energy plants still results in a net energy *deficit* of seven barrels of oil (equivalent) per ton of garbage. Reuse and recycling preserves much more of the embodied energy value than any form of waste disposal, which is a complete, or nearly complete, write-off of all the investment of resources and energy that was used to produce the products.

The illusion that garbage is a renewable fuel ignores the fact that our cities don't produce the materials that end up in their waste. A city is an open system; products and packaging flow in from somewhere else. This creates the politically challenging problem that a local community burning its waste receives economic benefits (heat and power generation, avoided cost of landfilling), whereas the distant communities where replacement products are manufactured are burdened with social and environmental costs (resource extraction, factory and transportation pollution). Politicians naturally favor a course of action that benefits their own constituencies. Nevertheless, communities that invest in waste incinerators become locked into supplying those facilities with waste in order to earn the energy revenues on which the economic viability of waste-to-energy depends. It's a vicious cycle that shuts out waste reduction. Where is the incentive to produce or consume reusable and recyclable products if the energy infrastructure relies on throwaways to operate?

Landfills—A Major Source of Uncontrolled Greenhouse Gas Emissions

It's not just the incineration industry that is on board the waste-to-energy bandwagon. Landfill operators are trying to exploit the gas that is produced by decomposition of the organic fraction of garbage, which includes paper, food scraps, and yard trimmings.[31]

Methane is generated in landfills and open dumps as waste decomposes without oxygen; landfill gas contains about 50 percent methane, which can be combusted as a fuel. This may seem like a smart use of our otherwise useless landfills, but it can also create incentives for decisions that are not so smart. For example, in late 2009 the State of Michigan, which banned yard waste from landfills a generation ago, was pressured by the landfill industry to repeal the yard-waste ban so they can "convert grass to gas."[32] Similarly, the waste industry is seeking to reverse long-standing practices that were put in place to delay landfill gas generation and introduce practices to *speed up* the production of landfill gas for use as fuel. Unfortunately, adding more organic matter to our landfills will also increase the rate at which they fill up, meaning local governments will need to spend more money and sooner to build new landfills (usually farther away).

More important, while landfill-generated methane is a potential energy source, it's also a potentially devastating greenhouse gas, and gas capture systems are far from perfect. Methane is twenty-three to seventy-five times more potent than carbon dioxide, depending on the timescale over which it is measured.[33] Landfills are the second-largest human-related source of methane in the United States, accounting for 23 percent of all methane emissions in 2007.[34] When actual operating conditions are taken into account over the lifetime of a landfill with gas-recovery systems in place, as much as 80 percent of the methane may still end up being released into the atmosphere.[35] As a recent Sierra Club report on landfill gas-to-energy practices states:

> Contrary to conventional wisdom, it appears the relatively small carbon dioxide reduction benefit that might be achieved by replacing fossil fuel electricity with electricity [generated from landfill gas] is greatly outweighed by the increase in fugitive methane emissions resulting from altered landfill management practices.[36]

Finally, landfill gas does not burn cleanly—some studies suggest dioxin emissions from landfill gas flaring are thirty times higher than from state-of-the-art waste incinerators.[37] Whether from incinerators or landfills, the risk to human health from waste combustion, despite advances in pollution control, is far from zero. Along with the well-known effects of dioxins and heavy metals in incinerator emissions, there are new and less well-characterized threats to health from nanoparticles that can move through tissues into the brain.[38] And in the end, landfilling, like incineration, removes products from circulation so that the destructive production process must be repeated again and again.

The European Union introduced tough measures in 1999 for reducing the quantity of biodegradable materials going into landfills in order to prevent methane emissions.[39] But Europe's approach had the unintended consequence of encouraging waste incineration with its own attendant greenhouse gas impacts. North America is in a position to learn from European experience by rejecting end-of-pipe solutions and emphasizing prevention.

THE ZERO-WASTE VISION

Our waste management policies and practices rest on the assumption that waste is inevitable—an assumption that became a self-fulfilling prophecy. What if we start from the assumption that most, if not all, of the waste in our communities is a symptom of massive market failure caused by misguided (if well-intentioned) policies? Once we accept this assumption, we are well on the way toward *denormalizing waste*.

Zero waste is an approach directed at preventing waste rather than managing it. Its scope is the entire production and consumption system, not just the back-end activities of our economy that have traditionally been carried out by local governments and the waste industry. It is a holistic focus on global resource flows, rather than a myopic focus on local waste management. Zero waste is the design principle best articulated by William McDonough and Michael Braungart in their 2002 book *Cradle to Cradle:* Instead of "cradle-to-grave" resource flows, zero-waste design produces safe products and closed-loop "cradle-to-cradle" flows.[40]

The Community's Responsibility

Strong federal and even international regulation will be required to reduce today's unsustainable global materials and energy flows and to channel them into closed-loop systems where wasting is discouraged. But change can be driven from the local level, through a conscious rethinking by citizens about the role of their local communities in the global system of producing and discarding goods.

Zero waste offers communities a practical alternative to IWM, a strategy to begin correcting decades of neglect both at the front (production) and back (disposal) ends of our throwaway economy. The Product Policy Institute proposed in 2005 that communities focus on two zero-waste objectives that should be pursued together.[41] The first is eliminating the municipal subsidy that communities provide to producers of throwaway products and packaging, which is enabling waste growth. The second is curbing the emission of methane and other harmful substances caused by landfilling of organic wastes. This is an area where local communities can take immediate action. The need is urgent in North America because more than 80 percent of our waste that is buried or burned ends up in landfills.[42]

Local governments in North America have already had striking success diverting yard trimmings from landfills. Within a decade of introduction, yard trimmings diversion programs were recovering almost two-thirds of available supply.[43] Food and food-contaminated paper products remain the unfinished business of our municipal recycling system.[44] Less than 3 percent of food scraps (which comprise 20 percent of the discards in landfills) are currently being diverted; fortunately, major cities in the United States have recently begun collection of food scraps.[45] In October 2009, San Francisco became the first city in the United States to require residents and businesses to separate organic material from their waste. Seattle has a similar requirement that applies only to single-family homes. The Canadian province of Quebec, with federal government support, is investing over $500 million in four new municipal composting infrastructure projects to divert organics from disposal.[46]

The Producer's Responsibility

The other great task of local communities is to give back to producers and consumers the responsibility for the management of throwaway products and packaging. This is being done through an internationally recognized policy called "extended producer responsibility" (EPR), also known as "product stewardship" in North America.[47] EPR establishes a legal chain of producer custody extending through the entire product life cycle.

Ultimately, there could be a significant reduction in the overall flows of materials and energy if producers rethink their products and supply chains to avoid the costs that are currently incurred in waste management. Indeed, we are already seeing rapid development of new recycling services where EPR has been introduced. In Canada every province has adopted EPR legislation, and this has given rise to a whole range of new programs provided at no cost to local communities for recycling electronics, tires, used oil, paint, solvents, pesticides, pharmaceuticals, and beverage containers.[48]

An early precursor to the system we now call EPR was the system used in the first half of the twentieth century for marketing nationally branded soft drinks and beer. At one time, every town had several bottling plants. These were local businesses that would produce one or more brand-name beverages using syrup concentrates that were supplied by the brand owner. The bottlers would package the beverages using distinctive bottles and caps that were also specified by the brand owner; consumers received cash refunds for bringing their bottles back to the store.

But this system was abandoned in the mid-twentieth century due to another well-meaning government program that had unintended consequences. The Interstate Highway System, construction of which began in the 1950s, made it more profitable for the brand owners to switch to no-deposit, no-return bottles and cans that could be filled at large regional bottling plants and trucked on the new highways to local markets. The results were roadside litter, growing quantities of throwaway bottles and cans in local landfills, and the loss of many small bottling businesses as well as small local brands of beer and soft drinks (which used to compete successfully against national brands).

Our municipal recycling programs, at their best, do no more than deliver bales of low-value commodities back into the global marketplace, with the municipality taking the risk of fluctuating market prices. Since the 1970s some state and provincial governments have introduced "bottle bills" requiring beer and soft drink companies to reinstitute cash refunds on bottle and can returns, shifting the cost of beverage container recycling from the public to the beverage industry. These states have the best recycling rates for beverage containers in North America.[49]

This example hints at the possibilities for renewed local economic development through EPR. Local bottling businesses have not yet made a comeback in bottle bill states. However, a return to local production could ensue as energy prices rise post–peak oil because EPR levels the playing field between national brands and local brands. Moreover, EPR not only can help put the brakes on waste and global materials and energy flows, it can also drive the development of more economically productive manufacturing, repair, and recycling infrastructure in local communities.

The Activist's Responsibility

The zero-waste concept has energized a new generation of community activists across North America and beyond. A number of broad citizen-based campaigns are pushing for EPR and programs to divert organics from landfills.

In 2008 the Institute for Local Self-Reliance, the Global Alliance for Incinerator Alternatives, and Eco-Cycle produced a seminal report, *Stop Trashing the Climate*, which examined the link between reform of the waste management system and broader issues of peak oil, climate change, and corporate globalization.[50] The report called for an end to new investment in landfills and incinerators and the expansion of EPR and local recycling. Similarly, the Sierra Club adopted a zero-waste policy in 2008 promoting EPR.[51] COOL 2012 is a new and growing campaign to keep "compostable organics out of landfills."[52]

In addition, the Electronics TakeBack Coalition, the Texas Campaign for the Environment, and other state-level advocacy groups have pressed nineteen states to adopt tough EPR legislation targeted at electronic products. The Container Recycling Institute and ad hoc groups in communities across North America are putting pressure on high-profile beverage producers to expand bottle bills, scoring one new program in the United States (Hawaii in 2002) and significant expansion of the scope of bottle bills in other jurisdictions. Eight out of ten Canadian provinces have bottle bills that are much broader in scope than those in the United States (for example, the province of Alberta requires cash refunds on *all* beverage containers, including milk containers).

Local governments are also increasingly activist in their call for EPR. The Product Policy Institute has organized local governments to press for state EPR legislation, building on the effective model of the Northwest Product Stewardship Council. That regional council of local governments, established in 1998, lobbied successfully for legislation introduced in Washington State in 2006 requiring producers to set up recycling programs for electronic products. Product Stewardship Councils have been formed in California, New York, Texas, and Vermont and organizing is continuing in other states. The councils have adopted common "framework principles" for product stewardship policy, and they are promoting these as the basis for harmonized statewide legislation.[53]

GOVERNMENT AND THE MARKET

A citizens' movement, supported by growing advocacy from local governments, is pressing for change in our waste policy. But national policy is still shaped by the dominant neoconservative economic paradigm that the market economy is the life force of our civilization and that *consumption* is the purpose of that economy, creating jobs and wealth and material prosperity. It also holds that producers will act for the common good once they are guided by "sovereign" consumers without interference from government. By this thinking, if we just exhort *individual consumers* to purchase green products we will eventually arrive at a greener form of capitalism.

There is some truth within this notion, but there are also the practical realities of corporate power and self-interest. Corporations by nature seek freedom to pursue profit for their shareholders as their first priority, and to keep environmental and other nonmarket obligations to a minimum. Author Samantha MacBride is concerned that the recycling movement is being co-opted by corporations.[54] As an example, these corporations have insinuated themselves into Keep America Beautiful (KAB), a supposedly grassroots organization that promotes entirely nonmarket solutions—volunteer cleanups and municipal recycling—to our waste problem. KAB's most prominent donors ("social responsibility partners") are a garbage company (Waste Management), an opponent of bottle bills (Pepsico), and a major source of cigarette butt litter (Philip Morris).[55] The lower tiers of corporate sponsorship are populated by a who's who of the corporations enjoying the greatest subsidies from municipal taxpayers in avoiding their waste management responsibilities. These corporations spare no expense in an effort to build public acceptance of status quo municipal recycling as an initiative that satisfies public yearning for change while not threatening the practices that have led to excessive production, consumption, and waste.

Added to this is the distrust of government that pervades North America at both ends of the political spectrum. The Right trusts corporations more than governments to ensure that we will continue to enjoy the material benefits to which some have become accustomed, while the Left blames governments for decades of inaction against self-interested corporations. This has led especially in the United States to a tolerance of corporate greenwashing rather than tough, fair government regulation.

But there seems to be a growing realization, expressed by Michael Maniates in *Confronting Consumption*, that today's market failure can be addressed effectively only through civic reform rather than voluntary solutions ("collective citizen action as opposed to individual consumer behavior"). To redirect the market toward practices that protect the common good, Maniates emphasizes, we will need "strong and sustained intervention at large scales to regulate the freedom of the firms that control extraction, production and distribution of goods that end up as waste."[56]

Along with the Product Stewardship Councils' advocacy of framework EPR legislation, the Institute for Local Self-Reliance is leading a comprehensive New Rules Project that explores ways of "designing rules as if community matters."[57] Their work in municipal waste management is a good starting place to find examples of interventions at all levels to change the status quo and hold corporations accountable for their waste.

NEW RULES, NEW PATH

Reforming waste policy is an important part of the broader work on transitioning to a post-carbon economy, both to reduce materials and energy flows and to build resilient communities through a return to local production and product stewardship. It would be irrational to repeat the mistakes of the nineteenth century with public investment in municipal incinerators and landfills supporting unsustainable flows of materials and energy, and simply hope that consumers and producers will of their own accord do in this new century what they failed to do in the last one. Instead, we can set new rules and hold producers responsible for obeying them. If we get waste policy right, we can leverage profound changes in how our society manages materials and energy and how we function as communities. If we fail, then "business as usual" will lead to further acceleration of material and energy throughput and ensuing destabilization of the climate and human society.

Part Thirteen

HEALTH

HUMAN HEALTH AND WELL-BEING IN AN ERA OF ENERGY SCARCITY AND CLIMATE CHANGE

CINDY L. PARKER, MD, MPH, AND
BRIAN S. SCHWARTZ, MD, MS

CINDY PARKER *is on the faculty at the Johns Hopkins Bloomberg School of Public Health, where she co-directs the Program on Global Sustainability and Health. Her professional interests include education, policy work, practice, and research on the global environmental topics of climate change, peak petroleum, and global sustainability. She is a frequent speaker on the health effects of global climate change and recently co-authored* Climate Chaos: Your Health at Risk *(2008). Parker is a Fellow of Post Carbon Institute.*

BRIAN SCHWARTZ *is a professor in the Department of Environmental Health Sciences in the Johns Hopkins Bloomberg School of Public Health, where he co-directs both the Program on Global Sustainability and Health and the Environmental Health Institute. He has conducted extensive research on the health effects of chemicals via occupational, environmental, and molecular epidemiology studies. His career has included research, teaching, and training, as well as clinical and public health practice. Schwartz is a Fellow of Post Carbon Institute.*

❖

In the past hundred years, we have created lifestyles, communities, food systems, water systems, transportation systems, and health systems that are entirely reliant on cheap and plentiful oil and that assume a favorable and stable climate. Our health and well-being have been shaped by these lifestyles and systems, but they have not necessarily been well served: Climate change and the threat of energy scarcity now pose serious challenges to our "health system," specifically health care services and public health services.

The consequences of climate change and energy scarcity will be wide ranging and complex, will affect all aspects of our lives, and will touch all people—some more so than others. Energy scarcity will result primarily in reduced capacity, capabilities, and services in the health care and public health systems. Climate change will cause new and increased demands on our current capabilities and services. Without preparation, early responses to these challenges will likely be motivated simply by rising and volatile energy prices—and characterized by trial and error, incorrect decisions, and highly politicized debate. Fortunately, we can plan ahead to provide communities with the essential capabilities and resources they'll need to be resilient, safeguarding individual and family health in an increasingly uncertain future.

HEALTH AND ITS MANY DETERMINANTS

Health is a state of complete physical, mental and social well-being and not merely the absence of disease or infirmity.
—WORLD HEALTH ORGANIZATION, 1948

Physical, Mental, and Social Well-Being

A definition of health as merely the absence of disease is much too limiting. The broad definition of health above was formulated more than sixty years ago and has remained widely useful. Although *physical* health is important to well-being, humans also need *mental* health, which starts with the absence of mental illness but also includes such concepts as freedom from fear of personal harm, freedom from fear about not meeting basic needs (food, water, shelter, safety), and so on. In addition, we are *social* creatures and require a sense of community: stimulating, trusting, and regular interactions with others, plus a sense of usefulness, satisfaction, and security in what we do and how we live our lives as members of groups. Without all three kinds of well-being—physical, mental, and social—we are not healthy.

When health and well-being have been defined broadly, it becomes easier to understand what the health impacts of energy scarcity and climate change are likely to be. Many things that are not considered to be "health related" *per se* are nevertheless important determinants of health;

all of the factors below contribute to physical, mental, and social well-being—or lack thereof—and each of these is likely to be influenced by the coming energy and climate challenges:

- Community economic vitality
- Employment rate
- Social stability
- Neighborliness
- Dependability and affordability of basic needs like food and water
- Urban planning and design
- Reliable transportation systems
- Discrimination
- Political/military conflict
- Population dislocation/mass migration
- Confidence/worry about the future
- Equity/inequity
- Freedom of/restrictions on movement
- Disaster preparedness (how communities respond to droughts, floods, and heat waves)
- Availability of public health and health care services

Researchers studying what affects the health of society as a whole (as well as the health of smaller social groups) have identified "large-scale" factors far outside of an individual's control that can have profound influences on health.[1] For example, while tobacco smoking, inactivity, high-fat diets, high-salt diets, and obesity account for a large share of the world's incidence of heart disease, there is also substantial risk associated with adverse socioeconomic conditions. Thus, while many of us acknowledge that our behaviors influence our health in good ways and bad, few recognize the social context in which health-related behaviors occur and become socially patterned.[2] These social determinants of health are critically important and go a long way toward explaining different rates of disease across populations.

Risk Regulators

Human actions and behaviors are influenced by many different dynamics and at many different scales. Here are just a few:

Dynamics	*Scales*
Cultural	School
Economic	Family
Environmental	Individual
Historical	Global
Political	National
Religious	Community
Social	Workplace

The opportunities and constraints created by these dynamics are called *risk regulators*, defined as features and phenomena of the social and built environments that shape, channel, motivate, and induce behavioral risk factors for adverse or good health outcomes.[3] For example, the ongoing war in the Congo that began in 1998 has been responsible for more than 5 million civilian deaths through 2009. Many of these persons did not die of war *per se*, but rather from the collapse of social and environmental life-support systems such as housing, public health, food, and water. The conditions created by the war exacerbated risks to public health beyond the immediate effects of the war itself.

The health threats of climate change and energy scarcity can be thought of in the same way. Climate change and energy scarcity have direct effects on health, such as through extreme weather events and the impacts of rising fuel prices on dietary choices. But they will also increasingly affect other systems that are essential to public health around the world, from food and water to economic activity and political stability. In addition, they will change the advantages and disadvantages different populations have for dealing with these crises. Some people and communities will find new opportunities in the changes brought by climate change and energy scarcity, but many more will be confronted with new and greater constraints. Most especially, populations that are already starting out disadvantaged in terms of resources, health, and political power—or with less of what might be termed *resilience*—will be more severely impacted.

Health at Risk

One of the most important determinants of risk to our health in the United States has turned out to be the spatial organization of our communities. We have spent the last sixty years building a physical infrastructure—including highways, office buildings, housing subdivisions, and shopping malls—that was entirely shaped by the availability of cheap and plentiful oil. Homes are far removed from jobs, services (including health services), and even places for recreation and social gathering—all things we need for our well-being. Thus our built environment becomes an important health risk regulator as energy scarcity makes distance more of an obstacle.

Another unexpected determinant of health risk is what might be termed our "provisioning system"—that is, the ways in which we provide our communities with the goods they need. The manufacture and transport of most goods will be impacted in obvious ways by the challenges ahead, but the health risk of the food system is probably the most worrisome. Our food generally comes to us from industrial models of food production, thousands of miles away and completely dependent on fuel, pesticides, herbicides, fertilizers, and plastics made from petroleum and natural gas—a very vulnerable situation in a future of oil prices double or even triple what they are today. In addition, climate change threatens to bring not just more crop-damaging extreme weather (especially droughts/floods) but major shifts in agricultural zones and pest ranges.

Climate change and energy scarcity will create direct challenges for our health system, but they will also create myriad *indirect* problems for health simply because of how we have built and provisioned our communities and economies up until now.

Sustainable Well-Being

Dr. John Holdren, currently the lead science and technology policy adviser in the Obama administration, has argued that human well-being rests on a foundation of three pillars of conditions and processes[4]:

- *Economic:* production, employment, income, wealth, markets, and trade.
- *Sociopolitical:* national and personal security, liberty, justice, law, education, health care, science, arts, civil society, and culture.
- *Environmental:* air, water, soils, mineral resources, living organisms, and climate.

For sustainable human well-being, each is indispensable, none can be identified as the most important, and the three are highly interdependent. What Holdren did not make explicit was that energy scarcity and climate change will adversely influence each of the three pillars and limit options for responding to the tremendous challenges they create. He highlighted the "energy-economy-environment dilemma" that reliable and affordable energy is essential for meeting human needs, but the way we currently use energy is responsible for many challenging environmental problems. According to Holdren, "energy is the hardest part of the environment problem; environment is the hardest part of the energy problem; and resolving the energy-economy-environment dilemma is the hardest part of the challenge of sustainable well-being for industrial and developing countries alike."

Recent U.S. national-security reports state that climate change will pose serious threats to national security because it will likely increase poverty, lead to serious environmental degradation, and weaken national governments—findings that are interestingly similar to Holdren's three pillars and the idea of risk regulation.[5] A growing number of analysts are viewing climate change and energy scarcity through these lenses and the conclusion is unmistakable: Climate change and energy scarcity pose unprecedented challenges to human health and well-being.

HEALTH CARE AND PUBLIC HEALTH

Philosophy and Practice

Most people are familiar with the *health care system*—its primary function is to take care of us when we get sick, and as such is often referred to as the "illness care system." Your doctor's office, clinics, hospitals, medical laboratories, outpatient surgical facilities, and diagnostic centers such as for MRIs are all part of the health care system. It focuses on the health of an *individual* who seeks the advice of a health care practitioner for a specific health problem. The practitioner then typically takes a history, completes a physical examination, performs some laboratory or other diagnostic tests, formulates a diagnosis, and then offers a treatment plan. While the health care system usually focuses on persons who are sick, it also offers clinical preventive services to detect disease early (e.g., colonoscopy for colon cancer, mammogram for breast cancer) or prevent it (e.g., immunization for influenza).

In contrast, people are generally less familiar with the *public health system* and how it differs from the health care system. The goal of the public health system is to improve and maintain well-being in *communities and populations* rather than in individuals. In the United States it is made

BOX 29.1 SARS and the Public Health System

The events surrounding the severe acute respiratory syndrome (SARS) epidemic of 2002–2003 provide a good example of the public health system in action, and also a good example of what can happen if it doesn't work well. The SARS epidemic began in Guangdong Province, China, in late 2002. For a variety of reasons, the response of the Chinese public health system was not adequate, and SARS spread rapidly, eventually infecting people in thirty-seven countries. Once the World Health Organization learned what was going on, however, public health professionals sprang into action to research and identify the cause of the illness, determine how it was transmitted and how to stop its spread, and inform public health agencies around the world. Here in the United States, monitoring and surveillance systems were set up to detect the first cases, make sure adequate treatment was obtained, and prevent the spread of the disease to others by tracing contacts and keeping infected persons separated from others. What could have become a global epidemic was reined in and successfully stopped by the public health system.

up of local and state health departments, public health laboratories, and the Centers for Disease Control and Prevention (CDC), all staffed with specially trained public health professionals. The public health system is most visible in its work to detect and stop outbreaks of infectious diseases (see box 29.1), but its functions also include:

- Working with government agencies to monitor air and water quality.
- Preparing for and providing services after a disaster (e.g., the provision of food, water, and shelter for affected residents).
- Enforcing health laws, such as by conducting restaurant inspections, to ensure health and well-being.
- Educating communities about good health-maintenance practices and informing the public about potential health hazards.
- Detecting, tracking, and responding to disease outbreaks.
- Mobilizing community members and organizations for health-related activities.
- Researching innovative solutions to health problems.

These are all useful functions not only for dealing with the consequences of climate change and energy scarcity, but also for working with the public to develop strategies for stabilizing the climate and preventing some of the negative consequences of energy scarcity.

Challenges Facing the Health Care System

> We have seen the impact of acute shortages on the health care system in patient transport via ambulance. After Hurricanes Gustav and Ike compromised refinery and transport capacity in the Gulf, the Southeast experienced a short-term fuel shortage, and in Atlanta our ambulances had to travel much farther than usual to fuel up. While service was maintained, this demonstrated for us the need to consider fuel storage for EMS organizations to maintain supplies in the face of acute shortages. It's the long-term price increases that are ultimately a greater concern, however, as they will ramify throughout the health care system and are likely to cause significant inflation in health care costs above and beyond what we're already seeing from other sources. It's a strain that our health care system likely cannot bear.
>
> —DR. JEREMY HESS, *emergency room physician*[6]

Hospitals are energy intensive, requiring high-technology diagnostic and patient-care equipment—and personnel to operate them—around the clock. Furthermore, concerns about spreading infection have led to the reliance on disposable single-use supplies and equipment, which contributes to the resource use of hospitals. Rising energy costs will add a significant burden to the future cost of providing illness care.

One of the most energy-intensive aspects of the health care system is emergency medical assistance. Current practice guidelines recommend that only the level of care required to stabilize the patient be provided in the field. The patient is then transported to a hospital emergency room or tertiary care provider such as a burn center or a trauma center to receive the majority of his or her medical care. Emergency transportation typically occurs in helicopters, with an average fuel mileage rate of about 10 miles per gallon (range is 1 to 15 miles per gallon, depending on flying conditions and the size and power of the helicopter), or ambulances, with an average fuel mileage rate usually less than 10 miles per gallon (although newer designs can approach 20 miles per gallon). Emergency medical transport companies faced economic hardship during the summer of 2008 when gasoline exceeded $4 per gallon. With petroleum prices increasing, the long-term feasibility of this system as currently configured is questionable.

Petroleum-based transportation of patients is also important to the health care system in non-emergency situations. Patients must typically transport themselves to clinics and hospitals to receive care, medical personnel must transport themselves to work every day, and patients are transported from one medical facility to another for specialty medical care or to be closer to family. Many rural areas are already experiencing what suburbs and urban areas might expect to see in a future of energy scarcity, with more difficult access to health care and more cost associated with transit to and from the hospital for routine or urgent care.

Petroleum is a basic manufacturing material for many medications and therefore its increasing scarcity could well make medications more expensive. Many people will likely be willing to bear the added cost for necessary medications; patients on fixed incomes, however, will find it more difficult to pay for needed prescriptions and their health will suffer accordingly. Petroleum is also a basic material in many medical supplies, especially those made of plastic such as intravenous bags and tubing, syringes, and oxygen masks. Plant-based alternatives may provide acceptable substitutes but will require testing for potential negative interactions with pharmaceuticals and body fluids.

Challenges Facing the Public Health System

> The connections among the global just-in-time economy, energy availability, and public health are far more extensive than almost anyone can imagine. . . . [T]he public health community has been largely absent from this consideration and discussion of energy issues.
>
> —DR. MICHAEL OSTERHOLM, *director of the Center for Infectious Disease Research and Policy (CIDRAP) at the University of Minnesota*[7]

The public health system will face unprecedented challenges from energy scarcity and climate change. Threats to population health and the public health system's inability to deal with them will be even greater challenges than the already formidable issues facing individual health care.

The backbone of the public health system is the network of health departments in every state and locality. Energy scarcity will likely be felt first by these agencies in their budgets; transportation costs will be the first spike, but upstream transportation costs involved in providing materials and supplies will also rise, stressing already tight budgets in practically every area. Eventually, services will have to be cut and/or models of delivery redesigned.

Many communities are located in areas at risk from extreme weather, seismic or volcanic activity, sea-level rise, and freshwater floods. When such risks become actual events, immediate disaster response usually involves the rapid transport of massive amounts of medical supplies and personnel into an affected area. Disaster preparation for some events also involves the rapid evacuation of the population. With transportation costs rising as a result of energy scarcity, however, disaster planners will need to design new models for preparation and response.

Transportation is an integral component of the public health system. Although some direct services rely on individuals going to a clinic or office, many local and state health departments provide services that require department personnel to travel regularly. For example:

- Food inspectors must travel around to the places where food is stored, prepared, and sold.
- Outreach workers must travel to the homes of tuberculosis patients for many months to observe them taking their medicine—even after their symptoms are gone—so as to avoid spread of the disease.
- Investigations of disease outbreaks require health professionals to gather information from many sources in the community to ascertain the cause of the outbreak and devise a plan to stop it.

CHALLENGES FOR HEALTH IN GENERAL

Until recently, most public discussion of the adverse health impacts of fossil fuels has focused on their combustion (i.e., air pollution) rather than on the overwhelming fossil-fuel dependence of the systems that influence our health.[8] This discussion needs to change, as discussed above, and it also needs to broaden to include climate change in particular and the interaction of energy scarcity with environmental challenges in general. The problem is that we are entering the era of energy scarcity at the same time that the effects of climate change, ecosystem degradation, and species and biodiversity losses are accelerating.

For more than a century, we have used cheap and plentiful energy to insulate ourselves from the negative health consequences of our environmental destruction. If we depleted fish stocks in one area, we trawled deeper and farther using cheap energy to harvest other species. If we degraded ecosystem services such as capturing, purifying, and storing freshwater, we used cheap energy to drill deeper into aquifers or built desalination plants, a direct way of converting energy into potable water. If drought adversely affected food production in one locale, we used cheap energy to transport food great distances from elsewhere. If severe storms impacted our cities, we used cheap energy to bring in relief supplies, rebuild, and, in some cases, put in place structures to lessen the effects of the next storm.

We will soon no longer be able to use cheap and plentiful energy to mask the effects of the massive environmental changes we've caused. Global climate change is occurring and if left unchecked will have severe consequences for the health and well-being of citizens of every nation. Even under the best-case scenarios, an average global temperature increase of 2 degrees Celsius (3.6 degrees Fahrenheit) above pre-industrial averages is inevitable. Even that seemingly small amount of average global warming will have significant health impacts.

Finally, energy scarcity and climate change have important implications for health disparities—that is, large differences in rates of disease for populations that differ by race/ethnicity or socioeconomic status. These concerns are already a key challenge for public health but are likely to get much worse as populations face the local effects of climate change, increasing or volatile energy prices, and international population movements forced by these challenges. Local movements of people, including wealthier, previously suburban-dwelling families returning to cities and displacing predominantly poorer minority families, will also influence population health.

Heat Stress and Worsening Air Quality

Global warming is tracked by following the average global temperature, but averages can be misleading. For example, relatively small average temperature increases mask one of the hallmarks of climate change: more frequent and longer-lasting severe heat waves. In 1995, a heat wave hit Chicago resulting in more than 700 deaths; more than 45,000 people died in heat waves during the summer of 2003 in Western Europe; and the summer of 2006 brought scorching heat to much of the United States and Canada, killing 300 in California alone and sending tens of thousands to emergency rooms and hospitals.[9]

Some people are more vulnerable to heat than others, including babies, children, the elderly, the poor, those who live in inner-city neighborhoods, and the socially isolated (again highlighting the importance of social well-being). More Americans die every year from heat stress than from any other weather-related event, with the exception of Hurricane Katrina. Computer models suggest that if climate change occurs unabated ("climate chaos"), by 2040 heat waves as severe as the 2003 event that killed so many people in Europe could occur every other year.[10]

Heat waves are especially deadly because warmer temperatures worsen air quality. For example, higher temperatures increase concentrations of ground-level ozone (the primary component of smog and an important contributor to global warming), which damages the lungs, blood vessels, and heart. People who have asthma and other breathing disorders are especially vulnerable to the effects of ozone, requiring more medications and leading to more emergency-room visits and hospitalizations. The combination of high temperatures and high ozone concentrations is especially deadly and plays an important role in the numbers of people who die during heat waves.[11] Other kinds of air pollution are expected to get worse with climate change as well.

Air conditioning is a partial and temporary fix for heat waves but requires substantial amounts of electricity. With the majority of the American electricity supply coming from burning coal, the use of air conditioning over the long term will only exacerbate the climate problem. Making matters worse, power plants themselves become overheated during heat waves and are sometimes forced to shut down, as happened in Greece during heat waves in 2007 and in the U.S. Southeast during the 2006–2008 drought. Energy production is also expected to be constrained by climate change because of impacts on local precipitation cycles, reducing river flows. We simply cannot solve our climate-related health challenges by increasing our energy use.

BOX 29.2 Climate Change and Dengue Fever

Bill McKibben, as quoted in
"Americans Who Tell the Truth"

I wrote the first book [*The End of Nature*] on climate change in 1989, so I've been writing and speaking about it for a long time. But some years ago I took a trip to Bangladesh to do some reporting. And while I was there they were having their first big outbreak of dengue fever, a mosquito-borne disease now spreading like wildfire because of global warming. Since I was spending a lot of time in the slums, I got bit by the wrong mosquito myself.

I was as sick as I've ever been, but because I was healthy going in, I didn't die. Lots of people did, mostly old and young. I remember standing in the hospital ward looking at rows of cots of shivering patients, and thinking to myself: these people did nothing to deserve this.

You can barely measure how much carbon Bangladesh produces: a nation of 140 million, but most of them don't have electricity or cars. Whereas in the U.S. 4% of us manage to produce 25% of the world's carbon dioxide. A quarter of those hospital beds were our fault.

When I figured that out in my gut, I came home and started organizing, and that's what I've been up to ever since.

Source: Americans Who Tell the Truth, "Bill McKibben," http://www.ameri canswhotellthetruth.org/pgs/portraits/bill_mckibben.php.

Infectious Diseases

Warmer temperatures, milder winters, precipitation changes, and other effects of climate change can influence the distribution and risk of many infectious diseases. Debilitating and deadly insect-borne diseases such as malaria, dengue fever, and Lyme disease are especially sensitive to changes in temperature, humidity, and rainfall patterns and will likely increase their ranges and possibly their transmissibility (see box 29.2). Waterborne infectious diseases will also be influenced by warmer temperatures, changes in precipitation patterns, and the compromised ability of degrading ecosystems and suboptimal built environments to deal with heavy precipitation events.

Threatened Water and Food Supplies

Clean water is vital to life and health, but climate change will seriously threaten water supplies around the world. In general, regions that are typically wet now will get wetter and those that are dry now will likely get drier. Even wetter regions, however, may still experience frequent bouts of water shortages because more of the precipitation will come in the form of heavy precipitation events, leading to greater runoff of stormwater and longer periods of droughts in between rain events.[12]

Much of the world's population gets its freshwater from glaciers and mountain snowpack. Mountain ranges collect water, purify it, store it as ice or snow, and release it over time into streams and rivers. Global warming has already caused many of these glaciers and snowpacks to melt far more rapidly than expected. If glaciers in the Andes continue melting at present rates, they will likely disappear completely within one or two decades. The Himalayas are melting so fast that Chinese and Indian farmers are seeing more river water than usual, making it even harder to motivate the water-conserving changes necessary as these glaciers—which provide freshwater for more than one-sixth of the world's population—disappear. Much of the western United States is in a similar situation, relying on the threatened snowpack of the Rocky Mountains, the Sierra Nevadas, and the Cascade Range for much of its water. This has serious implications for the entire country: The farms of California alone account for approximately half of U.S.-grown fruits, nuts, and vegetables and more than one-fifth of the milk supply.[13]

There are many reasons why the effects of climate change could lead to diminished food supplies. Plants require certain amounts of moisture and nutrients and can live only in particular temperature ranges. With climate change, previously productive agricultural zones are becoming too hot or too dry to grow some traditional crops, forcing the production of those crops northward or eliminating their cultivation altogether. For example, by the end of the century the climate of New Hampshire is projected to be like that of North Carolina today.[14] Unfortunately, the plant and animal species in New Hampshire evolved over hundreds and thousands of years to take advantage of the climate of northern New England, not the climate 800 miles to the southwest.

Other negative climate effects on agriculture include:

- More frequent, longer-lasting, and more severe droughts and floods
- Warmer temperatures
- Chronic water shortages
- Higher concentrations of ozone and other air pollutants that hamper plant growth
- Stronger and more resistant plant pests and diseases

Energy scarcity promises to further compound our food-production challenges. The American food supply has become reliant on fewer and larger farms using a number of fossil-fuel inputs in the form of fertilizers, pesticides, pump irrigation, heavy machinery, and long-distance transport to accomplish what was once done by many people, locally, without the various fossil-fuel inputs. Constant erosion of topsoil and cultivation of single-plant crops have led to a reliance on chemical fertilizers created from natural gas and chemical pesticides largely derived from petroleum. Practically all communities now rely on food produced using these methods and transported long distances—frequently from other regions of the United States, other countries, or even from the other side of the world—to arrive at our grocery stores. Without a steady supply of inexpensive fossil fuels, especially petroleum, the current American food system will not function—and health depends on an adequate supply of nutritious food.

Extreme Weather Events

The most well-known effect of climate change is rising sea levels, which threaten coastal areas with inundation. Climate change also promises to bring more severe and potentially more frequent extreme weather events such as hurricanes, tornadoes, and heavy rainfall, all of which increase the risk of injury and death and cause social disruption (itself an important cause of adverse health impacts). With more of our precipitation coming in less-frequent, heavy-rainfall events, freshwater flooding is becoming a greater problem, creating both immediate and long-term risks. A recent study documented that the majority of outbreaks of waterborne disease in the United States occurring between 1948 and 1994 followed heavy-rainfall events that overwhelmed water treatment facilities.[15] Another study found that flood survivors often experience greater risk of chronic diseases such as diabetes and heart disease long after the floodwaters have subsided.[16] For decades, evidence has mounted that centuries of building levees and draining wetlands has increased the risk of flooding—another example of how the decisions we make about our communities and economies can indirectly but profoundly affect public health risks.

Other evidence of how failed ecosystems wreak havoc on human settlements, compromising health and well-being, includes the finding that intact coastal wetland ecosystems might have reduced the height and/or speed of the storm surge created by Hurricane Katrina in 2005 and possibly prevented the resultant flooding that devastated New Orleans.[17] The loss of these coastal wetland ecosystems is largely due to human activities such as offshore oil drilling and refining, importation of invasive species, and boxing in the Mississippi River so that it is no longer able to deposit sediment to replace coastal land lost to erosion.

Conflict and Health

Competition for shrinking environmental resources, especially the necessities of water, food, and housing, could potentially result in greater conflict within and between geopolitical entities. There is ample evidence that the scarcity of environmental resources has played an important role in many areas of conflict, such as the genocides that devastated Rwanda and continue to occur in Darfur, the ongoing clashes between Zapatista rebels and the federal government in Mexico, and the decades-long modern Israeli-Palestinian conflict.[18] That is, what have been termed "ethnic conflicts" have actually been exacerbated by, if not directly caused by, environmental scarcity. Such conflicts will increase in the era of energy scarcity and climate change. In addition, the number of environmental refugees created by rising sea levels and failure of the local ecosystems to meet basic needs could increase by many hundreds of millions.[19] These refugees will face a greater risk of attack and conflict if they must cross political or cultural borders and will face the same hardships in many countries as those who flee war zones. As climate change worsens the gap between those with resources and those without, social unrest may worsen and spread into previously stable areas. This is another example of a risk regulator. If left unchecked, environmental degradation and the challenges it creates can ultimately threaten the basis of society itself.

Mental Health Effects

The risks to mental well-being in a future of energy scarcity and climate change are quite significant. Examples include persons forced from their homes due to extreme weather events; the inability of the environment to provide sufficient food and water; individuals faced with job loss, separation from family and friends, and concern about the future; and persons coping with the various disruptions to life caused by an unstable climate. Such mental health outcomes as depression, anxiety, and post-traumatic stress disorder are expected to increase as a result.[20]

THE FUTURE OF HEALTH CARE AND PUBLIC HEALTH

What health care and public health services will look like in a world constrained by energy scarcity and climate change depends on the choices we make in response to these challenges—and what happens to economies and communities as a result.

Energy prices will influence where people live and how they transport themselves from place to place. It is likely that these changes will influence future communities to be more compact, higher density, and more walkable; to contain a mixture of residential, commercial, and even recreational uses; and to be transit accessible. At the same time, populations will be on the move from the effects of climate change, including extreme weather events, drought, sea-level rise, declining food production in some areas, and the inability to make environments hospitable owing to energy costs. To meet the needs of an energy-constrained future, the public health system as well as the health care system will need to be redesigned.

Unfortunately, policy discussions about reforming the health care system have not mentioned energy scarcity or climate change. The next iteration of our health care system must nevertheless be designed to meet these challenges and function within their constraints. In general, the allocation of financial resources, personnel, and energy should be shifted to favor public health and preventive services—for all members of society—instead of focusing primarily on illness care. More than anything else, this would result in lower energy requirements for the health care system while building more resilient communities nationwide, benefiting all citizens at all socioeconomic levels.

There are many other opportunities to improve health care and public health while preparing for the energy- and climate-constrained future. Of these, the three largest have to do with delivery of services, disaster response, and food.

Delivery of Services

The most immediate challenge to health in the United States is the sheer energy intensity of our current health care system. We present four basic ways in which this challenge could be met. In reality, a combination of many approaches will likely be needed.

1. *Reorganize where care is provided.* For many years the trend has been to centralize health services in larger hospitals and reduce services in or even close smaller hospitals. Care for rare or complicated illnesses will need to remain in centralized high-level hospitals, but smaller hospitals and care centers that could care for most medical problems could be more numerous and located at midlevel transportation hubs for easier access. Health services could even be brought directly into neighborhoods, through many small, scattered, local "pods" of public health workers who are able to perform many functions in their specific neighborhoods. Many of these changes would require reworking the way public health professionals are educated and trained.

2. *Use technology to decentralize more services.* Remote imaging and video-conferencing technologies, which allow specialists at larger institutions to diagnose and treat patients remotely, can be used to improve care at decentralized facilities. These technologies can also be used to develop and monitor skills in localities and to transfer skills there. Of course, such high-tech solutions would require energy and resources to put into place and to maintain. As transportation becomes more expensive, new models of health service delivery will be required.

3. *Practice medicine differently.* Some energy-intensive procedures may not be medically necessary. We recommend reducing reliance on energy-intensive diagnostic procedures when those procedures are

used only to confirm what a physician knows from a physical exam and less invasive tests. This would require changes to how health care providers are reimbursed and might also require a change in the liability laws so that health providers do not feel obligated to defend their clinical judgment from potential lawsuits with unnecessary diagnostic tests.

4. *Plan for smart decision-making about energy usage.* As fossil-fuel supplies decline, the costs of transporting goods and people, powering facilities and machines, and manufacturing synthetic products will all rise. The health care industry should follow the example of most other industries and push for greater energy efficiency in its facilities and technologies. It may also be necessary to consider how the increasingly scarce resources will be apportioned for energy use (e.g., emergency medical transport) versus materials use (e.g., pharmaceuticals, plastics).

Disaster Response

Disaster responses currently rely on the ability to ship in resources and personnel from afar and to evacuate large populations if necessary. As energy prices rise, disaster preparedness will need to focus far more on building local resources and training local personnel. Emphasis should shift from disaster response to disaster prevention and preparedness based on a community's specific areas of vulnerability. Typical efforts to reduce future impacts of disasters, such as building more and taller seawalls or drainage systems, may also be limited by energy scarcity. Alternative— and often smarter—approaches will be required, such as changing zoning regulations to disallow additional development in high flood-risk areas and using native vegetation along wetlands and waterways to buffer storm surges and reduce erosion.

Food

Like most other industrialized countries, the United States will need to redesign its methods of producing, importing, and distributing food. Our eating habits will need to change. No longer will much of the nation be able to eat fresh fruits and vegetables flown in from California, South America, and elsewhere in the dead of winter. Instead, during natural harvest times, produce will have to be canned, dried, or otherwise pre-served for consumption during the off-season. The public health system can play an essential role in building local food resilience by supporting and educating about:

- Localized food production and processing
- Farmers' markets and regional purchasing by groceries and supermarkets
- Gardening and farming projects in schools and by community groups
- Regional and seasonal cuisine
- Safe food handling and food preservation (canning, drying, etc.)

One significant benefit of increasing local food production is a greater supply of fresh food (if only seasonally for some locations), which often is less processed, better tasting, and more nutritious. Food production may ultimately need to occupy a greater proportion of time for many individu-als than has become the norm over the last hundred years. Yet another potential benefit of this is the building of social capital as communities work together to grow and process food, securing a mutually shared food future.

HOW WE CAN ADAPT

The effects of climate change will create new demands on our health care system and for public health services. We must prepare for this reality, while also doing everything we can to reduce our contributions to global warming. All the health system adaptations we can envision and all the ways to enhance community resilience that we can call for—much less implement—will not be enough if the climate is not ultimately stabilized.

All forms of energy, other than passive warming from the sun, have an environmental and a societal cost. Therefore, using less energy or using it more efficiently should be a primary societal goal, regardless of where that energy comes from. To accomplish this goal, housing patterns, trans-portation options, food and water provisioning, and many other aspects of our lives will all have to be redesigned to require substantially less energy from any source. Energy scarcity will force these decisions upon us, but hasty decisions to replace petroleum with other liquid fuels, such as ethanol, biodiesel, or oil from oil sands, will only forestall the inevitable for a short time and will greatly aggravate other problems, such as climate change and food and water insecurity.

Some options, however, for addressing the dual challenges of climate change and energy scarcity could make our communities better places to live. A stronger sense of community, greater emphasis on family and friends, less time spent in cars and commuting, and localization of economic activity and food production will all benefit health and well-being.

Transforming our health care and public health systems will require significant policy changes. It's essential that citizens educate their elected officials about the issues and demand prompt, well-informed, forward-looking solutions. This will not be easy, because the necessary changes will likely be seen as politically unpopular and volatile energy prices will encourage actions that do not necessarily serve society well in the long run. But if we make the right choices now, we can maximize the benefits and lessen the risks. The transition to the energy-scarce, climate-constrained future will create significant hardship if tough decisions about how to proceed are not made soon. However, the end result of a more self-sufficient, cohesive, resilient, and healthy society is worth the effort.

Part Fourteen

EDUCATION

SMART BY NATURE

Schooling for Sustainability

MICHAEL K. STONE AND ZENOBIA BARLOW

MICHAEL STONE *is senior editor of the Center for Ecoliteracy. He is the primary author of* Smart by Nature: Schooling for Sustainability *(2009) and co-editor of* Ecological Literacy: Educating Our Children for a Sustainable World *(2005). He has written for the* Toronto Star *and the* New York Times, *and he was managing editor of* Whole Earth *magazine.*

ZENOBIA BARLOW *is executive director and co-founder of the Center for Ecoliteracy and one of the nation's pioneers in creating models of schooling for sustainability. She co-edited* Ecological Literacy *(2005) and* Ecoliteracy: Mapping the Terrain *(2000). In 2009 she served on an international team of experts that advised the Bhutan government on integrating "gross national happiness" principles into education. Barlow is a Fellow of Post Carbon Institute.*

❖

What can educators do to foster real intelligence? . . . We can attempt to teach the things that one might imagine the Earth would teach us: silence, humility, holiness, connectedness, courtesy, beauty, celebration, giving, restoration, obligation, and wildness.

—DAVID W. ORR[1]

There is a bold new movement under way in school systems across North America and around the world. Educators, parents, and students are remaking K–12 education to prepare students for the environmental challenges of the coming decades. They are discovering that guidance for living abundantly on a finite planet lies, literally, under their feet and all around them—in living soil, food webs and water cycles, energy from the sun, and everywhere that nature reveals her ways. Smart by Nature schooling draws on 3.8 billion years of natural research and development to find solutions to problems of sustainable living, make teaching and learning more meaningful, and create a more hopeful future for people and communities.

School gardens bloom in wintry climates and on former asphalt lots. Students learn good nutrition while eating healthy lunches of farm-fresh food. At independent schools in New Jersey, public schools in California, and charter schools in Wisconsin, education comes alive as children discover the wonders of nature while restoring rural landscapes, protecting endangered species, and creating city habitats. Classroom buildings in schools on the South Side of Chicago, in central Arkansas, and in suburban Oregon become living laboratories for energy conservation and resource stewardship.

Schools from Washington to Florida have transformed into model communities. Utilities, governments, and educators have become partners in designing energy-efficient, safe, and healthy schools that promote the welfare of students and school staff while teaching wise resource use and care of our Earth. In small towns and large cities, students practice the arts of citizenship while improving the lives of their neighbors.

This movement responds to the realization that the young people in school today will inherit a host of pressing—and escalating—environmental challenges: threats of climate change; loss of biodiversity; the end of cheap energy; depletion of resources; environmental degradation; gross inequities in standards of living; obesity, diabetes, asthma, and other environmentally linked illnesses. This generation will require leaders and citizens who can think ecologically, understand the interconnectedness of human and natural systems, and have the will, ability, and courage to act.

The movement goes by many names: green schools, eco-schools, high-performance schools. We call it schooling for sustainability to underline its kinship with other global movements reshaping the relationships between human societies and the natural world. At the same time, we acknowledge that "sustainability" is problematic to some people.

"The word 'sustainability' has gotten such a workout lately that the whole concept is in danger of floating away on a sea of inoffensiveness," wrote Michael Pollan in late 2007. "Everybody, it seems, is for it—whatever 'it' means."[2] Paradoxically, many people remain unaware of the concept, while others have already concluded that it is on its way to joining "natural" and "ecological" as words that can simultaneously mean anything and nothing. "If a man characterized his relationship with his wife as sustainable," wrote architect William McDonough and chemist Michael Braungart, "you might well pity them both."[3] After reviewing the alternatives, though, writer and consultant Alan AtKisson concluded, "As a name for the future of our dreams, sustainability may be 'the worst word, except for all the others.' "[4]

To stay useful, however, *sustainability* must mean more than merely surviving or trying to keep a degraded world from getting worse. Otherwise, why bother? Invoking nature's capacity for sustaining life, as physicist and systems theorist Fritjof Capra suggests, is critical. A sustainable community worth imagining is alive, in the most exuberant sense of that word—fresh, vital, evolving, diverse, and dynamic. It cares about the quality as well as the continuation of life. It is flexible and adaptive. It draws energy from its environment, celebrates organic wholeness, and appreciates that life has more to reveal than human cleverness has yet discovered. It teaches its children to pay attention to the world around them, to respect what they cannot control, and to embrace the creativity with which life sustains itself.

OVERCOMING OBSTACLES

Few question the need to prepare students for the complex world into which they will graduate, but the schooling-for-sustainability movement nevertheless encounters obstacles: School systems are notoriously slow to change. Responsibilities for schools' operations are often dispersed through multiple levels of authority, from the local principal to the federal government, with mandates that sometimes conflict. Virtually all schools and districts face financial challenges. Schooling for sustainability competes with other priorities, including standardized testing in public schools and pressure to focus on Advanced Placement in independent schools.

Schools across the country are creatively overcoming barriers to schooling for sustainability. Over the past two decades, the Center for Ecoliteracy, a public foundation in Berkeley, California, dedicated to education for sustainable living, has worked with hundreds of educators committed to this vision. In our 2009 book *Smart by Nature: Schooling for Sustainability* we set out to document the accomplishments of schools of all types and sizes from every geographic region, to share the lessons they have learned, and to further the discussion that has begun among the many parties to this movement.

We discovered that schooling for sustainability is a winning proposition with many direct and indirect benefits. What is good for the future of the environment and for communities is also good for schools and students now. Students who learn nature's principles in gardens and serve their communities through civic participation become more engaged in their studies and score better in diverse subjects, including science, reading and writing, and independent thinking.

Designing buildings to conserve energy and water can save enough money to convince finance-minded school boards. Going green helps competitive independent schools to attract students, and local communities to attract residents and business. Students and staff members who eat better meals and spend their days in buildings with better air quality are absent less often, report higher satisfaction, and perform better. Schools become better appreciated as assets to their communities.

WHAT IS EDUCATION FOR?

We have sought to identify schools that, in their own ways, are rising to the challenges posed by David W. Orr in "What Is Education For?"—to teach students how they are part of the natural world; to emphasize self-understanding and personal mastery; to recognize the responsibility to use knowledge well in the world; to understand the effects on people and communities of the application of knowledge; to provide role models of integrity, care, and thoughtfulness in institutions whose actions embody their ideals; and to recognize that the process of education is as important as its contents.[5]

There is no single schooling-for-sustainability blueprint that is appropriate for all schools. Increasingly, though, we find ourselves drawn to affirmations that we have distilled into principles we describe in detail in *Smart by Nature*:

- Nature is our teacher.
- Sustainability is a community practice.
- The real world is the optimal learning environment.
- Sustainable living is rooted in a deep knowledge of place.

The goal of education conducted according to these principles is cultivation in students of competencies of the head, heart, hands, and spirit.

To nurture communities that are in concert with nature, we must understand nature's principles and processes, the deep facts of life: for instance, that matter cycles continually through the web of life, while living systems need a continual flow of energy; that diversity assures resilience; that one species' waste is another species' food; that human needs and achievements are both supported by and limited by the natural world.

Teaching this ecological knowledge, which is also ancient wisdom, requires seeing the world from the perspective of relationships, connectedness, and context. This way of thinking is emerging at the forefront of science through the evolving theory of living systems, which recognizes the world as a network of patterns of relationships and the planet as a living, self-regulating system.

Ecological study is inherently multidisciplinary, because ecosystems connect the living and nonliving worlds. Therefore, it is grounded not only in biology, but also in geology, chemistry, thermodynamics, and other branches of science. Human ecology, meanwhile, entails a range of other fields, including agriculture, economics, industrial design, and politics.

Knowledge and intellectual understanding are crucial, but they are never enough. Students also need to be able to adapt their knowledge to new circumstances and to use it to solve problems. To do so requires critical and creative thinking, as well as the ability to recognize the unquestioned assumptions and habits of thinking that can lead well-intentioned people to make ecologically catastrophic decisions.

It also requires competencies of the hands—for instance, the capacity to apply ecological knowledge to ecological design; practical skills to create and use tools and procedures for design and building; and the ability to measure, assess, predict, and alter energy and resource consumption.

More, still, will be needed. Creating and maintaining sustainable communities will entail hard work over long periods, in the face of conflicting interests and passionate advocates. The strength to persist and the ability to succeed will call for competencies of the heart: deeply felt, not just understood, concerns for the well-being of Earth and of living things; empathy and the ability to see from and appreciate multiple perspectives; commitments to equity, justice, inclusivity, and respect for all people; and skills in building, governing, and sustaining communities.

Finally, we have identified a number of competencies of the spirit that we believe will characterize people who will be effective agents for sustainable living: a sense of wonder; the capacity for reverence; a felt appreciation of place; a sense of kinship with the natural world; and the ability to invoke that feeling in others.

CURRICULUM IS ANYWHERE THAT LEARNING OCCURS

Nurturing these competencies depends on a definition of "curriculum" that is broader and more holistic than "a set of courses." A team of educators from Yap, a South Pacific atoll, once visited the Center for Ecoliteracy. As a parting gift, they left a poster proclaiming "Curriculum Is Anywhere Learning Occurs." We concur wholeheartedly. The campus, the life of the school community, and that community's relationships with the larger communities in which it is embedded are not just the context for curriculum. They *are* curriculum.

Schooling is everything the school does that leads to students' learning—whether that learning is intended or not (the unintended learning is often the most powerful, especially when it contradicts the designed curriculum). Students learn from what the school serves for lunch, how it uses resources and manages waste, who is included in its decisions, and how it relates to the surrounding community.

In *Smart by Nature* we explore four domains—food, the campus, community, and teaching and learning—that offer multiple avenues for the transformative work of schooling for sustainability. Each chapter includes profiles of schools or districts that have creatively addressed these topics and the strategies they have employed to overcome obstacles, create change within institutions, and incorporate schooling for sustainability into curricula.

THE SUSTAINABLE SCHOOLS PROJECT: BURLINGTON, VERMONT

Lawrence Barnes Elementary School had a horrendous reputation. According to former principal Paula Bowen, "It's in the inner city, with high poverty. It's where refugees are first resettled. Anybody who had the wherewithal to get their kids into some other school typically did." Now, though, "Barnes is the groovy school, the cool school. Test scores are up. Parents are asking for variances to get *into* Barnes."

The spark behind the turnaround was the Sustainable Schools Project (SSP), a collaboration with nearby Shelburne Farms, a 1,400-acre working farm, National Historic Landmark, and national leader in schooling for sustainability. The project demonstrates the power of combining place-based learning, schoolwide curriculum collaboration, partnerships with community organizations, and hands-on civic engagement.

In 2000 Vermont became the first state to incorporate sustainability and understanding of place into its standards. In response to requests for assistance in teaching the new standards, Shelburne Farms designed professional development workshops and contributed the bulk of the writing of *The Vermont Guide to Education for Sustainability.*[6]

The state standards had intentionally left the definition of "sustainability" broad, out of a belief that communities should create homegrown definitions. Shelburne Farms' formulation, "Improving the quality of life for all—socially, economically, and environmentally—now and for future generations," reflects the work of the Burlington Legacy Project, a citywide effort to envision a sustainable Burlington.

For Shelburne Farms, the link between sustainability and schooling is civic engagement. Former Sustainable Schools Project coordinator Erica Zimmerman identifies three elements essential to successfully grounding education in civic engagement:[7]

- *Understanding connections.* Learning gains meaning and depth and students begin to comprehend how human and natural systems work when they see the networks of interconnection within their community.
- *Connecting to place.* Students need to know their own place before they can make the leap to thinking globally. With such knowledge, they have more reason to care for this world and become stewards of it.
- *Making a difference.* In order to become motivated and engaged citizens, students need to know that they can make a difference. Schooling for sustainability depends on projects that are meaningful, are developmentally appropriate, have academic integrity, and can be completed with the time and resources available to students.

Big Ideas and Essential Questions

Colleen Cowell, a dynamic fourth- and fifth-grade teacher at Champlain Elementary School on Burlington's suburban fringe, attended one of Shelburne's workshops. The content resonated with her, but she wanted to go beyond individual teachers' putting the ideas of sustainability into practice. What if a whole school worked together? With Cowell's enthusiasm and strong support from principal Nancy Zahnhiser, Champlain and Shelburne Farms launched the Sustainable Schools Project. Three years later, it migrated to Lawrence Barnes.

Working with Shelburne Farms consultants, teachers identified nine "big ideas of sustainability" as a framework for curriculum integration: diversity, interdependence, cycles, limits, fairness and equity, connecting to place, ability to make a difference, long-term effects, and community. They created curriculum maps tracing these ideas from grade to grade and from the classroom to the schoolyard, the neighborhood, and the wider community. They identified "essential questions" that connect sustainability concepts across subject-matter boundaries. For instance:

- What do all living things need in order to live a safe, healthy, and productive life?
- What does it mean to be a citizen in our community?
- What connections and cycles shape our Lake Champlain ecosystem?
- How do we take care of the world, and how does the world take care of us?

The big ideas and essential questions helped recapture portions of the curriculum that testing mandates such as No Child Left Behind had squeezed out, connecting science to social studies and literacy. "We hoped to demonstrate how using the big ideas of sustainability to enhance existing curriculum was engaging and something they were already doing— with a slight twist," says Shelburne Farms Sustainable Schools Project staff member Tiffany Tillman.[8] "Instead of a unit on living organisms," explains Lawrence Barnes third-grade teacher Anne Tewksbury-Frye, "you're looking at it as a unit on systems and how those systems interact and how you can address other systems in a more global fashion."

Teachers discovered the teaching potential of their own place. "Something I never did before SSP was to look at what resources we have on the school property," one first-grade teacher told a researcher. "Now that I have some knowledge about vernal pools, I know I can make use of them. Before it was just a big wet spot in the playground, and now I know it is teeming with life."[9] Teachers discovered that children can learn more about nature from the squirrels they observe every day than from exotic animals they see only in books. The project connected teachers with local farmers, experts on the indigenous Abenaki people, artists, businesspeople, and myriad other community members, who have spoken to classes, lent resources, and contributed to student projects.

Healthy Neighborhoods/Healthy Kids

Place-based education, community connections, and civic engagement converge in Healthy Neighborhoods/Healthy Kids, a fourth- and fifth-grade project within the Sustainable Schools Project. Students brainstorm quality-of-life indicators in a neighborhood. Their lists have included green places with plants and flowers, habitat for animals, more trees for better air, healthy food, speed bumps to calm traffic, murals instead of graffiti, safe places to play, and spots for neighbors to meet.

Then they conduct neighborhood walks and create report cards, which they use to grade their communities. The walks can be eye-openers. Children from higher-income parts of the city discover that some classmates live without parks, tennis courts, stop signs, or other amenities they take for granted. But they also find features that are absent in their own neighborhoods, like community centers where kids can hang out.

The report cards become the starting point for civic engagement, leading to student-generated projects such as creating habitat for local birds, cleaning up streams, or organizing block parties to bring neighbors together. Students present their report cards to local government bodies. State Senator Tim Ashe, a former Burlington city council member, observed, "I think we grown-ups tend to take many things for granted, both good and bad, because we've learned to live with them. Kids are able to see for the first time a broken sidewalk, graffiti on a building wall, or a faltering street light and ask, with legitimate confusion, 'Does it have to be this way?' "[10]

The Case of the Missing Park

The students sometimes discover that they know more about the city than the authorities responsible for it. Lawrence Barnes students found a park that the city had forgotten. They contacted the Parks and Recreation Department about this park, where they didn't feel safe at night, to suggest installing lights. "We don't have a park on South Champlain Street," they were told. "Yes, you do. There's a sign there that says 'Parks & Rec Department.' We want to tell you about it."

Another time, children from Lawrence Barnes reported that the street in front of the school had no School Zone sign, making for dangerous traffic. The city council drafted a resolution to put in a sign. The director of the public works department, a city council member, and the mayor came to unveil the sign and praise the students' initiative. A small matter, perhaps, but the response and the media coverage were important to a neighborhood used to finding itself in news stories about crime and drugs.

After Lawrence Barnes joined the Sustainable Schools Project, reading scores rose 22 percent and math scores rose 18 percent, parents became more involved, residents began to take pride in the neighborhood and to see the school as a resource within it, *and* Barnes became the "cool school." In 2008 the school that parents once shunned was chosen by the district to become the nation's first K–5 magnet school with a sustainability theme.

COMMUNITY COLLEGES

A Vital Resource for Education in the Post-Carbon Era

NANCY LEE WOOD

NANCY LEE WOOD *is a professor of sociology and director of the Institute for Sustainability and Post-Carbon Education (ISPE) at Bristol Community College in Fall River, Massachusetts. After winning her college's prestigious Presidential Fellowship in 2007, she developed ISPE and spearheaded a new course of study, the Organic Agriculture Technician Certificate Program, which premiered in fall 2009. She lectures frequently throughout southeastern Massachusetts.*

❖

The post-carbon era is going to require knowledge and skills that are not commonly acquired in most formal educational settings today. There are numerous areas in which people will need to be educated, not only to meet the needs of an energy-constrained future but to develop their own useful livelihoods:

- Training in organic growing and permaculture
- Retrofitting old housing and building stock
- Refashioning metals for practical tools and machinery
- Setting up and running local businesses
- Reindustrializing for small-scale local production of needed goods
- Developing health-care delivery alternatives and establishing local currencies

The key question is, "Where in our current educational system is it possible to develop and institutionalize the kinds of education needed to prepare people for work in the post-carbon economy—and to do so relatively quickly?"

Fortuitously, the Obama administration has recognized the role that community colleges can play in the near-term future. In July 2009, President Obama announced the American Graduation Initiative (AGI), a ten-year, $12 billion plan to invest in the 1,200 community colleges across the country. Focused on a declining industrial base and the need to reeducate the American workforce, AGI is intended to increase graduation rates and prepare students for new employment in well-paying, community-based jobs.

WHY THE FOCUS ON COMMUNITY COLLEGES?

There are currently 6.5 million students enrolled in community college credit programs throughout the United States, with another 5 million enrolled in noncredit options.[1] These students account for nearly half of all students in college in the country today. The rise in popularity of community colleges during the last half century is due to several factors.

From the individual's perspective, there are several reasons to look to the community college as an attractive educational setting. Community colleges provide students with the opportunity to acquire remedial instruction, training for specific careers, and the foundations for continuing education at four-year institutions if they wish to work toward baccalaureate degrees. The community colleges' open-door policies allow all students entry into a college experience. In addition, many community colleges offer attractive transfer packages to four-year institutions, including excellent financial deals for those students who maintain a high grade-point average.

From the societal perspective, there are several characteristics that make the community college a vital institution:

- Community colleges are *local*. Most students who attend a community college reside in the vicinity served by that institution. Very few students cross the country to attend a community college three thousand miles away. Rather, the typical community college student is tied to the local community via job and/or family and tends to remain in the geographic area of the community college after completing his or her academic work.

  The rise in costs related to future energy constraints is going to result in people seeking more local options, whether it be for work, for buying local produce, or for education. The community college's local presence in an area makes it an attractive option for students as they seek education and training opportunities within their geographic reach.

- They are *affordable*. In 2008, the average yearly combined tuition and fees at public community colleges was $2,402 (with some states, such as California, charging as little as $20 per credit or less for residents).[2] Typically, the revenue sources for public community colleges come from state funds (38 percent), local funds (21 percent), and federal funds (15 percent), with only 17 percent coming from tuition and fees. Nearly half of all community college students (47 percent) receive some form of financial aid, making higher education possible for many students who otherwise could not afford to attend college.

  Rising energy costs, putting greater stress on personal and household budgets, will lead many people to seek education and training programs that are at as low a cost as possible. Community colleges, already providing the "biggest bang for the buck," are likely to become even more of an attractive option as students and their families feel squeezed by rising energy costs.

- They offer *practical training*. While a liberal arts education is available at most community colleges, much of the pedagogy is focused on practical knowledge that leads to immediate employment (e.g., nursing, dental hygiene, culinary arts, criminal justice) upon graduation. Many community colleges offer certificate programs (e.g., fire science, human services, computer technology skills), qualifying students for some aspect of a specific job in less time than it takes to complete an associate degree. The benefits of practical knowledge that leads to specific immediate work opportunities are especially attractive to students seeking to enhance their workforce credentials in a relatively short period of time and at minimal expense.

  Moreover, the emphasis on work-related practical knowledge coincides with the kind of short-term training programs that will be required in the post-carbon future and that readily could be adopted within the structure of most community colleges.

- They are *agile*. Because the primary focus at community colleges is teaching, these colleges are geared toward putting new courses and programs into place relatively quickly in order to meet existing and emerging educational needs of the community. This is an important asset because while we can predict some obvious educational needs in the post-carbon era, there are likely to be some circumstances that currently are unrecognizable and, thus, unforeseen. Rapid and facile development of educational options can help to ensure relatively smooth transitioning to a post-carbon existence.

· Finally, as institutions, community colleges are *connected to the community.* They pride themselves in responding to local economic and societal needs apparent within the specific geographic area of the college. They develop degree and certificate programs as well as noncredit educational opportunities in response to local realities. Moreover, they often work in active partnerships with local and regional groups and organizations on service learning programs, civic engagement experiences, regional projects, and conference/ colloquial gatherings.

Overall, community colleges already meet several of the requisites needed for the relocalization efforts anticipated in the post-carbon era.

RETHINKING CURRICULA FOR A POST-CARBON WORLD

The post-carbon era is going to require our reconceptualizing many already existing programs, extending some programs to include new areas of knowledge, and, in some cases, developing entirely new programs of study. Below are a few examples of the kinds of changes in curricula that will be needed.

Agriculture

The dominant industrial agriculture model, which is dependent on fossil fuels, is unsustainable—not only in terms of its enormous consumption of nonrenewable energy sources, but also in terms of its detrimental impact on the environment and the resulting nutrient failures. This globalized food system, racking up thousands of "food miles," is extremely vulnerable to impending energy scarcity and thus threatens public food security.

As calculated by Richard Heinberg, some 50 million prospective farmers need to be trained in organic growing within the next twenty years if we are to stave off worst-case scenarios of food shortages.[3] Over the last half century, thousands of small-scale farms have been forced out of production, unable to compete with huge fossil-fuel-based agribusinesses. The average age of farmers in the United States today is fifty-nine and, until recently, young people have had little incentive to go into farming. Thanks in part to the works of Michael Pollan[4] and Joel Salatin,[5] new interest in relocalizing agriculture via organic and free-range farming has emerged. Many communities and individuals are willing to devote land to local food production but cannot find people with the skills and knowledge to operate successful farms.

These realities point to the urgent need for community colleges to develop organic agriculture and/or permaculture certificate or degree programs. Every community must reconnect with local food production as a necessity. No program is in greater need of immediate implementation than that of teaching future farmers the basics of sustainable agriculture.

Culinary Arts

These programs typically train students for employment in conventional food settings, preparing them to work as chefs, cooks, and managers of food services such as restaurants, cafeterias, hospital kitchens, and school lunchrooms. Culinary arts in the future may have to extend their programs to include the basics in canning, root cellaring, and "know-your-foods" courses in which students learn about the vitamin and mineral properties of different foods, as well as how to prepare them to maximize their nutritional value.

One can envision culinary arts intersecting with agriculture where students learn, for example, the basics of growing vegetables, fruits, and herbs as an integral part of their training and preparation for jobs in the food industry. Courses in organic farming, greenhouse production, vermiculture, and beekeeping could become invaluable classes to budding chefs who are seeking to bring healthy and nutritionally dense food at affordable prices to their restaurants, cafeterias, and kitchens. One also can envision culinary arts and agriculture intersecting with the health-care sciences with emphases, for instance, on healing through herbs and on sound nutrition.

Health Sciences

Current health-care training programs in community colleges prepare students for employment in traditional medical sectors, all of which are heavily dependent on nonrenewable petroleum-based products and services, from analgesics and antibiotics to surgical plastics and petrochemicals for radiological dyes and films. In the meantime, public health dollars are spread unevenly across states and are eroding as the recession hits state and local public health departments alike.

These realities necessitate a rethinking and an extension of educational programs preparing people for work in the health-care sector. Holistic preventive education via courses focused on healthy eating that promote good nutrition as the first step toward sound health practices may become required curricula. Health-maintenance programs that deal with issues such as stress management, emotional balance, violence prevention, physical activity, personal hygiene, and sanitation health may become integral parts of health-care training, thus preparing students to be practitioners and community public health counselors within local and even micro-level health service agencies. As federal and state budgets shrink, more responsibility will be foisted onto communities and local public health practitioners to fill the widening gaps.

Business and Finance

Business as usual will be hard-pressed to continue in a post-carbon economy. As consumerism (characterized by energy inefficiencies and mega-waste) declines out of necessity, new forms of business will have to emerge to meet consumer needs. The community college, with its agile character and connectedness to local environs, is well positioned to help localities (re)discover local manufacturing as small, locally based businesses emerge to meet public needs. Thus, courses on how to develop and run small businesses that emphasize sustainability and that function through cooperation and interdependence via regional networking will become highly valued. The strategies initiated within the Business Alliance for Local Living Economies (BALLE)—the mission of which is to "catalyze, strengthen and connect networks of locally owned independent businesses dedicated to building strong local living economies"[6]—could become the core of academic training for business majors at community colleges.

In addition, courses and programs focused on the functions and operations of publicly owned and controlled banking systems (such as credit unions, as well as regional banks and state-owned banks) will be in demand, as will educational programs on how to set up time-shares, time-banks, local currencies, and other public finance innovations.

Engineering and Industry

"Green jobs" is the growing mantra as people across the country begin to grapple with impending environmental problems brought on by climate change. Such new and alternative employment is especially attractive in the face of recessionary double-digit unemployment and the fear of mounting job losses from traditional employment sectors.

Community college engineering programs are ripe for developing both degree and nondegree opportunities to train students in "green engineering." Such work would include job training for employment in photovoltaic installation and much-needed retrofitting skills to transform the millions of already-existing buildings and houses into energy-efficient structures. Many communities and individuals are willing to convert to these new sustainable technologies but, as in agriculture, cannot find local people trained in the skills and knowledge to do this work.

Moreover, there is a plethora of opportunities to learn and invent within the realm of low-tech engineering, which readily could become core curricula of engineering programs at community colleges. For example, Amy Smith, a senior lecturer in the Department of Mechanical Engineering at MIT who specializes in engineering design and appropriate technology, has produced several inventions that are sustainable and useful in poor, resource-constrained countries[7]—technologies that we may find suited to our own energy-constrained needs in the future.

Conflict Resolution

Several four-year colleges and universities have academic programs in peace studies and conflict resolution. However, only 1 percent of such programs are available at community colleges. Undoubtedly, numerous disputes and conflicts are likely to arise as we transition from the current large-corporate dominant system to a post-carbon energy system. For example, much of agriculture, out of necessity, is going to have to become local and urban, disturbing the "normality" of green lawns, open spaces, and public lands. Land use will have to be reconceptualized as well as rezoned to meet the new food-production needs. Such changes are likely to induce conflicts, especially, for example, as some residents in neighborhoods attempt to turn their green lawns into agricultural plots or small animal-production sites. There will be numerous incidents calling for the skills of mediators and arbitrators who are locally based to help manage and negotiate these community and neighborhood disputes. In addition, larger-scale environmental-impact conflicts, such as a recent dispute in Massachusetts over the placement of wind turbines for the offshore wind farm in Nantucket Sound,[8] will become more numerous as we confront the challenges of transitioning to a sustainable, post-carbon energy system.

Community colleges could provide the necessary training and expertise for relatively short-term, two-year degree programs that prepare students for careers in conflict management and dispute resolution of local neighborhood, community, and regional issues. Such a program could have tracks—agriculture, environmental, social welfare—in which students concentrate their area of expertise. Furthermore, even shorter-term training via certificate programs could be established, preparing students for micro-level dispute resolution such as conflict between neighbors.

COMMUNITY COLLEGES CAN BEGIN POST-CARBON EDUCATIONAL TRANSITIONS NOW

While the curricula of most community colleges have yet to reflect the growing energy constraints awaiting us, the educational structure of the community college makes it a viable medium through which to offer majors and programs that will be necessary in the future. A workforce trained in these areas will be needed as we begin the descent from the peak of global oil production. The time to put such critical programs into place is now, while we still have a window of opportunity to prepare for the imminent challenges of a post-carbon future. The community college can and should be at the center of these efforts.

Part Fifteen

BUILDING
RESILIENCE

PERSONAL PREPARATION

CHRIS MARTENSON

CHRIS MARTENSON *is the creator of the Crash Course, a twenty-chapter online video seminar about our broken economic system, the crisis of our aging popula-tion, and peak oil. Since its launch in 2008, the Crash Course has been viewed more than 1.5 million times and has sold over 25,000 DVD copies. Previously, Martenson was a vice president at a Fortune 300 company and spent more than ten years in corporate finance and strategic consulting. He has a PhD in pathology from Duke University and an MBA from Cornell University. Martenson is a Fellow of Post Carbon Institute.*

❖

It can feel pretty personally overwhelming to learn about all the eco-nomic, environmental, and energy challenges in store for us for the rest of this century. There's plenty of work to be done by governments and businesses, sure—but what about preparing yourself and your family for this quickly changing world? The choices seem overwhelming. Where does one begin?

Six years ago, I began to address these questions for myself and my family. I'll be honest; my first motivation came from a place of fear and worry. I worried that I could not predict when and where an economic collapse might begin. I fretted that the pace of the change would over-whelm the ability of our key social institutions and support systems to adapt and provide. I darkly imagined what might happen if a Katrina-sized financial storm swept through the banking system. I was caught up in fear.

But I am no longer in that frame of mind. Here, six years later, I am in a state of acceptance about what the future might bring (although I am concerned), and I have made it my life's work to help others achieve a similar measure of peace. While I am quite uncertain about what might unfold and when, I am positive that anyone can undertake some basic preparations relatively cheaply, and will feel better for having done so.

I am passionately interested in helping others to gracefully adapt their lifestyles and adjust their expectations to a very different-looking sort of future. I have no interest in scaring you further, or having you approach the future with trepidation, anxiety, or fear. Quite the opposite. I want to let you know that adjusting and adapting can be one of the most rewarding and fulfilling journeys you could undertake. It has been so for our family.

Just so you have a sense of the scope and the pace of these changes in our lives I should mention that in 2003 I was a VP at a Fortune 300 company, forty-two years of age with three young children (the oldest was nine), living in a six-bedroom waterfront house, and by every conventional measure I had it all. Today I no longer have that house, that job, or that life. My "standard of living" is a fraction of what it formerly was, but my quality of life has never been higher. We live in a house less than half the size of our former house, my beloved boat is gone, and we have a garden and chickens in the backyard.

Peering in from the outside someone might conclude that our family had fallen off the back of the American-dream truck with a thud. But from the inside they would observe a tight, comfortable, confident, and grounded family. We owe much of our current state of unity to the fact that we embarked on a journey of becoming more self-sufficient and discovered the importance of resilience and community along the way.

Anyone can do the same. But first, we must lay some groundwork and address the question, "Why prepare?" After that, we can delve into the details.

THE BASICS OF PREPARING

Becoming Resilient

The point of personal (and community) preparedness can be summed up in one single word: resilience.

We are more resilient when we have multiple sources and systems to supply a needed item, rather than being dependent on a single source. We are more resilient when we have a strong local community with deep connections. We are more resilient when we are in control of how our needs are met and when we can do things for ourselves.

We are more resilient if we can source water from three locations—perhaps from an existing well, a shallow well, and rainwater basins—instead of just one. If we throw in a quality water filter (essential for the rainwater anyway), then just about any source of water becomes potentially drinkable.

We are more resilient if we can grow a little bit more of our own food, rather than rely on a single grocery store. Our community gains food resilience when we demand local food, perhaps by shopping at a farmers' market or purchasing a farm produce subscription (also known as "community-supported agriculture"), and thereby increase our local supply of food and farming skills.

We are more resilient when our home can be heated by multiple sources and systems, perhaps wood and solar to complement oil or gas.

For my family, resilience now stretches well beyond our four walls and physical things and deep into our local networks and community. But it began with focusing our initial efforts within our household.

Resilience, then, becomes the lens through which we filter all of our decisions. It is a great simplifying tool. Should we buy this thing? Well, how does it make us more resilient? Should we invest in developing this new skill? Well, how will that help us be more resilient? Should we plant these trees or those? Well, which ones will add the most to the natural diversity and abundance around us?

It's really that simple. Instead of finding ourselves overwhelmed by all the things we could or should be doing, we find our lives simpler and easier.

The first concept of becoming prepared is resilience.

Insufficient, but Necessary

We must become the change we wish to see. If we just sit back and wait for a world where people are living with a reduced footprint and in balance with our economic and natural budgets, that world will never come. It is up to each of us to inspire others by first inspiring ourselves. The good news is that you are not and will never be alone on this journey.

But let's be perfectly honest: Any steps we might take to prepare for a potential environmental, societal, or economic disruption, no matter how grand, are nearly certain to be insufficient. Nevertheless, they are still necessary.

They will be insufficient because being perfectly prepared is infinitely expensive. But actions are necessary because they help us align our lives with what we know about the world. In my experience, when gaps exist between knowledge and actions, anxiety (if not fear) is the result. So it's not the state of the world that creates the anxiety quite as much as it is someone's lack of action.

To put it all together, we take actions because we must. If we don't, who will? We change the world by changing ourselves. We reduce stress, fear, and anxiety in our lives by aligning our thoughts and our actions and by being realistic about what we can preserve, setting our goals and plans accordingly.

The second concept of preparation is that actions are both necessary and insufficient.

Set Targets

When considering preparation the first question is usually, "How much?" Here I recommend setting a realistic goal given the amount of money and time you have to devote.

My family's goal has never been to be 100 percent self-sufficient in meeting *any* of our basic needs. Instead our goal has been to increase our self-sufficiency to something, anything, greater than "none." For example, until we got our solar panels we were 100 percent dependent on the utility grid. Now we are something laughably less than that, perhaps 3 percent, but we can manufacture and use our own electricity. What's the difference between being zero percent self-reliant and 3 percent? Night and day. We can charge batteries, have light at night, and, most important, prevent our fully stocked freezer from thawing during a power outage.

There's an enormous difference between being zero percent and 10 percent self-sufficient for food production. In the former case you rely on the existing food-distribution system. In the latter case you have a garden, local relationships with farmers, fruit trees in the yard, perhaps a few chickens, and a deep pantry. Developing even a limited percentage of your own food production does not take a lot of money, but it does take time. So set a realistic target that makes sense for you and your family and then find a way to get there.

The third concept of preparation is to set realistic goals.

Being in Service

Reducing my own anxiety was reason enough to prepare but an equally important objective was to be of service to my community. Should a crisis occur, I expect to find many unprepared people scrambling around in a desperate bid to meet their needs and many others paralyzed by the situation and unable to effectively act. I feel it is my duty to not be among them.

Some have commented that they think of personal preparation as a selfish act, possibly involving guns and bunkers, but that's not what this is about. My experience in life tells me that being a good community member means having your own house in order. If you do, you'll be in a better position to add valuable resources and skills to any future efforts.

My expectation is that communities will rally in the face of a disruption, an act I've witnessed several times having lived through hurricanes in North Carolina. But some communities will fare better than others and the difference between them will be dictated by the resilience of their respective citizen populations. I wish to live in a resilient community, which means I must become more resilient.

The fourth concept of preparation is that your community needs you to get yourself prepared.

Step Zero

Many people, when daunted by the potential magnitude of the coming change, immediately jump to some very hard conclusions that prove incapacitating. For example, they may have thoughts such as, "*I need to go back to school to get an entirely different degree so I can have a different job!*" or "*I need to completely relocate to a new area and start over, leaving all my friends behind!*" or "*I need to abandon my comfortable home and move to a remote off-grid cabin!*" These panic-driven conclusions may feel so radical that they are quickly abandoned. As a result, nothing gets accomplished. Further, nearly everyone has hidden barriers to action lurking within.

My advice here is crisp and clear. Find the smallest and easiest thing you can do, and then do it. I don't care what it is. If that thing for you is buying an extra jar of pimentos because you can't imagine life without them, then buy an extra jar next time you are shopping and put them in the pantry. I am only slightly joking here. I call this "step zero" to symbolize something minor that might precede step one.

The point is that small steps lead to bigger steps. If you have not yet taken *step one* toward personal preparation and resilience, then I invite you to consider taking *step zero*.

Examples might be taking out a small bit of extra cash to store outside of the bank in case of a banking disruption, buying a bit more food each week that can slowly deepen your pantry, or going online to learn something more about ways you can increase your resilience with regard to water, food, energy, or anything else you deem important to your future. It doesn't so much matter what it is, as long as an action is taken.

The fifth concept of preparation is to start with small steps.

The Importance of Community

My community is the most important element of my resilience.

In my case, I joined up with eight other gentlemen, and, as a group, over the course of a year we went through each and every "bucket" of a self-assessment we designed covering nine basic areas of our lives. We took a good, hard look at our then-current situations, made plans for preparation and change, and held each other accountable for following through with our plans. The support we shared was, and still is, invaluable.

My wife, Becca, and our children are deeply hooked into a wider community of people actively engaged in nature awareness, permaculture, native skills, fruit collection, and other pastimes that to them seem recreational, but also offer deeper local connections to people and nature.

I would recommend working with people you trust or with whom you already share basic values. The closer they live to you geographically, the better. One of my core values is this: I have no interest in living in fear, and my plan is to live through whatever comes next with a positive attitude and with as much satisfaction and fun as I can possibly muster. So it has always been important to me to be in community with others who share this outlook. And even now that I've experienced the pleasures (and joys and frustrations) of working in a group setting on matters of preparation, I would still immediately join or start another one if I happened to move away.

I now count this group as one of the most important elements in my life. I know who I can talk to about next steps, I know who I can count on in an emergency, and I know who will look after my family should I happen to be out of town when something big goes awry.

It is incredibly helpful to find people to join forces with as you step through the basics of self-preparation. I encourage you to consider seeking like-minded locals with whom to form such a group, if you have not already done so, and to encourage others to do the same.

My preparation group is now working outside of our group and exploring ways to help get our larger community into a more resilient position. I am only as secure as my neighbor is, and we are only as secure as our town, and our town is only as secure as the next town over. But it all begins at the center, like a fractal pattern, with resilient households determining how the future unfolds.

The sixth concept of preparation is that community is essential.

THE BASICS OF RESILIENCE

Now that we've covered the reasons why becoming more resilient is generally important, it is time to examine how we can best prepare to meet our basic physical needs for food, water, shelter, and warmth, and our modern need for electricity.

Long-Term Food Storage

Everyone should have a minimum of three months of food stored. It's cheap; it's easy; it's a no-brainer.

The three main reasons for storing some food are:

1. Because it's cheap.

2. Because it's prudent.

3. Because your great-grandparents would yell at you for not doing it.

Once upon a time, there was a person in every community whose job it was to ensure that sufficient food stocks existed in their town to carry the people through the winter. Their job was to travel to all the farms and granaries, total up all the food, divide by the number of people in town, and assess whether they were going to make it through the winter. In fact, it is only very recently that we have lost this function, and today most people think it rather odd to even wonder about food security.

But for all of human history, up until about a hundred years ago in the United States, this was not odd at all. In fact the reverse—going into winter without a local store of food sufficient to feed the community—would have been considered insane.

Once I examined the "just-in-time" delivery system that keeps us fed in this country, I began to grow concerned. Most communities have, at most, a total of three to five days' worth of food on hand in their local grocery stores and supermarkets. In other words, if trucks stopped rolling into town, and then everyone went down to the store to buy what they needed, the stores would be stripped bare in no time at all. I've seen this happen several times living down in hurricane country—which were formative experiences I can tell you—but for people who haven't seen this dynamic at play it may sound quite foreign.

The list of things that could disrupt the food-distribution chain is frightfully long. Fuel scarcity, flu epidemics, terrorist events, martial law, and economic breakdown are but a few of them. So our food-distribution system is best described as both highly cost-efficient (with low inventories and rolling stock) and extremely brittle.

Given this, Becca and I decided that putting some food into storage made sense. Having researched food storage for a while, we discovered that we could store food in a manner that would last for thirty years and would cost us less than $3 per person per day's worth of food.

So we made that a priority, and instead of sweating it out alone we held a food-storage packing day with fourteen local families and made a grand old time of it. Many people opt to buy the food already prepackaged for long shelf storage and there are many sources providing such products.

Today we have eight months' worth of food stored for our entire family, plus additional food set aside in case it will be needed by anybody else. It's been a year since the food-packing day and I have neither worried nor thought about food security or storage since, and I won't have to for twenty-nine more years. All for $3 per person per day. That is the cheapest peace of mind one can buy.

There are a lot of resources to help you decide what foods to store, how much, and where to get them. I've collected quite a few of them at my Web site (chrismartenson.com), but you can also locate plenty of helpful tips and information quite easily off of the Internet with a short amount of searching.

A simpler step than arranging for many months of food that will last for thirty years is to simply deepen your pantry. This means buying more of the very same foods that you already eat and putting them into rotation in your pantry. I am only talking about those foods that will keep for a year (or more), not things like bread or what's in your refrigerator. Mainly dry goods like spaghetti, and whatever you eat that comes in cans or jars.

Whether you decide to store a little or a lot, I encourage you to get started right away. And start small.

Growing and Storing Food

For us, the next step after getting some food stored away was to increase our local sources of food. Our primary local sources include the farmers who produce our meat and raw milk and the community-supported agriculture (CSA) vegetable operation to which we belong. Our local demand translates into more local food—a worthy outcome by itself, but we also happen to get superior food as part of the bargain.

And there's more. Our CSA is run by two fabulous young farmers whom we adore, it employs a crew of young local people, and they grow everything organically. We are getting tastier and healthier food, increasing demand for local food, and supporting our local community, all in one fell swoop. If you do not yet belong to a CSA and have the opportunity, it is well worth pursuing. If a CSA is not available or affordable to you, then at the very least, make connections with local farmers and food producers and purchase food from them directly whenever possible.

For the past six years we've also been growing a vegetable garden at what can only be termed "hobby level," and our learning process has been steep. While we enjoy and preserve the fruits of our labors, it seems that each year brings new challenges to surmount. The spring of 2009 here in the U.S. Northeast was the wettest and coldest in living memory, leading to all sorts of problems and plant diseases. The year before that it was extremely dry and hot. When I asked a local organic farmer if there was some book or internship that could accelerate my learning process he laughed and remarked, "Nope. It's ten years for everybody." By this he meant that there's no substitute for experience. One must live through the wettest year and the driest year and the year with funny yellow bugs and so on. So my advice is to get started.

Whether the food is grown by us or by our CSA, our family has developed a practical plan for food storage. We have fashioned a workable root-storage cellar out of our basement bulkhead for use over the late fall and winter months. All of our various root crops (potatoes, beets, turnips, carrots, etc.) are stored there until we use them. Effective storage in a root cellar requires a bit of learning and experimenting, with the variables being the method of storage, varieties being stored, temperature and humidity control, and culling to ensure minimal spoilage.

We keep chickens, which handily convert our kitchen waste into eggs and fertilizer. We also raise a few turkeys for the freezer every year. Over the years, we have gained increasing experience with butchering and processing our own birds, and now people come to us to learn this skill. This, too, has become a point of community for us.

After several years of practice, Becca has become a master canner and works throughout the fall to can many different kinds of fruits and vegetables. As with our informal food-storage and butchering outreach, I often find her sharing the kitchen with friends as they work side by side. This kind of sharing has the benefit of nurturing relationships within our community. It also introduces local friends to new skills that may be useful to them on their own path toward personal preparation and increased food independence.

Each of these areas represents a more direct relationship with our food and each requires a different set of skills and knowledge. I wish I could tell you that a smart and dedicated person could pick these skills up more rapidly than others, should the need arise, but it turns out that there really isn't any shortcut to becoming a gardener, or a canner, or a butcher, or a food preservationist. The vagaries of each growing season and the environmental variations of each year ensure your food-production education will be anything but dull.

Wherever you live, do what you can to learn about the specific growing conditions there and the varieties of food plants that particularly thrive in your area. You may want to start by adjusting your eating habits and expectations to match what is easy to grow and obtain locally.

Our family's goals from this point forward are to plant a wide variety of hardy, semi-dwarf fruit trees—apples, pears, plums, peaches, and cherries, along with hardy kiwis and grapes (on trellises). Further, we intend to work with local permaculture experts to design a system of growing food on our land that will require the least amount of energy to produce the largest possible gains. Our goal is to produce as much food as we can on our plot of land using the least amount of our personal energy. If everybody did this, think how much more resilient we'd be, and probably healthier too.

Whether you can begin to grow your own food or not, I highly recommend that you figure out how to obtain as much of your food locally as you can while it's in season, and then learn how to store it so that it lasts as long as possible. Set a goal. How about 10 percent?

Water

Clean water is a necessity of life. For most Americans, drinking and washing water comes either from a municipal (town/city) water supply or from a private well. Storing water is an enormous inconvenience, because stored water takes up a great deal of space, it's heavy, and it needs to be replaced with a fresh supply every couple of years.

Fortunately for me, I've never had to worry about water much because each place I've lived has had potable surface water nearby. Our house has a deep well, but I plan to invest in a second, shallow well by drilling down 80 to 90 feet to a water-holding gravel layer that sits under our land. I intend to attach both a windmill (for relatively continuous pumping for gardening purposes) and a hand pump capable of drawing from that depth. We will also be installing rainwater catchment systems. Clean water is critical for sustaining life, no matter what your standard of living.

We also have a ceramic filter based on a very old technology that can render the most foul pond water into clean drinking water. You just pour water in and let gravity do the rest. These filters remove all bacteria, all other little critters, and even a host of noxious chemicals. We even use it to treat our well water right now, because it removes even slight impurities and improves the flavor—but it also gives us familiarity and practice in using this system of filtering water.

Knowing that our family will always have clean drinking water, no matter what economic or weather emergency may arise, adds to our resilience. It also gives us a peace of mind that is invaluable.

Shelter and Warmth

The primary goal in meeting the need for shelter and warmth is to make your house as efficient and self-sustaining in energy as possible so that you are not completely reliant on imported energy to function—energy that could be either very expensive or intermittently available in the future.

For us, this means having three ways of heating our house and heating water: We have an oil furnace, we have a woodstove, and we are about to install a solar hot-water system. Our goal here is to cut our oil use by 50 percent in the first year after installation of the solar hot-water system.

However, our very first step after buying our house was to ensure that the house was as insulated and airtight as possible. With the number of states offering tax credits and other forms of assistance to help make houses more energy efficient, there is little excuse not to button up your home if you own it yourself. Check out the programs and get busy if you haven't already done so. When it comes to energy, saving it is far easier, and cheaper, than creating it, so you might as well invest first in conservation.

When it comes to selecting systems and components, one of my new criteria is that they be as simple as possible. I will gladly give up some efficiency or pay a little more if the system has fewer moving parts and seems like it could be fixed without flying in a Swedish engineer. Unless someone local can service and fix the system, I want no part of it. Simplicity now has a very high premium in my decision-making processes.

After we are done getting our house into shape with respect to energy, I anticipate utility bills that are half what they used to be, a less drafty and more comfortable house, and the security of knowing that hot water will always be a part of our lives.

Electricity

Next, we also have solar photovoltaic (PV) arrays to create a modest amount of electricity and a modest battery bank for limited storage. The primary purpose of this system is to provide a 100 percent fail-safe source of electricity to run our 25-cubic-foot freezer, the failure of which would result in a devastating food loss if the power went out in the early fall when it is most packed with food.

Our PV array provides about 2 kilowatts, which is far more than the freezer needs but far less than our house uses. Still, in a pinch, it would be sufficient to recharge batteries and run a laptop computer and drive a solar pump on our shallow well.

Our home is on the grid, but, at the very least, I am comfortable knowing that we have a source of electricity on the property that could serve a wide range of purposes if necessary. Again, the difference between being zero percent self-sufficient and slightly self-sufficient is simply enormous.

PERSONAL AND LOCAL RESILIENCE BEGINS AT HOME

We've just covered the six basic concepts of personal preparation and the areas of food growing and storage, water, shelter, warmth, and electricity. I strongly encourage you to make progress in each of these areas before moving on to others.

Six years ago my family lived in a big house by the sea, and we were completely dependent on outside systems and efforts to deliver to us our daily bread, our daily water, our daily warmth, and our daily electricity. Perhaps even more worryingly, we had a relatively narrow community defined by the people with whom we worked or we knew through our children's lives and activities.

Today we have a garden, chickens, food-preservation skills, solar hot water and electricity, local food connections, and a deep network of relationships around each of these elements and many more besides. We did not do this all at once but over a period of years, and I invite you to consider starting your own journey toward personal and local resilience as soon as you can.

Personal preparation is prudent, rational, liberating, and necessary. Remember the airplane emergency rule: Put on your oxygen mask first before assisting others. Start with small steps. Your community needs you.

WHAT CAN COMMUNITIES DO?

ROB HOPKINS

ROB HOPKINS *is the originator of the Transition Town concept, which promotes community-driven responses to peak oil that focus on cooperative effort to meet basic needs as sustainably and close to home as possible; in just a few years, his work has inspired an international movement of hundreds of communities. He is co-founder of the Transition Network and author of* The Transition Handbook: From Oil Dependency to Local Resilience *(2008). He is a trustee of the Soil Association (U.K.), the winner of the 2008 Schumacher Award, and a Fellow of Ashoka International. Hopkins is a Fellow of Post Carbon Institute.*

❖

AN EVENING AT THE BRIXTON–POUND LAUNCH

It's mid-September 2009, and I am standing in Lambeth Town Hall in Brixton, London. The hall is packed, the audience reflecting the area's rich cultural diversity. We are all there for the launch of the Brixton pound, an initiative of Transition Town Brixton (TTB), itself part of a quickly growing worldwide network of grassroots groups called the Transition movement. TTB was the first urban Transition initiative, starting in 2007, and has done amazing work in pioneering Transition in an urban context. They also host great events. This was no exception.

The Brixton pound is a printed local currency, specific to the Brixton area. It is a brave and bold idea; no one in this part of the world has ever done it before, and the context of the worst financial crisis the United Kingdom has faced since the 1930s adds an impetus and sense of urgency to the proceedings. One of the evening's speakers is the leader of the local council, who tells the audience, "I want this to become the currency of choice for Brixton," and later tells me that, of course, people will be able to pay their council tax in it, a national first. The notes, Brixton's best-kept secret until that point, are unveiled to rapturous applause; they feature notable former Brixtonians such as Vincent van Gogh, James Lovelock, journalist and historian C. L. R. James, and Olive Morris, who set up the Brixton Black Women's Group and who died aged only twenty-seven. (Brixtonians David Bowie and local dub poet Linton Kwesi Johnson had both declined to grace the notes.)

What comes through stronger than anything else is that this is a large group of people not waiting for permission to begin their responses to peak oil and climate change, and not waiting for distant economic forces to lay waste to their local economy. They are not assuming that central government will do everything for them, but are initiating change from the bottom up, in a way that is creative and even playful, that is not trying to place blame, and that feels historic. They are not seeing these challenges as disastrous calamities, but rather as the opportunity for a once-off rethink of many basic assumptions about how their society and economy function. They recognize that the future of fossil-fuel scarcity and a changing climate will require us to think ever more locally, and they are starting to make it happen. Welcome to the world of Transition.

WHY COMMUNITY MATTERS

Given the scale of the challenges humanity faces in the early twenty-first century, already outlined in great detail in earlier sections of this book, it is clear that a range of responses is required. Government is part of the solution, but it tends to be reactive rather than proactive. Local government is often so focused on meeting immediate needs with limited resources that it doesn't feel it can be imaginative or take much initiative. Local citizens often feel disempowered after years of being ignored in the decisions made about their community.

However, any sufficient response to these challenges requires all of the levels of response working together, driven by the twin objectives of massively reducing carbon emissions and building resilience. The Transition movement embodies this approach with an attitude that might be summarized this way: "If we try and do it on our own it will be too little, if we wait for government to do it it will be too late, but if we can gather together those around us—our street, our neighborhood, our community—it might just be enough, and it might just be in time."

Community matters when we are looking for responses to peak oil and climate change because of the power that emerges from working together and creating meaningful change through shared action. In a world where social capital and a sense of connection to community are in decline, it is the taking of practical action that enables us to rediscover meaningfulness and community. It is my observation, through seeing what groups inspired by Transition have done, that happiness and fulfillment are achieved though meaningful activity, and meaningful activity needs to happen with other people. If we see climate change and peak oil as purely environmental and energy problems that someone else will fix, we give away our potential to create change, and we close ourselves away and feel powerless—and the last thing we need at this point in history is people feeling powerless.

The Transition movement is, in effect, about the application of engaged optimism to the challenges we face. What does it look like if we use Transition to create what social entrepreneur Jeremy Leggett calls "scalable microcosms of hope"? How might it be if the energy that propels people into action isn't distress, fear, and despair, but the things that they are passionate about? That sense of optimism and "can-do" activism that was so palpable at the launch of the Brixton pound is being felt around the world by communities who are deciding that they want to be a part of shaping the future.

In the United Kingdom, where central government still dismisses the concept of peak oil, Transition initiatives are doing hugely valuable work in asking the questions and doing the thinking that government agencies are still unable to do. However, by doing so in a way that focuses on opportunities and possibilities rather than crises, this work is increasingly engaging organizations, businesses, and local government in exploring the potential that, when looked at through Transition glasses, offers an economic, social, and cultural renaissance the likes of which we have never seen. Part of that work is about shifting the scale on which we implement solutions from the global to the local.

LOCALIZATION

The age of cheap energy, which we are now leaving behind, made many things possible, one of the most impactful being economic globalization.

The ability to cheaply transport people and goods over huge distances has massively changed how the world does business. Western nations have dispensed with the quaint idea that they might actually make anything, specializing instead in ideas and services. The U.K. government's definition of "resilience" in terms of food is that it is gotten from as wide a range of sources as possible, rather than as locally as possible. Comedian David Mitchell once described the U.K. economy as now being based on "ringtones and lattes."[1] A recent report suggested that the three main areas of economic activity that were predicted to pull the United Kingdom out of recession are offshore wind farms, yacht building, and . . . cheese.[2] The age of a dynamic manufacturing sector has passed.

While economic globalization has brought huge benefits (albeit inequitably distributed ones), its key flaw is its vulnerability to high fuel prices. During the age of cheap energy, our economic success and our individual sense of prowess and well-being have been directly linked to how much oil and energy we consume. We are now rapidly moving into a time where our degree of oil dependency is equal to our degree of vulnerability.

The concept of localization suggests that the move away from globalized distribution systems is not a choice but an inevitable change in direction for humanity. The rebuilding of local economies offers a response to the challenges presented by peak oil, as well as a tremendous opportunity to rethink and reinvent local economies. Localization is not, as Michael Shuman puts it, about "walling off the outside world"; rather it is about meeting needs that can be met locally, locally.[3] David Fleming sums up the case for relocalization nicely when he writes: "Localisation stands, at best, at the limits of practical possibility, but it has the decisive argument in its favour that there will be no alternative."[4]

THE TRANSITION CONCEPT

The Transition response to peak oil and climate change is based on the following assumptions:

1. Life with dramatically lower energy consumption is inevitable, and it is better to plan for it than to be taken by surprise.

2. Our settlements and communities presently lack the resilience to enable them to weather the severe energy shocks that will accompany peak oil.

3. We have to act collectively, and we have to act now.

4. By unleashing the collective genius of those around us to creatively and proactively design our energy descent, we can build ways of living that are more connected and more enriching and that recognize the biological limits of our planet.

From its beginnings in Kinsale in Ireland, then Totnes in England, and now globally, Transition has emerged as a process that acts as a catalyst, creating enthusiasm in communities to begin exploring and implementing the practicalities of rebuilding local economies in all their aspects. It is a process that has several qualities. It is:

- *Viral:* It spreads rapidly and pops up in the most unexpected places.
- *Open source:* It is a model that people shape and take ownership of and is made available freely.
- *Self-organizing:* It is not centrally controlled; rather it is something people take ownership of and make their own.
- *Solutions focused:* It is inherently positive, not campaigning against things, but rather setting out a positive vision of a world that has embraced its limitations.
- *Iterative:* It is continually learning from its successes and its failures and is continually redefining itself, trying to research what is working and what isn't.
- *Clarifying:* It offers a clear explanation of where humanity finds itself based on the best science available.
- *Sensitive to place and scale:* It looks different wherever it goes.
- *Historic:* It tries to create a sense of this moment as being a historic opportunity to do something extraordinary—and perhaps most important of all . . .
- *Joyful:* If it's not fun, you're not doing it right.

A model known as the "12 Steps (or Ingredients) of Transition" has emerged from the experience of early Transition initiatives. This model supports Transition initiatives through the process of forming their groups, engaging their community, and working toward the creation of an Energy Descent Action Plan (EDAP), a kind of Plan B for the community that sets out how it could move toward a lower-carbon, resilient future. The term "viral" is not used lightly. Transition has grown exponentially, from just a handful of initiatives in 2007 to more than 300 official groups in

TABLE 33.1 Formal Transition Initiatives as of Spring 2010

United Kingdom

Andover	Dorchester	Horsham	Marsden and Slaithwaite	South Petherton
Arran and Holy Isle	Dorking	Hull	Matlock	Southwell Area
Ashburton	Downham Market	Ipswich	Mayfield	St Albans
Ashtead	Downton	Isle of Man	Melrose	Stafford
Bangor	Dunbar	Isle of Wight	Mersea Island	Stamford
Bassingbourn	Ely	Isles of Scilly	Minehead and Alcombe	Stoke Newington
Bath	Evesham Vale	Ivybridge	Moffat	Stratford
Bedford	Exeter	Kendal and South Lakes	Monmouth	Stroud
Belsize	Exmouth	Kensal to Kilburn	Nayland	Taunton
Berkhamsted	Eynsham Area	Kingston-upon-Thames	New Forest Transition	Tavistock
BH Hub	Falmouth	Kirkbymoorside	Newent	Tayport
Biggar	Farnham	Ladock and Grampound	Newton Abbot	Thornbury
Black Isle	Faversham	Road	North Howe	Thorncombe
Brampton	Finsbury Park	Lampeter	North Queensferry	Tooting
Brighton & Hove	Forest of Dean	Lancaster	Norwich	Totnes
Bristol	Forest Row	Langport	Nottingham	Wivenhoe
Bro Ddyfi	Forres	Lavenham	Omagh	Tring
Bro Festiniog	Frome	Leamington Spa	Ottery St Mary	Tunbridge Wells
Bro Gwaun	Glastonbury	Leek	Oxford	Tynedale
Bungay	Groningen	Leicester	Penwith	Wandsworth
Buxton	Haslemere	Letchworth	Portobello (Edinburgh)	West Kilbride
Calon Teifi	Hastings	Lewes	Presteigne	West Kirby
Cambridge	Hawick	Liskeard	Redland	Westcliff-on-Sea
Canterbury	Haywards Heath	Liverpool - South	Rhayader	Weymouth and Portland
Chepstow	Helston & District	Llandeilo	Richmond	Whitstable
Chester	Hemel Hempstead	Llantwit Major	Saltash	Wigan
Chesterfield	Henley on Thames	London - Brixton	Sampford Peverell	Wolverton
Chichester	Hereford	Lostwithiel	Seaton	Woodbridge
Clitheroe	Hertford	Louth	Sevenoaks	Worthing
Coventry	High Wycombe	Maidenhead	Sheffield	Wrington
Crediton	Highbury	Malvern Hills	Sherborne	York
Derby	Holywood	Market Harborough	Shoreham-by-Sea	
Diss	Horncastle	Marlow	Sidmouth	

United States

Albany, CA	Denver, CO	Media, PA	Portland, ME	Shelburne, VT
Anderson, OH	New Haven, CT	Micanopy, FL	Portland (PDX), OR	Staunton Augusta, VA
Ann Arbor, MI	Hancock Cty., ME	Monterey, CA	Portland (Sunnyside), OR	Stelle, IL
Ashland, OR	Hardwick, VT	Montpelier, VT	Putney, VT	Seattle (Northeast), WA
Austin, TX	Houston, TX	Newburyport, MA	Reno, NV	Transition Colorado
Berea, KY	Keene, NH	Northfield, MN	Richmond, CA	Tucson, AZ
Bloomington, IN	Ketchum, ID	Oklahoma City, OK	San Francisco, CA	Van Buren-Allegan, MI
Carrboro / Chapel Hill, NC	Laguna Beach, CA	Olympia, WA	San Luis Obispo, CA	West Marin, CA
Chelsea, MI	Los Angeles, CA	Paso Robles, CA	Sandpoint, ID	Westminster, CO
Cotati, CA	Louisville, CO	Pittsburgh, PA	Santa Barbara, CA	Whatcom, WA
Culver City, CA	Louisville, KY	Pima, AZ	Santa Cruz, CA	Whidbey, WA
	Lyons, CO	Pine Mountain, CA	Sebastopol, CA	

Australia

Adelaide West, SA	Bellingen, NSW	Eumundi Markets, QLD	Maleny, QLD	Sydney Epping, NSW
Anglesea, VIC	Blue Mountains, NSW	Far North Queensland, QLD	Newcastle, NSW	Tamborine Mtn., QLD
Armidale, NSW	Cooran, QLD	Hervey Bay, QLD	North Sydney, NSW	Torquay, VIC
Banyule, VIC	Darebin, VIC	Kenmore, QLD	South Barwon, VIC	Transition East, QLD
Barraba, NSW	Denmark, WA	Kurilpa, QLD	Sunshine Coast, QLD	Wingecarribee, NSW
Bell, VIC	Eudlo, QLD		Sydney, NSW	

Canada

Barrie, ON	Guelph, ON	Ottawa, ON	Poplar Hill / Coldstream, ON	Salt Spring Island, BC
Cocagne, NB	London, ON	Peterborough, ON	Powell River, BC	Vancouver, BC
Dundas, ON	Nelson, BC			Victoria, BC

New Zealand

Brooklyn	Waiheke Island
Kapiti	Whanganui
Nelson	
Opotiki	
Orewa	
Timaru	

Elsewhere

El Manzano, Chile	Witzenhausen, Germany	Fujino, Japan
Syltemae, Denmark	Kildare Town, Ireland	Hayama, Japan
Siirtymäliike, Finland	Kilkenny, Ireland	Deventer, Netherlands
Bielefeld, Germany	Kinsale, Ireland	
Friedrichshain-Kreuzberg, Germany	Monteveglio Città di Transizione, Italy	

Source: Transition Network Web site, http://www.transitionnetwork.org/initiatives.

2010 (table 33.1). There are national Transition organizations in Sweden, Ireland, Italy, New Zealand, Japan, and the United States, and individual initiatives (including "mullers" considering becoming official) number in the thousands. But what inspires them, and what tangible outcomes have emerged from their work thus far?

IS RESILIENCE THE NEW SUSTAINABILITY?

The study of resilience has been covered elsewhere in this book. It is most often explained as referring to the ability of a system to withstand a shock and return to its original functions. It is a lens through which many disciplines—disaster management, human development, psychology, and organizational development—explore the implications of shock. An emerging area within resilience thinking is known as adaptive or transformational resilience, which argues (as does the Transition movement) that change offers huge potential to rethink assumptions and build new systems.

Human communities differ from ecological communities in that they are able to see change coming, and to anticipate and plan for that change. Brigit Maguire and Sophie Cartwright articulate how social resilience is different from ecological resilience, describing resilience as "the ability of a community to respond to change *adaptively*. Rather than simply returning to a pre-existing state, this can mean transforming to a new state that is more sustainable in the current environment."[5]

For Transition, when peak oil and climate change are overlapped and looked at together, it becomes clear that resilience is, alongside the drastic reduction in carbon emissions, a dynamic and useful way of looking at the way forward from here. One of the questions explored in Transition is whether or not resilience can be measured. In Totnes, the process of creating an Energy Descent Action Plan also involved the creation of some "resilience indicators," measures that could be revisited regularly to check that the community is moving in the right direction. These measures might include things like the percentage of food consumed locally that was produced locally, the percentage of trading done using local currencies, the degree to which people felt involved in community activities, and so on.

WHERE TRANSITION STARTS AND WHERE IT NEEDS TO GO

Transition initiatives often start with food projects, as they offer (excuse the pun) the low-hanging fruit—the projects that can get under way the fastest.[6] These take many forms, from community-supported agriculture to urban fruit and nut tree plantings, from community gardens to re-skilling workshops around food production.

Some of the more mature initiatives in the United Kingdom are starting to broaden out and step up to larger-scale projects:

- Totnes, Lewes, Stroud, and Brixton have launched Transition currencies. The Brixton pound, launched in September 2009, issued more than £30,000 worth of notes into circulation in the first month, and became the first local currency to be accepted by its local council to pay council tax.
- Transition Taunton Deane in Somerset worked with its local council and ran a weeklong visioning process with its city planners, producing *Towards a Resilient Taunton Deane*, an extraordinary document.[7]
- Transition Stroud worked with its local authority and produced *Food Availability in Stroud District*,[8] a report that went on to underpin the council's food policy. The deputy leader of the council said, "If Transition Stroud didn't exist we'd have to make [the policy] up."
- Transition Town Totnes just published its *Energy Descent Action Plan*, the first community-generated "Plan B," based on a yearlong community consultation process.[9]

In the United States, the organization Transition US is sponsoring initiatives, supplying materials, and providing technical assistance for groups nationwide. Launched in 2008, Transition US had more than sixty-five formally recognized Transition initiatives in twenty-four states by mid-2010—and for every official Transition initiative there were at least four groups mulling over whether to become official. The number of formal initiatives, as well as the number of people completing the "Training for Transition" course, is expected to increase significantly in the next few years.

Transition initiatives are under way in all regions of the country:

- The San Francisco Bay Area is home to six official Transition initiatives (with more on the way), several of which are collaborating to build diverse leadership and establish an area-wide convergence. The Los Angeles region has a city hub coordinating support, mentoring, and collaboration with seven initiatives throughout the area.
- A bioregional Transition hub is emerging in the Puget Sound/Salish Sea region, with initiatives in Olympia, Seattle, and Whidbey Island (Washington) collaborating across the border with initiatives in Victoria and Vancouver (British Columbia). Portland, Oregon, has both a citywide initiative and one of the first official neighborhood-level groups.
- The western mountain states are home to the three earliest U.S. initiatives, in Boulder, Colorado, and in Sandpoint and Ketchum, Idaho. The Great Plains and Texas are seeing initiatives emerge in rural, suburban, and urban settings, with official groups in Austin, Houston, and Oklahoma City.
- The Ohio River Valley has official initiatives in four cities, and groups have formed in Tennessee, North Carolina, and Florida. The Northeast has only a handful of official initiatives, but more than thirty groups are beginning to form.

Wherever they are located, it is hoped that Transition initiatives will grow to become agents of relocalization, social enterprises dedicated to guiding their communities through the decline of fossil fuels.

A VISION OF WHERE THIS COULD ALL GO

The age of cheap energy led to the idea that our economies can grow indefinitely, forever, in complete contradiction to any notion of ecological or energy limits. Increasingly, though, the awareness has been growing that economic growth has not been accompanied by social growth; that is, it has not led to our being happier, more relaxed, less indebted, more skilled, and better connected with a stronger sense of community. As the global economy now enters a period where any degree of economic growth is becoming infeasible, it is clear there is a choice: either to try to use the same thinking that got us into this situation to get us back out again or to replace the idea of growth—as Tim Jackson sets out in

Prosperity without Growth[10]—with the idea of prosperity in the widest sense of the word.

In scaling up the Transition movement, we hope to see the allied and inseparable concepts of drastic carbon reduction and resilience building underpin policy-making, business planning, and community development. We also hope to see many more communities themselves taking ownership of their development, becoming their own banks, developers, energy companies, and so on.

One day when I was eighteen, I went with my friends to collect our final exam results from school. I remember sitting in the sunshine on the school steps and looking round at my friends, who had just received grades of varying quality, and thinking what a useless lot we were. None of us knew how to garden, build, repair, or do anything of any great value. If we had washed up on a desert island together, we wouldn't even have known how to feed each other.

In the same way, I think that when two people, two communities, two regions, or two nations meet each other and interact from positions of mutual dependency, mutual need, a lack of real skills, and an inability to turn their hands to anything, it is a very different quality of relationship than when both are able, adaptable, and resilient. We cannot respond to peak oil and climate change by putting up fences, drawing up drawbridges, and retreating into survivalism and a rejection of society. The Transition approach argues, and indeed is actively demonstrating, that the solutions we need will, in large part, emerge from those around us, from the networks and relationships we build, and from the sense of "engaged optimism" that we are able to generate. That will be the dynamic free energy source that will actually sustain us long into the future.

Part Sixteen

CALL TO ACTION

34

WHAT NOW?

The Path Forward Begins with One Step

ASHER MILLER

ASHER MILLER *is executive director of Post Carbon Institute. Previously he served as partnership director at Plugged In, international production coordinator at Steven Spielberg's Shoah Foundation, ghostwriter for a Holocaust survivor, and consultant for a number of other nonprofit groups. He currently serves on the board of Transition US, the hub of the Transition movement in the United States.*

❖

So, what now? In the face of these enormous and complex challenges, it's easy to throw one's hands up in disgust, despair, or denial and walk away. I know. I do it at least seven times a day. And yet I always come back.

There's a reason why you've picked up *The Post Carbon Reader*, and a reason why its authors, and so many others, have dedicated their lives to pushing that proverbial rock up the hill. Call it hope, call it morality, call it stubbornness, call it whatever you wish. But it all boils down to one fundamental belief—that we *can* do something.

These times will test our courage, capacity, and commitment. These are also exciting times, when broken paradigms can be discarded and communities can become grounded in deeper relationships. Some (perhaps you or someone you know) have already begun this journey. Some have lived it for decades or generations.

Quietly, a small but growing movement of engaged citizens, community groups, businesses, and elected officials has begun the transition to a post-carbon world. These early actors have worked to reduce consumption, produce local food and energy, invest in local economies, rebuild skills, and preserve local ecosystems. You've gotten a glimpse of them throughout this book.

For some citizens, this effort has merely entailed planting a garden, riding a bike to work, or no longer buying from "big-box" stores. Their motivations are diverse, including halting climate change, environmental preservation, food security, and local economic development. The essence of these efforts, however, is the same: They all recognize that the world is changing and the old way of doing things, based on the idea that consumption can and should continue to grow indefinitely, no longer works.

Alone, these efforts are not nearly enough. But taken together, they can point the way toward a new economy. This new economy would not be a "free market" but a "real market," much like the one fabled economist Adam Smith originally envisioned; it would be, as author David Korten has said, an economy driven by Main Street and not Wall Street.[1]

Thus far, most of these efforts have been made voluntarily by exceptional individuals who were quick to understand the crisis we face. But as our current paradigm continues to fail, more and more people will be searching for ways to meet even basic needs. Families reliant on supermarkets with globe-spanning supply chains will need to turn more to local farmers and their own gardens. Many corporations—unable to provide a continuous return on investment or to rely on cheap energy and natural resources to turn a profit—will fail, while local businesses and cooperatives of all kinds will flourish. Local governments facing declining tax revenues will be desperate to find cheap, low-energy ways to support basic public services like water treatment, public transportation, and emergency services.

What we need now are clarity, leadership, coordination, and collaboration. With shared purpose and a clear understanding of both the challenges and the solutions, we *can* manage the transition to a sustainable, equitable, post-carbon world.

So what does this world look like? What is our vision for the post-carbon century? In January 2010, Post Carbon Institute brought our Fellows, board, and staff together in part to try to answer this question (figure 34.1).

VISION FOR A POST-CARBON CENTURY

Our vision is of a world worth inheriting, where people not only survive, they thrive. In this future, we have emerged from a period of uncertainty,

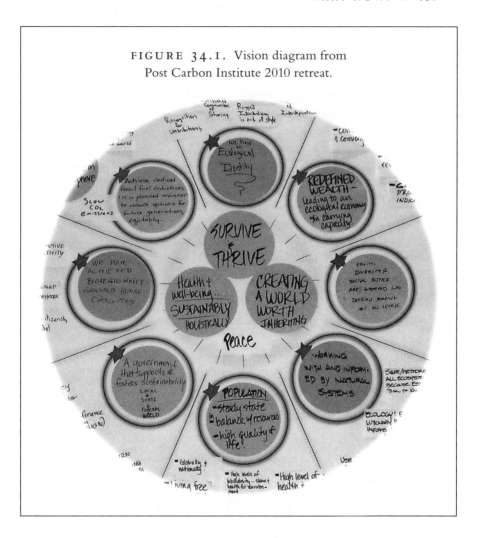

FIGURE 34.1. Vision diagram from
Post Carbon Institute 2010 retreat.

confusion, and questioning with a new understanding of what it means to
be human. This understanding is manifested in the following ways:

· We've developed an ecological identity, a recognition that begins in
  early childhood of our interdependence on the natural world.
· We've redefined prosperity—wealth is counted by the extent of our
  relationships and knowledge, not the amount of things we own.
  We've abandoned the false god of economic growth and look to
  genuine progress indicators (GPIs) rather than gross domestic product (GDP) as our measure of economic well-being. Businesses make

natural resource conservation and local sourcing core tenets of their work, not the costs of business or a responsibility to avoid.

· We've rediscovered democracy—government that is responsive to an engaged public, with institutions composed of engaged citizens, not representatives for hire—where equity, diversity, and a deep understanding of natural systems are woven into decision-making at all levels.

· We've redesigned our homes and communities to live efficiently, comfortably, and in beauty. People live in passively powered dwellings in human-scaled neighborhoods. Our communities are connected to one another by post-automobile modes of transport and powered by locally sourced renewable energy. We eat food grown locally, organically, and seasonally.

· World population is at a steady state, in balance with natural resources and free from conflict, and with high quality of life across the globe.

· We have achieved radical reductions in fossil-fuel use in a planned and equitably distributed way, and we have reduced fossil-fuel emissions to such an extent that, despite unavoidable climate changes, we've managed to not, as David Orr says, "evict ourselves from the only paradise we've ever known."

If you've read this list and wondered to yourself, "How in the world are we ever going to achieve this?" you're not alone.

The bad news is that, no matter what we do, it won't be enough to "solve" the problems outlined in the preceding chapters. The good news is that, no matter what we do, it *can* make a difference. Such is the scale and extent of our predicament. We may not be able to fully realize this vision, or it may be a long and painful journey to reach it, but that does not mean things are hopeless. If they were, you and me, we wouldn't be having this conversation.

Now put this book down and go do something. Anything.

NOTES

FOREWORD

1. Richard Heinberg, "Peak Oil Day," July 3, 2009, http://www.postcarbon.org/blog-post/40804-peak-oil-day.

2. U.S. Bureau of Labor Statistics, http://www.bls.gov/data/.

3. Don Peck, "How a New Jobless Era Will Transform America," *Atlantic*, March 2010, http://www.theatlantic.com/magazine/archive/2010/03/how-a-new-jobless-era-will-transform-america/7919/.

4. The Associated Press, "Uh, Oh, Higher Jobless Rates Could Be the New Normal," October 23, 2009, http://www.nydailynews.com/money/work_career/2009/10/19/2009-10-19_uh_oh_higher_jobless_rates_could_be_the_new_normal.html.

5. Robert Reich, "When Will the Recovery Begin? Never," July 9, 2009, http://robertreich.blogspot.com/2009/07/when-will-recovery-begin-never.html.

6. John Michael Greer, *The Long Descent: A User's Guide to the End of the Industrial Age* (Gabriola Island, BC: New Society, 2008). Richard Farson attributes the idea that "problems can be solved; predicaments can only be coped with" to philosopher Abraham Kaplan; Richard Farson, *Management of the Absurd: Paradoxes in Leadership* (New York: Free Press, 1997), 42.

7. See http://www.transitionus.org and http://www.transitionnetwork.org.

CHAPTER 1. BEYOND THE LIMITS TO GROWTH

1. Donella Meadows, Dennis Meadows, Jorgen Randers, and William Behrens III, *The Limits to Growth* (New York: Universe Books, 1972).

2. A recent study by the Australian Commonwealth Scientific and Industrial Research Organization (CSIRO) concluded: "[Our] analysis shows that 30 years of historical data compares favorably with key features of [the *Limits to Growth*] business-as-usual scenario." Graham Turner, *A Comparison of the Limits to Growth with 30 Years of Reality*, CSIRO Working Paper, June 2008, www.csiro.au/files/files/plje.pdf; Justin Lahart, Patrick Barta, and Andrew Baston, "New Limits to Growth Revive Malthusian Fears," *Wall Street Journal*, March 24, 2008.

3. The amount of energy, in British thermal units (Btu), required to produce a dollar of GDP has been dropping steadily, from close to 20,000 Btu per dollar in 1949 to 8,500 Btu in 2008. Praveen Ghanta, "U.S. Economic Energy Efficiency: 1950–2008," Seeking Alpha, January 10, 2010, http://seekingalpha.com/article/181818-u-s-economic-energy-efficiency-1950-2008.

4. The *Limits to Growth* scenario study has been rerun repeatedly in the years since the original publication, using more sophisticated software and updated input data. The results each time have been similar. See Donella Meadows, Jorgen Randers, and Dennis Meadows, *Limits to Growth: The 30-Year Update* (White River Junction, VT: Chelsea Green, 2004).

5. David Korten, *Agenda for a New Economy: From Phantom Wealth to Real Wealth* (San Francisco: Berrett-Koehler, 2009).

CHAPTER 2. WHAT IS SUSTAINABILITY?

1. Eric T. Freyfogle, *Why Conservation Is Failing and How It Can Regain Ground* (New Haven: Yale University Press, 2006).

2. United Nations World Commission on Environment and Development (known as the Brundtland Commission), *Our Common Future* (Oxford: Oxford University Press, 1987), http://www.un-documents.net/wced-ocf.htm.

3. Albert A. Bartlett, "Reflections on Sustainability, Population Growth, and the Environment—Revisited," *Renewable Resources Journal* 15, no. 4 (winter 1997–1998), 6–23, http://www.hubbertpeak.com/bartlett/reflections.htm.

4. The Natural Step, "The Four System Conditions," http://www.naturalstep .org/en/the-system-conditions.

5. William E. Rees and Mathis Wackernagel, *Our Ecological Footprint: Reducing Human Impact on the Earth* (Gabriola Island, BC: New Society, 1995).

6. Richard Heinberg, *Peak Everything: Waking Up to the Century of Declines* (Gabriola Island, BC: New Society, 2007).

7. Joseph Tainter, *The Collapse of Complex Societies* (Cambridge, UK: Cambridge University Press, 1988).

8. Jared Diamond, *Collapse: How Societies Choose to Fail or Succeed* (New York: Viking/Penguin, 2005).

9. Julian Simon, "The State of Humanity: Steadily Improving," *Cato Policy Report* 17, no. 5 (September/October 1995), 131.

10. This is Albert Bartlett's first law of sustainability, reproduced verbatim—I found it impossible to improve upon. Albert A. Bartlett, "Reflections on Sustainability, Population Growth, and the Environment," *Population & Environment* 16, no. 1 (September 1994), 5–35.

11. Efforts to refine this essential principle of sustainability are ongoing.

12. This principle was first stated, in a more generalized and more mathematically rigorous form, by Albert A. Bartlett in his 1986 paper "Sustained Availability: A Management Program for Non-Renewable Resources," *American Journal of Physics* 54 (May 1986), 398–402. The article's abstract notes: "If the rate of extraction declines at a fixed fraction per unit time, the rate of extraction will approach zero, but the integrated total of the extracted resource between t = 0 and t = infinity will remain finite. If we choose a rate of decline of the rate of extraction of the resource such that the integrated total of all future extraction equals the present size of the remaining resource then we have a program that will allow the resource to be available in declining amounts for use forever." Annually reducing the rate of extraction of a given nonrenewable resource by its yearly rate of depletion effectively accomplishes the same thing, but requires only simple arithmetic and layperson's terms for its explanation.

13. The fourth axiom encapsulates Bartlett's seventh and eighth laws of sustainability. It is also the basis for the Oil Depletion Protocol, first suggested by petroleum geologist Colin J. Campbell in 1996 and the subject of one of my books: Richard Heinberg, *The Oil Depletion Protocol: A Plan to Avert Oil Wars, Terrorism and Economic Collapse* (Gabriola Island, BC: New Society, 2006). The aim of the Oil Depletion Protocol is to reduce global consumption of petroleum to avert the crises likely to ensue as a result of declining supply—including economic collapse and resource wars. Under the terms of the Oil Depletion Protocol, oil-importing countries would reduce their imports by the world oil-depletion rate (calculated by Campbell at 2.5 percent per year); producers would reduce their domestic production by their national depletion rates.

CHAPTER 3. THINKING "RESILIENCE"

1. Even in the United States, life expectancy increased by thirty years during the twentieth century.

2. In effect, heavy resource exploitation implies the effective integration of the human enterprise with the corresponding ecosystem. Indeed, people are often the most ecologically significant consumer organism in managed ecosystems. We refer to the resultant hybrid system as a socio-ecosystem.

3. Brian Walker and David Salt, *Resilience Thinking: Sustaining Ecosystems and People in a Changing World* (Washington DC: Island Press, 2006).

4. Julian Simon, "The State of Humanity: Steadily Improving," *Cato Policy Report* (September/October 1995). Available at http://www.cato.org/pubs/policy_report/pr-so-js.html.

5. Albert A. Bartlett, "Forgotten Fundamentals of the Energy Crisis," *American Journal of Physics* 46, no. 9 (1978), 876–888.

6. The now-discredited concept of "maximum sustainable yield" is a classic example of this equilibrium-oriented management approach.

7. C. S. Holling, Lance H. Gunderson, and Donald Ludwig, "In Quest of a Theory of Adaptive Change," in *Panarchy: Understanding Transformations in Human and Natural Systems*, C. S. Holling and Lance H. Gunderson, eds. (Washington DC: Island Press, 2002), 6.

8. The capacity for continuous self-organization and self-production is sometimes called "autopoiesis." Living systems from individual cells to the entire ecosphere are "autopoietic" systems.

9. Walker and Salt, *Resilience Thinking*, 8.

10. C. S. Holling, "Understanding the Complexity of Economic, Social and Ecological Systems," *Ecosystems* 4 (August 2001), 390–405.

11. The domain over which key systems variables can safely range while maintaining specific systems characteristics is sometimes called a systems "regime."

12. For example, mean global temperature may be lagging behind rising greenhouse gas levels by 20 to 60 years.

13. Consider the many freshwater lakes—once prized for sport fishing and other water-based recreation—that we have seen suddenly "flip" into a eutrophic state characterized by noxious algae, anoxic water, and dead fish. Decades of excess nutrient runoff from agriculture and municipal sewage plants can push a lake beyond hidden thresholds where the negative feedbacks that kept the lake "clean" are overwhelmed

by positive feedbacks that drive it into an alternative undesirable (from the human perspective) stable regime.

14. Walker and Salt, *Resilience Thinking*, 9.

15. That said, we must recognize that not all systems adaptation and resilience is obviously beneficial to humans. The increasing resistance of crop pests to biocides and the increasing resistance of bacteria to antibiotics are examples of resilient adaptations that frustrate human purposes. Similarly, in human societies, the resistance of powerful vested interests to needed changes to the status quo frustrates sustainability planning.

16. Holling, "Understanding the Complexity of Economic, Social and Ecological Systems," 404.

17. Ibid., 392.

18. Climate change is possibly one such shock. Interestingly, the phenomenon of human-induced climate change is an example of one level in the global hierarchy (the human enterprise, an intermediate-speed subsystem) "feeding up" and reconfiguring a higher level (the global climate, a slower subsystem).

19. Joseph Tainter, "Sustainability of Complex Societies," *Futures* 27, no. 4 (May 1995), 397–407.

20. The "constant-capital-stocks criterion" for sustainability states that a society is sustainable if its wealth-producing assets per capita are adequate, and are constant or growing. There are two versions. Economists tend to prefer a "weak sustainability" version in which the aggregate dollar value of different forms of capital is maintained. This assumes, among other things, that natural capital and manufactured capital are substitutes and that there is no penalty associated with liquidating natural capital to acquire an equivalent or greater market value of manufactured capital. Ecologists and ecological economists prefer a "strong sustainability" version in which constant, adequate, per capita physical stocks of both natural capital and manufactured capital are maintained in separate accounts. Monetary commensurability is denied on grounds that some forms of natural capital are nonsubstitutable and that their loss would be irreversible and potentially catastrophic.

21. See the discussion on "night soil" in Herbert Girardet, *Cities, People, Planet: Liveable Cities for a Sustainable World* (Chichester, UK: Wiley-Academy, 2004).

22. Note that the guidelines are fully compatible with the well-developed bioregional philosophy of living as much as possible "in place" and could be used as a further argument in support of the contemporary relocalization movement.

CHAPTER 4. A NEW WORLD

1. Andrew Revkin, "Puberty on the Scale of a Planet," *New York Times*, August 7, 2009.

2. Robert Poole, "For the Apollo Astronauts, A Small World," *Los Angeles Times*, July 19, 2009.

3. Rosslyn Beeby, "Warming Fuels Rise in Tropical Storms," *Canberra Times*, December 27, 2008.

4. "NASA Study Links Severe Storm Increases, Global Warming," *Pasadena Star News*, January 23, 2009.

5. Brian K. Sullivan, "California Fire Season Now Year Round in Era of Mega Blazes," *Bloomberg News Service*, November 18, 2008.

6. Jonathan Leake, "Arctic Ice Melting Even in Winter," *Times (London)* online, October 26, 2008.

7. Joseph Romm, "First Commercial Ship Sails Through Northwest Passage," ClimateProgress.org, November 29, 2008, http://climateprogress.org/2008/11/29/.

8. Lisa M. Jarvis, "Kindling for Climate Change," *Chemical and Engineering News* 87, no. 33 (August 17, 2009).

9. Mason Inman, "Arctic Ice in 'Death Spiral,' Is Near Record Low," National Geographic News, September 17, 2008, http://news.nationalgeographic.com/news/.

10. Joseph Romm, "Two Trillion Tons of Land Ice Lost Since 2003, Rate of Greenland Summer Ice Loss Triples 2007 Record," ClimateProgress.org, December 19, 2008, http://climateprogress.org/2008/12/18/greenland-antarctica-ice-loss-sea-level-rise/.

11. "The Curse of Carbon," *Economist*, December 30, 2008.

12. Paul Roberts, *The End of Oil* (Boston: Houghton Mifflin Harcourt, 2004), 125.

13. Steve Connor, "Expanding Tropics 'A Threat to Millions,'" *Independent*, December 3, 2007.

14. Zoological Society of London, "Coral Reefs Exposed to Imminent Destruction from Climate Change," news release, July 6, 2009, http://www.zsl.org/.

15. William Branigin, "Obama Plans to Overhaul Environmental Policies," *Washington Post*, January 26, 2009.

16. Richard Harris, "Global Warming Is Irreversible, Study Says," *All Things Considered*, National Public Radio, January 26, 2009.

17. Jonathan Weisner, "Global Warming Goal Set," *Wall Street Journal*, July 3, 2009.

18. Steve Connor, "Exclusive: Methane Time Bomb," *Independent*, September 23, 2008.

19. Volker Mrasek, "A Storehouse of Greenhouse Gases Is Opening in Siberia," *Spiegel Online*, April 17, 2008.

20. Melissa Block, "Scientist Measures an Overlooked Greenhouse Gas," *All Things Considered*, National Public Radio, September 10, 2007.

21. Fred Pearce, "Arctic Meltdown Is a Threat to Humanity," *New Scientist*, March 25, 2009.

22. "Sinking Feeling: Hot Year Damages Carbon Uptake by Plants," Agence France-Presse, September 17, 2008.

23. David Adam, "Sea Absorbing Less Carbon Dioxide, Scientists Discover," *Guardian*, January 12, 2009.

24. Global Carbon Project, *Carbon Budget and Trends 2007*, September 26, 2008.

CHAPTER 5. THE INTERNATIONAL RESPONSE TO
CLIMATE CHANGE

1. David Adam, "Roll Back Time to Safeguard Climate, Expert Warns," *Guardian*, September 15, 2008.

2. Helene C. Muller-Landau, "Carbon Cycle: Sink in the African Jungle," *Nature* 457 (February 19, 2009), 969–970.

3. The author helped design the cap-and-share approach in 2006.

CHAPTER 6. THE ECOLOGICAL DEFICIT

1. David Archer, *The Long Thaw: How Humans Are Changing the Next 100,000 Years of Earth's Climate* (Princeton: Princeton University Press, 2009), 146–147.

2. Sanford Levinson, *Our Undemocratic Constitution: Where the Constitution Goes Wrong (And How We the People Can Correct It)* (New York: Oxford University Press, 2006), 173; Larry Sabato, *A More Perfect Constitution: 12 Proposals to Revitalize Our Constitution and Make America a Fairer Country* (New York: Walker & Company, 2007), 198–220.

3. Sabato, *A More Perfect Constitution*, 199–200.

4. The U.S. Supreme Court is apparently losing a large share of its international audience who finds its decisions, perhaps, too ideological, aloof, formulaic, and remote from lived reality. See Adam Liptak, "U.S. Court, a Longtime Beacon, Is Now Guiding Fewer Nations," *New York Times*, September 18, 2008.

5. Christopher Stone, *Should Trees Have Standing? And Other Essays on Law, Morals and the Environment* (Los Altos: William Kaufmann, 1974).

6. It is worth studying the similarities between slavery and our use of fossil fuels as a matter of intergenerational law. See, for example, David Orr, "2020: A Proposal," in David Orr, *The Nature of Design: Ecology, Culture, and Human Intention* (New York: Oxford University Press, 2002), 143–151, and Jean-François Mouhot, "Historical and Contemporary Links and Parallels in Slave Ownership and Fossil Fuel Usage," unpublished manuscript, 2008.

7. David Korten, "Only One Reason to Grant a Corporate Charter," speech given at Faneuil Hall, Boston, November 13, 2007, available at http://www.common dreams.org/archive/2007/12/08/5710.

8. Peter Barnes, *Capitalism 3.0: A Guide to Reclaiming the Commons* (San Francisco: Berrett-Koehler, 2006); Peter Barnes et al., "Creating an Earth Atmospheric Trust," *Science* 319, no. 5864 (February 8, 2008), 724.

9. Mark Schaefer et al., "An Earth Systems Science Agency," *Science* 321, no. 5885 (July 4, 2008), 44–45.

10. Robert Ornstein and Paul Ehrlich, *New World, New Mind* (New York: Doubleday, 1989). Ornstein and Ehrlich proposed the creation of a "foresight institute" charged with evaluation of long-term trends and their consequences.

11. Bill McKibben, *Hope, Human and Wild: True Stories of Living Lightly on the Earth* (Boston: Little Brown, 1995).

12. With the leadership of Tony Cortese and his staff at Second Nature, hundreds of colleges and universities, including Oberlin, have responded to the challenge by signing commitments to move toward carbon neutrality and are taking steps to reduce the use of fossil fuels. Reaching the goal of carbon neutrality will be easier where sunlight and hydropower are abundant and more difficult in regions like our own that are highly dependent on coal. In any event, the case for moving rapidly toward levels of energy efficiency that lower carbon emissions includes lower costs as the price of fossil energy rises, resilience in the face of price shocks and supply interruptions, and the moral obligation not to damage the world in which our graduates and our children will live.

CHAPTER 7. WATER

1. Intergovernmental Panel on Climate Change (IPCC), *Climate Change 2007: The Physical Science Basis* (Cambridge, UK: Cambridge University Press, 2007); IPCC, "Summaries for Policymakers," in *Climate Change 2007: Impacts, Adaptation and Vulnerability* (Cambridge, UK: Cambridge University Press, 2007).

2. Tim Pearce, ed., "Natural Disasters Displacing Millions—U.N. Study," Reuters, September 22, 2009; Robert Draper, "Australia's Dry Run," *National Geographic*, April 2009, 35–59; Heather Timmons, "Half a Million Are Stranded by India Flood," *New York Times*, September 1, 2008; Mian Ridge, "India's Farmers Struggle without Crucial Monsoon Rains," *Christian Science Monitor*, August 25, 2009; Paul Rodgers, "Millions Facing Famine in Ethiopia as Rains Fail," *Independent*, August 30, 2009.

3. "Iowa Flood, Midwest Flooding: Videos, Maps, News and Background," Geology.com, June 13, 2008, http://geology.com/events/iowa-flooding/; "Governor Sonny Perdue Prays for Rain in Georgia," WDEF.com, November 14, 2007; Robbie Brown and Liz Robbins, "Rain Stops, but 8 are Dead in Southeast Floods," *New York Times*, September 22, 2009.

4. P. C. D. Milly et al., "Stationarity Is Dead: Whither Water Management?" *Science* 319 (February 1, 2008), 573–574.

5. Ibid., for $500 billion annual global investment figure.

6. Stuart Bunn, presentation at the 94th Annual Meeting of the Ecological Society of America, Albuquerque, NM, August 2–7, 2009; for an excellent narrative on the Australian drought, see Robert Draper, "Australia's Dry Run," *National Geographic*, April 2009, 35–59.

7. Tim Barnett and David Pierce, "When Will Lake Mead Go Dry?" *Water Resources Research* 44 (March 29, 2008).

8. Richard Seager et al., "Model Projections of an Imminent Transition to a More Arid Climate in Southwestern North America," *Science* 316 (May 25, 2007), 1181–1184.

9. Population figures from Population Reference Bureau (PRB), *2009 World Population Data Sheet*, http://www.prb.org/.

10. Just six countries (Brazil, Russia, Canada, Indonesia, China, and Colombia) account for half the water annually flowing back toward the sea in rivers, streams, and underground aquifers—what hydrologists call "runoff"—according to the United Nations Food and Agriculture Organization (FAO), *Review of World Water Resources by Country* (Rome: FAO, 2003).

11. Number of large dams (those at least 15 meters high) from World Commission on Dams, *Dams and Development* (London: Earthscan, 2000); Jamie Pittock et al., "Interbasin Water Transfers and Water Scarcity in a Changing World—A Solution or a Pipedream?" (Frankfurt: World Wildlife Fund Germany, August 2009).

12. Sandra Postel, "Where Have All the Rivers Gone?" *World Watch* 8 (May/June 1995); Fred Pearce, *When the Rivers Run Dry* (Boston: Beacon Press, 2006).

13. Sandra Postel, *Pillar of Sand: Can the Irrigation Miracle Last?* (New York: W. W. Norton, 1999).

14. Matthew Rodell, Isabella Velicogna, and James S. Famiglietti, "Satellite-based Estimates of Groundwater Depletion in India," *Nature* 460 (August 20, 2009).

15. V. L. McGuire, *Ground Water Depletion in the High Plains Aquifer, Predevelopment to 2005*, U.S. Geological Survey Fact Sheet 2007-3029, 2007, http://pubs.er.usgs .gov/; 30 percent figure from USGS, "High Plains Regional Ground Water (HPGW) Study," http://co.water.usgs.gov/nawqa/hpgw/HPGW_home.html.

16. Jamie Pittock et al., "Interbasin Water Transfers and Water Scarcity in a Changing World"; total transfer volume from Ruixiang Zhu, "China's South-North Water Transfer Project and Its Impacts on Economic and Social Development," People's Republic of China Ministry of Water Resources (2008).

17. Kenneth Pomeranz, "The Great Himalayan Watershed: Agrarian Crisis, Mega-Dams and the Environment," *New Left Review* 58 (July/August 2009); estimates of India's irrigated area vary widely depending on the source and estimation method per Prasad S. Thenkabail et al., "Irrigated Area Maps and Statistics of India Using Remote Sensing and National Statistics," *Remote Sensing* 1, no. 2 (April 17, 2009), 50–67.

18. Brian D. Richter, "Lost in Development's Shadow: The Downstream Human Consequences of Dams," World Commission on Dams, forthcoming.

19. Robert Wilkinson, *Methodology for Analysis of the Energy Intensity of California's Water Systems, and an Assessment of Multiple Potential Benefits through Integrated Water-Energy Efficiency Measures*, Environmental Studies Program, University of California, Santa Barbara (2000), 6; QEI, Inc., *Electricity Efficiency through Water Efficiency, Report for the Southern California Edison Company* (Springfield, NJ: 1992), 23–24.

20. Debbie Cook, former mayor of Huntington Beach, CA, has said, "The next worst idea to turning tar sands into synthetic crude is turning ocean water into municipal drinking water," quoted in "Desalination—Energy Down the Drain," The Oil Drum, March 2, 2009, http://www.theoildrum.com/node/5155.

21. Quirin Schiermeier, "Purification with a Pinch of Salt," *Nature* 452, no. 7 (March 20, 2008), 260–261.

22. National Academy of Sciences (NAS), Water Science and Technology Board, *Desalination: A National Perspective* (Washington DC: National Academy Press, 2008); 15,000 figure from Schiermeier, "Purification with a Pinch of Salt."

23. NAS, Water Science and Technology Board, *Desalination*.

24. Sandra Postel, *Liquid Assets: The Critical Need to Safeguard Freshwater Ecosystems*, Worldwatch Paper 170 (Washington DC: Worldwatch Institute, 2005).

25. Sandra Postel and Barton H. Thompson Jr., "Watershed Protection: Capturing the Benefits of Nature's Water Supply Services," *Natural Resources Forum* 29, no. 2 (May 2005), 98–108.

26. Cara Goodman, "South America: Creating Water Funds for People and Nature," The Nature Conservancy, http://www.nature.org/. For more examples and a fuller description of Quito's fund, see Postel, *Liquid Assets*.

27. National Research Council, *Valuing Ecosystem Services: Toward Better Environmental Decision-Making* (Washington DC: National Academy Press, 2005); $366 million figure from David G. Killam, "Sacramento District Project Wins Public Works Project of the Year," Web site of the U.S. Army, February 12, 2009, http://www .army.mil/.

28. Will Hewes and Kristen Pitts, *Natural Security: How Sustainable Water Strategies Are Preparing Communities for a Changing Climate* (Washington DC: American Rivers, 2009).

29. Emily Pilloton, "Chicago Green Roof Program," Inhabitat, August 1, 2006, http://www.inhabitat.com/2006/08/01/chicago-green-roof-program/.

30. Number of 430 dams is from Rebecca Wodder, "Tolling Bells Ushered in Kennebec River's Rebirth," *Kennebec Journal & Morning Sentinel*, June 28, 2009; $65 million figure is from Hewes and Pitts, *Natural Security*; for more on dams and rivers, see Sandra Postel and Brian Richter, *Rivers for Life: Managing Water for People and Nature* (Washington DC: Island Press, 2003).

31. A. Y. Hoekstra and A. K. Chapagain, "Water Footprints of Nations: Water Use by People as a Function of Their Consumption Pattern," *Water Resources Management* 21, no. 1 (2006), 35–48.

32. For this calculation, I assumed that the 1.2 billion people who will join humanity's ranks over the next fifteen years will eat low-meat diets, and I made no allowance for the 850 million people who don't have enough food today or for the increasing dietary water requirements in China and elsewhere as incomes rise; hence it is very conservative.

33. Postel, *Pillar of Sand*; 2025 calculation based on withdrawal estimates in William J. Cosgrove and Frank R. Rijsberman, *World Water Vision: Making Water Everybody's Business* (London: Earthscan, 2000).

34. David Molden, ed., *Water for Food, Water for Life: A Comprehensive Assessment of Water Management in Agriculture* (London: Earthscan and Colombo: International Water Management Institute, 2007).

35. For a fuller description, see Postel, *Pillar of Sand,* chap. 9; useful Web sites include those of the International Water Management Institute, www.iwmi.cgiar.org, which also has many informative publications; for more on rainwater harvesting, see the Web site of the Centre for Science and Environment in Delhi, India, www.cse india.org, especially its site www.rainwaterharvesting.org; for examples of affordable, small-plot irrigation, see especially International Development Enterprises, www .ideorg.org.

36. Dietary water requirement from D. Renault and W. W. Wallender, "Nutritional Water Productivity and Diets," *Agricultural Water Management* 45 (2000), 275–296; calculation assumes average annual dietary water requirement drops from 1,971 cubic meters per person to 1,242; U.S. 2025 population of 358.7 million is the medium variant estimate of the Population Division of the Department of Economic and Social Affairs of the United Nations, *World Population Prospects: The 2008 Revision*, http://esa.un.org/unpp.

37. Analysis of grain import dependence based on data from U.S. Department of Agriculture, Foreign Agricultural Service, "Production, Supply and Distribution Online," http://www.fas.usda.gov/psdonline.

38. Jing Ma et al., "Virtual versus Real Water Transfers within China," *Philosophical Transactions of the Royal Society B* 361 (2006) 835–842.

39. Postel, *Pillar of Sand*; Sandra Postel, "But Who Will Export Tomorrow's Virtual Water?" in *The Truth about Water Wars*, SEED, May 14, 2009, http://seedmagazine .com/.

40. Sandra Postel and Amy Vickers, "Boosting Water Productivity," *State of the World 2004* (Washington DC: Worldwatch Institute, 2004), 46–65; Unilever example from *Sustainable Development Report 2007: Environmental Sustainability* (Unilever, 2007).

41. For conservation methods and examples, see Amy Vickers, *Handbook of Water Use and Conservation: Homes, Landscapes, Businesses, Industries, Farms* (Amherst, MA: WaterPlow Press, 2001); Boston example from Sandra Postel, *Liquid Assets*, and Sandra Postel, "Lessons from the Field—Boston Conservation," *National Geographic* Web site, March, 2010, http://environment.nationalgeographic.com/environment/freshwater/lessons-boston-conservation/.

42. Cristina Milesi et al., "Mapping and Modeling the Biogeochemical Cycling of Turf Grasses in the United States," *Environmental Management* 36 (September 2005), 426–438; Dara Colwell, "Our Love Affair with Our Lawns Is Hurling the U.S. toward Water Crisis," AlterNet, October 2, 2009, http://www.alternet.org/; Las Vegas figures from Robert Glennon, *Unquenchable: America's Water Crisis and What to Do about It* (Washington DC: Island Press, 2009).

43. Personal e-mail communication with Katherine M. Yuhas, water conservation officer, Albuquerque Bernalillo County Water Authority, Albuquerque, NM, October 12–13, 2009. Between 1995 and 2008, Albuquerque's total water production declined from 40.775 billion gallons to 32.247 billion gallons, while the population served increased from 445,167 to 559,828.

44. iStaq example from Matthew Power, "Peak Water: Aquifers and Rivers Are Running Dry: How Three Regions Are Coping," *Wired* 16, no. 5 (April 21, 2008); "iPhone App Offers Remote Water Sensing for Farmers," *New York Times*, June 30, 2009; see the Web site for Question Box, http://questionbox.org, and Ron Nixon, "Dialing for Answers Where Web Can't Reach," *New York Times*, September 28, 2009.

45. Jamie Pittock et al., "Interbasin Water Transfers and Water Scarcity in a Changing World."

46. For more examples, see Sandra Postel and Barton H. Thompson Jr., "Watershed Protection: Capturing the Benefits of Nature's Water Supply Services," *Natural Resources Forum* 29 (May 2005), 98–108.

47. Edwards Aquifer Authority Web site, www.edwardsaquifer.org; water use from San Antonio Water System, *2008 Annual Report*.

48. U.S. Congress, Energy Independence and Security Act of 2007, 110th Congress, 1st session, 2007.

49. R. Dominguez-Faus et al., "The Water Footprint of Biofuels: A Drink or Drive Issue?" *Environmental Science & Technology* 43 (May 1, 2009), 3005–3010.

50. Todd Woody, "Alternative Energy Projects Stumble on a Need for Water," *New York Times*, September 30, 2009.

CHAPTER 8. PEAK NATURE?

1. Lynn Margulis and Dorion Sagan, *What Is Life?* (New York: Simon & Schuster, 1995), 56.

2. Michael Rosenzweig, *Win-Win Ecology: How the Earth's Species Can Survive in the Midst of Human Enterprise* (New York: Oxford University Press, 2003), 130.

3. Joe Roman et al., "Facing Extinction: Nine Steps to Save Biodiversity," Solutions, February 24, 2009, http://www.thesolutionsjournal.com.

4. Michael E. Soule and Gordon H. Orians, eds., *Conservation Biology: Research Priorities for the Next Decade* (Washington DC: Island Press, 2001), 3.

5. Lynn Margulis, *The Symbiotic Planet: A New Look at Evolution* (New York: Basic Books, 1998), 120.

6. G. Tyler Miller Jr. and Richard Brewer, *Living in the Environment*, 15th ed. (Belmont, CA: Wadsworth Publishing, 1988), 293.

7. Scott Hoffman Black and Matthew Shepard, "Small Animals that Pack a Big Punch," *Wings* 31, no. 2 (fall 2008), 4, available at http://www.xerces.org/wings-archive/.

8. Black and Shepard, "Small Animals that Pack a Big Punch," 7.

9. Stephen L. Buchmann and Gary Paul Nabhan, *The Forgotten Pollinators* (Washington DC: Island Press, 1996), 49–51.

10. Jerry Melillo and Osvaldo Sala, "Ecosystem Services," in *Sustaining Life: How Human Health Depends on Biodiversity*, Eric Chivian and Aaron Bernstein, eds. (New York: Oxford University Press, 2008), 75.

11. Jane Goodall, *Hope for Animals and Their World: How Endangered Species Are Being Rescued from the Brink* (New York: Grand Central Publishing, 2009), 98–99.

12. Melillo and Sala, "Ecosystem Services," 106.

13. "Chickadee, Nuthatch Presence in Conifers Increases Tree Growth," News Centre, University of Colorado at Boulder, August 1, 2007, http://www.sciencecentric.com/news/article.php?q=07080102.

14. Daniel Hillel and Cynthia Rosenzweig, "Biodiversity and Food Production," in *Sustaining Life: How Human Health Depends on Biodiversity*, Eric Chivian and Aaron Bernstein, eds. (New York: Oxford University Press, 2008), 330.

15. David H. Molyneux et al., "Ecosystem Disturbance, Biodiversity Loss, and Human Infectious Disease" in *Sustaining Life: How Human Health Depends on Biodiversity*, Eric Chivian and Aaron Bernstein, eds. (New York: Oxford University Press, 2008), 293–294.

16. Hillel and Rosenzweig, "Biodiversity and Food Production," 347–348.

17. Bruce Pavlik, *The California Deserts: An Ecological Rediscovery* (Berkeley: University of California Press, 2008), 91.

18. United Nations Millennium Ecosystem Assessment, *Ecosystems and Human Well-Being: Biodiversity Synthesis* (Washington DC: World Resources Institute, 2005), 11–12.

19. Ann Vileisis, *Discovering the Unknown Landscape: A History of America's Wetlands* (Washington DC: Island Press, 1997), 316; United Nations Millennium Ecosystem Assessment, *Ecosystems and Human Well-Being*, quoted in Viqi Wagner, ed., *Endangered Species*, Opposing Viewpoints Series (Detroit: Greenhaven Press/Thomson Gale, 2008), 45.

20. Melillo and Sala, "Ecosystem Services," 92.

21. Brian Tissot, "The Importance of Deep-Sea Coral Communities," *Wings* 32, no. 1 (spring 2009), 24, available at http://www.xerces.org/wings-archive/.

22. Severin Carrel, "Ocean Acidification Rates Pose Disaster for Marine Life, Major Study Shows," *Guardian*, December 10, 2009.

23. Scripps Insitute of Oceanography, "Beyond the Obituaries: Successful Fish Stories in Ocean Conservation," Scripps News, February 13, 2009, http://scrippsnews.ucsd.edu/Releases/?releaseID=961.

24. United Nations Millennium Ecosystem Assessment, *Ecosystems and Human Well-Being*, 70.

25. Wagner, ed., *Endangered Species*, 17.

26. Stuart L. Pimm et al., "What Is Biodiversity?" in *Sustaining Life: How Human Health Depends on Biodiversity*, Eric Chivian and Aaron Bernstein, eds. (New York: Oxford University Press, 2008), 23.

27. Anthony D. Barnosky, *Heatstroke: Nature in an Age of Global Warming* (Washington DC: Island Press/Shearwater Books, 2009), 42–43.

28. T. Edward Nickens, "Paper Chase," Audubon Magazine Web Exclusive, January–February 2009, http://www.audubonmagazine.org/.

29. Jeffrey A. McNeely, Eleanor Sterling, and Kalemani Jo Mulongoy, "What Individuals Can Do to Help Conserve Biodiversity," in *Sustaining Life: How Human Health Depends on Biodiversity*, Eric Chivian and Aaron Bernstein, eds. (New York: Oxford University Press, 2008), 407–424.

30. Alan Weisman, *The World Without Us* (New York: St. Martin's Press, 2007), 115–116.

31. Fatal Light Awareness Program, "Make Windows Safe for Birds," http://www.flap.org/flap_home.html.

32. United Nations, *Principle 15 of the Rio Declaration*, United Nations Conference on Environment and Development (the "Earth Summit"), 1992.

33. Elizabeth Kolbert, "The Sixth Extinction?" *New Yorker*, May 25, 2009, 59–60.

34. Wagner, ed., *Endangered Species*, 14.

35. Ibid., 16.

36. Ibid., 14.

37. Soule and Orians, eds., *Conservation Biology*, 3.

38. Yvonne Baskin, *A Plague of Rats and Rubbervines: The Growing Threat of Species Extinctions* (Washington DC: Island Press/Shearwater Books, 2002), 78.

39. United Nations Millennium Ecosystem Assessment, *Ecosystems and Human Well-Being,* 3.

40. Ibid., 64–67.

41. John M. Randall and Janet Marinelli, eds., *Invasive Plants: Weeds of the Global Garden* (Brooklyn, NY: Brooklyn Botanic Garden, 1996), 9–10.

42. Baskin, *A Plague of Rats and Rubbervines*, 103.

43. Michael Soule, "Nature's Aspirin: A Cure for Many of Nature's Ills," speech given at the Western Conservation Summit, January 2009, available at http://www.michaelsoule.com/.

44. Barnosky, *Heatstroke*, 54–55.

45. Ibid., 199.

46. Soule, "Nature's Aspirin."

47. Ibid.

48. Caroline Fraser, *Rewilding the World: Dispatches from the Conservation Revolution* (New York: Metropolitan Books/Henry Holt, 2009), 48.

49. Edward O. Wilson, *The Future of Life* (New York: Alfred A. Knopf, 2002), 160–164.

50. Roman et al., "Facing Extinction."

51. Cor Kwant, "The Gingko Pages: History," http://www.xs4all.nl/~kwanten/history.htm; Eric Chivian and Aaron Bernstein, "Threatened Groups of Organisms Valuable to Medicine," in *Sustaining Life: How Human Health Depends on Biodiversity*, Eric Chivian and Aaron Bernstein, eds. (New York: Oxford University Press, 2008), 249.

52. Weisman, *The World Without Us*, 184–186.

53. Fraser, *Rewilding the World*, 98.

54. Craig Childs, "The Memory of Water: Life in Ephemeral Water Holes," *Wings* 32, no. 1 (spring 2009), 4, available at http://www.xerces.org/wings-archive/.

55. Richard Louv, "A Walk in the Woods: Right or Privilege?" *Orion* 28, no. 2 (March–April 2009), 70.

56. Daniel Imhoff, *Farming with the Wild: Enhancing Biodiversity on Farms and Ranches* (San Francisco: Sierra Club Books, 2003), 21–25.

57. Fraser, *Rewilding the World*, 283.

CHAPTER 9. GETTING FOSSIL FUELS OFF THE PLATE

1. Karl Finison, *Energy Flow on a Nineteenth Century Farm,* Anthropology Research Report 18 (Amherst: University of Massachusetts, 1979).

2. Between 1845 and 1905 primary energy consumption in the United States increased from 1.8 quadrillion to 13 quadrillion Btu, and the nonrenewable proportion of this energy increased from zero to 83 percent. Energy Information Administration, table E1, "Estimated Primary Energy Consumption in the United States, 1635–1945," *Annual Energy Review 2008.* Machines first outworked animals in 1870; by 1900 machines were doing 3.4 times as much useful work as animals. See R. U. Ayres, L. W. Ayres, and B. Warr, "Exergy, Power and Work in the US Economy, 1900–1998," *Energy* 2 (March 2003), 219–273.

3. Martin C. Heller and Gregory A. Keoleian, *Life Cycle-Based Sustainability Indicators for Assessment of the U.S. Food System,* Center for Sustainable Systems Report CSS00-04 (Ann Arbor: University of Michigan, 2000).

4. Annika Carlsson-Kanyama, Marianne Pipping Ekstrom, and Helena Shanahan, "Food and Life Cycle Energy Inputs: Consequences of Diet and Ways to Increase Efficiency," *Ecological Economics* 44, no. 2 (March 2003), 293–307.

5. Heller and Keoleian, *Life Cycle-Based Sustainability Indicators for Assessment of the U.S. Food System.*

6. J. D. Wood et al., "Effects of Fatty Acids on Meat Quality: A Review," *Meat Science* 66, no. 1 (January 2004), 21–32.

7. Carlsson-Kanyama et al., "Food and Life Cycle Energy Inputs."

8. H. Kim, D. Y. Kwon, and S. H. Yoon, "Induction of Phenolics and Terpenoids in Edible Plants Using Plant Stress Responses," in *Biocatalysis and Agricultural Biotechnology,* Ching T. Hou and Jei-Fu Shaw, eds. (Boca Raton, FL: CRC Press, 2009).

9. G. Tong, D. M. Christopher, and B. Li, "Numerical Modeling of Temperature Variations in a Chinese Solar Greenhouse," *Computers and Electronics in Agriculture* 68, no. 1 (August 2009), 129–139.

10. A Ford Explorer uses almost a third of a gallon of gasoline to drive four miles in the city (see U.S. Department of Energy/Environmental Protection Agency, www.fueleconomy.gov), consuming about 36 megajoules of fossil energy—enough to carry two pounds of bananas around the world eight times on a full container ship. International Maritime Organization, "International Shipping: Carrier of World Trade," 2005, http://www.imo.org/includes/blastDataOnly.asp/data_id%3D13168/background paper%28E%29.pdf. A Toyota Prius can make the four-mile trip using 0.08 gallon of gasoline, which still contains enough energy for those bananas to circle the world twice.

11. Christopher L. Weber and H. Scott Matthews, "Food-Miles and the Relative Climate Impacts of Food Choices in the United States," *Environmental Science and Technology* 42, no. 10 (2008), 3508–3513.

12. "Designs," Vertical Farm Project, 2009, http://www.verticalfarm.com/designs.html.

13. Heller and Keoleian, *Life Cycle-Based Sustainability Indicators for Assessment of the U.S. Food System.*

14. Horace Herring and Richard York, "Jevons Paradox," Encyclopedia of Earth, October 8, 2006, http://www.eoearth.org/article/Jevons_paradox.

CHAPTER 10. TACKLING THE OLDEST ENVIRONMENTAL PROBLEM

1. United Nations Millennium Ecosystem Assessment, *Ecosystems and Human Well-Being: Biodiversity Synthesis* (Washington DC: World Resources Institute, 2005).

CHAPTER 12. POPULATION

1. United Nations Children's Fund, *The State of the World's Children*, 2009, http://www.unicef.org/rightsite/sowc/.

2. While birth rates and death rates were both high in these countries, they were at the same level, so population growth rates were zero or close to zero.

3. David Pimentel et al., "Will Limits of the Earth's Resources Control Human Numbers?" *Environment, Development and Sustainability* 1, no. 1 (March 1999), 19–39.

4. Ibid.; Peter Goodchild, "The Century of Famine," Culture Change, March 2, 2010, http://culturechange.org/cms/index.php?option=com_content&task=view&id=610&Itemid=1.

5. Union of Concerned Scientists, *World Scientists' Warning to Humanity*, 1992, http://www.ucsusa.org/about/1992-world-scientists.html.

6. "Science Summit on World Population: A Joint Statement by 58 of the World's Scientific Academies," *Population and Development Review* 20, no. 1 (March 1994), 233–238, available at http://www.prosperityagenda.us/node/3116.

7. Paul A. Murtaugh and Michael G. Schlax, "Reproduction and the Carbon Legacies of Individuals," *Global Environmental Change* 19 (2009), 14–20.

8. Frederick A. B. Meyerson, "Population Growth Is Easier to Manage than Per-Capita Emissions," Population and Climate roundtable discussion held by the *Bulletin of the Atomic Scientists*, January 17, 2008, http://www.thebulletin.org/web-edition/roundtables/population-and-climate-change.

9. John P. Holdren, "Population and the American Predicament: The Case against Complacency," *Daedalus* 102, no. 4 (fall 1973), 31–43. Full text at http://www.npg.org/notable%20papers/JohnPHoldrenpaper.html.

10. Lester Brown, Gary Gardner, and Brian Halweil, *Beyond Malthus: 19 Dimensions of the Population Challenge* (New York: W. W. Norton, 1999).

11. Ansley J. Coale, "Population and Economic Development," in *The Population Dilemma*, Philip M. Hauser, ed. (Englewood Cliffs, NJ: Prentice-Hall, 1963), 46–69.

12. Bruce Sundquist, "The Controversy over U.S. Support for International Fam-

ily Planning: An Analysis," at The Earth's Carrying Capacity: Some Related Reviews and Analyses, http://home.windstream.net/bsundquist1/ (accessed November 2005).

13. See Demographic Health Surveys, http://www.measuredhs.com/countries/.

14. Virginia Abernethy, "The Demographic Transition Revisited: Lessons for Foreign Aid and US Immigration Policy," in *People and Their Planet: Searching for Balance,* Barbara Sundberg Baudot and William R. Moomaw, eds. (New York: St. Martin's Press, 1999).

15. Lant H. Pritchett, "Desired Fertility and the Impact of Population Policies," *Population and Development Review* 20, no. 1 (March 1994), 1–55.

16. United Nations Population Fund, "Reproductive Health: Ensuring that Every Pregnancy Is Wanted," http://www.unfpa.org/rh/planning.htm.

17. Ndola Prata, "The Need for Family Planning," *Population and Environment* 28, nos. 4–5 (May 2007), 213–214.

18. Ibid. In Bangladesh there was a 51 percent prevalence of contraception use among people with no education and 59 percent prevalence among those who received secondary education, whereas in the Philippines these figures were 11 percent and 58 percent, respectively.

19. Heidi Noel Nariman, *Soap Operas for Social Change: Toward a Methodology for Entertainment-Education Television* (Westport, CT: Praeger Publishers, 1993).

20. Institute for Communication Research A.C. (Televisa), "Towards the Social Use of Commercial Television: Mexico's Experience with the Reinforcement of Social Values through TV Soap Operas," paper presented at the annual conference of the International Institute of Communications, Strasbourg, France, September 1981, 51.

21. Everett M. Rogers et al., "Effects of an Entertainment-Education Radio Soap Opera on Family Planning Behavior in Tanzania," *Studies in Family Planning* 30, no. 3 (1999), 193–211.

22. Jeffrey D. Sachs, *Commonwealth: Economics for a Crowded Planet* (New York: Penguin, 2008), 188.

23. For a full proposal outlining these positions, see William N. Ryerson, "Concept Paper for an Office of Special Assistant to the President for Population and Sustainability Issues in the White House," available at Population Media Center, February 9, 2009, http://www.populationmedia.org/2009/02/09/my-revised-idea -for-the-new-administration/.

CHAPTER 13. DANGEROUSLY ADDICTIVE

1. Horatio Alger Jr. (1834–1899) was a prolific author of "rags-to-riches" adventure stories for boys.

2. El Dorado, "the golden one" (Spanish), was the legendary City of Gold sought by Spanish conquistadors in their conquest of the Americas in the sixteenth century.

CHAPTER 15. THE HUMAN NATURE OF UNSUSTAINABILITY

1. Union of Concerned Scientists, *World Scientists' Warning to Humanity*, 1992, http://www.ucsusa.org/about/1992-world-scientists.html.

2. Millennium Ecosystem Assessment, *Living Beyond Our Means: Natural Assets and*

Human Well-Being, statement from the board, March 2005, http://www.millennium assessment.org/en/BoardStatement.aspx.

3. W. E. Rees, "The Ecological Crisis and Self-Delusion: Implications for the Building Sector," *Building Research and Information* 37, no. 3 (2009), 300–311.

4. Andrew Nikiforuk, "At War with Our Planet," review of *The Weather Makers: How We Are Changing the Climate and What It Means for Life on Earth*, by Tim Flannery, *Globe and Mail*, March 4, 2006.

5. Theodosius Dobzhansky, "Biology, Molecular and Organismic," *American Zoologist* 4 (1964), 449.

6. W. E. Rees, "Are Humans Unsustainable by Nature?" Trudeau Lecture, Memorial University of Newfoundland, St. Johns, Newfoundland, January 28, 2009.

7. The argument may be stated from a system-dynamics perspective in this way: "Unsustainability is an inevitable 'emergent property' of the systemic interaction between contemporary techno-industrial society and the ecosphere. Contributing factors include both genetically-programmed behavioral strategies that heretofore assured human survival and contemporary socio-economic norms that reinforce these now-negative attributes" (Rees, "Are Humans Unsustainable by Nature?").

8. E. R. Pianka, "On 'r' and 'K' selection," *American Naturalist* 104 (1970), 592–597; E. G. Matthews and R. L. Kitching, *Insect Ecology* (Brisbane: University of Queensland Press, 1984).

9. Within-group (e.g., family, tribe, or nation) cooperative behavior increases between-group competitive success.

10. C. W. Fowler and L. Hobbs, "Is Humanity Sustainable?" *Proceedings of the Royal Society of London, Series B: Biological Sciences* 270 (2003), 2579–2583.

11. Rees, "Are Humans Unsustainable by Nature?" This is no small irony. Many economists and other technological optimists argue falsely from monetary analyses that the ecological crisis may ease because the human enterprise is "dematerializing" and "decoupling" from nature.

12. Richard G. Wilkinson, *Unhealthy Societies: The Afflictions of Inequality* (London and New York: Routledge, 1996).

13. People not only deplete *real* resources, but also create *virtual* resources—bank loans and credit cards, for example—and use these to capacity as well.

14. Richard Dawkins, *The Selfish Gene* (Oxford: Oxford University Press, 1976).

15. W. E. Rees, "Globalization and Sustainability: Conflict or Convergence?" *Bulletin of Science, Technology and Society* 22, no. 4 (2002), 249–268.

16. There is actually a second layer of nature-nurture interaction in play here. Humans are natural storytellers, genetically predisposed to myth making. The social construction of (perceived) reality, including disciplinary paradigms, political ideologies, and cultural myths, is a universal property of human societies (C. Grant, *Myths We Live By* [Ottawa: University of Ottawa Press, 1998]). The key point is that while the tendency to mythologize is yet another vessel cast from our genes, what we put into it is determined by sociocultural context.

17. H. W. Arndt, *The Rise and Fall of Economic Growth* (Sydney: Longman Cheshire, 1978), cited in Peter A. Victor, *Managing without Growth: Slower by Design, Not Disaster* (Cheltenham: Edward Elgar, 2008), 13.

18. Herman E. Daly, "The Circular Flow of Exchange Value and the Linear Throughput of Matter-Energy: A Case of Misplaced Concreteness," in Herman Daly,

Steady-State Economics, 2nd edition with new essays (Washington DC: Island Press, 1991), 195–210.

19. E.g., Julian Simon, "The State of Humanity: Steadily Improving," *Cato Policy Report* (September/October 1995), available at http://www.cato.org/pubs/policy _report/pr-so-js.html.

20. W. E. Rees, "Ecological Footprints and Bio-Capacity: Essential Elements in Sustainability Assessment," in *Renewables-Based Technology: Sustainability Assessment,* Jo Dewulf and Herman Van Langenhove, eds. (Chichester, UK: John Wiley & Sons, 2006), 143–158; Mathis Wackernagel and W. E. Rees, *Our Ecological Footprint: Reducing Human Impact on the Earth* (Gabriola Island, BC: New Society, 1996); World Wildlife Fund, *Living Planet Report 2008* (Gland, Switzerland: WWF–World Wide Fund for Nature, 2008).

21. To facilitate comparisons among regions with different eco-productivities, ecological footprints are converted to "standardized" hectares of world average productivity known as global average hectares (gha).

22. World Wildlife Fund, *Living Planet Report 2008.*

23. Ibid.

24. Cited in Mark Buchanan, "What Made You Read This?" *New Scientist* 195, no. 2611 (2007), 36–39.

25. Paul D. MacLean, *The Triune Brain in Evolution: Role in Paleocerebral Functions* (New York: Plenum, 1990).

26. Antonio Damasio, *Descartes' Error: Emotion, Reason and the Human Brain* (New York: Avon Books, 1994), 192.

27. Ibid., 123.

28. Robert E. Lane, *The Loss of Happiness in Market Democracies* (New Haven: Yale University Press, 2000); Preservation Institute, *The End of Economic Growth*, Charles Siegel, Preservation Institute Policy Study (2006), available at http://www.preserve net.com/endgrowth/; Victor, *Managing without Growth.*

29. Ernst von Weizsäcker, Amory B. Lovins, and L. Hunter Lovins, *Factor Four: Doubling Wealth, Halving Resource Use: A Report to the Club of Rome* (London: Earthscan /James & James, 1997).

30. There is a counterargument for all-out conflict. Some people will survive any human-induced apocalypse, most likely the richest and most militarily powerful. In these circumstances, the ancient intelligence of the reptilian complex and limbic system wins out once again (but it wouldn't be a pretty sight).

31. Brian E. Wexler, *Brain and Culture: Neurobiology, Ideology and Social Change*, Bradford Books (Cambridge: MIT Press, 2006), 180.

32. Damasio, *Descartes' Error*, 121.

33. Wexler, *Brain and Culture.*

CHAPTER 16. MAKING SENSE OF PEAK OIL AND ENERGY UNCERTAINTY

1. Global *discoveries* of conventional oil peaked in the 1960s and are uniformly expected to continue declining; thus the future of conventional-oil *production* is relatively straightforward to forecast. Indeed, practically all analysts (including the major

oil companies) agree that conventional-oil production will be in permanent decline by 2015 at the latest.

2. Terry Macalister, "US Military Warns Oil Output May Dip Causing Massive Shortages by 2015," *Guardian*, April 11, 2010; Richard Heinberg, "Quacks Like a Duck," March 29, 2010, http://www.postcarbon.org/blog-post/85699-quacks-like-a-duck; UK Industry Taskforce on Peak Oil & Energy Security, "The Oil Crunch: Securing the UK's Energy Future," October 2008, http://www.peakoiltaskforce.net.

3. For an in-depth exploration of the net-energy constraints of both renewable and nonrenewable fuels, see Richard Heinberg, *Searching for a Miracle: "Net Energy" Limits & the Fate of Industrial Society* (San Francisco: International Forum on Globalization, 2009).

4. Robert Hirsch et al., "Peaking of World Oil Production: Impacts, Mitigation, & Risk Management" (Washington DC: U.S. Department of Energy, 2005), 4.

5. Andrew Farrell, "Ethanol Demand Burns Meat Producers," *Forbes*, March 9, 2007.

6. See "The HPL Timeline of Airline Bankruptcies, Mergers, Acquisitions, and Fiascos" in Howard Lichtman, "The Crash of Commercial Aviation and Telepresence," September 8, 2008, http://www.telepresenceoptions.com/2008/09/the_collapse_of_commercial_avi/.

7. Hirsch et al., "Peaking of World Oil Production," 5.

8. Numerous books and studies describe these market-limiting factors; one recent summary is Phil Hart and Chris Skrebowski, "Peak Oil: A Detailed and Transparent Analysis," Energy Bulletin, May 30, 2007, http://www.energybulletin.net/node/30537. For discussion on the more recent development of price constraints on oil production, see Richard Heinberg, "Goldilocks and the Three Fuels," Reuters Environment Forum, February 18, 2010, http://blogs.reuters.com/environment/2010/02/18/goldilocks-and-the-three-fuels/.

CHAPTER 17. HYDROCARBONS IN NORTH AMERICA

1. Calculations from data provided in U.S. Energy Information Administration (EIA), *International Energy Outlook 2009*, May 27, 2009, http://www.eia.doe.gov/oiaf/ieo. Other statistics in this paragraph derived from data at this source.

2. A major portion of the renewable energy sector is large hydropower, which by some definitions is nonrenewable in the longer term, and certainly is not without its environmental impacts.

3. U.S. Energy Information Administration, *International Energy Outlook 2009*; International Energy Agency (IEA), *World Energy Outlook 2009*, http://www.iea.org/weo/2009.asp.

4. Data from spreadsheet available with BP's *Statistical Review of World Energy 2009*, June 2009, http://www.bp.com/productlanding.do?categoryId=6929&contentId=7044622.

5. U.S. Geological Survey, "3 to 4.3 Billion Barrels of Technically Recoverable Oil Assessed in North Dakota and Montana's Bakken Formation—25 Times More than 1995 Estimate," press release, April 10, 2008, http://www.usgs.gov/newsroom/article.asp?ID=1911.

6. A. K. Gupta, M. C. Herweyer, and C. A. S. Hall, "Appendix E: Oil Shale:

Potential, EROI and Social and Environmental Impacts," The Oil Drum, April 15, 2008, http://www.theoildrum.com/node/3839.

7. David Luhnow, "Mexico's Fading Oil Output Squeezes Exports, Spending," OilOnline, September 16, 2009, http://www.oilonline.com/News/NewsArticles/ctl/ArticleView/mid/517/articleId/22144/categoryId/16/Mexicos-fading-oil-output-squeezes-exports-spending.aspx.

8. Canada is also an oil importer, as its east coast provinces are highly dependent on offshore oil. This makes Canada a relatively small net exporter of about 1 million barrels per day.

9. Canada National Energy Board, "Continuing Trends," chap. 4 in *Canada's Energy Future: Reference Case and Scenarios to 2030*, http://www.neb.gc.ca/clf-nsi/rnrgyn fmtn/nrgyrprt/nrgyftr/2007/nrgyftr2007chptr4-eng.html#s4_5 (accessed November 2007).

10. Canada National Energy Board, *2009 Reference Case Scenario: Canadian Energy Demand and Supply to 2020*, July 2009, http://www.neb.gc.ca/clf-nsi/rnrgynfmtn/nrgyrprt/nrgyftr/2009/rfrnccsscnr2009-eng.pdf.

11. Canadian Association of Petroleum Producers (CAPP), *Crude Oil: Forecast, Markets and Pipeline Expansions*, June 2009, http://www.capp.ca/getdoc.aspx?DocId=152951&DT=NTV.

12. Kjell Aleklett, "Comments on Guardian Article: 'Key Oil Figures Were Distorted by US Pressure, Says Whistleblower,'" Energy Bulletin, November 10, 2009, http://www.energybulletin.net/50662.

13. The 32 percent decline rate for natural gas is found in the chart "US Natural Gas Production History," prepared by EOG Resources, Inc. from IHS Energy data; see slide 3 of the PowerPoint presentation "Washington Energy Information Meetings," American Exploration and Production Council, July 11, 2007, http://www.dpcusa.org/natural/ppt/070711.ppt.

14. Shannon Nome and Patrick Johnson, *From Shale to Shining Shale: A Primer on North American Natural Gas Plays*, Deutsche Bank, July 22, 2008.

15. J. David Hughes, "The Energy Sustainability Dilemma: Powering the Future in a Finite World," public lecture given in Ottawa, Ontario, September 10, 2009, http://www.aspocanada.ca/images/stories/pdfs/ottawa_sept_10_2009.pdf.

16. America's Natural Gas Alliance, http://www.anga.us/; American Clean Skies Foundation, http://www.cleanskies.org/index.html.

17. Aubrey McClendon's testimony to the U.S. Congress, Select Committee on Energy Independence and Global Warming, July 30, 2008, http://www.globalwarm ing.house.gov/tools/2q08materials/files/0125.pdf.

18. Pickens Plan, http://www.pickensplan.com/act/.

19. Scott Simpson, "Kitimat LNG Pipeline Takes Another Step Forward," *Vancouver Sun*, April 9, 2009, available at http://www.pacifictrailpipelines.com/sites/ptp/files/VanSun_KLNG_Apr09.pdf; proposed British Columbia West Coast liquefaction terminal, "Project Description," Kitimat LNG Terminal, http://www.kitimatlng.com/code/navigate.asp?Id=10.

20. Nome and Johnson, *From Shale to Shining Shale*.

21. Arthur Berman, "Lessons from the Barnett Shale Suggest Caution in Other Shale Plays," commentary, Association for the Study of Peak Oil and Gas–USA, August 10, 2009, http://www.aspousa.org/index.php/2009/08/lessons-from-the-barnett-shale-suggest-caution-in-other-shale-plays/.

22. Arthur Berman, "World Oil Editor Fired Over Oil Shale Columns," Petroleum Truth Report, November 5, 2009, http://petroleumtruthreport.blogspot.com/2009/11/world-oil-editor-fired-over-shale.html.

23. Ohio Valley Environmental Coalition, "High Resolution Mountaintop Removal Pictures," http://www.ohvec.org/galleries/mountaintop_removal/007/.

24. Richard Heinberg, *Blackout: Coal, Climate and the Last Energy Crisis* (Gabriola Island, BC: New Society, 2009).

25. Leslie Glustrom, *Coal: Cheap and Abundant: Or Is It? Why Americans Should Stop Assuming that the US Has a 200-Year Supply of Coal*, February 2009, lglustrom@gmail.com.

26. U.S. Energy Information Administration, *Annual Energy Outlook 2010 Early Release with Projections to 2035*, DOE/EIA-0383(2010), December 14, 2009, http://www.eia.doe.gov/oiaf/aeo/index.html.

27. Massachusetts Institute of Technology, *The Future of Coal: Options for a Carbon-Constrained World* (Boston: Massachusetts Institute of Technology, 2007), http://web.mit.edu/coal/The_Future_of_Coal.pdf.

CHAPTER 18. NINE CHALLENGES OF ALTERNATIVE ENERGY

1. Canadian Association of Petroleum Producers, *Crude Oil: Forecast, Markets & Pipeline Expansions*, June 2009, http://www.capp.ca/.

2. International Energy Association, *World Energy Outlook 2008*, http://www.worldenergyoutlook.org/.

3. Bengt Söderberg et al., "A Crash Program Scenario for the Canadian Oil Sands Industry," *Energy Policy* 35, no. 3 (March 2007), 1931–1947.

4. U.S. Energy Information Administration, *Annual Energy Outlook 2008 (First Release)*, DOE/EIA-0383 (2008), January 2008. Note that subsequent revisions of *Annual Energy Outlook 2008* changed the cited figures for gasoline demand.

5. Robert L. Hirsch, Roger Bezdek, and Robert Wendling, *Peaking of World Oil Production: Impacts, Mitigation, & Risk Management,* U.S. Department of Energy report, February 2005, http://www.netl.doe.gov/publications/others/pdf/oil_peaking_netl.pdf.

6. John Whims, "Pipeline Considerations for Ethanol," Agricultural Marketing Resource Center, http://www.agmrc.org/media/cms/ksupipelineethl_8BA5CDF1FD179.pdf.

7. David Cohen, "Earth's Natural Wealth: An Audit," *New Scientist* 23 (May 2007), 34–41.

8. A megajoule equals 239 food calories; a typical adult male requires 10 MJ of food energy per day.

9. As coined by user HeIsSoFly, comment on "Drumbeat," The Oil Drum, March 7, 2007, http://www.theoildrum.com/node/2344.

10. For a more in-depth discussion of energy return on investment, see Richard Heinberg, *Searching for a Miracle: "Net Energy" Limits & the Fate of Industrial Society* (San Francisco: Post Carbon Institute/International Forum on Globalization, 2009). Note that EROI is sometimes also referred to as "energy returned on energy invested" (EROEI).

11. Charles A. S. Hall, Robert Powers, and William Schoenberg, "Peak Oil, EROI, Investments and the Economy in an Uncertain Future," in *Biofuels, Solar and*

Wind as Renewable Energy Systems: Benefits and Risks, David Pimentel, ed. (New York: Springer, 2008), 109–132.

12. The often-cited 8:1 return on Brazilian ethanol and the high return estimated for cellulosic ethanol are not energy calculations; in these studies, the energy provided from biomass combustion is ignored. See, for example, Suani Teixeira Coelho et al., "Brazilian Sugarcane Ethanol: Lessons Learned," *Energy for Sustainable Development* 10, no. 2 (June 2006), 26–39.

CHAPTER 19. PEAK OIL AND THE GREAT RECESSION

1. Throughout this chapter, oil-production statistics should be understood to include both what is known as "conventional oil" (e.g., light crude) and "unconventional oil" (i.e., tar sands, shale oil, natural gas liquids, heavy crude, etc.).

2. Two of the most important of these organizations were the Association for the Study of Peak Oil, of which the author is an advisory board member, and Post Carbon Institute, of which the author is a Fellow.

3. World gross domestic product is the total of all nations' GDPs.

4. "Real wages" are wages that have been adjusted for the effects of inflation on purchasing power.

5. "Real GDP" is GDP adjusted for inflation.

6. Steve Andrews, "The First Peak Oil Recession: Interview with Steven Kopits," Energy Bulletin, September 14, 2009, http://www.energybulletin.net/node/50109.

CHAPTER 20. ECOLOGICAL ECONOMICS

1. In a competitive market, no single buyer or seller of a commodity has sufficient market power to set prices. Economic actors are price takers, not price makers. However, so-called competitive markets actually require extensive cooperative behavior—for example, to defend property rights.

2. Monetary policy is basically how the government influences the supply and availability of money in an economy, as well as the interest rate at which it can be borrowed or loaned. Fiscal policy is basically how much money a government spends and how much it collects in taxes.

3. U.S. Department of Commerce, Bureau of Economic Analysis, "Current-Dollar and 'Real' GDP," National Economic Accounts spreadsheet, 2007, http://www.bea.gov/national/.

4. A resource is scarce when there is not enough available for all desirable ends, hence the competition among ends.

5. John Gowdy, ed., *Limited Wants, Unlimited Means: A Reader on Hunter-Gatherer Economics and the Environment* (Washington DC: Island Press, 1998).

6. Manfred Max-Neef, "Development and Human Needs," in *Real-Life Economics: Understanding Wealth Creation*, Paul Ekins and Manfred Max-Neef, eds. (London: Routledge, 1992); Robert Costanza et al., "Quality of Life: An Approach Integrating Opportunities, Human Needs, and Subjective Well-Being," *Ecological Economics* 61, nos. 2–3 (March 1, 2007); Joshua Farley and Robert Costanza, "Envisioning Shared Goals for Humanity: A Detailed, Shared Vision of a Sustainable and Desirable USA in 2100," *Ecological Economics* 43, no. 2 (December 2002), 245–259.

7. Joshua Farley et al., "Synthesis: The Quality of Life and the Distribution of Wealth and Resources," in *Understanding and Solving Environmental Problems in the 21st Century: Toward a New, Integrated Hard Problem Science*, Robert Costanza and Sven Erik Jørgensen, eds. (Amsterdam: Elsevier, 2002).

8. Ernst Fehr and Klaus M. Schmidt, "The Economics of Fairness, Reciprocity and Altruism: Experimental Evidence and New Theories," in *Handbook on the Economics of Giving, Reciprocity and Altruism,* vol. 1, Serge-Christophe Kolm and Jean Mercier Ythier, eds. (Amsterdam: North-Holland/Elsevier, 2006).

9. Robert M. Solow, "The Economics of Resources or the Resources of Economics," *American Economic Review* 64, no. 2 (May 1974), 1–14; Julian Simon, *The Ultimate Resource 2* (Princeton: Princeton University Press, 1996); Wilfred Beckerman, *Small Is Stupid: Blowing the Whistle on the Greens* (London: Duckworth, 1995).

10. Matthew Savinar, "How Much Human Energy Is Contained in One Barrel of Oil?" Life After the Oil Crash, http://www.lifeaftertheoilcrash.net/Research.html#anchor_71.

11. Emilie Alberola, Julien Chevallier, and Benoit Chèze, "Price Drivers and Structural Breaks in European Carbon Prices 2005–2007," *Energy Policy* 36, no. 2 (February 2008), 787–797.

12. Herman E. Daly and Joshua Farley, *Ecological Economics: Principles and Applications*, 1st ed. (Washington DC: Island Press, 2004); Ida Kubiszewski, Joshua Farley, and Robert Costanza, "The Production and Allocation of Information as a Good that Is Enhanced with Increased Use," *Ecological Economics* 69, no. 6 (April 1, 2010), 1344–1354.

13. While public provision may involve coercion, in a democratic society it is mutual coercion mutually agreed upon, and hence cooperative. Hereafter, "public" will be treated as a subset of "cooperative."

14. Nicholas Stern, *The Economics of Climate Change: The Stern Review* (Cambridge, UK: Cambridge University Press, 2006).

15. Daly and Farley, *Ecological Economics*, 1st ed.

16. Wind is slightly rival, because one wind farm can reduce wind flows to a downstream farm.

17. Currently, efficient solar energy capture and storage depend on several scarce rare minerals, for which competition is intense, but new technologies need not be dependent on these.

18. Michael A. Heller and Rebecca S. Eisenberg, "Can Patents Deter Innovation? The Anticommons in Biomedical Research," *Science* 280, no. 5364 (May 1, 1998), 698–701.

19. David Korten, *Agenda for a New Economy: From Phantom Wealth to Real Wealth* (San Francisco: Berrett-Koehler, 2009); Herman E. Daly and Joshua Farley, *Ecological Economics: Principles and Applications*, 2nd ed. (Washington DC: Island Press, 2010).

20. Donella H. Meadows, *Leverage Points: Places to Intervene in a System* (Hartland, VT: Sustainability Institute, 1999).

21. Richard Layard, *Happiness: Lessons from a New Science* (New York: Penguin, 2005); Robert E. Lane, *The Loss of Happiness in Market Democracies* (New Haven: Yale University Press, 2000).

22. Joseph E. Stiglitz, Amartya Sen, and Jean-Paul Fitoussi, *Report by the Commission on the Measurement of Economic Performance and Social Progress*, Commission on

the Measurement of Economic Performance and Social Progress (CPMEPSP) Issues Paper (Paris: 2008).

23. Peter Victor, *Managing without Growth: Slower by Design, Not Disaster* (Cheltenham: Edward Elgar Publishing, 2008); Tim Jackson, *Prosperity without Growth? The Transition to a Sustainable Economy* (Sterling, VA: Earthscan, 2009).

24. David Sloan Wilson and Edward O. Wilson, "Rethinking the Theoretical Foundations of Sociobiology," *Quarterly Review of Biology* 82, no. 4 (December 2007), 327–348.

25. David Sloan Wilson, *Evolution for Everyone: How Darwin's Theory Can Change the Way We Think about Our Lives* (New York: Delacorte Press, 2007).

26. For a review of key literature, see Fehr and Schmidt, "The Economics of Fairness, Reciprocity and Altruism"; Elinor Ostrom, *Governing the Commons: The Evolution of Institutions for Collective Action* (Cambridge, UK: Cambridge University Press, 1990); Daniel W. Bromley, ed. *Making the Commons Work: Theory, Practice, and Policy* (San Francisco: ICS Press, 1992).

27. Samuel Bowles and Herbert Gintis, "The Evolution of Strong Reciprocity: Cooperation in Heterogeneous Populations," *Theoretical Population Biology* 65, no. 1 (February 2004), 17–28.

28. Peter Barnes, *Capitalism 3.0: A Guide to Reclaiming the Commons* (San Francisco: Berrett-Koehler, 2006).

29. Daly and Farley, *Ecological Economics*, 2nd ed; Korten, *Agenda for a New Economy*.

30. Rachel Beddoe et al., "Overcoming Systemic Roadblocks to Sustainability: The Evolutionary Redesign of Worldviews, Institutions and Technologies," *Proceedings of the National Academy of Sciences* 106, no. 8 (February 24, 2009), 2483–2489.

31. U.S. Department of Commerce, "Current-Dollar and 'Real' GDP."

CHAPTER 21. MONEY AND ENERGY

1. Glyn Davies, *A History of Money from Ancient Times to the Present Day* (Cardiff: University of Wales Press, 2002). According to Davies's mammoth study, the Yap used their stone money until the 1960s.

CHAPTER 22. THE COMPETETIVENESS OF LOCAL LIVING ECONOMIES

1. U.S. Census Bureau, *The 2010 Statistical Abstract*, PDF version, http://www.census.gov/compendia/statab/2010edition.html.

2. Total annual payroll of the businesses discussed here is used as a measure of their "market share" of the national economy.

3. Downloadable at U.S. Census Bureau, *Statistics of U.S. Businesses (SUSB)*, http://www.census.gov/econ/susb/.

4. Thomas L. Friedman, *The World Is Flat: A Brief History of the Twenty-First Century* (New York: Farrar, Straus & Giroux, 2005).

5. David G. Savage, "Supreme Court Overturns Ban on Direct Corporate Spending on Elections," *Los Angeles Times*, January 22, 2010.

CHAPTER 23. THE DEATH OF SPRAWL

1. Peter Hong, "Housing Crunch Becomes Literal in Victorville," *Los Angeles Times,* May 5, 2009.

2. More than 3,600 of Victorville's estimated 4,983 homes for sale (one in ten of all *existing* housing units) in July 2009 were in foreclosure. City-data.com, http://www.city-data.com/city/Victorville-California.html (accessed August 3, 2009); Yahoo! Real Estate, http://realestate.yahoo.com/California/Victorville/foreclosures (accessed July 17, 2009).

3. Patrick Thatcher, "New Homes Demolished," *Victorville Daily Press,* May 1, 2009.

4. Paul R. LaMonica, "Economic Oil Spill on the Horizon?" The Buzz, CNN Money.com, August 3, 2009.

5. U.S. Census Bureau, *American Community Survey,* 2007, http://www.census.gov/acs/www/.

6. U.S. Department of Labor, Bureau of Labor Statistics, "State and County Employment and Wages (Quarterly Census of Employment & Wages)," 2007, http://www.bls.gov/data/#employment; U.S. Census Bureau, *American Community Survey,* 2007.

7. U.S. Census Bureau, *American Community Survey,* 2007.

8. "U.S. Vehicle Miles Traveled: 1936–2005," Pew Center for Global Climate Change, http://www.pewclimate.org/global-warming-basics/facts_and_figures/us_emissions/vmt.cfm. The rate of vehicle ownership increased from 411 per 1,000 people in 1960 to 812 per 1,000 in 2002. Joyce Dargay et al., "Vehicle Ownership and Income Growth, Worldwide: 1960–2030," December 2007, http://www.econ.nyu.edu/dept/courses/gately/research.htm.

9. TransForm, *Windfall for All: How Connected, Convenient Neighborhoods Can Protect Our Climate and Safeguard California's Economy,* November 2009, http://transformca.org/resources/reports.

10. For home-size information, see Infoplease.com, http://www.infoplease.com/askeds/us-home-size.html.

11. The embodied energy of an automobile and supporting infrastructure (construction and upkeep of roads, bridges, parking) can be 50 percent or more than the energy required for direct fuel use. One estimate is that 15 percent extra energy in addition to fuel energy use is required for manufacturing of the car and 35 percent extra energy for infrastructure. Philip Camill, "Watch Your Step: Understanding the Impact of Your Personal Consumption on the Environment," National Center for Case Study Teaching in Science, August 2002, http://ublib.buffalo.edu/libraries/projects/cases/case.html.

12. Alex Steffen, "My Other Car Is a Bright Green City," Worldchanging.com, January 23, 2008, http://www.worldchanging.com/archives/007800.html.

13. Robert E. Lang and Jennifer B. LeFurgy, *Boomburbs: The Rise of America's Accidental Cities* (Washington DC: Brookings Institution, 2007), 6.

14. Urban Land Institute and PricewaterhouseCoopers, "Emerging Trends in Real Estate 2010," October 2009, http://www.uli.org/ResearchAndPublications/EmergingTrends/Americas.aspx.

15. As the nation's second-largest county, San Bernardino spans 215 miles from west to east and 150 miles from north to south; it can hold four Connecticuts. Well

after the lawsuit and the subsequent real estate crash, the county's Web site boasted that six of the nation's fifty fastest-growing cities after the 2000 census were in San Bernardino County. County of San Bernardino, "Population Growth Accelerates," http://www.co.sanbernardino.ca.us/OpportunityCA/build_business/gr_pop Growth.html (accessed June 22, 2009); California Office of the Attorney General, "Brown Announces Landmark Global Warming Settlement," August 21, 2007, http://ag.ca.gov/newsalerts/release.php?id=1453.

16. California Office of the Attorney General, "Brown Announces Landmark Global Warming Settlement."

17. See Daniel Lerch, *Post Carbon Cities: Planning for Energy and Climate Uncertainty* (Sebastopol, CA: Post Carbon Press, 2007), for a full discussion of the ramifications of peak oil for communities and local governments.

18. Tim Chinn, "Got Arsenic?" September 1, 2002, http://americancityandcounty .com/mag/government_arsenic/.

19. UK Industry Taskforce on Peak Oil and Energy Security, *The Oil Crunch: A Wake-Up Call for the UK Economy*, February 2010, http://peakoiltaskforce.net/.

20. Edward L. Glaeser and Matthew E. Kahn, *Sprawl and Urban Growth*, National Bureau of Economic Research Working Paper No. 9733, May 2003, http://www .nber.org/papers/w9733. See also Glaeser's foreword to Lang and LeFurgy, *Boomburbs*.

21. Glaeser has since toned down his defense of sprawl. In 2006 he authored a paper with UCLA's Matthew Kahn arguing that sprawling cities such as Houston pollute more and consume more energy than more compact cities; see Edward L. Glaeser and Matthew E. Kahn, *The Greenness of Cities*, Rappaport Institute Policy Brief (Boston: Harvard University, 2008).

22. For a history of the pre-modern suburbs in the late-nineteenth and early-twentieth centuries in England and the United States, see Richard Harris and Peter Larkham, eds., *Changing Suburbs: Foundation, Form and Function* (London: Routledge, 1999).

23. Lang and LeFurgy, *Boomburbs*, ix.

24. Dana E. King et al., "Adherence to Healthy Lifestyle Habits in U.S. Adults, 1988–2006," *American Journal of Medicine* 122, no. 6 (June 2009), 528–534.

25. Roni Caryn Brown, "Bad Habits Asserting Themselves," *New York Times*, June 9, 2009.

26. U.S. Department of Transportation, Federal Highway Administration, "Travel to School: The Distance Factor," National Household Travel Survey Brief, January 2008, http://nhts.ornl.gov/publications.shtml.

27. One of the first publications to bring awareness of peak oil and its ramifications for cities and suburbs to lay audiences was James Howard Kunstler's *The Long Emergency* (New York: Grove/Atlantic, 2005).

28. Urban Land Institute and PricewaterhouseCoopers, "Emerging Trends in Real Estate 2010."

29. "Bringing Urban and Rural Leaders Together," Roots of Change, November 3, 2008, http://www.rocfund.org/.

30. San Francisco is inventorying where its food is imported from in the state and region, so it can collaborate on providing protection for important regional food sources, and is issuing a "buy local food" directive for city departments. Len Richard-

son, "First-Ever Regional Food Policy," *California Farmer*, September 2009, available at http://magissues.farmprogress.com/CLF/CF09Sep09/clf007.pdf.

31. "Clean-tech" jobs grew at a rate of almost two and a half times the average job-growth rate from 1999 to 2007, according to a Pew Charitable Trust study. "Pew Finds Clean Energy Economy Generates Significant Job Growth," Pew Charitable Trust, press release, http://www.pewtrusts.org/news_room_detail.aspx?id=53254.

32. Toledo's new solar skill base has been optimized with federal and state funding, as well as local private industry and educational research-and-development support; see Joan Fitzgerald, "Cities on the Front Lines," *American Prospect*, April 13, 2009. Metro-area employment figures from U.S. Census Bureau, *American Community Survey*, 2007; see also Joan Fitzgerald, *Emerald Cities: Urban Sustainability and Economic Development* (New York: Oxford University Press, 2010).

33. "10.7 Billion Trips Taken on U.S. Public Transportation in 2008," American Public Transportation Association, March 9, 2009, http://apta.com/mediacenter/pressreleases/2009/Pages/090309_ridership.aspx.

34. Pedal Pushers Online, "Bike Ridership Up in 2008," ppolnews.com, November 18, 2008, http://www.ppolnews.com/?id=84077&keys=New-York-Bicycling-Coalition. In 2008, 8 percent of Portland, Oregon, commuters used a bicycle as their primary means of transportation.

35. "Green Choice Renewable Energy Program," austinenergy.com, http://tinyurl.com/2q6t2b.

36. "City and County of San Francisco Municipal Solar Installations," posted on sfenvironment.org, May 2009, http://sfenvironment.org/downloads/library/sfpuc_solar_map_presentation.pdf.

37. "Top Ten Alternative Fueled City Fleets," Sustainlane.us, 2006, http://www.sustainlane.us/articles/Top_Ten_Alternative_Fueled_City_Fleets.jsp.

38. John Cote, "Market Street Poised for Car Restrictions," sfgate.com, July 28, 2009, http://www.sfgate.com/cgi-bin/blogs/cityinsider/detail?entry_id=44416; Rachel Gordon, "Market St. Traffic Test Starts," *San Francisco Chronicle*, September 30, 2009.

39. Pew Center on Global Climate Change, "Climate Techbook: Transportation Overview," May 2009, http://www.pewclimate.org/climate-techbook.

40. Josh Flory and Ed Marcum, "Fuming over Gas Questions," Knoxvillebiz.com, October 5, 2008, http://www.knoxnews.com/news/2008/oct/05/fuming-over-gas-questions/.

41. Marilyn A. Brown et al., *Shrinking the Carbon Footprint of Metropolitan America*, Brookings Institution, Blueprint for American Prosperity Policy Briefs (May 29, 2008), 11–12.

42. Warren Karlenzig, "Ranking US Cities' Oil Addiction: Sprawl and Car Commuting Emerge as Real Estate Risk Factors," presented at the Behavior, Energy and Climate Change conference, Stanford University, November 17, 2008, available online at http://tinyurl.com/ygzb5c9.

43. Urban Land Institute and PricewaterhouseCoopers, "Emerging Trends in Real Estate 2010."

44. Density for efficient public transit requires about thirty people per acre, which is about three times more dense than the average U.S. suburb; see Paul Spreiregen and Beatriz La Paz, eds., *Pre-Design* (LaCrosse, WI: Kaplan AEC Education, 2007), 103.

45. In late 2009, developers in Portland, Oregon, and other locations reported increased demand for smaller homes, more multifamily dwellings, and homes with access to public transit options. Ryan Frank, "Portland Area Developers Shift to Small, Efficient Homes," *Oregonian* (October 31, 2009), http://www.oregonlive.com/business/index.ssf/2009/10/portland-area_builders_shift_t.html.

46. See ICLEI–Local Governments for Sustainability, "The STAR Rating System," http://www.icleiusa.org/programs/sustainability/star-community-index/concept-overview/rating-system/the-star-rating-system; Global Footprint Network, "Footprint for Cities," http://www.footprintnetwork.org/en/index.php/GFN/page/footprint_for_cities/.

47. Tim Barnett and David Pierce, "When Will Lake Mead Go Dry?" *Water Resources Research* 44 (March 29, 2008).

48. Lewis Knight and William Riggs, "Nourishing Urbanism: A Case for a New Urban Paradigm," *International Journal of Agricultural Sustainability* (February 2010), 116–126; author's personal travels; David Holmgren, "Retrofitting the Suburbs for Sustainability," *Energy Bulletin*, March 30, 2005, http://www.energybulletin.net/node/5104.

49. Jason Blevins, "Agriburba Sprouts in Colorado's Front Range," *Denver Post*, October 24, 2009.

50. Urban system metabolism depends largely on how energy, water, food, and materials are acquired, used, and (where possible) reused. From these ingredients, and through processes like labor and the use of knowledge, come products, services, waste, and pollution (the last two being minimal if the system is efficient). Christopher Kennedy, "Urban Metabolism," *Encyclopedia of Earth*, April 18, 2007, http://www.eoearth.org/article/Urban_metabolism.

51. From a speech by California governor Arnold Schwarzenegger, Commonwealth Club of San Francisco, September 24, 2009, available online at http://tinyurl.com/2bljhyy.

52. Todd Woody, "Alternative Energy Projects Stumble on a Need for Water," *New York Times*, September 29, 2009.

CHAPTER 24. SMART DECLINE IN POST-CARBON CITIES

1. Deborah E. Popper and Frank J. Popper, "Small Can Be Beautiful: Coming to Terms with Decline," *Planning* 68, no. 7 (July 2002), 20–23.

2. Peter Hall, *Cities of Tomorrow: An Intellectual History of Urban Planning and Design in the Twentieth Century*, 3rd ed. (Malden, MA: Blackwell, 2002), 13–47.

3. For proof, see for instance Christopher G. Duerksen, C. Gregory Dale, and Donald L. Elliott, *The Citizen's Guide to Planning*, 4th ed. (Chicago: American Planning Association, 2009).

4. Hall, *Cities of Tomorrow*, 427–468.

5. Michael Gecan, "On Borrowed Time: Urban Decline Moves to the Suburbs," *Boston Review*, March/April 2008, http://bostonreview.net/BR33.2/gecan.php; David A. Graham, "What's the Matter with Ohio?" *Newsweek*, January 22, 2010, http://blog.newsweek.com/blogs/thegaggle/archive/2010/01/22/what-s-the-matter-with-ohio.aspx.

6. Rich Exner, "Metro Cleveland is 3rd Nationally in Population Loss: Search

the Latest Numbers," Cleveland.com, March 19, 2009, http://www.cleveland.com/datacentral/index.ssf/2009/03/metro_cleveland_is_third_natio.html.

7. Justin B. Hollander et al., "Planning Shrinking Cities," *Progress in Planning* 72 (2009), 223–232.

8. City of Youngstown, Ohio, *Youngstown 2010 Citywide Plan*, 2005, http://www.cityofyoungstownoh.com/about_youngstown/youngstown_2010/index.aspx.

9. Hollander et al., "Planning Shrinking Cities," 223.

10. "Brave Thinkers: John Fetterman," *Atlantic*, November 2009, http://www.theatlantic.com/magazine/archive/2009/11/brave-thinkers/7692/10/.

11. Byron W. Brown, "Mayor Brown's '5 in 5' Demolition Plan," city of Buffalo, August 2007, http://www.ci.buffalo.ny.us/files/1_2_1/Mayor/PublicPolicyPublication/5in5_DemoPlan.pdf.

12. Margot Carmichael Lester, "Sign of the Times—Five Cities Bringing New Life to Abandoned Sites," Developer Online, August 11, 2008, http://www.developeronline.com/sign-of-the-times-five-cities-turning-around-abandoned-sites/.

13. Kristen Longley, "Tale of Shrinking Cities," *Flint Journal*, March 7, 2010, http://www.mlive.com/news/flint/index.ssf/2010/03/tale_of_two_shrinking_cities_f.html.

14. Detroit Vacant Property Campaign, http://officemanager.law.officelive.com/default.htm.

15. Suzette Hackney, "Bing: Demolition Project Begins April 1: Plan Is to Raze Homes in Stages," *Detroit Free Press*, March 25, 2010.

16. Deborah E. Popper and Frank J. Popper, "An America without Farmers?" *Publications: Prairie Writers*, Land Institute, April 4, 2004, http://www.landinstitute.org/vnews/display.v/ART/2004/04/08/4076b2169776a?in_archive=1.

17. Stephen G. Wilson, *Population Dynamics of the Great Plains, 1950–2007: Population Estimates and Projections* (Washington DC: U.S. Census Bureau, 2009).

18. Deborah E. Popper and Frank J. Popper, "From Dust to Dust: A Daring Proposal for Dealing with an Inevitable Disaster," *Planning* 53, no. 5 (December 1987), 13–18.

19. Deborah E. Popper and Frank J. Popper, "The Buffalo Commons: Metaphor as Method," *Geographical Review* 89, no. 4 (October 1999), 491–510.

20. Anne Matthews, *Where the Buffalo Roam: Restoring America's Great Plains*, 2nd ed. (Chicago: University of Chicago Press, 2002).

21. Frank Popper chairs the Great Plains Restoration Council board.

22. Deborah E. Popper and Frank J. Popper, "A New Park to Save the Plains," *Kansas City Star*, November 14, 2009; "How to Save Plains," *Wichita Eagle*, November 22, 2009, www.kansas.com/950/story/1066544.html.

23. Popper and Popper, "The Buffalo Commons," 491–510.

24. Deborah E. Popper and Frank J. Popper, "Looking Forward: Adding the Buffalo Commons to the Grasslands Mix," in *Farming with Grass: Achieving Sustainable Mixed Agricultural Landscapes*, Alan J. Franzluebbers, ed. (Ankeny, IA: Soil and Water Conservation Society, 2009).

25. Hackney, "Bing: Demolition Project Begins April 1."

CHAPTER 25. TOWARD ZERO-CARBON BUILDINGS

1. "The New York City Greener, Greater Buildings Plan," NYC.gov, http://www.nyc.gov/html/planyc2030/html/plan/buildings_plan.shtml.

2. Clay G. Nessler, "Renovation of the Empire State Building," presentation to the U.N. Economic Commission for Europe's Committee on Housing and Land Management, September 23, 2009, http://www.unece.org/hlm/sessions/docs2009/presentations/11.CNC.Rode.pdf; for U.S. EPA/DOE Energy Star program, see http://www.energystar.gov/.

3. Anthony Malkin, "Empire State Building," press conference, New York, April 6, 2009, http://www.esbsustainability.com/SocMe/Content/Files/Empire%20State%20Building%20Co%20Statement.pdf.

4. National Science and Technology Council, *Federal Research and Development Agenda for Net-Zero Energy, High-Performance Green Buildings*, October 28, 2008, http://www.bfrl.nist.gov/buildingtechnology/documents/FederalRDAgendaforNetZeroEnergyHighPerformanceGreenBuildings.pdf, 11.

5. U.S. Environmental Protection Agency Green Building Workgroup, *Buildings and the Environment: A Statistical Summary* (Washington DC: Environmental Protection Agency, 2004), 2.

6. U.S. Energy Information Administration, *Annual Energy Outlook 2006*, DOE/EIA-0383 (2006), February 2006, http://www.eia.doe.gov/oiaf/archive.html. Building emissions are currently at 658 million metric tons of carbon dioxide annually; U.S. Environmental Protection Agency, *Inventory of U.S. Greenhouse Gas Emissions and Sinks: 1990–2002*, EPA/430-R-04-003 (Washington DC: Environmental Protection Agency, 2004), 3–7 and table 3-6.

7. Marilyn Brown, Frank Southworth, and Therese Stoval, *Towards a Climate-Friendly Built Environment*, report for the Pew Center on Global Climate Change (Arlington, VA: Pew Center, 2005), 52.

8. Green Globes, formed by groups in Canada and the United States as an alternative to LEED, emphasizes "ease of use, low cost, and user education through its Web-based application." The National Association of Home Builders and the International Codes Council partnered in 2008 to establish a National Green Building Standard compliant with the American National Standards Institute (ANSI); see http://www.nahbgreen.org/guidelines/ansistandard.aspx.

9. U.S. Green Building Council, "LEED Initiatives in Government and Schools," September 2009.

10. Rob Watson, ed., *Green Building Impact Report 2008* (Oakland, CA: Greener World Media, 2008), 3. It's unclear whether this growth in market penetration for new buildings will continue (more likely it will level out).

11. Norm Miller, Jay Spivey, and Andrew Florance, "Does Green Pay Off?" *Journal of Sustainable Real Estate*, July 8, 2008, http://www.costar.com/JOSRE/default.htm. The study cites rent premiums of $11.33 and $2.40 per square foot, and a 4.1 and 3.6 percent higher occupancy for LEED-certified buildings and Energy Star buildings, respectively. Sales premiums include $171 and $61 per square foot.

12. As quoted in *Green Building Materials in the U.S.*, a report from market research publisher SBI Energy.

13. Commission for Environmental Cooperation, *Green Building in North America:*

Opportunities and Challenges (Montreal: Commission for Environmental Cooperation Secretariat, 2008), 17.

14. U.S. Environmental Protection Agency Green Building Workgroup, *Buildings and the Environment*.

15. Per a worldwide study by the World Business Council for Sustainable Development, *Energy Efficiency in Buildings: Business Realities and Opportunities*, http://www.wbcsd.org/plugins/DocSearch/details.asp?type=DocDet&ObjectId=MjU5MTM.

16. Ibid., 56.

17. U.S. Energy Information Administration, "Energy Consumption by Sector and Source," table 2 in *Annual Energy Outlook 2010*, December 2009, http://www.eia.doe.gov/oiaf/aeo/excel/aeotab_2.xls.

18. Martin Adelaar et al., *Green Building Energy Scenarios for 2030*, Green Building Background Papers (Commission for Environmental Cooperation, 2008), http://www.cec.org/Page.asp?PageID=1180&SiteNodeID=468.

19. John A. Laitner, *The Positive Economics of Climate Change Policies: What the Historical Evidence Can Tell Us* (Washington DC: American Council for an Energy-Efficient Economy, July 2009); Hannah Choi Granade et al., *Unlocking Energy Efficiency in the U.S. Economy* (McKinsey & Company, July 2009).

20. Gordon V. R. Holness, "Improving Energy Efficiency in Existing Buildings," *ASHRAE Journal* (January 1, 2008), 1.

21. Brown et al., *Towards a Climate-Friendly Built Environment*, 11.

22. McGraw-Hill Construction, *Smart Market Report, Green Building Retrofit & Renovation: Rapidly Expanding Market Opportunities through Existing Buildings*, October 2009.

23. U.S. Green Building Council, "Green Building Consultant's Top 10 Predicts Green Building Growth Despite Economy," February 2, 2009, from *Contractor* magazine, http://www.usgbc.org/News/USGBCInTheNewsDetails.aspx?ID=3966. LEED O&M is the U.S. Green Building Council's rating tool for building systems upgrades.

24. P. Komor, "Space Cooling Demands from Office Plug Loads," *ASHRAE Journal* 39, no. 12 (December 1997), 41–44.

25. Adelaar et al., *Green Building Energy Scenarios for 2030*.

26. Greg Rosenquist et al., *Energy Efficiency Standards for Residential/Commercial Equipment and Buildings: Additional Opportunities*, LBNL-56207 (Berkeley: Lawrence Berkeley National Laboratory, 2004), 19.

27. "The New York City Greener, Greater Buildings Plan," NYC.gov, http://www.nyc.gov/html/planyc2030/html/plan/buildings_plan.shtml.

28. Intergovernmental Panel on Climate Change, "Residential and Commercial Buildings," in *Working Group III Report: Mitigation of Climate Change*, Bert Merz et al., eds. (New York: Cambridge University Press, 2007), www.ipcc.ch/ipccreports/ar4-wg3.htm.

29. B. Griffith et al., *Assessment of the Technical Potential for Achieving Net-Zero Energy Buildings in the Commercial Sector,* National Renewable Energy Laboratory, NREL/TP-550-41957 (2007), 64.

30. Ibid., 38.

31. Architecture 2030, "The 2030 Challenge," http://www.architecture2030.org/2030_challenge/index.html.

32. Cascadia Region Green Building Council, *The Living Building Challenge: In Pursuit of True Sustainability in the Built Environment*, 2006, http://www.livingshelter.com/Lb-challenge-v1-2.pdf.

33. Lew W. Pratsch, "Zero Energy Buildings," presentation at the Residential Energy Services Network 2003 RESNET Conference, San Diego, www.resnet.us/conference/2003/presentations/Pratsch.PDF.

34. Commission for Environmental Cooperation, *Green Building in North America*, 42.

35. American Society of Heating, Refrigerating, and Air-Conditioning Engineers, www.ashrae.org.

CHAPTER 26. LOCAL GOVERNMENT IN A TIME OF PEAK OIL AND CLIMATE CHANGE

1. Abraham Lincoln, July 1, 1854, quoted in "Fragment on Government," in *The Wisdom of Abraham Lincoln,* Temple Scott, ed. (New York: Brentano's, 1909), 89.

2. Richard Heinberg, *Searching for a Miracle: "Net Energy" Limits & the Fate of Industrial Society* (San Francisco: Post Carbon Institute/International Forum on Globalization, 2009).

3. Daniel Lerch, *Post Carbon Cities: Planning for Energy and Climate Uncertainty* (Sebastopol, CA: Post Carbon Press, 2007), 63–66.

4. City of Portland Peak Oil Task Force, *Descending the Oil Peak: Navigating the Transition from Oil and Natural Gas*, Final Report, March 2007, available at http://www.portlandonline.com/bps/index.cfm?c=42894.

5. ICLEI–Local Governments for Sustainability USA, *2009 Annual Report: Measuring Up* (Boston: ICLEI USA, 2009), http://www.icleiusa.org/library/documents/.

CHAPTER 27. TRANSPORTATION IN THE POST–CARBON WORLD

1. For oil's share of all transport fuel, see International Energy Agency, *World Energy Outlook 2009* (Paris: OECD/IEA, 2009), 622.

2. Richard Gilbert and Anthony Perl, *Transport Revolutions: Moving People and Freight without Oil*, 2nd ed. (Gabriola Island, BC: New Society, 2010).

3. Ibid.

4. See, for example, Jane Jacobs, *Dark Age Ahead* (New York: Random House, 2004); Jared Diamond, *Collapse: How Societies Choose to Fail or Succeed* (New York: Viking/Penguin, 2005); James Howard Kunstler, *The Long Emergency: Surviving the Converging Catastrophes of the Twenty-First Century* (New York: Grove/Atlantic, 2005). In reprising his recent book, *The Upside of Down*, Thomas Homer-Dixon described the crux of the current predicament as this: "Our global system is becoming steadily more complex, yet the high-quality energy we need to cope with this complexity will soon be steadily less available." See Thomas Homer-Dixon, *The Upside of Down: Catastrophe, Creativity, and the Renewal of Civilization* (Washington DC: Island Press, 2006); Thomas Homer-Dixon, "Prepare Today for Tomorrow's Breakdown," *Toronto Globe & Mail*, May 14, 2006.

5. The GCV is subject to a distribution loss of about 10 percent, which could fall with improved technology. A BEV with current (nickel hydride) batteries is subject to

an additional charge-discharge loss of about 30 percent. Julian Matheys et al., "Comparison of the Environmental Impact of 5 Electric Vehicle Battery Technologies Using LCA," in *Proceedings of the 13th CIRP International Conference on Life Cycle Engineering* (held May–June 2006, Leuven, Belgium), 97–102. The charge-discharge loss could be below 10 percent with advanced lithium-ion batteries. Lars Hedström et al., "Key Factors in Planning a Sustainable Energy Future Including Hydrogen and Fuel Cells," *Bulletin of Science, Technology & Society* 26, no. 4 (2006), 264–277.

6. Michael Taplin, "A World of Trams and Urban Transit," Light Rail Transit Association, January 2006, http://www.lrta.org/world/worldind.html; Trolley Motion at http://www.trolleymotion.com/en/.

7. For details on this high-speed rail revolution, see "Learning from Past Transport Revolutions" and "Leading the Way Forward" in Gilbert and Perl, *Transport Revolutions.*

8. Hutnyak Consulting, "1970–1977—Quebec Cartier Mine, Canada," Hutnyak. com, Trolley History, 2001, http://hutnyak.com/Trolley/trolleyhistory.html#QCM.

9. The averages are based on data from the U.S. Federal Transit Administration in *National Transit Database,* http://www.ntdprogram.gov/ntdprogram/data.htm.

10. The logic for seeking a 44 percent reduction is developed fully in the chapter "The Next Transport Revolutions" in Gilbert and Perl, *Transport Revolutions.* It takes into account anticipated oil supply in 2025 and provides for larger reductions in consumption for developed than for developing countries.

11. For the analysis behind this estimate of world oil production in 2025, see figures 3.7 and 3.8, and the discussion of petroleum-liquids production, in "Transport and Energy" in Gilbert and Perl, *Transport Revolutions.*

12. Table 5.1 of Gilbert and Perl, *Transport Revolutions,* shows that richer countries were actually responsible for 74 percent of total oil consumption in 1990, and that the 2025 shortfall of expected supply in relation to "business-as-usual" consumption will be 11.3 billion barrels. Allocating this shortfall as proposed in the text, richer countries would use about 7.5 billion barrels less than the business-as-usual projection, and poorer countries would use about 3.7 billion barrels less. For richer countries, this would represent an annual decline in consumption of about 3.6 percent. For poorer countries, it would represent an annual increase in consumption of about 1.2 percent.

13. For nonfuel uses of oil, see tables 1.15 and 1.3 of U.S. Energy Information Administration, *Annual Review of Energy 2006,* DOE/EIA-0384 (2006), June 2007, http://www.eia.doe.gov/emeu/aer/contents.html.

14. The U.S. population estimate and projection are from United Nations, Department of Social and Economic Affairs, Population Division, *World Population Prospects: The 2008 Revision* (New York: United Nations, 2009), highlights available at http://www.un.org/esa/population/.

15. The average megajoules per passenger-kilometer is a conservative suggestion based on information in table 3.3 of Gilbert and Perl, *Transport Revolutions.*

16. The promise and prospects for personal rapid transport are discussed in "Transport and Energy" in Gilbert and Perl, *Transport Revolutions.* For anticipated energy consumption by personal rapid transport, see Eva Gustavsson, "Energy Efficiency of Personal Rapid Transit," in *The Energy Efficiency Challenge for Europe: ECEEE Summer Study Proceedings 1995,* Mandelieu, France, 1995, http://www.eceee.org/conference_proceedings/eceee/1995/Panel_6/p6_1/Paper/.

17. The suggested unit fuel use by airships is speculative. A current operating company reports use of 1.3 megajoules per passenger-kilometer for a fifteen-passenger vehicle (see Airship Management Services, "FAQs," Airshipman.com, http://www .airshipman.com/faq.htm). Larger airships and use of solar power from canopy-mounted connectors could reduce liquid fuel consumption substantially.

18. For towing kite applications for ships, see SkySails GmbH & Co, "Turn Wind into Profit," 2009, http://www.skysails.info.

CHAPTER 28. CLIMATE CHANGE, PEAK OIL, AND THE END OF WASTE

1. For a thorough history of the origins of municipal waste collection summarized here, see Martin V. Melosi, *Garbage in the Cities* (College Station, TX: Texas A&M University, 1981).

2. Steven Mintz, "Housework in Late 19th Century America," Digital History, http://www.digitalhistory.uh.edu/historyonline/housework.cfm (accessed January 1, 2010).

3. Susan Strasser, *Waste and Want: A Social History of Trash* (New York: Metropolitan Books, 1999).

4. Elizabeth Grossman, *Chasing Molecules: Poisonous Products, Human Health, and the Promise of Green Chemistry* (Washington DC: Shearwater/Island Press, 2009). The U.S. Environmental Protection Agency defines "commercial quantity" as more than 25,000 pounds used per facility per year.

5. See Annie Leonard, *The Story of Stuff*, www.storyofstuff.org.

6. Jennifer Clapp, "The Distancing of Waste: Overconsumption in a Global Economy," in *Confronting Consumption*, Thomas Princen et al., eds. (Cambridge, MA: MIT Press, 2002).

7. Mathis Wackernagel and William Rees, *Our Ecological Footprint: Reducing Human Impact on Earth* (Gabriola Island, BC: New Society, 1996).

8. Thomas Princen, Michael Maniates, and Ken Conca, eds., *Confronting Consumption* (Cambridge, MA: MIT Press, 2002), 4–7.

9. U.S. Environmental Protection Agency, *Opportunities to Reduce Greenhouse Gas Emissions through Materials and Land Management Practices*, EPA 530-R-09-017 (September 2009), http://www.epa.gov/oswer/publication.htm.

10. While there are technical differences between *systems*-based and *consumption*-based greenhouse accounting, both focus on the end users: consumers in the economic sense of households and government.

11. *Goods*, or products and packaging, includes building materials and passenger automobiles.

12. Joshuah Stolaroff, "Products, Packaging and U.S. Greenhouse Gas Emissions" (Athens, GA: Product Policy Institute, September 2009), http://www.productpolicy .org/content/climate-change-epr.

13. J. Jeswiet and M. Hauschild, "EcoDesign and Future Environmental Impacts," *Materials & Design* 26, no. 7, Sustainable Design (2005), 629–634.

14. R. W. Beck, *Size of the U.S. Solid Waste Industry*, Environmental Research and Education Foundation (Alexandria, VA: Chartwell Information Publishers, 2001).

15. Garrick E. Louis, "A Historical Context of Municipal Solid Waste Management in the United States," *Waste Management and Research* 22, no. 4 (2004), 306–322.

16. Paula J. Meske, "The Solid Waste Dilemma: Municipal Liability and Household Hazardous Waste Management," *Environmental Law* 23 (1993).

17. U.S. Environmental Protection Agency, *Municipal Solid Waste Generation, Recycling, and Disposal in the United States: Facts and Figures for 2008*, EPA-530-F-009-021 (Washington DC: Environmental Protection Agency, November 2009), table 3, http://www.epa.gov/wastes/nonhaz/municipal/pubs/msw2008rpt.pdf.

18. Harold Crooks, *Giants of Garbage: The Rise of the Global Waste Industry and the Politics of Pollution Control* (Toronto: James Lorimer, 1993).

19. Peter Anderson, "Endgame: Consolidation and Competition in the Solid Waste Industry," in *MSW Elements 2000*, 24–28. Accessed January 12, 2010, at http://www.competitivewaste.org/reports/CCWEndgamet.PDF.

20. Neil Seldman, "History of Recycling," in *Encyclopedia of Energy, Technology and Environment* (New York: Wiley, 1995).

21. The EPA refers to the policy as integrated *solid* waste management. See U.S. Environmental Protection Agency, *Solid Waste Management: A Local Challenge with Global Impacts*, May 2002, http://www.epa.gov/waste/nonhaz/municipal/pubs/ghg/f02026.pdf.

22. *AB 939 (Sher)—The Integrated Waste Management Act*, 1989, at "History of California Solid Waste Law, 1985–1989," http://www.ciwmb.ca.gov/Statutes/Legislation/CalHist/1985to1989.htm (accessed January 1, 2009).

23. U.S. Environmental Protection Agency, *Municipal Solid Waste Generation, Recycling, and Disposal in the United States*; Statistics Canada, *Waste Management Industry Survey: Business and Government Sectors*, catalog no. 16F0023X (2006), 9.

24. Anderson, "Endgame."

25. Samantha MacBride, *Diversion: The Progress and Promise of Recycling in the United States* (Cambridge, MA: MIT Press, forthcoming 2011).

26. Statistics Canada, *Waste Management Industry Survey*, reports that the amount of waste disposed in public and private disposal facilities increased 8 percent between 2004 and 2006, following an increase of 5 percent during the previous two-year period.

27. For instance, a January 8, 2010, report to the Metro Vancouver board projected an increase in annual waste generation from 3.7 million metric tonnes in 2010 to 5 million metric tonnes by 2020 as the basis for scaling an increase in waste disposal capacity in the region's new Solid Waste Management Plan.

28. Covanta Energy Corporation, "EfW Solutions," http://www.covantaholding.com/site/solutions/efw.html.

29. CBC News, "Garbage a Burning Issue in Metro Vancouver," June 23, 2009, http://www.cbc.ca/canada/british-columbia/story/2009/06/23/bc-garbage-burning-gvrd.html.

30. Jeffrey Morris, "Why the Vancouver Region Should Fund & Promote 3Rs not 2Ds," presentation to Vancouver Board of Trade, July 2009, available at http://rcbc.bc.ca/files/u7/ZW_JeffMorrisReport_0907.pdf.

31. Current EPA regulations under the Clean Air Act require many landfill owners/operators to collect and combust landfill gas. U.S. Environmental Protection Agency, "Landfill Methane Outreach Program," http://www.epa.gov/lmop/faq/lfg.

html#07. Likewise, some Canadian provinces have similar requirements—see for example, British Columbia, "Landfill Gas Management Regulation," http://www .env.gov.bc.ca/epd/codes/landfill_gas/.

32. Detroit News, December 21, 2009, http://detnews.com/article/20091221/ POLITICS02/912210317.

33. Sierra Club Landfill Gas-to-Energy Task Force, Sierra Club Report on Landfill Gas-to-Energy, January 5, 2010, http://www.sierraclub.org/policy/conservation/ landfill-gas-report.pdf.

34. U.S. Environmental Protection Agency, 2009 U.S. Greenhouse Gas Inventory Report: Inventory of U.S. Greenhouse Gas Emissions and Sinks: 1990–2007, April 2009, http://epa.gov/climatechange/emissions/usgginventory.html.

35. Intergovernmental Panel on Climate Change (IPCC), 2006 IPCC Guidelines for National Greenhouse Gas Inventories: vol. 5, Waste (Hayama, Japan: Institute for Global Environmental Strategies, 2006), 3.19, http://www.ipcc-nggip.iges.or.jp/ public/2006gl/vol5.html.

36. Sierra Club Landfill Gas-to-Energy Task Force, Sierra Club Report on Landfill Gas-to-Energy.

37. AECOM Canada Ltd., Management of Municipal Solid Waste in Metro Vancouver, June 2009, http://public.metrovancouver.org/boards/GVSDD%20Board/GVSDD _Board-June_12_2009-AECOM_FULL_REPORT.pdf.

38. Vyvyan Howard, "Incinerator Health Risk 'Unacceptable,'" BBC News, March 31, 2005; Louise Roseingrave, "Expert Challenges Safety Risk Study for Incinerator," Irish Times, June 10, 2009.

39. European Union Council Landfill Directive, articles 5.1 and 5.2, Official Journal of the European Communities, April 26, 1999, http://eur-lex.europa.eu/LexUriServ/ LexUriServ.do?uri=OJ:L:1999:182:0001:0019:EN:PDF.

40. William McDonough and Michael Braungart, Cradle to Cradle: Remaking the Way We Make Things (New York: North Point Press, 2002).

41. Helen Spiegelman and Bill Sheehan, "The Next Frontier for MSW," BioCycle 47, no. 2 (February 2006), 30, http://www.jgpress.com/archives/_free/000781.html.

42. U.S. Environmental Protection Agency, Municipal Solid Waste Generation, Recycling, and Disposal in the United States.

43. Spiegelman and Sheehan, "The Next Frontier for MSW."

44. It can be argued that branded, or brand-name, food products also require producer responsibility. Likewise, compostable products may require producer financing of a fair share of composting costs.

45. U.S. Environmental Protection Agency, Municipal Solid Waste Generation, Recycling, and Disposal in the United States.

46. "Green Infrastructure Projects for Montreal," Solid Waste and Recycling: News, February 1, 2010, http://www.solidwastemag.com/issues/story.aspx?aid=1000 356947.

47. The Organisation for Economic Co-operation and Development (OECD) carried out extensive analysis of EPR during the 1990s and in 2001 produced a guidance manual, to help member states understand and implement it, as well as a fact sheet, "Extended Producer Responsibility," which can be accessed at http://www .oecd.org/document/53/0,3343,en_2649_34395_37284725_1_1_1_1,00.html.

48. Bill Sheehan and Helen Spiegelman, "Extended Producer Responsibility Poli-

cies in the United States and Canada: History and Status," in *Governance of Integrated Product Policy: In Search of Sustainable Production and Consumption*, Dirk Scheer and Frieder Rubik, eds. (Sheffield, UK: Greenleaf Publishing, 2005).

49. Businesses and Environmentalists Allied for Recycling (BEAR), "Understanding Beverage Container Recovery: A Value Chain Assessment Prepared for the Multi-Stakeholder Recovery Project," a project of Global Green USA, January 2002, http://www.container-recycling.org/publications/reports/bear.htm.

50. Brenda Platt, David Ciplet, Kate M. Bailey, and Eric Lombardi, *Stop Trashing the Climate*, Institute for Local Self-Reliance, June 2008, http://www.stoptrashingthe climate.org/.

51. Sierra Club, "Zero Waste: Cradle-to-Cradle Principles for the 21st Century," approved by the board of directors, February 23, 2008, http://www.sierraclub.org/policy/conservation/ZeroWasteExtendedProducerResponsibilityPolicy.pdf.

52. COOL 2012, "Compostable Organics Out of Landfills by 2012," http://www.cool2012.com/.

53. Product Policy Institute, *Product Stewardship Policy and Framework Principles*, January 2010, http://www.productpolicy.org/content/framework-principles.

54. MacBride, "Diversion."

55. Keep America Beautiful, Inc. (KAB), "Corporate and Foundation Partners," http://www.kab.org/site/PageServer?pagename=Corporate_contributors.

56. Michael Maniates, "Individualization: Plant a Tree, Buy a Bike, Save the World?" in *Confronting Consumption*, Thomas Princen et al., eds. (Cambridge, MA: MIT Press, 2002).

57. Product Policy Institute, "EPR Framework," http://www.productpolicy.org/content/epr-framework; Institute for Local Self-Reliance, "Recycling and Solid Waste," New Rules Project, http://www.newrules.org/environment/rules/recycling-and-solid-waste.

CHAPTER 29. HUMAN HEALTH AND WELL-BEING IN AN ERA OF ENERGY SCARCITY AND CLIMATE CHANGE

1. Thomas A. Glass and Matthew J. McAtee, "Behavioral Science at the Crossroads in Public Health: Extending Horizons, Envisioning the Future," *Social Science and Medicine* 62, no. 7 (2006), 1650–1671.

2. In the public health field, "social patterning" is the idea that differences in states of health across populations are determined by differences in the distribution of a variety of advantages and disadvantages in those populations.

3. Glass and McAtee, "Behavioral Science at the Crossroads in Public Health."

4. John P. Holdren, "Science and Technology for Sustainable Well-Being," *Science* 319, no. 5862 (January 25, 2008), 424–434.

5. House Select Committee on Energy Independence and Global Warming of the House Permanent Select Committee on Intelligence, *National Intelligence Assessment on the National Security Implications of Global Climate Change to 2030*, statement for the record of Dr. Thomas Fingar, deputy director of National Intelligence for Analysis and chairman of the National Intelligence Council, June 25, 2008.

6. Dr. Jeremy Hess, personal communication with the authors, February 17, 2010.

7. M. T. Osterholm and N. S. Kelley, "Energy and the Public's Health: Making the Connection," *Public Health Rep* 124, no. 1 (2009), 20–21.

8. Charles A. S. Hall and John W. Day, "Revisiting the Limits to Growth after Peak Oil," *American Scientist* 97, no. 3 (May/June 2009), 230–237.

9. Jan C. Semenza et al., "Heat-Related Deaths during the July 1995 Heat Wave in Chicago," *New England Journal of Medicine* 335, no. 2 (July 11, 1996), 84–90; Tom Kosatsky, "The 2003 European Heat Waves," *Eurosurveillance* 10, no. 7 (July 1, 2005), 148–149; Kim Knowlton et al., "The 2006 California Heat Wave: Impacts on Hospitalizations and Emergency Department Visits," *Environmental Health Perspectives* 117, no. 1 (January 2009), 61–67; Bart D. Ostro et al., "Estimating the Mortality Effect of the July 2006 California Heat Wave," *Environmental Research* 109, no. 5 (July 2009), 614–619.

10. P. A. Stott, D. A. Stone, and M. R. Allen, "Human Contribution to the European Heatwave of 2003," *Nature* 432 (December 2, 2004), 610–614.

11. Mercedes Medina-Ramon and Joel Schwartz, "Temperature, Temperature Extremes, and Mortality: A Study of Acclimatisation and Effect Modification in 50 United States Cities," *Occupational and Environmental Medicine* 64 (2007), 827–863.

12. Anil V. Kulkarni et al., "Glacial Retreat in Himalaya Using Indian Remote Sensing Satellite Data," *Current Science* 92, no. 1 (January 10, 2007), 69–74.

13. California Department of Food and Agriculture, "Agricultural Statistical Review," in *California Agricultural Resource Directory 2007* (2008).

14. U.S. Global Change Research Program, *Our Changing Planet: The U.S. Climate Change Science Program for Fiscal Year 2009* (Washington DC: U.S. Global Change Research Program, 2008).

15. Frank C. Curriero et al., "The Association between Extreme Precipitation and Waterborne Disease Outbreaks in the United States, 1948–1994," *American Journal of Public Health* 91, no. 8 (2001), 1194–1199.

16. Mike Ahern et al., "Global Health Impacts of Floods: Epidemiologic Evidence," *Epidemiologic Reviews* 27, no. 1 (2005), 36–46.

17. Pat J. Fitzpatrick et al., "The Impact of Louisiana's Levees and Wetlands on Katrina's Storm Surge," presented at the 28th Conference on Hurricanes and Tropical Meteorology, American Meteorological Society, May 2008, http://ams.confex.com/ams/28Hurricanes/techprogram/paper_137224.htm.

18. Jared Diamond, *Collapse: How Societies Choose to Fail or Succeed* (New York: Penguin, 2005); Thomas F. Homer-Dixon, *Environment, Scarcity, and Violence* (Princeton: Princeton University Press, 2001).

19. Intergovernmental Panel on Climate Change (IPCC), "Summary for Policymakers," in *Climate Change 2007: Impacts, Adaptation and Vulnerability*, M. L. Parry et al., eds. (Cambridge, UK: Cambridge University Press, 2007), 7–22.

20. A. E. Kazdin, "Psychological Science's Contributions to a Sustainable Environment: Extending Our Reach to a Grand Challenge of Society," *American Psychologist* 64, no. 5 (July/August 2009), 339–356; Robert Gifford, "Psychology's Essential Role in Alleviating the Impacts of Climate Change," *Canadian Psychology* 49, no. 4 (November 2008), 273–280; R. C. Kessler et al., "Trends in Mental Illness and Suicidality after Hurricane Katrina," *Molecular Psychiatry* 13, no. 4 (April 2008), 374–384.

CHAPTER 30. SMART BY NATURE

1. David. W. Orr, "Some Thoughts on Intelligence," in David W. Orr, *Earth in Mind* (Washington, Covelo, and London: Island Press, 2004), 48–53.

2. Michael Pollan, "Our Decrepit Food Factories," *New York Times Magazine* (December 16, 2007), http://www.nytimes.com/2007/12/16/magazine/16wwln -lede-t.html?pagewanted=1.

3. William McDonough and Michael Braungart, *Cradle to Cradle: Remaking the Way We Make Things* (New York: North Point Press, 2002), 155.

4. Alan AtKisson, *Believing Cassandra: An Optimist Looks at a Pessimist's World* (White River Junction, VT: Chelsea Green, 1999), 148.

5. David. W. Orr, "What Is Education For?" in David W. Orr, *Earth in Mind* (Washington, Covelo, and London: Island Press, 2004), 7–15.

6. *The Vermont Guide to Education for Sustainability*, http://www.vtefs.org/resources/ EFS%20GuideComplete-web.pdf.

7. Erica Zimmerman, "Education for Sustainability," *Community Works Journal* (summer 2004), 4.

8. *Sustainable Schools Project Newsletter* (spring/summer 2006), 8.

9. Place-Based Education Evaluation Collaborative, "Examining the Staying Power of the Sustainable Schools Project: A Program Evaluation Focused on Champlain Elementary School," http://www.peecworks.org/PEEC/PEEC_Reports/ S00686CFB-0069AC2C.

10. Quoted in Tiffany Tillman, *Healthy Neighborhoods/Healthy Kids Project Guide* (a publication of Shelburne Farms' Sustainable Schools Project, in partnership with Smart Growth Vermont, 2007), 57.

CHAPTER 31. COMMUNITY COLLEGES

1. American Association of Community Colleges, "CC STATS," http://www2 .aacc.nche.edu/research/index.htm (accessed April 1, 2010).

2. The College Board, *Trends in College Pricing 2008* (Washington DC: 2008), http://professionals.collegeboard.com/profdownload/trends-in-college-pricing -2008.pdf.

3. Richard Heinberg, "Fifty Million Farmers," from a lecture delivered to the E. F. Schumacher Society in Stockbridge, MA, on October 28, 2006, http://www .energybulletin.net/node/22584.

4. See, for example, Michael Pollan, *In Defense of Food* (New York: Penguin, 2008) and *The Omnivore's Dilemma* (New York: Penguin, 2006).

5. See Tom M. Purdum, "The High Priest of Pasture," *New York Times*, May 1, 2005.

6. See http://www.livingeconomies.org/aboutus/mission-and-principles.

7. Logan Ward, "MIT's Guru of Low-Tech Engineering Fixes the World on $2 a Day," *Popular Mechanics*, August 1,2008, http://www.popularmechanics.com/ technology/engineering/gonzo/4273674.

8. See http://www.capewind.org/.

CHAPTER 33. WHAT CAN COMMUNITIES DO?

1. David Mitchell, "I've Always Wondered about Woolies," *Observer*, November 23, 2008.

2. BDaily Business News Network, "Wind Farm 'Driving Economy,'" November 9, 2009, http://bdaily.info/news/technology-and-science/09-11-2009/wind-farm-driving-economy/.

3. Michael H. Shuman, *Going Local: Creating Self-Reliant Communities in a Global Age* (New York: Routledge, 2000).

4. David Fleming, "Lean Logic: The Dictionary of Environmental Manners," 2007, unpublished.

5. Brigit Maguire and Sophie Cartwright, *Assessing a Community's Capacity to Manage Change: A Resilience Approach to Social Assessment* (Canberra: Australian Bureau of Rural Sciences, 2008).

6. Tamzin Pinkerton and Rob Hopkins, *Local Food: How to Make It Happen in Your Community* (Totnes, UK: Green Books/Transition Books, 2009). See http://www.transitionbooks.net.

7. Transition Culture, "Transition Taunton and Their Local Council Produce a Transition Vision for 2026," November 11, 2009, http://transitionculture.org/2009/11/11/transition-taunton-town-and-their-local-council-produce-a-transition-vision-for-2026/.

8. Fi Macmillan and Dave Cockcroft, *Food Availability in Stroud District*, Transition Stroud, December 16, 2008, http://community.stroud.gov.uk/_documents/34_Food_Availability_in_Stroud_District.pdf.

9. Transition Town Totnes, *Transition in Action: Totnes & District 2009–2030: An Energy Descent Action Plan*, 2010, http://www.totnes.transitionnetwork.org/edap/home.

10. Tim Jackson, *Prosperity without Growth: Economics for a Finite Planet* (London: Earthscan, 2009).

CHAPTER 34: WHAT NOW?

1. David Korten, *Agenda for a New Economy: From Phantom Wealth to Real Wealth* (San Francisco: Berrett-Koehler, 2009).

INDEX

EDITORS

RICHARD HEINBERG is widely regarded as one of the world's most effective communicators of the urgent need to transition away from fossil fuels. He is the author of nine books, including *The Party's Over: Oil, War and the Fate of Industrial Societies* (2003), *Powerdown: Options and Actions for a Post-Carbon World* (2004), and *Blackout: Coal, Climate and the Last Energy Crisis* (2009). He has authored scores of essays and articles, is featured in many documentaries, and has appeared on numerous television and radio programs. Heinberg is Senior Fellow-in-Residence at Post Carbon Institute.

DANIEL LERCH is program director of Post Carbon Institute and the author of *Post Carbon Cities: Planning for Energy and Climate Uncertainty* (2007), the first major guidebook for local governments on peak oil and global warming. He has delivered presentations and workshops on local responses to peak oil to elected officials, planners, and other audiences across the United States, as well as in Canada, the British Isles, and Spain.

"For a comprehensive, integrated overview of the relationship between the human species and its planetary home circa 2010, look no further. *The Post Carbon Reader* is an invaluable primer, resource, and textbook. This is what you need to know—period."

—LESTER R. BROWN, Earth Policy Institute

Visit postcarbonreader.com to access additional material,
learn more about the authors, and connect with other readers.